★ NEW ENGLAND STUDIES ★
Edited by John Putnam Demos, David Hackett
Fischer, and Robert A. Gross

EDWARD BYERS
The Nation of Nantucket

RICHARD RABINOWITZ
The Spiritual Self in Everyday Life

JOHN R. MULKERN
The Know-Nothing Party in Massachusetts

DANIEL P. JONES
*The Economic and Social Transformation of Rural
Rhode Island, 1780–1850*

CONRAD EDICK WRIGHT
*The Transformation of Charity in Postrevolutionary
New England*

THE
Transformation of Charity in Postrevolutionary New England

CONRAD EDICK WRIGHT

Northeastern University Press

BOSTON

Northeastern University Press

Library of Congress Cataloging-in-Publication Data

Wright, Conrad Edick.
   The transformation of charity in postrevolutionary
New England / Conrad Edick Wright.
      p.   cm.—(New England studies)
   Includes bibliographical references and index.
   ISBN 1-55553-123-7
      1. Charities—New England—History—18th century.
   2. Charities—New England—History—19th century.
   I. Title.   II. Series
   HV98.N38W75   1992
   361.7'0974—dc20   91-40405

Designed by Richard C. Bartlett and Ann Twombly

Composed in Perpetua by The Composing Room of Michigan, Inc.,
Grand Rapids, Michigan. Printed and bound by The Maple Press,
York, Pennsylvania. The paper is Sebago Antique, an acid-free sheet.

MANUFACTURED IN THE UNITED STATES OF AMERICA
96   95   94   93   92   5   4   3   2   1

TO MY FATHER AND MOTHER

Contents

Acknowledgments

IN 1732 Samuel Mather, Cotton Mather's youngest son and successor at Boston's Second Church, delivered "An Essay Concerning Gratitude." According to the younger Mather, gratitude was close kin to charity, a reciprocal virtue "*which consists in a grateful Sense of received Benefits, in a free Acknowledgment of them, in speaking well of the Donor, and in endeavouring to requite him.*" In the fullness of that spirit, I am grateful to the many individuals and institutions that contributed to this project.

The research that resulted in this book began while I was a graduate student at Brown University. Gordon S. Wood supervised the dissertation out of which the present study has grown; William G. McLoughlin and John L. Thomas served as readers. Each offered careful criticism of my dissertation, and this book, which differs substantially from my thesis, is a better work thanks to their advice. The following contemporaries of mine at Brown also provided help and encouragement: Paul A. Gilje, A. G. Roeber, and E. Bruce Tucker. I owe a special debt of thanks to Bruce Tucker, who read not only the dissertation, but also an advanced draft of this work and offered insightful comments on both occasions. The New World Colloquium at Harvard Divinity School discussed aspects of my research on two occasions, and I am grateful to its members, especially to William R. Hutchison, for these opportunities to present my work.

If this book differs in some respects from previous studies of organized charity, its novelty is due in part to my slightly eccentric career path, not into teaching but into historical administration. I have had valuable opportunities to learn about the operation of institutions and the mechanics of fundraising everywhere I have worked, and I owe debts of thanks to Thad W. Tate, Jr., formerly of the Institute of Early American History and Culture, James B. Bell, formerly of The New-York Historical Society, and Louis L. Tucker, of the Massachusetts Historical Society, for their lessons in the management of non-profit organizations. I owe special thanks to the Institute and to the M.H.S. for allowing me to devote some of my work time to this project and to the

M.H.S. for financial support. While at the Institute, I benefited from comments from and conversation with William K. Breitenbach, Thomas M. Doerflinger, Norman S. Fiering, Michael McGiffert, John E. Selby, Daniel F. Vickers, and the members of the Institute's Williamsburg Seminar; at the M.H.S., I have received welcome help from Peter Drummey, Edward W. Hanson, and Mary Beth LaDow. Peter Virgadamo, whose own research on charity intersects with mine, provided useful advice while he held a short-term fellowship at the Society. C. C. Goen commented incisively on many of the ideas offered in the first chapter when I presented them in a different form at the annual meeting of the American Society for Church History in 1980. William Pencak set aside his work to comment on my manuscript when I was in the midst of revising it. Lilian Handlin read the entire manuscript at a later date and Pauline Maier read the first chapter, and each offered welcome encouragement.

The note on sources at the back of this volume indicates the institutions at which I conducted research in manuscript collections. I am grateful to staff members at each of these repositories. I owe a special word of thanks to Norman S. Novack, formerly of Widener Library at Harvard and now of the Smithsonian Institution, for his help over the course of several years. I must also thank Jane Tucker of Wiscasset, Maine, who secured the records of the Wiscasset Female Charitable Society for me and allowed me to read them at her dining-room table in "Castle Tucker." Professor Gary B. Nash generously loaned me materials he had gathered on the Society for Encouraging Industry and Employing the Poor.

Robert A. Gross, of the College of William and Mary, who edited this book, offered many important insights growing out of his own research and writing. Ann Harrer, a gradeschool classmate of mine, drew the maps in chapter two. I am grateful to both and to the staff of Northeastern University Press—notably William A. Frohlich, Susan M. Kuc, Deborah Kops, and Ann Twombly—for their great assistance in seeing this book through production.

Finally, I must thank my mother (for her encouragement), my father (both for a careful reading of a late draft of this book and for the example he has set over many years), and my wife (for her patience, her support, and much more).

Boston, Massachusetts
June 1991

THE TRANSFORMATION OF CHARITY IN
POSTREVOLUTIONARY NEW ENGLAND

Introduction

On AUGUST 9, 1820, Ward Stafford left home for an extended tour of New England.[1] Thirty-two years of age, a graduate of Yale, and a Presbyterian minister, Stafford had been employed for several years as an agent of the Female Missionary Society for the Poor of the City of New York. He had carried the gospel door to door in the city's worst neighborhoods, trying to serve New York's growing numbers of poor and dependent men and women. Such work, he felt certain, expressed the sincere compassion of affluent Christians toward those who were less fortunate. Now, however, Stafford had another project in mind. In 1817 he had taken part in the organization of the New York Marine Bible Society, an association to spread the gospel among seamen.[2] The ambitious aim of his present journey was to extend such institutions to New England's principal towns.

Stafford's first port of call was Nantucket, which he reached on August 11. After consulting a clergyman "with whom I had some previous acquaintance," as well as the island's other ministers and "several of the principal men of different denominations," the New Yorker determined to call a meeting for that evening. Notices were posted, and at 7:00 o'clock many of the island's leading citizens assembled in a room above the Union Insurance office. Stafford explained the nature of the proposed organization, "a resolution to form the society was offered, and, after some remarks by different gentlemen, *was* unanimously carried." At this point, Stafford produced a constitution for the new society, previously prepared, which those in attendance circulated. Without waiting for a second meeting scheduled for a later date to consider the document, Stafford secured passage for New Bedford, where he repeated his performance.

Between August 11 and October 13, Ward Stafford visited every New England state except landlocked Vermont. From New Bedford he traveled west to Newport, Bristol, and Providence, and then north to Boston. From there he continued along the coast to Portland, touching half a dozen large and small seaports along the way, including Salem, where "a large number of

3

respectable citizens" assembled on September 1.[3] After a meeting on September 11 in Portland, where he "made some interesting Remarks on the Good effects that had arisen, from the formulation of similar Societies in other places"[4] and oversaw the establishment of the Portland Marine Bible Society, he followed the Kennebec River inland to Hallowell. Here, at the head of the Kennebec, he met a merchant from Bangor "who earnestly desired me to visit that place." It took Stafford nearly a week by horse and foot to cover the distance from Hallowell to Bangor, sixty miles away across forbidding and largely unsettled terrain at the head of the Penobscot. When his business was done in Bangor on September 21, he seized an opportunity to travel down the river by sailboat to Castine on the coast. He spent several days in the small port towns northeast of Portland, returned briefly to Boston, then set out for Connecticut, where he passed slightly more than a week. On October 15 Stafford returned to New York City, nearly ten weeks after he had left.

Most of Stafford's visits had been very brief. He had remained in Boston, "the capital of New England," for a week, since he believed that success there was especially important "on account of the influence which such an example will have on the other ports." But he had allotted less time to the other communities he had passed through, often no more than a day. Events had moved so quickly in Belfast, a town on Maine's Penobscot Bay, that he had been able to complete the organization of a marine Bible society during the morning of the day of his arrival, September 23, and leave for Waldoborough, several miles down the coast, in time to hold a meeting there the same evening.

By October 15, Stafford's tally read: twenty-four ports visited, twenty-two marine Bible societies organized or in the process of establishment. This Johnny Appleseed of marine Bible societies had traveled about 1,600 miles to towns he had never previously visited, had arrived unannounced in most cases, and had ordinarily dealt with people whom he had not previously met. Once or twice he had overcome the initial doubts of a town's residents. In New London, where the citizens had formed a Bible society to serve the county the year before, one civic leader "remarked, that he had come . . . not disposed to unite in forming a new Society" that might compete with the new county Bible society, "but he was convinced that it was important, and, therefore, moved, that it is expedient to form a Marine Bible Society." Looking back on his travels, Stafford could only thank God for the success He had brought to the mission.

Ward Stafford's journey had been far more successful than he had dared hope for when he had set out. Yet his achievement was only somewhat out of the ordinary. The clergyman had benefited from one of the most important developments of his day, the rise of organized charity. In 1820 New England rode the crest of a wave. Half a century before, New Englanders could count only about 50 charitable institutions of any kind. By 1820, however, there were at least 1,500 Bible societies, missionary societies, masonic lodges, orphanages, and other kinds of charitable institutions, and possibly more than 2,000. Organized charity now reached into every corner of New England, small and remote towns like Hallowell and Bangor as well as metropolises like Boston and Providence. Initial resistance had forced Stafford to call on his apparently formidable powers of persuasion only occasionally; most of the civic leaders with whom he dealt were ready and eager to help this stranger promote a cause so obviously worthwhile. Like New Englanders everywhere, they were caught up in a frenzy of organization.

This book is a history of the transformation of charity in New England between the mid-1780s and the 1820s. Within this brief period New Englanders substantially redefined charity—both its principles and its practices. Their efforts prepared the way for the great initiatives of the antebellum era by providing philanthropists and reformers with both the means and the confidence to act. The story involves both the rise of organized charity and the consequent emergence of new beliefs and assumptions about the nature of human relationships and duties.

To the extent that it is a history of institutions, this book may be read as a case study in the structural reorganization, or "modernization," of the United States during the early years of the republic. New England experienced an institutional revolution after the War for Independence, a transformation as important as any technological development during the era, and organizations fundamentally reshaped charity. Between the mid-1780s and the 1820s the New Englanders who are at the center of this story established, spread, and operated institutions that seemed remarkably large and wealthy at the time. In these attributes, however, New England's charitable institutions were not unique. New Englanders ran into many of the same problems in their efforts to institutionalize charity that politicians, capitalists, and denominational leaders encountered at about the same time, not to mention charitable organizers in the middle Atlantic, southern, and western states. Politicians, entrepreneurs, church leaders, and philanthropists all struggled to build and operate large institutions, attract resources and supporters, and maintain lines of communication over great distances. Associating for charity was no easy matter. Success depended on the ability of organizers to learn about the institutions they were establishing and to accommodate them both to the conditions they encountered and to the needs they hoped to serve.

This book is also a case study of the effects of social and institutional reorganization on a stable structure of deeply held beliefs and assumptions. The ideas with which it is concerned were commonplaces, beliefs so basic that virtually all New Englanders held them, no matter what their class, religion, occupation, sex, or politics. Such fundamental ideas are rarely challenged, or even thought about. They never change without a revolution.

The rise of organized charity called into question colonial New England's assumptions about the nature and extent of each individual's interpersonal obligations. New Englanders struggled to understand how their personal needs—their self-interest—could coexist with their duties to God and to the wider society. Steeped in teachings dating back at least as far as St. Augustine, almost all colonial New Englanders shared a common understanding of the true believer's charitable responsibilities. At its center was an apologetic tradition, an intricate and enduring set of explanations for the individual Christian's natural inability to fulfill the Bible's injunctions to emulate the purity of Jesus, the universal love of the good Samaritan. The rise of organized charity raised doubts about much of this apologetic heritage, however. Without abandoning their inheritance, New Englanders found ways to accommodate it to radically new circumstances. Drawing on this heritage they developed a new understanding of charity, one fundamentally shaped by institutionalization.

Candor requires every historian who tries to see events as men and women of a bygone day did to admit the ultimate impossibility of the task. In 1973 Clifford Geertz warned his fellow anthropologists of the dangers inherent in the "long-distance mind reading or cannibal-isle fantasizing" that sometimes passes for analysis when ethnographers deceive themselves into believing that they are capable of " 'seeing things from the actor's point of view.' "[5] Geertz's caveat applies equally to historians. We can bury ourselves in the texts that New England ministers studied and pore through the sermons that laymen heard, but we can never completely recreate the broad range of influences that shaped their thought.

There are ways, however, to narrow the inevitable gap between scholar and subject. Geertz urged his fellow ethnographers to confine their analysis to a reliable core of direct statements, myths, and observed events.[6] For historians, who usually rely heavily on the written word, careful attention to the nuances of language can help to recover at least a portion of the past. I have tried, consequently, to be as sensitive as possible to the language of revolutionary and postrevolutionary New England. Because this concern has shaped my book in several important respects, leading me to define my subject in ways that require explanation, a brief, preliminary discussion of a few key words is in order.[7]

Probably as a result of their extended training in the classics, New England writers in the eighteenth and early nineteenth centuries were very precise in their use of a number of words important to the history of charity. The distinction between "beneficence" and "benevolence," for example, is sometimes lost in modern speech and writing, but when New Englanders used the former term they meant "doing good" and by the latter they meant "wishing good." "Benevolent institutions," as far as most New Englanders were concerned, were consequently not simply almsgiving organizations, but agents of compassion as well. "Philanthropy," a word rarely used before the 1780s, meant "love" as well as "alms" and implied universality, a "Love to the humane Kind" according to the Reverend Peter Clark of Salem Village.[8] As we shall see, a vogue for the term "philanthropy," related to the rise of organized benevolence, was a reflection of New England's growing hopes and self-confidence at the close of the eighteenth century.

For the purposes of this book, "charity" itself is at once the most important and most complicated key word. My use of the term diverges from customary twentieth-century practices, and it even takes issue with the judgments of a few well-informed eighteenth-century observers. Modern Americans usually equate "charity" with "alms" and "almsgiving," although most of us also recognize a second, slightly archaic meaning, "compassion" or "kindness." Scholars have often assumed that over the years the common definition of "charity" evolved from an identification with emotions to actions.[9] In fact, by the middle of the eighteenth century a few contemporaries on each side of the Atlantic had begun to comment that the word's meaning was changing. In England the latitudinarian clergyman Samuel Clarke lamented before his death in 1729 that in "common Speech" his countrymen now typically used the word "to signify, *Alms* or *Charity to the Poor.*" And in Massachusetts the Reverend Jonathan Ashley of Deerfield, echoing Clarke, noted in 1742 "that Use and Custom in these latter Days has confined the Term *Charity* to *Alms-Deeds,* or giving our Wealth to the Poor and distressed."[10]

Such observations notwithstanding, after considerably more than a decade of reading manuscript and printed sermons, addresses, and discourses by the thousands as well as constitutions and by-laws, minutes of meetings, diaries, and letters, written both by laymen and by ministers, it seems clear to me that at least in writing, most New Englanders in the eighteenth and early nineteenth centuries defined "charity" as neither an emotion nor an act, but as something intermediate—an emotion necessarily requiring an action. In

1767 Samuel Johnson, the Anglican missionary stationed in Stratford, Connecticut, described "charity" as "an habitual Temper or Frame of the Soul, from whence as flows a Fountain, every Virtue flows."[11] Johnson's definition captures, I believe, the essence of "charity" as most of his contemporaries— laymen as well as clergymen, Congregationalist and Baptist as well as Anglican—understood the term, and I have tried my best to follow this usage.

It is important to recognize that this definition encompasses some activities that modern historians have often differentiated from "charity," and it also distinguishes the virtue more clearly from certain other activities than they have sometimes felt necessary. On the one hand, charity was not merely almsgiving; New Englanders found it wherever certain emotions and actions were present. They recognized it in such varied settings as families, friendships, churches, masonic lodges, missionary societies, and temperance associations, as well as in secular almsgiving institutions. Good advice, a kind word, and an exhortation to piety could all express charity. Nor was charity the exclusive province of the affluent; impoverished men and women who treated others with compassion were as charitable as wealthy almsgivers. On the other hand, no later than the 1690s New Englanders began to distinguish between the public dole and charity. To be sure, well-motivated officials could administer poor relief in a spirit of charity. As early as 1695, though, Cotton Mather differentiated between paying "the *Publick Charges* of the Place in which we live," which were "*Debts* which *Honesty* rather than *Charity* binds us to the Payment of," and "The *Giving* of what may supply the Necessities and Relieve the Calamities of the *Indigent*." "Charity" according to Mather's definition was manifested in such "*Spiritual Beneficence*" as "*Contributions* for the Propagation of the Gospel," "*Subscriptions* towards the Education of Poor, but Good *Scholars* in the University," "the *Dispersion* of Bibles," and such "*Temporal Beneficence*" as efforts "To Comfort the *Sick,* to Nourish *Widows* and *Orphans,* to Redeem *Captives,* and *Prisoners,* and make mourning Hearts sing."[12] Throughout this book I have tried to allow contemporaries to define the subject for me, finding charity wherever they did and following their lead in otherwise ignoring public poor relief.

Attention to the contemporary understanding of charity has required two other divergences from the historian's traditional path—reconsideration of the common identification of evangelical Protestantism with certain forms of beneficence, and review of customary descriptions of the relationship between organized charity and domestic socioeconomic conditions.

Recognizing that the rise of organized charity took place at the same time that religious infighting was producing the first organized denominations, scholars have often postulated a causal link between the two developments. Students of the post-1815 "united front" of nationwide missionary, Bible, tract, education, and reform institutions have found this assumption especially seductive. Evangelical Protestants, we are told, drawn largely from Presbyterian, Methodist, Baptist, Episcopal, Dutch Reformed, and orthodox Congregational circles, fearful of the disruptive effects of the growth of cities, the expansion of the frontier, and the rising tide of New England Unitarianism and French deism, banded together in voluntary associations at the end of the eighteenth century to preserve religion and reform society. Theories about the regenerate Christian's obligation to practice "disinterested benevolence," advanced by the Reverend Samuel Hopkins, a disciple of Jonathan Edwards, provided a theological meeting ground for the faithful of the orthodox denominations, so the story goes, and roughly two decades later their combined efforts resulted in the establishment in 1816 of the American Bible Society and the formation between 1819 and 1833 of the rest of the institutions of the "united front."[13]

Such accounts of the origins of the united front have seemed reasonable because most of the national organizations established after 1815 were formed by evangelical Christians, who used them to advance the cause of orthodoxy. Although many of these organizations opened admission without reference to denominational affiliation to anyone who supported their aims and paid the annual dues, institutional officers often worried about the growth of religious liberalism. John Pintard, the American Bible Society's recording secretary and accountant between 1816 and 1832, for example, decried the efforts of Unitarians (or Socinians as he called them) to form a church in New York City, and expressing his "christian charity for every denomination of believing Christians," he qualified his remarks with the admission that he feared "the baleful effects of this rational system" and found that he could not "patiently endure" the liberal Christians.[14]

When the focus of attention is shifted from the united front and its origins to New England's own varied charitable activities, however, it soon becomes clear that especially in the commercial towns along the Atlantic coast from Portsmouth to Newport the link between organized beneficence and evangelical Christianity was neither as direct nor as complete as scholars have sometimes assumed. Although the earliest missionary, tract, and education societies ordinarily served the needs of individual denominations, before 1815 only a few associations imposed creedal tests for membership and many enjoyed the support and leadership of the liberals as well as of the orthodox. Moral reform societies and almsgiving institutions found support in every quarter and almost never adopted religious barriers to membership or aid.

Before the late 1820s only one humanitarian association, the Boston Episcopal Charitable Society, organized in 1724, ever used denominational criteria to restrict its services. Bible societies, which were established to distribute the scriptures "without note or comment," drew for support on Protestants of virtually every theological leaning. Moses Brown, the Quaker merchant, helped to organize the Rhode Island Bible Society, and a number of leading Unitarians, including Joseph Stevens Buckminster and James Freeman, took part in the founding of the Massachusetts Bible Society.[15] Although I have made an effort to trace the growing importance over time of the connection between evangelical Protestantism and some forms of organized beneficence, I have consequently assumed that doctrinal tests were the exception, not the rule, and have written by and large about ideas, institutions, and events that spanned rather than divided the emerging denominations.

Much as some scholars have seen the rise of organized charity as an outgrowth of the emergence of evangelical denominations, others have attributed it to contemporaneous social and economic conditions. Such interpretations have taken two basic shapes. Some historians have proposed a cause-and-effect formulation depicting institutional beneficence as an immediate and direct response either to growing poverty, irreligion, and moral decay, or to the mobility and anonymity of increasingly atomized nineteenth-century society.[16] Others, sometimes influenced by Marxian insights, have offered a materialist version which portrays the emergence of organized charity as a consequence of the rise of capitalist economic relationships and modes of production. Interpretations within this second school have taken a couple of forms,[17] some suggesting that organized charity grew out of the proto-Victorian desire of middle-class Americans to maintain "social control" over the less fortunate (who were presumably predisposed to immoral behavior),[18] and others asserting that these voluntary associations were cynical and purposeful capitalist ploys to turn the poor into a permanently dependent underclass and source of cheap labor.[19]

Years of studying charity have persuaded me of the perils of drawing straightforward correlations between socioeconomic circumstances and the emergence of institutional beneficence. While it would be folly to contend that there was no connection at all between charitable institutions and the social, spiritual, and moral problems their officers and members hoped to relieve, as we will see, the relationship was neither as simple nor as direct as some have led us to believe. In investigating the connection between organized charity and domestic conditions, the years this book covers are especially instructive. For in contradiction to cause-and-effect interpretations, they reveal that many forms of organized charity developed at a time when the need for them was constant or diminishing. Anomie and community needs were necessary preconditions for the establishment of some, but not all, charitable organizations; they were not ordinarily the immediate or primary causes. And in contradiction to materialist accounts, the evidence of these years shows that far from being purposeful and certain in their efforts to repress the lower orders, New England's pioneers in charity often floundered in their search for ways to serve those in need. With only a rudimentary understanding of the conditions they hoped to ameliorate, New England's early charitable organizers often spent years simply learning about these circumstances before they could formulate sensible courses of action.

PART ONE

The Charitable World of
Prerevolutionary New England

━━

The Lawyer's Question

ON A WINTER'S DAY in Galilee or Judea sometime around the year 30 A.D., so the story goes, an itinerant rabbi was addressing a small audience. One of those in attendance, a lawyer by profession, was worried about salvation. "What shall I do to inherit eternal life?" he asked.

The teacher, Jesus of Nazareth, replied with two questions of his own: "What is written in the law? how readest thou?"

"Thou shalt love the Lord thy God with all thy heart, and with all thy soul, and with all thy strength, and with all thy mind," the lawyer returned, "and thy neighbor as thyself."

"Thou hast answered right," Jesus confirmed, "this do, and thou shalt live."

The lawyer remained troubled and confused, however, and "willing to justify himself," he pressed further. "And who is my neighbor?" he asked. Jesus responded with a story of pure and universal compassion, the parable of the good Samaritan.[1]

The gospel of Luke fails to record whether the parable allayed the lawyer's fears. Certainly, his were the worries of a reasonable man, one well aware of his own limitations and insecure about his ability to emulate the Samaritan in his daily life. Who could fail to empathize with him? Not New Englanders in the third quarter of the eighteenth century. More than 1,700 years after the start of the Christian era, in the face of the rabbi's demands for self-denying love New Englanders still shared the lawyer's doubts.

Gideon Hawley knew how difficult it was to play the part of the Samaritan. A man of "amiable and unexceptionable" character, "pious and benevolent, zealous and candid, firm and gentle, sedate and cheerful,"[2] Hawley in 1757 was ending his fifth year of missionary service on New England's western frontier. His first two years, 1752 and 1753, he had spent under the supervision of Jonathan Edwards as a teacher at the Stockbridge, Massachusetts, Indian settlement. Persistent quarreling between two local factions, however, had encouraged him in 1754 to look for a more peaceful station to practice the "self-denials" attending missionary work.[3] In Onoquage among the Six Nations he believed he had found such a place. After ordination in Boston's Old South Church on July 31, 1754, he had settled there among the Iroquois under the financial sponsorship of the Boston Board of Commissioners of the New England Company, a London missionary society.

By the start of 1756, though, life in Iroquois country had begun to lose its allure. Hawley had not achieved the easy missionary successes for which he prayed, and when the Seven Years' War broke out between the English and the French he had found himself in "a Wilderness surrounded with Enemies."[4] By May the conflict had forced him to withdraw from Onoquage.

Late in 1756, when hostilities in the vicinity of the outpost had cooled, Hawley's sponsors had urged him to resume his station. Early in December the missionary had returned to his post, but "quite weary of journeying" and finding "Little or no purpose" in his efforts, he had begun to wonder whether he should "quit Indian Business and lay aside the Tho'ts of my Mission."[5] By the end of the month he had returned to Springfield, Massachusetts, to meditate on his future and on his obligations to the Indians he served, to his sponsors in London and Boston, and to God.

Hawley had a great deal to consider. Letters from Boston expressed "great lothness"[6] at his apparent intention to give up his mission. Friends around him—among them Edwards and his wife—also urged his return. Hawley looked deep inside himself and "prayed to God for a spirit of self-denial." On Friday night, February 11, 1757, he went to bed at eight o'clock, "lay till near 12 without a Wink," then rose for several hours of "praying to God and examining my heart, full of suspicions of myself."[7]

Within a few days, Hawley's troubled mind began to relax. On February 16 he recorded that he felt "extremely languished." "My spirits are down," he added, "and I feal easie—I can't see that I can blame myself in Point of Conduct respecting my Mission." Hawley reassured himself: "If I had ever so much zeal and were it ever so pure I don't think I should have done more—I have not had the Love to God . . . which I ought to have but I have done all that outward visible Conduct which God and man require of me except . . . to wait and see if providence won't open a Door for my return to my Mission." "I see no prospect of doing good by it," he concluded: "We must act upon *probabilities* not *possibilities.*"[8] Gideon Hawley had determined to give up his mission.

The next day, the seventeenth, Hawley rode over to Stockbridge to tell Jonathan Edwards of his decision and to say good-bye. Edwards and his wife tried once again to dissuade Hawley from leaving. Sarah Edwards was a "good Woman," Hawley recognized, but she did not "know eno' of my Mission to give her advice to one so perfectly acquainted." Edwards himself was "a hearty well wisher to the affair," but he had "blind Notions about Things and no Wonder seeing he knows nothing but by hearsay and half has never been told him." He was "a very good man . . . but capible of being biased."[9]

The pleas of friends, neighbors, and sponsors were to no avail. On the eighteenth, now easy of mind, Gideon Hawley set out for Boston and a new life.

Chapter One

"Our Powers are Limitted"

LIKE GIDEON HAWLEY, in their more practical moments most New Englanders on the eve of the American Revolution acknowledged the impossibility of their primary charitable ambition. Their aim was marvelous in its simplicity: in the words of the Reverend Jonathan Mayhew of Boston, a love that was "infinitely . . . noble, generous, and disinterested,"[1] a love of humanity much like the reborn Christian's love for his maker. There were times when such an emotion seemed almost within their grasp, periods of intoxication and exhilaration. Yet when enthusiasm waned and passions cooled, it was obvious to most how far short of their ideal of selfless and universal charity they had fallen. How could human beings actually feel the heavenly sentiments and perform the divine acts that perfect charity required? Even "The oldest and best of the Ministers, and Servants of CHRIST," as the Reverend Solomon Williams of Lebanon, Connecticut, admitted, felt ". . . Stirrings of inordinate Desires after worldly Things, immoderate Attachments to Creature Relations and Connections, whereby they are hindered in the Exercise of Faith and Holiness."[2]

At the same time that they pledged a love of "all mankind; all who partake of the common nature with ourselves whatever dispers'd," most New Englanders consequently added a coda, a charitable apology: as a practical matter this goal was beyond them "because our powers are limitted."[3] High ambition and the reluctant acknowledgment that their hopes were impossibly utopian, then, were the two predominant traits of charity as prerevolutionary New Englanders knew it, and the tension at the conjunction of their aspirations and their abilities shaped every aspect of their understanding of charity both as it was and as it ought to be.

Christian Love

"Love is the very essence of christianity," the Reverend Andrew Eliot of Boston instructed in 1774: "There is not a greater contradiction in nature than a christian without love."[4] Eliot might have added that Christianity was the essence of love, at least in the minds of most New Englanders. On the eve of the American Revolution their aspirations for charity rose inevitably out of their religious beliefs. If love were "the very essence of christianity," then Christian doctrines also molded the consensus on love. At the core of New England's teachings about the nature of love was a set of assumptions, sometimes voiced, often tacit. Of these, the most fundamental was that charity was an obligation owed to God, a duty that required Christians first to determine God's will.

What was God's will? No challenge was more preoccupying to eighteenth-century theologians, preachers, and committed laymen—and no enterprise filled them with greater optimism—than their search for ways to determine the Lord's wishes on moral and spiritual subjects. Eighteenth-century New Englanders believed that their own spiritual inquiries, aided by the insights of the western world's greatest minds, present and past, gave them hope of discovering God's plans for them and His expectations of them. Where charity was concerned, New Englanders agreed, the Lord had made His will known to all Christians who cared to pay attention.

Most Christians of every age, before and since, have assumed God's ultimate inscrutability and admitted their inability to determine His intentions as precisely as they wished. Eighteenth-century New Englanders and the British thinkers whom they most admired did not, for the most part, take issue with this assumption. Yet there seemed to be good reason to hope that they were coming closer than ever before to learning the Lord's innermost desires. Toward the end of the seventeenth century a number of skeptical and deistic philosophers and writers in England tried to cast doubt on many of the axioms of Christian faith, those beliefs that Christians had always accepted without thought or proof.[5] Their challenge was unsuccessful, but in British circles, at any rate, it led to a reconsideration of the bases of authority on which Christians rested their faith. By the early eighteenth century, most British writers and their American followers were becoming more confident than ever of the validity of their beliefs.

The Bible had always been one authoritative source of wisdom about the Lord and His wishes, and many of the modern British clergymen whom New Englanders especially respected—for example John Tillotson, Samuel Clarke, and Joseph Butler—combed the scriptures carefully for evidence of God's instructions to them. Britons everywhere believed, however, that the Bible had recently been supplemented by the extraordinary scientific discoveries of Isaac Newton and by the philosophical insights of John Locke and a host of contemporaries and students who were sweeping away the haze that had always obscured the workings of the human mind. In forums like the annual Boyle lectures, begun in 1692 through a bequest from the great chemist Sir Robert Boyle, speakers like Clarke, William Derham, and William Whiston proclaimed that the Lord had revealed His aspirations for humanity as surely in His natural creation as in His written revelation. It now seemed possible—through the Bible and the new learning of Newton and Locke—to uncover the fundamental principles of God's universe. It was only a short step, perhaps through reasoning by analogies, eighteenth-century Britons told themselves, from the discovery of the structure of the natural world or the shape of the human mind to insights into the structure of the moral world and God's aspirations for mankind.[6]

Most eighteenth-century New Englanders agreed that to discover religious truth about a moral concern like charity, their surest course was to turn simultaneously to what the Reverend Jared Eliot of Killingsworth, Connecticut, referred to as "The Two Witnesses,"[7] revealed religion and natural religion. The Bible codified Christian faith: it was "the standard; the rule which Christians are to appeal." Nevertheless, Christians also found divine answers to their questions in "the book of nature": as Andrew Eliot asserted in 1771, "The great truths of Religion are founded in the reason and nature of things."[8] Through their understanding of the Bible's teachings about charity, New Englanders learned the goals for which God demanded them to strive; His injunctions became their aspirations. Through their reason or common sense they learned how far human nature actually allowed them to go.

What did New Englanders learn from the Bible about charity? The burden of centuries of scriptural exegesis from St. Augustine's time in the sixth century to their own seemed clear. It taught selflessness. John Calvin layed out the basic premises in his *Institutes* in 1536. "How difficult it is to perform the duty of seeking the good of our neighbour!" Calvin exclaimed: "Unless you leave off all thought of yourself, and in a manner cease to be yourself, you will never accomplish it." It was impossible, Calvin taught, to practice scriptural charity "unless you renounce yourself, and become wholly devoted to others."[9] This selfless devotion was to be extensive, comprehending "the most remote stranger." The Lord enjoined "that the whole human race, without exception, are to be embraced with one feeling of charity . . . here there is no distinction of Greek or Barbarian, worthy or unworthy, friend or foe, since all are to be viewed not in themselves, but in God."[10] It was also to be undertaken actively: "in regard to everything which God has bestowed upon us, and by which we can aid our neighbour, we are his stewards, and are bound to give account of our stewardship."[11] It was difficult to draw any other conclusion: scriptural charity was "the christian temper itself,"[12] a state of mind with three fundamental characteristics—it was selfless, universal, and active.

"The love and esteem we entertain for each other," Charles Brockwell, an Anglican missionary stationed in Boston instructed, "must be neither sordid nor mercenary, but free and unconfined as the open and ambient air."[13] Selfless love was a sincere desire for *"the Good and Welfare of our Neighbour"* unclouded by base motives.[14] Gospel love required Christians to look out for the interests of their neighbors as well as their own; sometimes it even required them to forego their own advantage to benefit others.[15]

When they studied the Bible, New Englanders found it filled with texts urging pure and selfless love as well as with practical examples to emulate. The most direct injunction appeared in Paul's first epistle to the Corinthians, the apostle's definition of love or charity: "Charity suffereth long, and is kind; charity envieth not; charity vaunteth not itself, is not puffed up. Doth not believe itself unseemly, seeketh not her own, is not easily provoked, thinketh no evil."[16] God's meaning here seemed clear to the Reverend David Mac-Gregore of Londonderry, New Hampshire: "Love dilates the good man's heart," MacGregore commented, "so that he no longer makes himself his chief end, but he has a sincere concern for the good of others. 'Tis one of the characters of charity, that 'she seeketh not her own.'" A good Christian was never happier than "when he is employed as an instrument, in the hand of God, in promoting the good of others."[17] This sincere and selfless love was a rare commodity, and more vile urges often masqueraded as charity. Mere *"External or apparent Virtue* is such an external Conduct as may seem to be the visible Effect or Expression of this inward divine Principle," President Thomas Clap of Yale admonished, "but, in Reality, is not; and proceeds from some *lower* Motive, such as Self-Interest, Honour, Fancy, or the like."[18]

There were two perfect examples of divine charity in the Bible, those of the Lord and His Son. The world itself was a product of God's selfless love toward its creatures: "It was . . . pure disinterested love that prompted him to bring forth this great something out of nothing."[19] And it was this same spirit that led God to send His Son to redeem humanity. No matter what an individual's religious leanings, New Englanders before the Revolution accepted without challenge the doctrine that unregenerate people were by nature miserable sinners. The Lord's compassion for such unworthy wretches was the ultimate in selfless love. Moreover, Jesus had been a living exemplar of holy love. In 1722 the Reverend Benjamin Wadsworth of Boston urged that *"All Christians should indeavour to Imitate the Example of our blessed Lord Jesus Christ,"* and New Englanders echoed this call often over the next half century. No doubt it was impossible to achieve the divinity of Jesus. No one could mediate as He had between God the Father and humanity. "But, as Christ the Son of God *appear'd in our nature,* liv'd on earth among Men, he was a *perfect pattern* of *holy Obedience* to God's commands." Because *"Our blessed Lord Jesus was compassionate and beneficent,"* Wadsworth indicated, His children were obliged to *"have the same care one for another."*[20] Who, "influenced by the force of so great an example," could selfishly "sit down first, and compute what account our good intentions, kind offices, or *works and labour that proceedeth of Love* to our indigent brothers, will turn to"?[21] "Our charity," admonished the Reverend Arthur Browne, Portsmouth's Anglican missionary, "must consist in imitating our Lord and Saviour."[22]

The universality of pure charity was a corollary of its disinterestedness. As Jonathan Mayhew explained, much as "the charity which is injoined in revelation" was selfless, so also "to love our neighbour, in the sense of scripture, is to love the world."[23] Christian charity was the antithesis of self-centeredness. "Since it does not take its rise in natural relations or worldly connections," the Reverend Amos Adams of Roxbury instructed, "so it disregards all distinctions of the world. It cordially embraces rich and poor, high and low, bond and free, friends and foes, good and bad, saints and sinners."[24] This spirit could "not be confin'd within the narrow Precincts of our own Nation, Land, Town, Church, Neighbourhood, Kindred or Family, nor limited to those of our particular Party, of our Way, Principles, and Humour," the Reverend Thomas Foxcroft of Boston pointed out in 1720: "It must reach unto all, whether our own Countrymen, Acquaintances and Relatives, or Strangers, Aliens and Foreigners."[25]

The parable of the good Samaritan provided the best evidence that God expected universal charity. The intention of the story was obviously to "teach the unbounded extent of the command, enjoining to love of his neighbour."[26] Like the lawyer in the parable, New Englanders wondered who their "neighbors" were. The word's primary definition was "those who dwell *near us.*" But of course the parable implied that this was not the meaning Jesus had in mind. Jonathan Mayhew consequently recognized that the term also had a broader sense, "all those with whom we have any thing to do,"[27] and other New Englanders offered even more sweeping exegeses. The consensus was that "every man breathing" was " . . . our neighbour,"[28] and that "love to our neighbour," a comprehensive duty, included "virtually all the offices of justice and charity, and whatever we are obliged to, with reference to one another."[29]

Could everyone achieve Christian charity? No, but everyone could strive for it. New Englanders distinguished between disinterested love and two other emotions, the *"natural tenderness"*[30] or natural love of moral but once-born men and women, and unrestrained greed. A "right *Charitable* and liberal Spirit," according to the Reverend Benjamin Colman of Boston, was not ". . . . meerly a *humane,* tender, generous *natural Temper,* or *acquired* Disposition towards a necessitous or compassionable Object," but rather "a distinguishing *Gift* of Providence."[31]

Everyone felt a natural affection toward friends, relatives, and neighbors, at least to a degree, but New Englanders warned that without regeneration this spirit grew out of self-concern rather than a sincere interest in the well-being of others. True Christian charity was impossible "where the fleshly principle rules, and acts," Arthur Browne warned, "For all its motions and suggestions have respect only to self: the pleasures, the honours, the riches *of this life.*"[32] Moved by a self-centered love, unregenerate men and women naturally favored those who could serve their own needs—for example, parents, children, siblings, and acquaintances. Natural tenderness was a virtue in its own right, an important tool for the maintenance of society's moral order. Moreover, it was preferable to unchecked greed, the sentiment that egoist philosophers like Thomas Hobbes and Bernard Mandeville believed inevitably to be at the base of all human conduct.[33] Nevertheless, everyone agreed that there was necessarily a stark contrast between unregenerate emotions of either sort and those of the twice-born. "Meer Self-love, without one Spark of the Love of God," [34] led to hatred and greed; "Works without Faith" were a "mere lifeless Carcase."[35] "Tenderness, Compassion, Benevolence, and Charity" flourished, however, in the presence of the "Genius and Spirit of the Gospel."[36]

True charity was best described, in the tradition of St. Augustine, as a love of humanity through God. "Love of our Neighbour," the Reverend Nathaniel Appleton of Cambridge taught, ". . . proceeds from, and is the effect of, a supreme Love to GOD."[37] Charity could take on an infinite number of forms, but as long as it expressed the love that regenerate Christians felt for their maker, then it was what God required of His children. Such charity came naturally to no one, but it was the inevitable result of regeneration and an evidence of the Lord's acceptance. No one could will it, no one could achieve it on his own no matter how hard he tried, just as no one could earn his own salvation, though it was natural to strive for it. Yet the regenerate Christian expressed it effortlessly, inexorably. Those whom God had chosen opened their hearts to the world.

Or so the theory went. But there was a hitch, one that became apparent only when it came time to implement charity. It was one thing to aspire to universal love and something else entirely to achieve it. New Englanders could learn about ideal charity from the Bible, but the gospel of John also instructed that Christians had to practice it. They were not to "love in word only, neither in tongue, but in deed and truth."[38] This was a demanding injunction, the extent of which New Englanders recognized with increasing clarity as time passed. For a variety of reasons, the practical problems the obligation entailed slipped to the farthest recesses of the minds of New England's first settlers. By the end of the seventeenth century, however, New Englanders were becoming conscious of the commonsense difficulties the injunction presented and aware of the distance separating their aspirations from their achievements, revelation's view of charity from nature's.

The Active Principle

Seventeenth-century New Englanders never doubted their obligation to do good works, but except for the obvious responsibility to treat friends and relatives with consideration, until the 1680s this duty was never more than an occasional concern. Ezechiel Carré, a Huguenot clergyman, spoke for New Englanders of all nationalities when he reminded them in Boston in 1689 of the connection between Christian charity and practical charity. Throughout the rest of the colonial period New Englanders agreed that faith and works had to be joined together. Carré condemned those hypocrites who "made their *Charity* consist onely in *words,*" and he reminded that the good Samaritan's example demonstrated "that it consists in *real actions* and in the good Service which we perform."[39] Colonial New Englanders concurred: "Our Affections," Cotton Mather observed, "must produce Affectionate Resolutions to do all the *Good* that we can."[40] New Englanders believed that Jesus's compassion for sufferers led Him to act,[41] and it appeared to them a basic "property of love to contribute what lies in its Power to the Welfare and Benefit of it's Beloved."[42] Yet it was easier to proclaim that good works were the responsibility of Christians[43] than it was to carry them out.

Throughout much of the seventeenth century the practice of charity in New England was striking for two characteristics: its wide-reaching ambition and the infrequency with which New Englanders actually had to act on their principles. To a degree that later generations of New Englanders could never approach, the founding fathers and their children were almost able to approximate comprehensive charity. Perhaps because they kept in regular contact with friends in England and led generally prosperous lives in a society starved for labor,[44] New Englanders through the middle of the seventeenth century almost never had to test the practical limits of their charity. Geography seemed a minor barrier to people who were keeping in touch with friends and relatives at home, and New Englanders maintained especially strong ties with the motherland through the Puritan Commonwealth and Protectorate periods between 1649 and 1660. Religious and political leaders corresponded frequently with their English counterparts,[45] and some New Englanders even returned to the old country to assist the Puritan cause when revolution broke out. Moreover, as long as there was "seldom any want, because labour is dear" and "because provisions are cheap,"[46] as one Connecticut governor reported to the Board of Trade in 1680, hardly anyone needed assistance but a few "impotent poor"—orphans, elderly widows, accident victims, and the ill.

Seventeenth-century New Englanders were remarkably generous toward needy strangers—in large measure because close to home the demands on their resources were so modest. In Dorchester and Roxbury between 1650 and 1683, for example, more than two-thirds of all church collections were for causes outside the community, including some for beneficiaries as far away as the Bahamas, Cape Fear, Dublin, and London.[47]

As early as the 1660s, however, New Englanders began to see the outer limits of their open-handed approach to charity, and by the end of the century most were beginning to change their ways. Emotional attachments to the mother country started to fray, and the prosperity that was the basis of their generosity faltered. Although neither correspondence with England nor English migration to New England ever entirely ceased, the restoration to the throne of an Anglican king, Charles II, isolated New Englanders from English circles of political and religious power after 1660. Migration from England to New England, moreover, dropped off in the early 1640s, never to revive. After the outbreak of the English Revolution, as John Winthrop noted, encouraging developments in England led most Puritans to remain there in expectation of a "new world."[48] After 1660 this "new world" suddenly seemed so remote that Englishmen soured on utopia, and immigration to the Puritan "City on a Hill" hardly seemed worth the bother.

Meanwhile, the growth of a landless social stratum both in rural New England and in the region's ports indicated that economic conditions were deteriorating. By the end of the seventeenth century, seventy years of natural population growth had filled many of the farming communities of eastern Massachusetts and the Connecticut River valley. With too little land available to support the generation coming of age, New England faced a labor surplus.[49] A few sons, unprovided for, stayed on in New England's farm country, where they were the seeds of a new rural underclass; more set out for the frontier or moved in search of opportunity to such commercial towns as Boston, Newport, Portsmouth, New Haven, and Salem, where a small, rowdy, and restless transatlantic population of mariners had been disturbing the people since the first years of settlement. These ports grew rapidly, and by the turn of the century each was sheltering a significant class of marginal men and women who worked in boom times and depended on their neighbors when trade was off.[50]

It is impossible to determine precisely when New Englanders began to realize the implications for their charity of the convergence of a surplus of labor and the unraveling of transatlantic attachments. No doubt, the moment of recognition differed from town to town and individual to individual. By the early 1680s, however, many churches were starting to draw inward, perceiving that growing demands on their charity were outstripping their resources, both emotional and financial. At least one church, in Salem, determined as early as 1660 to give preference to the needs of its own members; between the mid-1680s and 1700 many others in such communities as Boston, Cambridge, and Dorchester also made special provisions for their own needy. Meanwhile, New Englanders began to grope for ways to explain to themselves and to everyone else how even the most faithful and selfless Christians had to ration their charity.[51]

New Englanders did not introduce Christian charity and common sense to each other, nor were they the first Christians to try to come to terms with the natural constraints under which they labored. As they looked to make sense of their responsibilities, New Englanders in the late 1600s and early 1700s drew on the fruits of centuries of theological and philosophical speculation on the nature of moral duties. During the second quarter of the eighteenth century, moreover, college-educated New Englanders also drew conclusions about charity from revolutions in the social and natural sciences, the work of several generations of British moral philosophers, physicists, and their popularizers. On the eve of the American Revolution most New Englanders assumed that the common wisdom about charity's natural limits was fully in agreement with the conclusions of the best minds of western civilization.

By the end of the seventeenth century, New Englanders were facing a form of what has since become the classic problem of modern economics: how to allocate scarce resources—in this case both compassion and alms—in the most efficient and practical fashion. The obvious answer was to adopt an order of priorities, but this course of action was complicated by the assumption that good Christians selflessly loved the entire human race. Here was a paradox, one that colonial New Englanders never entirely resolved. While they proclaimed their disinterested love of humanity as a whole, they also reassured themselves that God accepted the practical limits to their charity.

The priorities that New Englanders began to talk about in the early eighteenth century made two kinds of distinctions: among acquaintances and strangers and between the deserving and the undeserving. Neither distinction was original to New England; in fact, the more complicated of these sets of priorities—involving distinctions among acquaintances—had its immediate origins in Calvin's Geneva.

Well before the settlement of New England, leaders in the reformed Protestant tradition recognized that a strict application of the Bible's most visionary teachings on charity was impossible. In Geneva, John Calvin taught in the 1530s that although there was "a general command from God to relieve the necessities of all the poor," Christians still fulfilled this obligation "who with all that in view give succour to all whom they see or know to be in distress, although they pass by many whose wants are not less urgent, either because they cannot know or are unable to give supply for all."[52] By the end of the sixteenth century, leading English Puritans drew justification from such teachings and from the philosophical writings of Petrus Ramus for the introduction of priorities into the practice of charity. Ramus, a French logician, instructed that society, indeed the universe as a whole, was composed of paired opposites or "affirmative contraries." Social roles and duties were not immutable but defined only through relationships: a husband was a husband only if he had a wife, a servant could not be a servant without a master.[53] Under these influences, William Perkins taught in the 1580s that although every Christian had a spiritual duty to "love and pray" selflessly for all humanity, in temporal terms every man and woman was also "a person in respect of another." Human relationships determined earthly responsibilities. "Thou art husband, father, mother, daughter, wife, lord, subject," Perkins reminded: " . . . thou must do according to thine office."[54] On the eve of the settlement of New England, English Puritans particularly emphasized the special love and charity that reborn Christians owed each other.[55] And in the *Marrow of Sacred Theology,* first published in 1623, William Ames offered an extended list of love's natural priorities: spouses before parents, parents before children, relatives before strangers.[56]

These ideas belonged to New England's cultural patrimony, and they were at the root of attempts at the end of the seventeenth century to deal rationally yet humanely with growing social problems. The effects of a fluctuating labor market were most severe in the trading towns along New

England's eastern coast between Portsmouth and Newport, and throughout the rest of the colonial period it was in these communities, especially in Boston, that citizens were most ready to find practical answers for their problems. By the early 1690s a circle of ministers in Boston set about to determine how to cope with the decay that seemed to be eating away at New England's social stability. Led by Cotton Mather, they stressed the special obligations that each human relationship entailed. Mather's own *Bonifacius: An Essay upon the Good,* a 200-page tract, summarized this position when it was published in 1710. By virtue of their stations, Mather instructed, special mutual obligations necessarily existed between relatives, neighbors, clergymen and their parishioners, teachers and their students, magistrates and citizens, physicians and their patients, rich men and the poor, Christians and the unconverted.[57]

Because teachings about each Christian's "relative duties" had a long history in Puritan thought, and because they seemed faithfully to describe the daily experience of most men and women, it is probably fair to suppose that although clergymen addressed the subject most often, by the early eighteenth century most New Englanders, of all callings, socioeconomic backgrounds, and educations, accepted some version of the doctrines that preachers like Cotton Mather were expressing. The influence of the theories of such scholars as Isaac Newton, John Locke, and Francis Hutcheson on assumptions about love, compassion, and moral obligation probably filtered only slowly from the ranks of New England's college men through the rest of the population. Nevertheless, surviving evidence in newspapers, correspondence, and church records, among other sources, strongly suggests that well before the Revolution these ideas too had become standard wisdom throughout society.[58]

The views on human love and obligation that New Englanders borrowed directly from men like Newton, Locke, and Hutcheson, or indirectly through their popularizers, built in the public mind on the old Ramist "affirmative contraries," and in an important sense these beliefs are best understood as a new systematization of traditional doctrines. In much the same way that Nicholaus Copernicus's heliocentric model of the universe wiped out centuries of confusion over epicycles and brought theoretical order to astronomy,[59] new configurations of beliefs about interpersonal relationships, stimulated by the work of the era's leading natural and moral scientists, established a convincing new understanding of the affectionate bonds of human society.

Without, in most cases, ever braving the mathematical complexities of Isaac Newton's *Principia Mathematica,* college-educated New Englanders after 1725 came to believe that the physicist's gravitational equations held for the moral as well as the natural world. Provincial scholars like tutors Samuel Johnson of Yale and Jonathan Mayhew of Harvard generally found when they cracked the covers of the *Principia* that the physics of gravity were too intricate to comprehend.[60] The principal sources of information on the new science for most educated New Englanders, consequently, were popularizations by a group of writers often known collectively as the "physicotheologians." The lectures of William Derham and William Whiston, for example, introduced listeners in old England and avid readers in New England to the rudiments of Newton's scientific ideas and instructed that so perfect, so harmonious a natural order, could only have come about through the handiwork of a good, kind, benevolent God.[61]

Because the physicotheologians were most concerned with elucidating Newton's scientific discoveries and with the attendant spiritual implications, their reflections on moral issues were at times no more than brief and suggestive. Readers attuned to the moral visions of a treatise like *The Astronomical Principles of Religion,* published in London in 1717, could nevertheless find direction in Whiston's assertion that the *"Universe* appears . . . to be evidently *One Universe;* govern'd by *One Law of Gravity* through the whole" and his inference that the same "Proportion, Harmony, and Decorum every where provided for by the Supreme Being in the Natural World" also ruled "all his Living and Rational . . . Creatures."[62] Love was the moral world's equivalent to gravity, according to this line of thinking, and anyone who had read John Locke's *Essay Concerning Human Understanding* could imagine the emotion as an invisible force of attraction drawing together the loving minds that sensed it.

The writings of Francis Hutcheson confirmed for most New England college men the validity of the analogy between the workings of gravity in the natural world and love in the moral world. Between 1725 and 1728, Hutcheson published four major essays on moral topics. These works, as well as his three-volume text, *A System of Moral Philosophy* (1755), and his single-volume *Short Introduction to Moral Philosophy* (1747), provided much of the basis of moral education in New England's colleges throughout the rest of the colonial period. Hutcheson instructed "That there is a universal Determination to Benevolence in Mankind, even toward the most distant part of the Species." Nevertheless, he also acknowledged that "we are not to imagine that this Benevolence is equal, or in the same degree toward all."[63] "This universal Benevolence toward all Men," Hutcheson proposed, "we may compare to that Principle of Gravitation, which perhaps extends to all Bodys in the Universe; but, like the Love of Benevolence, increases as the Distance is diminish'd, and is strongest when Bodys come to touch each other."[64]

By the second quarter of the eighteenth century most New Englanders accepted some variant of a common understanding of the faithful Christian's obligation to do good, whether or not they consciously took the theories of Newton, Locke, and Hutcheson into account and believed that "Universal Charity" could be "compared to the great Law of Gravitation."[65] No one questioned, as the Reverend Joseph Sewall of Boston put it, that "*Every Man without Distinction of Nation, or outward Condition*" was "*our Neighbour.*" Yet like Sewall, most New Englanders added that "*Such are our Neighbours in an especial Manner, as stand in any peculiar Relation to us, whether natural, civil or religious.*"[66] These "peculiar Relations" took on an imagined appearance much like the solar system's in the mind of Copernicus or Newton. At the center of this "grand machine"[67] was the faithful Christian. Standing apart at varying distances, like so many Venuses, Jupiters, and Saturns, drawn to him by "the attractive Force of Love,"[68] were the people in his life. As the Reverend Samuel Andrews, an Episcopal clergyman, reminded an audience of Freemasons in Wallingford in 1770, "charity . . . must begin at home, and is extended from thence to our nearest friends; after them, to the most remote, till it finally reach the utmost limits of human nature."[69] Like the force of gravity, the force of love weakened with distance. Although a Christian's "Charity extends to the whole Family of Mankind, and he can never be persuaded to do any Thing contrary to the general Interest," the Reverend Samuel Cooper of Boston maintained, "yet as his Abilities are limited, he chiefly exerts himself for that Society in particular, to which he is most nearly related; in which his Influence will be most felt; and his benevolent Designs are most likely to take Effect."[70]

Once New Englanders agreed on the priorities that differentiated among acquaintances and strangers in need, they drew one more set of distinctions, between innocent sufferers and the dissolute. Fire, serious illness, and a host of other crises could throw good and decent men, women, and children on the mercy of others through no fault of their own. There were times, however, when the needy brought their problems on themselves.

In 1719 the Reverend Benjamin Wadsworth of Boston spoke for most New Englanders when he analyzed the varieties of poverty. "There are *degrees* of *Poverty,*" Wadsworth explained. Some were simply "*poor negatively,* that is, they are not rich, have not such *plenty* and *abundance,* as some of their Neighbours have. Yet possibly by God's Blessings on their prudent diligent Labours, they want neither *Food* nor *Raiment* convenient for them." Others were less lucky. Despite their hard work and blameless lives they were "*very poor* . . . not able to provide themselves a *comfortable Dwelling,* nor *comfortable Food or Raiment.*" They were "in pinching *straits, wants, necessities.*" For such people, he noted, "*this poverty is not a Sin, but a misery.*" "In its self condider'd," he added, "'*tis no Sin to be poor.*'" However, a third group combined sin with poverty. For as Wadsworth conceded, "very often vicious wicked practices, do evidently and directly bring *pinching Poverty* on persons."[71]

Each of these groups merited a different expression of charity. The "negatively poor" needed only advice, compassion, and encouragement. Thus fortified, they could learn to live with their lots, or even to improve them. The helpless, worthy poor, beset by disease, accident, or theft, were fit recipients of more concrete aid. "When Persons are Impoverish'd by such ways as these," Wadsworth noted, "they are not to be *blam'd* for, but rather pity'd and relieved in, their affliction." Slothful, vicious, and criminal men and women did not deserve this kind of support.[72] Quoting Second Thessalonians, the Reverend Charles Chauncy of Boston explained in 1752 what the debauched poor deserved: "Concerning these Poor, it is the Command of an inspired Apostle, *that they shall not eat,* i.e. be maintained at the Charge of others; shall not live upon the Charities of their Christian Friends and Brethren."[73]

There was a normative aspect to the distinction between the worthy and unworthy that Wadsworth, Chauncy, and their countrymen drew; the grounds for their judgments were the moral standards of their communities. Much as the spectrum of New England's priorities among classes of acquaintances was a consequence of the limits of their resources, however, distinctions based on virtue or the lack of it were important because there was neither enough compassion nor relief to go around.

New England's theories about charity implied that all sorts of good works, even limited or unsuccessful ones, expressed Christian compassion, or could if the conditions were right. The Christian who really lived his faith had no shortage of ways to live his charity as well, only powers that were limited. As long as he attempted to serve real needs and his heart was in the right place, a Christian's sympathy, moral admonitions, evangelism, alms, and patriotism could all convey his charity. He could act alone or with others. He could serve relatives, friends, neighbors, countrymen, complete strangers, or under certain circumstances even himself. He could aspire to do great things, yet do none but small ones, and still live in charity.

The gap between aspirations and achievements seemed the narrowest, and charity seemed to flourish the best, in the most intimate situations, among relatives, friends, and neighbors. The Reverend James Noyes expressed his "abundant Charity" best through the free medical care he provided his neighbors in Stonington, Connecticut. As the Reverend Eliphalet Adams of New London reminded Noyes's parishioners in a funeral eulogy in 1720, "when he came to your Sick beds . . . what tenderness and pity would he shew! more like a Father than a Physician, How would he *Chear* the *drooping spirit* by his *Encouraging Speeches, hearty Sympathy, wise Instructions and fervent Prayers.*"[74] Charity was also a "foundation of all moral rectitude,"[75] and through their sense of rectitude Christians met those duties imposed by God "which more immediately relate to *ourselves.*" It was the Lord's will, Thomas Clap maintained, that "every Man, considering himself as one of the Creatures of *God;* ought to endeavour to promote his *own* Happiness, as well as the Happiness of *others;* and therefore ought to cultivate and improve his rational Powers and moral Habits."[76] Loving Christians additionally were obliged to "*Watch over*" their families, friends, and neighbors.[77] Sloth and idleness could ruin an individual, his household, and his community.[78] In the early 1740s the Reverend Edmund March of Amesbury detailed the consequences of a failure of family love. " 'Tis not easy," March wrote, "to describe the Confusion and Misery of some families when one, or both, that are at the Head don't consider or regard the Obligations that they are under to seek the Good of the several Members of the House both in Body and Soul, for Time and Eternity." Such families spawned children who were "evil Doers," youths who were "ungovernable Creatures," and adults who "destroy themselves by a debauched Way of Living."[79]

There were certain community organizations in which charity could also thrive. As the Reverend William Balch of Bradford reminded the members of the newly established Second Church of Rowley in 1732, churches had a duty "*to manage all their affairs with charity.*" Communicants, Balch admonished, should behave "with a sincere and fervent Affection to each other, being influenced with a tender Regard to each others Good, and promoting it in all proper ways, to the uttermost of their power." They were to think, speak, and act compassionately toward each other, as well as to relieve each other in times of need.[80] In Boston, after 1720 the Congregational churches met one aspect of this responsibility by taking up a collection at a joint charity lecture held cooperatively every three months. The members of the Massachusetts Convention of Congregational Ministers began as well in the early eighteenth century to take up collections to relieve clergymen in need, their families, and their heirs.[81]

Members of mutual benefit societies also believed that a similar bond of Christian love could join them together. Mutual benefit societies were an English contribution to the institutional life of colonial America, the first known ones in the mother country having been established in the early seventeenth century to support dues-paying members in case of sudden calamities like illness or accident. By the early eighteenth century these fraternities, the most notable of which were the Freemasons, were spread across Great Britain, although they were concentrated in large cities and towns. By 1772 two competing grand lodges, both located in Boston, oversaw between them about two dozen masonic lodges, most of them in the region's ports. New England also had at least four marine societies composed of ships' captains and merchants and perhaps another half-dozen additional fraternities of various descriptions. Each association limited its membership, typically to forty or fewer brothers, and made new admissions on the basis of the vote of existing members. Many required unanimous approval for admission. Such institutions, as Balch recognized in 1732, were governed by the same divine principles that ruled the affairs of families, churches, precincts, and towns. Outsiders sometimes accused Freemasons of selfishness and Deism, and indeed the brotherhood ordinarily limited its relief to lodge mates, but members of the order maintained that their mutual love was of a piece with the broader "Universal love" that joined Christians to humanity as a whole.[82]

Three other associations combined mutualism with more impersonal relief for nonmembers who fell within narrowly defined categories. The organizers of the Scots' Charitable Society, New England's first formal beneficent association, founded in 1657, augmented their special interest in the welfare of subscribers with a concern for the condition of Scotsmen in need traveling through Boston. The Charitable Irish Society and the Episcopal Charitable Society, both of Boston, pledged to relieve Irishmen and Anglicans respectively, nonmembers as well as members.[83]

As attempts at charity grew increasingly impersonal, however, they became sporadic as well as less successful and less satisfying to those who took part in them. The rescue of Phillis Wheatley, America's first published black female poet, was so exceptional that its very success reveals the haphazardness and discontinuity of charity outside the household and neighborhood in colonial New England.

On an August day in 1761, Susanna Wheatley, the wife of an affluent Boston craftsman, was passing through the market when a slave sale caught her attention. Mrs. Wheatley was in need of domestic help, and as she watched the proceedings she was drawn to a gap-toothed, barely clothed girl of seven or eight. Mrs. Wheatley bought the girl, but instead of putting her to work full time as a household slave, the entire family befriended her and Susanna's daughter began to tutor her. Soon Phillis was reading and writing in several languages. Her first published poem appeared in print in 1767, six years after she entered the Wheatley home.[84]

Unique in its particulars, the story of Susanna and Phillis Wheatley is nevertheless revealing of impersonal charity in New England before the

American Revolution. An unplanned spasm of compassion in response to an accidental encounter, Susanna Wheatley's purchase of Phillis, like the Samaritan's good deed on the road from Jerusalem to Jericho, was a private, personal act of kindness. Were it not for the girl's remarkable abilities, the entire episode would have been without continuing significance outside the Wheatley household.

Unlike the rescue of Phillis Wheatley, most of colonial New England's other impersonal initiatives ultimately demonstrated the extent of the gulf between aspirations and achievements. Missionary work, for example, could be considered a kind of charity, as Benjamin Wadsworth recognized in 1718 when he called for "the Charitable Spreading of the Gospel." As early as 1655, President Charles Chauncy of Harvard, the great-grandfather of his namesake, the eighteenth-century Boston minister, recognized that New Englanders who lived on the frontier faced the possibility that their children might "go native." Far from churches and ministers, schools and teachers, many New Englanders in the backcountry risked isolation from the institutions that preserved a civilized and Christian way of life. Indians and pioneers alike needed the services of missionaries. Although these evangelists were to spread the faith and win reborn converts to Christ, they had a second, related objective, one of equal importance as far as most local observers were concerned, the charitable fostering of British mores in a cultural wasteland. At his mission station in Stockbridge, the Reverend John Sergeant, speaking of his Indian charges, explained this important goal of all New England missionaries, no matter for whom they cared: "to take such a *Method* . . . as shall in the most effectual Manner change their whole Habit of thinking and acting."[85] Colonial New Englanders never spared much energy or money for evangelism, however, although by the mid-1720s they were supporting it modestly. Missionaries themselves needed a charitable spirit, as Gideon Hawley well knew, but most New Englanders were not able to take such direct roles in the work and confined their participation to advice and contributions.

Domestic support for Indian missions was rarely substantial or reliable during the colonial period, but by the middle of the eighteenth century a few New Englanders were attending to evangelism. Although the first Indian missions were established in the 1640s by the Reverend John Eliot of Roxbury and the Mayhew family of Martha's Vineyard, New Englanders in general were oblivious to evangelism until the eighteenth century. Throughout the seventeenth century, New England's few missionaries depended for support almost entirely on a London missionary society, the Company for Propagacion of the Gospell in New England and the Parts adjacent in America, or as it was usually called, the New England Company.[86] Except for the missionaries themselves, the only New Englanders to take active roles in the conversion of the natives were the members of a small board of local notables set up to serve as trustees for and advisors to the Company's London officers. As late as the outbreak of the Revolution, New Englanders were still relying on the New England Company and a second British organization, the Society in Scotland for Propagating Christian Knowledge, which had underwritten its first New England missionaries in 1733,[87] as well as on fundraising campaigns in England and Scotland, to cover most of their missionary bills. Serious efforts to solicit local contributions started in the 1740s,[88] and by the 1760s these attempts began to meet with some success. Two early efforts, however, failed to establish missionary societies in Boston in 1749 and 1762, the second of these when the Privy Council in London refused to approve its proposed corporate charter.[89] In 1743 John Sergeant came to the discouraging conclusion that New Englanders had no interest in his work as a missionary in Stockbridge when almost no one responded to his appeal for support for a school for Indians.[90] By 1764, though, when Eleazar Wheelock solicited contributions for a second school for the natives, Moor's Charity School in Lebanon, Connecticut, his efforts resulted in £258 in donations, of which two-thirds came from New Englanders.[91]

The spiritual and moral needs of English settlements in tiny or isolated places were no better served than those of the Indians. A few New Englanders began to recognize as early as the 1690s that one frequent cost of settlement in such places was a kind of religious deprivation, an isolation from a community of Christians and the ministrations of a capable clergyman.[92] They did little to remedy this deficiency, however, until 1726, when the members of Boston's churches agreed to take up regular collections to subsidize clergymen in communities that could not afford to pay full salaries. Throughout the rest of the colonial period ministers in such places as Nantucket, Freetown, Tiverton, and Providence (where the Congregational minority was a tiny island in a sea of Baptists and Quakers) received small salary supplements.[93] Provincial ministerial associations also tried to provide for the needs of isolated settlements, taking up regular collections for the purpose at their annual meetings in Massachusetts beginning in the early 1700s and in New Hampshire starting in 1752.[94] With the establishment in 1769 of Dartmouth College by Eleazar Wheelock, who turned to domestic evangelism when he became discouraged by repeated failures among the Indians, New Englanders had a seminary the graduates of which were pledged to serve as frontier or Indian missionaries.

Such initiatives were useful as far as they went, but on the eve of the

Revolution the needs of isolated settlements obviously far outran the measures that New Englanders had considered to relieve them. At his school in
Connecticut, and later at Dartmouth in Hanover, New Hampshire, Eleazar
Wheelock frequently received pleas for help from frontier towns without
preachers. In 1763, two correspondents from Cornwallis, New Hampshire,
writing on behalf of "a Poor flok with out a Sheppard Scatter'd upon the
mountains," begged Wheelock to take "Compasinate Care and Consarne" for
them. Two years later in 1765, a resident of Orford, New Hampshire, twenty
miles up the Connecticut River from Hanover, making a similar plea to
Wheelock, estimated that in the vicinity there were "about a hundred town-
ships now granted and seteling verey fast and but one ordand minister in
them all and thay . . . greatly Desire to have the Gospel preacht amongst
them." By 1771, observers estimated that fully 200 new towns in northern
New England needed settled clergymen or missionaries.[95]

Whatever the cause of the failure to support Indian and domestic missions, the reason was not that New Englanders were devoting their energies
to reform activities. Despite the example of English reformers, whose efforts
were beginning to meet success by 1700, attempts by New Englanders
systematically to cure what they believed to be pressing moral problems were
generally ineffectual.

Although the most noteworthy outcome of England's Glorious Revolution
was its political settlement, the accession of William and Mary to the throne,
among its indirect fruits was what one historian has called "the moral
revolution of 1688." A veritable army of reform societies arose in major
English cities in the aftermath of the coup, some to cure social ills, others for
the self-improvement of their members. The first of these, an association to
close bawdy houses, appeared in London's East End about 1690. By 1701
there were "near twenty societies of various qualities and functions, formed
in subordination and corresponding with one another, and engaged in this
Christian design in and about this city and suburbs." Similar associations to
suppress vice in its various forms also took shape in such English communities as Gloucester, Leicester, Coventry, Shrewsbury, Hull, Tamworth,
and Portsmouth.[96]

Led by Cotton Mather, New Englanders began to organize societies on this
model almost immediately. By the early eighteenth century, several of these
institutions had come and gone. Mather established the first, a self-
improvement association for the black residents of Boston, in 1693. Other
societies for white residents appeared under Mather's aegis by 1702; two
were active between 1705 and 1711 but had probably dissolved by 1712. At
least one small reform society survived in Boston in the 1760s, though, and

elsewhere there are signs in the church records of such towns as Plymouth of the existence of local reform associations at various times before the War for Independence. Meanwhile, Ezra Stiles and Samuel Hopkins toyed briefly in Newport in the early 1770s with the idea of establishing an antislavery society. And several New Englanders, including John Lathrop of Boston and Jonathan Edwards, Jr., of New Haven, were involved at about the same time in a still-born attempt to establish a continental tract society, the American Society for Promoting Religious Knowledge among the Poor in the British Colonies.[97]

Large-scale efforts to relieve domestic poverty through charity met with only slightly more success. Throughout the colonial period New Englanders usually responded generously to ad hoc charitable subscriptions, but they were ineffective when it came to following British examples and establishing permanent programs. In times of crisis, seventeenth- and eighteenth-century governors often issued charity briefs for collections to be taken up at Sunday church services,[98] and when a disaster like the sinking in 1769 of a major portion of Marblehead's fishing fleet struck a town, neighbors came to the aid of victims and survivors.[99] By the middle of the eighteenth century, however, in many English cities and towns community leaders were establishing endowed charity schools, hospitals, and an assortment of other permanent institutions to take care of the poor and disabled. Between the early 1750s and the start of the Revolution, residents of Philadelphia and New York were quicker than New Englanders to follow suit.[100]

The most notable colonial charitable institution was the Pennsylvania Hospital, established in Philadelphia in 1751, with £4,750 in contributions to care for the sick poor and the demented. By 1776 Philadelphians had also established an organization to take care of insolvent debtors, the Philadelphia Society for the Relief of Distressed Prisoners, and Manhattan residents had followed Philadelphia's lead and built a hospital.[101] In Boston, though, an early proposal by Benjamin Colman in 1713 to establish charity schools for the town's poor was never implemented,[102] and many of those programs that were instituted led checkered histories.

Boston's most ambitious attempt to match the achievements of other communities on both sides of the Atlantic was the Society for Encouraging Industry and Employing the Poor, an organization of about 200 subscribers in 1754, which briefly met success in the early 1750s but terminated most activities by the late 1750s and disappeared by the mid-1760s, leaving scarcely a trace. Founded sometime between 1748 and 1751 (the surviving evidence is inconclusive), the Society was modeled on existing English and Irish associations. Like these organizations, the Society trained the unemployed at a "spinning school," then provided them with spinning wheels, looms, and flax. Thanks to a contribution from Benjamin Franklin, it also offered local farmers a prize for the most successful flax production.[103] Under ideal circumstances, the members believed, after an initial outlay the "linen manufactory" could be self-supporting. Revenues from the sale of finished cloth would cover the costs both of buying more flax and of paying the spinners and weavers stipends. Receipts apparently never matched expenses, however, and the Society closed its books sometime after 1760, possibly the ironic victim of a brief surge in the demand for labor during the Seven Years' War that made its work temporarily superfluous. At war's end, the increased demand for labor dried up, unemployment rose, and by 1768 Boston's selectmen were making arrangements with private contractors to use the Society's old facilities as a duck-cloth manufactory where the poor could be employed.[104]

Only two of colonial New England's major charitable activities even approximated unqualified success as far as contemporaries were concerned—a subscription in 1760 to relieve the victims in Boston of "the most terrible fire that has happened in this town or perhaps in any other part of North-America,"[105] and the appeal that went out in 1774 when Parliament closed the ports of Boston and Charlestown in response to the Boston Tea Party. The fire, which broke out at two in the morning of March 20, gutted much of the town. By the time it burned itself out it had destroyed 400 buildings worth somewhere between £100,000 and £300,000.[106] New Englanders recognized immediately that this loss was too severe to be made up by the town itself, so on March 22 the General Court of the province voted to ask Gov. Thomas Pownall to send out briefs to solicit contributions. The Court also voted to advance £3,000 from the public treasury.[107] When the town's committees toted up the contributions from Massachusetts, Connecticut, New Hampshire, Nova Scotia, New York, Pennsylvania, Maryland, and London they amounted to 17,576.15.8 pound (l.m.), or £13,317.11.9,[108] not enough, to be sure, to compensate fully for the losses of the 439 sufferers, but a prodigious sum nonetheless.[109]

Parliament's decision in March 1774 to close the ports of Boston and Charlestown on June 1, allowing only overland shipments of food and fuel, similarly threw the residents of the two towns on the mercy of their countrymen both in Massachusetts and throughout the North American colonies. Years of assiduous letter-writing, beginning in the mid-1760s as the imperial crisis was growing increasingly serious, had provided Boston's Committee of Correspondence, however, with a network of friends and sympathizers.[110] When word of Parliament's punitive actions became known, legislatures in many colonies drafted resolutions to express their concern.[111] In Massachusetts the General Court resolved on June 17, the day of its dissolution by Gov. Thomas Gage, to recommend that citizens of the province contribute to relieve the two towns. In Connecticut the legislature recommended general subscriptions on three separate occasions.[112] The response was a patriotic flood of compassion "towards the unhappy sufferers"[113] and a stream of contributions of all sorts. Nearly 3,000 sheep bleated along country roads to the slaughter in Boston. Other donations included cattle, oxen, swine, fish, butter, cheese, grain, cocoa, olive oil, wood, iron, shoes, and even a single handkerchief, as well as cash. Contributions came from nearly one hundred communities across New England and more than thirty towns and counties outside the region, from Savannah in the south to Montreal and Quebec City in the north. Between late June 1774 and the end of the following April, committees in Boston and Charlestown received and distributed donations worth a minimum of £9,850.[114]

The relief of Boston in 1760 and its provisioning with Charlestown in 1774 were major achievements, at least by provincial standards, ones that New Englanders were quick to herald. "The unexampled charity and munificence with which this distressed Town hath been treated by their brethren of the continent," one Boston official exclaimed in 1774, "must strike Europe with astonishment."[115] Fires and blockades were extraordinary events, though, and the public's response to them had been extraordinary as well. The story was different in more normal times, as almost everyone realized. Occasionally, to be sure, civic boosters, swept away by a moment's excitement, enthused that a New England community had "remarkably signalized its self, for its Charity and Compassion to the Poor."[116] But these were uncommon boasts. Before the Revolution most New Englanders were well aware of the limits of their charity.

By any standard New Englanders had fallen short. Their efforts paled in comparison with those of other Englishmen. Philadelphia's hospital far overshadowed any comparable organization New Englanders could claim, especially after the demise of the linen manufactory. Even John Adams, ever a New England chauvinist, conceded in 1774 that Philadelphia outdid Boston in its "charitable public foundations." It went without saying, moreover, that neither Boston nor Newport nor any of New England's other important commercial towns could boast any private infirmaries, asylums, or similar institutions to compare with those in London and the British outports. Nor were New England's efforts always adequate. Ad hoc expedients that worked for small towns were frequently insufficient to meet the needs of larger communities subject to the ebbs and flows of international commerce, and Boston's mixed experiences with textiles showed that New Englanders were not yet committed to that sort of activity. Most seriously of all for a people convinced of the Bible's literal truth, New England's charity failed Scripture's tests. Practical considerations obviously prevented the unlimited distribution of alms to the needy: as the Reverend Mather Byles of Boston recognized in 1740, it was "a Duty impossible to be perform'd."[117] And even Christian compassion had its limits.

Apologetic Charity

There was nothing left for New Englanders to do but to apologize for their shortcomings. Indeed, their apologies became formulaic, so often were they offered. The underlying premise was simple: "Perfection, in the strict sense of the Word," Byles pointed out in 1758, "is not attainable by us in our present State." No one, not the fallible sinner, not the reborn Christian, not the pious minister, nor even St. Paul, "who came as near the Character as any Man," was without failings and deficiencies.[118] Regeneration lifted converted Christians out of the deepest pit of depravity and closer to God than mortals could ever come by their own efforts, but it did not free them from human frailties. Even the very best Christians were "extremely deficient, and . . . sadly short of coming up to this amiable Character."[119] The converted could aspire to emulate the Lord and His son, but as Thomas Clap reminded, "all Perfection is originally in God"; it was only "communicated to the Creatures, in various limited Degrees, according to their several Ranks and Orders."[120] Not even a Christian with "a sincere, disinterested regard to the good of others" could "feel equally affected with their cases as with his own" because "the mind of man is a limitted thing. . . . more or less affected with objects, as they are more or less under view."[121]

Although the reborn Christian's compassion was infinitely purer than the natural person's, most New Englanders reluctantly admitted that in practice each was governed by the same priorities. The scholarly inquiries of trained theologians and the fruitless efforts of faithful laymen and women led to the same conclusion: nothing, not even a spirit filled with grace, could surmount nature's limitations.[122] This was an awkward, paradoxical realization in view of the Bible's apparent insistence on pure, selfless, and universal love, but most New Englanders tried to reconcile themselves to it.

There were various ways to try to explain away the incongruity between scriptural teachings and charity's natural limits, and New Englanders found comfort in several of them. Christians and philosophers had long wrestled with similar problems, and the heritage of their doubts underlay the rationales that most, if not quite all, New Englanders accepted.

Although the New Testament's apparent insistence on disinterested and universal love was at the root of the paradox, many New Englanders also found moral teachings in scripture to justify charity that was less than comprehensive. On the eve of the Revolution, New Englanders used such texts as Galatians 6:10, "As we have therefore opportunity, let us do good unto all men, especially unto them who are of the household of faith," and the story of the widow's mite, found both in Mark 12:41–44 and in Luke 21:2, to support their practices.

Galatians 6:10 was comforting on two scores. Following the lead of such Reformed divines as John Calvin, William Ames, and Richard Baxter, New Englanders seized on its first clause, "As we have therefore opportunity," to explain why at times their charity seemed to falter,[123] and its third clause, "especially unto them who are of the household of faith," to justify establish-ing practical priorities. Although Christian love was not to be confined to friends and acquaintances, faithful men and women were not expected to drop everything in order to travel the world providing relief and consolation to the needy. God's revealed Word plainly showed that all men and women were neighbors,[124] but it required nothing more than that Christians rise to the occasion as the Lord presented them with opportunities. Nor did God require the committed to bankrupt themselves in the name of Christian compassion. He recognized human frailty and accommodated Himself to it with His instructions to care especially for those of the "household of Faith." "With regard to the dispensing of *charity*," Arthur Browne instructed, the Lord expected His followers to be "governed by that *apostolic* rule . . . of prefering those, who are more nearly related to us; and then indiscriminately extending our relief to the necessitous and indigent, according to their several circumstances and recommendations."[125] New Englanders did not always agree on what constituted the "household of faith"—that is to say, they did not always accept precisely the same order of priorities. By the time of the Revolution, most followed the teachings of natural religion and identified it primarily with the family; others, however, associated it with the neighbor-hood and still others with the fellowship of reborn Christians.[126] Neverthe-less, almost everyone agreed that Galatians 6:10 gave Christians permission to be preferential in their charity.

The parable of the widow's mite reinforced the message of Paul's epistle to the Galatians. New Englanders identified readily with the condition of the old woman, whose two copper coins were a small contribution compared to the large sums of the wealthy but great in comparison to her own meager resources, and they sought similar approbation from their Savior: "Truly, I say unto you, this widow has put in more than all those who are contributing to his treasury. For they all contributed out of their abundance; but she out of her poverty has put in everything she had, her whole living."[127] Even in 1774, when the sum of their contributions to Boston and Charlestown made such an impressive show, the residents of many small New England towns invoked the story of the widow and her mite to explain why their offerings were not more grand.[128]

Many college-educated New Englanders also tried to justify their charity scientifically, with psychological theories about the nature of self-interest influenced by the speculations of seventeenth- and eighteenth-century moral philosophy. Despite the ingenuity of such moralists as Henry More, the Earl of Shaftesbury, and Francis Hutcheson, the science of the mind still suffered in the eighteenth century from areas of serious ambiguity and imprecision. The most relevant of these, New Englanders found, was the sometimes murky distinction that many philosophers drew between the affections—for example, gratitude, compassion, friendship, and the desire for universal good—and such passions as ambition, covetousness, hunger, lust, revenge, and anger.[129] Both the affections and the passions, moral philosophers taught, contained elements of self-concern, but the affections were moderate by nature, characterized by a spirit of *"calm Joy,"*[130] while the passions resulted "When more violent confused Sensations arise with the Affection." Calm affections and rampaging passions differed from each other principally in degree rather than nature, or so the philosophers taught. Tutored in a tradition filled with such cloudy concepts, New Englanders drew on an analogous distinction between two kinds of self-interest, the moderate, moral "spirit of self love in the Saints," a form of self-interest that was certainly compatible with divine love and perhaps even a part of it, and its extreme, egoistic cousin, the selfishness of the natural person.[131]

Samuel Willard's description of the two forms of self-interest, offered in 1701, was typical of the conclusions reached by most commentators throughout the century. Willard, a Boston minister, considered it self-evident "That every Man owes a Love to Himself." To be sure, there was "a sinful self-love which the Word of God condemns, it being irregular, and tending to Man's own hurt." But this selfish and hateful emotion was unlike the "Love which is due to a Man's self, without which he cannot perform the duties of the Law which belong to himself." God expected everyone "to seek his own Good," Willard pointed out: "He is to seek after his own Comfort, his Health, his comfortable Support in his Life, his own good Name, &c. Above all he is to seek his own Salvation, and give all diligence to secure it and work it out." All this was compatible, Willard believed, "with an entire view to the Glory of God."[132] As the Reverend Joseph Morgan, a Connecticut native settled in New Jersey, added in 1727, God had made everyone ultimately responsible for personal physical and spiritual needs. "We are not to exercise love in the same degree for our Neighbour as for ourselves," Morgan taught, "but in the same Sincerity and Truth."[133]

God had not prohibited self-interest, or a "Love to the World." It was "an *inordinate Love* to the World" that He condemned.[134] "To love ourselves and truly seek our own welfare," Isaac Backus maintained, "is both liberty and our indispensable duty."[135] "Were it possible for a rational Creature, to extinguish the Principle of Self-Love," Samuel Cooper argued in 1753, "far from being any Vertue or Perfection, this would at once appear a gross and monstrous Defect in his Constitution." "We are not," he instructed, " . . . to imagine that the benevolent Man divests himself of all Regard to his own Interest, and actuated by a kind of mad good Nature, becomes wholly devoted to the Gratification of others, without any Concern or Relish for his own private Happiness." Both "disinterested benevolence" and a proper self-love had been "design'd by the Author of Nature to exert themselves in us to a certain Degree," and the "Perfection of Vertue" lay in "maintaining them in a due Ballance, and allowing each it's proper Energy and Scope."[136]

If a "laudable self-love"[137] were part of God's design, New Englanders reasoned, then even a reborn Christian might be excused for being concerned first for himself, his friends, and his neighbors before looking farther afield. Self-interest was not an acceptable excuse for entirely ignoring the needs of the rest of mankind; one "ought not to let any *part* ingross *the whole* of his benevolence," Jonathan Mayhew warned. Nevertheless, if he wanted to avoid a benevolence that was "too vague, and diffuse" a Christian had to pay attention to the "gradations" that God had engraved on his heart, for "the order established by God" was "certainly the most conducive to the general happiness of mankind."[138]

Such explanations placed the great majority of New Englanders at the center of a tradition almost as old as Christianity itself, but it also opened them to criticism from certain contemporaries. From Augustine of Hippo to Thomas Aquinas to John Calvin to William Ames, Christians had worried about self-love. A few like Martin Luther had tried to write it out of the faith, but most had recognized a legitimate role for a well-tempered self-interest. Johann Wollebius, a Swiss divine whose *Compendium Theologiae Christianae*, published in 1626, served in the early eighteenth century as one of Yale's standard introductions to theology,[139] summed up the Reformed consensus: "Man's love for himself," he instructed, "is the quality by which, after God, every one of the faithful loves himself, and seeks his temporal and eternal welfare." This sentiment Wollebius contrasted with "perverse hatred and excessive self-love." "We see examples of perverse hatred," Wollebius commented, "in those who rebel against God and go to their own destruction. The vice of self-love is found in those who, intoxicated by too much esteem for themselves, not only contemn their neighbors in comparison with themselves, but also love themselves more than God."[140]

Most eighteenth-century New Englanders agreed, and although they differed among themselves at times in emphasis, in their concurrence they spanned most of the serious religious divisions of their day. Friends of the Great Awakening, the religious revival that shook New England during the early 1740s, were more likely to stress the universality of Christian love than its natural limits. Within New England's Congregational church, "New Lights" like Jonathan Parsons and Solomon Williams, as well as such allies as Gilbert Tennent of New Brunswick, New Jersey, and George Whitefield, the English evangelist who was at the center of the revival, emphasized the role of emotions in religion over practical concerns and stressed the universal love of the regenerate heart. Yet they also recognized the limits of their charity and the necessity of regulated self-love. "Old Light" opponents of the revival like Charles Chauncy pointed out the practical impossibility of universal love, but this did not prevent them from proclaiming it the reborn Christian's obligation. Revived "Separate Baptists" such as Isaac Backus, and resolutely rational Anglicans such as Charles Brockwell, agreed on the necessity of controlled self-love, although Backus paid special attention to altruism and Brockwell focused at far greater length on self-interest. To protect themselves from their own commonsense doubts, most New Englanders found it necessary to bend certain passages of scripture to suit their needs. For the Lord's will to seem reasonable, most were forced, in effect, to edit the Bible.

The Path Not Taken

A few New Englanders believed, however, that this scriptural reinterpretation had gone so far that it had trifled with God's Word. Under the leadership of Jonathan Edwards a small group of clergymen consequently attempted to reassert the primacy of the New Testament's message of pure and universal love. Between 1750 and the mid-nineteenth century, several generations of "Consistent Calvinist" or "New Divinity" ministers built an imposing, if esoteric, theological and philosophical system on an insight that Edwards first revealed in the late 1730s. For all the intriguing complexity of these doctrines in their mature form, however, the germinal idea was supremely simple. Edwards and his students disdained apologetic compromises, maintaining instead "That universal benevolence is the whole of holiness," and that "all sin consists in self-love."[141]

The history of Edwards's writings on charity may be divided conveniently into three phases, each corresponding with a significant statement on the subject. The first phase, before 1738, was by and large one of agreement with most contemporary ideas on the topic, reflected in a sermon written in 1733 but unpublished until 1809, "Christian Charity; or the Duty of Charity to the Poor, Explained and Enforced." By the late 1730s, however, Edwards had become dissatisfied with compromises. In the major statement of the second period, "Charity and Its Fruits," a series of sixteen sermons delivered in 1738 but also unpublished until the nineteenth century, Edwards drew a sharp distinction between Christian love for humankind and self-love. By the mid-1740s, the writings of Edwards's third phase had begun to reach the printer. In their final and most sophisticated form, his ideas about charity became part of a broader effort to create a new coherent and logical system of theology and moral philosophy. Edwards's aim, best expressed in *The Nature of True Virtue,* written in 1755 and published posthumously in 1765, was to distinguish philosophically and psychologically between the pure sentiments of the virtuous, and inevitably regenerate, person and the carnal emotions of the natural man or woman. After Edwards's death in 1758, a number of his students and admirers, the most prominent of whom was the Reverend Samuel Hopkins of Newport, continued to write in the Edwardsian tradition. Their efforts may be considered the fourth phase in the history of Edwardsian writing on charity.

At the center of Edwards's objections to common assumptions about charity was his belief that apologetic compromises blurred the critical distinction between regenerate and unregenerate love. Attempts to show how Christian love and a well-tempered self-love could both work toward the same end misled the unwary, Edwards believed, inducing them to draw the erroneous conclusion that there was very little difference between the two emotions. In "Christian Charity" in 1733, Edwards, himself, had minimized the distinction by indicating that unregenerate but beneficent men and women stood to gain in this life for their compassion, and that the reborn additionally would be "gainers" in the "hereafter."[142] By 1738, however, Edwards was drawing a sharp line between Christian love and natural love, and he adhered to this view throughout the rest of his life. In "Charity and Its Fruits," and later in *True Virtue,* Edwards tried to show that, contrary to popular belief, self-love could never be virtuous.

Edwards's description of charity in 1738 drew heavily on ideas common to his New England contemporaries, and it was, in fact, as distinctive for what he left unsaid as for what he said. Christian love in Edwards's view was a profound appreciation of all that was good in God and His children. This description of the virtue hinted of aesthetics almost as much as ethics, an inclination that would become even more clear in *True Virtue*. Despite this twist, disinterested benevolence as Edwards depicted it was much the same pure and universal love for God and humanity that New Englanders typically looked for in the regenerate. It was a composite of all that was truly good and beautiful and virtuous: "ALL THE VIRTUE THAT IS SAVING, AND THAT DISTIN-GUISHES TRUE CHRISTIANS FROM OTHERS," Edwards taught, "IS SUMMED UP IN CHRISTIAN LOVE."[143] Unregenerate love, by contrast, was the self-interested emotion that contemporaries believed nature instilled in every heart. Self-interest was completely distinct from the pure love of the reborn Christian, Edwards argued, and even the greatest act of beneficence performed under its influence was in vain without true charity.[144] "Let a man have what he will, and do what he will," he warned, "it signifies nothing without charity."[145] Edwards differed from his New England contemporaries in his denial that self-love had any real merit and in his unwillingness to recognize practical limits or priorities in regenerate love.

The distinction between real and counterfeit virtue was as clear in Edwards's mind in 1755 and the analysis was even more refined. In the 1740s and early 1750s Edwards had investigated a number of related issues, including the nature of pure religious affections,[146] the relationship of the theory of disinterested benevolence to its practice,[147] and the psychology of conversion.[148] These studies came together in *True Virtue* and resulted in an attempt to refute both the descriptions of benevolence of the British moral philosophers and New England's apologetic teachings. Following much the same line that he had hewed in 1738, but couching his discussion now in the vocabulary of aesthetics and moral philosophy rather than theology, Edwards described true virtue as "*benevolence to being in general*"[149] and self-love as "a man's regard to his confined private self," an emotion devoid of real merit.[150] True virtue was a pure and universal love; self-love was a "secondary" emotion which embodied "nothing of the nature of true virtue" and was "entirely a different thing."[151]

Samuel Willard, Solomon Stoddard, and generations of New Englanders past had urged each other to be vigilant against an unchained spirit of self-interest; Edwards and his students now warned against even the slightest whisper of self-love. "It has been said," Samuel Hopkins noted in 1773, that "though *inordinate* self-love is sinful, it is not so in itself, but when joined with love to God and our neighbor, and subordinate to the general good, it is a virtuous, holy affection." This was nonsense as far as Hopkins and the other Edwardsians were concerned. It seemed "utterly unaccountable" to them "that the same affection, when exercised in a certain limited degree, should be holiness, but when exercised in a higher and stronger degree should not only have less holiness, but change its nature and become sin." It was contrary to self-love's very nature, Hopkins argued, to serve the common good.[152] If reborn Christians seemed to take special interest in the needs of friends and neighbors, he added, it was not that self-interest guided their affections. God committed the regenerate Christian to care for himself because he was "under greater advantages to know his own state and circumstances" than anyone else, and to care for the rest of the community whenever it happened to "come under his notice."[153]

The basic beliefs the Edwardsians affirmed were not alien to other New Englanders; to the contrary, these doctrines were in important respects merely elaborations—albeit ingenious and incisive elaborations—of theories about Christian love and benevolence that were the common coin of popular thought in eighteenth-century New England. Nevertheless, most New Englanders found the Edwardsians' views too "extream,"[154] their pursuit of a single strand of thought too single-minded to accept. Although many of Edwards's writings, especially his edition of David Brainerd's diary, had great favor in evangelical circles over many decades,[155] most of Edwards's students failed to achieve very great popularity in the parish ministry, and most spent their lives in their only real colonial stronghold, the isolated rural communities of northwestern Connecticut and the western frontier of Massachusetts, where a shortage of preachers made welcome ministers of whatever theological views.[156] On the eve of the Revolution, Edwardsian doctrines had a relatively limited following among the New England clergy. Modern scholars agree with Ezra Stiles, who commented in 1773 that of approximately 600 preachers in New England there were only "about 20 or 25 ministers full in Mr. Hopkins's peculiarities; and 20 more who admire Mr. Edwards writings, and have a hearty Friendship for Mr. Hopkins, tho' rather as they are friends of all Calvinists than for his Singularities."[157] During the decade before the Revolution, the majority of colonial New Englanders maintained with a hard-headed, practical realism that even the most consistent of theories, if divorced from the real world, were "very wrong, and of a very evil tendency."[158]

Critiques of Edwards's philosophical teachings remained muted while the master was alive, confined in good measure to the muttered complaints of liberal clergymen who rejected not merely Edwardsian moral philosophy, but in broader terms all the New Light leader stood for.[159] The posthumous publication of True Virtue, however, triggered a vigorous reaction close to home. Although Boston liberals like Charles Chauncy undoubtedly found

Edwards's moral teachings impossible to accept, the most determined opposition came from a faction of Connecticut Calvinists, the most vocal of whom was William Hart, the combative pastor of the First Church of Saybrook.

Since the elaboration of Edwardsian views on disinterested benevolence resulted in an entire system of theology and moral philosophy, it is not surprising that critiques of the New Divinity covered a broad range of topics, from theodicy[160] to the Abrahamic covenant[161] to metaphysics.[162] For present purposes, however, the most relevant response was contained in a tract by Hart published in 1771, *Remarks on President Edwards's Dissertation Concerning the Nature of True Virtue.* Hart's "remarks" comprised a chapter-by-chapter refutation of *True Virtue,* crucial to which was his attempt to demonstrate "the destructive influence" of the Edwardsian "notion of virtue, upon virtue itself."[163] On a fundamental level, Hart took issue with Edwards's central premise, the identification of true virtue with benevolence to being in general. Hart incisively pointed out that since "God, and being simply considered, are exceedingly divers from each other," and since God, "a particular being," was less than the sum of all beings, then according to Edwards's logic "benevolence to God" had to be "but a secondary virtue, or a particular great branch of benevolence to being simply considered."[164] Edwards's views, Hart believed, led inevitably to the "shocking" conclusion that love to God was "but a *secondary* and *daughter* virtue," in effect "the first object of virtue's *secondary* love."[165]

Among Hart's more specific concerns was his fear that Edwards's reliance on benevolence to being in general implied "that men are under *no natural obligation to be virtuous.*"[166] Edwards had found no real merit in natural love or self-interest, but his theories did not convince Hart, who believed that such ideas encouraged libertine behavior among the unregenerate. "Virtue, as it respects our neighbour," Hart reminded the Edwardsians, "summarily consists in loving him *as ourselves.* Which implies that there is a love of ourselves, which is virtuous and approved by God: otherwise our loving our neighbour as ourselves could not be a virtuous love."[167] Truly virtuous actions had to be "sanctified by a spirit of religious regard to God,"[168] Hart admitted, but this did not mean that they had to be infused with the mystical love that Edwards described. Indeed, in Hart's view, true *"universal love"* grew out of a love to individuals which then extended outward, resulting in a "spirit of equitable friendly regard to the whole family of God."[169]

In rejecting Jonathan Edwards's teachings, William Hart spoke for most of his countrymen. Edwards's admirers and students, led by Hopkins and the Reverend Nathaniel Whitaker of Salem, rose to defend him from the criticism of Hart and others, including Moses Mather of Darien, Jedidiah Mills of

Huntington, and Israel Holly of Suffield, but without great popular suc-cess.[170] Edwardsian doctrines were too logical, too systematic, and too di-vorced from reality to represent anything but the road not taken for most New Englanders.

As long as most New Englanders continued to look simultaneously both to scripture and to the book of nature—that is, to Jared Eliot's "Two Witnesses"—it was inevitable that they would encounter inconsistency in their beliefs. Most assumed modestly that a measure of uncertainty and confusion was the natural condition of humankind. Attempts to resolve all religious doubts and ambiguities required the subordination of natural re-ligion to God's revealed word, but to the minds of most New Englanders the "Law" or "Rule of virtuous Practice" written in the "Volume of our own Nature" was too persuasive to ignore. They saw a danger in attempts to "depreciate and cry down Natural Religion, on Pretense of advancing the Honour of Revealed," and they reminded everyone that these were not "two opposite Religions." Perhaps reason and revelation seemed at times to collide, but most New Englanders believed that it was "owing to our Ignorance, or Misapprehension of Things hard to be understood in the Book of Nature, and the holy Bible, that we cannot reconcile" such apparent contradictions.[171]

If "charity" were an idea bound up in ambiguity, if its practice never approached the ideal, New Englanders could apologize and live with condi-tions as they were. They had done so in the past, and they would do so until Judgment Day. Or so it seemed to almost everyone on the eve of the American Revolution.

PART TWO

The Institutionalization of Charity

<hr>

The Blind Doctor Moyes

BLINDNESS, the result of a childhood case of smallpox, could not stop Henry Moyes. By his early thirties the Scotsman had accomplished far more than most sighted men and women achieve in a lifetime. College-educated, probably at the universities of Edinburgh and Glasgow, he had also received a medical degree and undertaken a successful career as a public lecturer on scientific subjects, first in Great Britain and then, beginning in 1784, in the United States.[1] To be sure, Moyes had developed some peculiar habits. Francisco de Miranda, a Spaniard on a tour of the new nation, dined with Moyes one evening at the home of President James Manning of Rhode Island College and discovered that "Succotash . . . was his favorite dish, in fact his only one." Nevertheless, Miranda was thoroughly taken by this "singular man!": "His deportment is highly becoming; his person and manner agreeable; his conversation festive, affable, erudite, and occasionally jocose."[2]

In December 1785 Moyes, who was now staying in Boston, invited a few friends to dine with him at his lodgings. The guest list consisted of the Reverend James Freeman of the Stone Chapel; Aaron Dexter, a Boston doctor; and Royall Tyler, a local lawyer. Each was young (about thirty), Harvard-educated, and on the brink of professional prominence.[3]

As the evening wore on, the conversation turned to the subject of "institutions established solely for the publick benefit." Moyes mentioned the British Royal Humane Society, an organization founded in London in 1774 in imitation of a Dutch association for resuscitating "such persons as were apparently dead from drowning, or any other sudden means of the extinction of life." One of the guests had also heard of the Society and knew that an acquaintance had recently received one of its promotional pamphlets. The gentlemen present decided to secure the publication, and they met the following evening to adapt it to local circumstances. Freeman drafted a proposal, and each man agreed to carry a subscription list to friends. On January 5, 1786, the subscribers met at the Bunch of Grapes Tavern on State Street, accepted a set of rules and regulations, and chose a slate of officers. The Humane Society of the Commonwealth of Massachusetts was born, as its twentieth-century historian later noted, almost but not entirely accurately, thanks "to a recently arrived Englishman [*sic*] and to his knowledge of an English institution."[4]

Chance had turned the conversation that first December evening to the subject of humane societies, but happenstance had nothing to do with events thereafter. At the end of the eighteenth century New Englanders were ready for organized charity. They flocked eagerly to these novel associations, even if at times they did not quite know what the institutions were or what they could do. By the early nineteenth century, New Englanders had taken British organizations like the humane society, the missionary society, and the mutual benefit society and begun to make them their own.

Chapter Two

The Rise of Organized Charity

THREE DECADES after the establishment of the Humane Society of the Commonwealth of Massachusetts, an interested observer, "Philo Pacificus" (a pseudonym for the Reverend Noah Worcester of Brighton, Massachusetts), surveyed charity in New England. In the intervening years New Englanders had set up hundreds more organizations. "This is the age of benevolent institutions," Philo Pacificus decided: "No former period will bear any comparison with the present with respect to the origin and establishment of societies, adapted to the improvement of the character and the condition of the human family."[1]

A generation's time had brought enormous changes to New England. Worcester, who was born in 1758, could remember a day before the American Revolution when organized charity's roots ran shallow and New Englanders did their best to help each other without formal assistance. Much as later generations of New Englanders have grown up with the automobile, the airplane, and the computer, however, by the 1810s boys and girls born in 1786 with the Massachusetts Humane Society had grown up with organized charity.

The maturing of a generation of men and women comfortable with organized charity shaped its subsequent history. The advantages of institutionalization—coordination and continuity of effort—were obvious. Thanks to voluntary association, the circumstances that had called for apologies no longer existed. As more and more New Englanders became experienced with charitable institutions, innovators found new ways to employ them and the number of societies grew at an accelerating pace. By 1816, when Philo Pacificus wrote, a new generation had come of age, one that was accustomed to organized charity and ready to make use of it.

The "Age of Benevolent Institutions"

For narrative purposes it would be convenient if the emergence by 1820 of perhaps as many as 2,000 charitable institutions across the length and breadth of New England had resulted from the initiative of a centralized movement, one with a single circle of acknowledged leaders and its own formal structure. This was not the case, however. Although coordinated campaigns played a part in the establishment of many institutions—and although some regional, national, and international organizations like the Freemasons and the American Board of Commissioners for Foreign Missions (ABCFM) actively encouraged the creation of local affiliates—each new lodge, cent society, and temperance association was ultimately the product of a local decision. It overstates the case only slightly to suggest that whatever coherence the "age of benevolent institutions" possessed existed solely in the minds of contemporaries who saw important changes taking place around them. It certainly was not to be found on a table of organization.

Instead of a single, coherent movement, organized charity in New England was the sum of many smaller initiatives. Some were entirely parochial; others involved greater or lesser degrees of cooperation and coordination across town, county, and state lines. By the late 1810s, a regional census of organized charity would have included marine societies, mechanic associations, masonic lodges, humane organizations, a dispensary, a hospital, a school for the deaf, several orphans' asylums, missionary societies, tract societies, Bible societies, education societies, Sunday schools, temperance associations, Sabbatarian groups, peace societies, and many more.[2]

Although there was no central administration to direct the institutionalization of charity, the process followed clear chronological and geographical patterns. Mutual benefit societies came first, growing in number approximately fourfold between 1787 and 1807. Humanitarian institutions developed more gradually, but by the end of the eighteenth century their number had also begun to increase steadily. A missionary society established in 1787 and two more in 1798 were New England's first agents of organized evangelism; the pace of formation picked up rapidly after 1805. And the creation in 1812 and 1813 of reform societies in Massachusetts and Connecticut began their rise, fitfully at first but more resolutely after 1820. Meanwhile, ripples of new institutions spread outward from the major commercial towns like Boston, Portsmouth, and New Haven, where the first were established, to large regional centers like Hallowell, Montpelier, and Greenfield, then to small and remote communities—for example, Paris, Maine, and Derby, Vermont.

By the late 1810s, New Englanders had established a large and seemingly comprehensive network of charitable institutions. Their efforts had been very ambitious, a fact that hardly escaped public notice. Indeed, if most of these institutions shared a common trademark it was their spirit of ambition. If fraternal organizations still made up an important segment of New England's charitable establishment in 1820, the apologies and the tentativeness that characterized the mutualists' cautious charity had given way to the growing self-confidence, and self-congratulation, of the humanitarians, evangelists, and reformers.

It is a measure of the changes that have taken place in popular thought since the eighteenth century that modern Americans rarely think of mutualism when they think of charity. The efforts of postrevolutionary marine societies, mechanic associations, masonic lodges, and similar organizations may seem more like insurance today than charity. Members paid periodic dues which entitled them or their heirs to draw on their fraternity's treasury in times of need. In postrevolutionary New England, however, hardly anyone doubted that these institutions gave "scope to all the ingenuous sensibilities and benevolent propensions."[3] Before the early nineteenth century, mutualism was New England's most common form of organized charity.

Of the region's mutual societies, masonic lodges were by far the most widespread and numerous. Almost by definition, New England's nine marine societies—composed of ships' captains, supercargoes, and merchants—were found only in seaports.[4] Mechanic associations developed where there was a critical mass of master artisans; of the nine mechanic associations in 1817, only the association in Warren, Rhode Island, was not in a principal port town.[5] The other independent mutual societies that New Englanders maintained in the late 1810s, about a dozen in all, were also limited to large towns, although one of these was established inland in Worcester. Masonic lodges, however, sprang up almost everywhere. By 1817, Freemasons had organized 273 "private" or "regular" or "secular" lodges, a grand lodge in each of the five New England states (a sixth was established in Maine shortly after its separation from Massachusetts in 1820), 33 Royal Arch chapters, and 5 Knights Templar encampments for Masons of advanced degrees as well as 4 grand chapters and a grand encampment. The fraternity had filled in the map of southern New England, and it was extending its reach into much of the northern part of the region.

The course that Freemasonry took in Connecticut was typical of its spread throughout southern New England. As late as 1772 there were only eight masonic lodges in Connecticut, all of them located along the Connecticut, East, and Thames rivers in towns of at least local importance—such seaports as New Haven and New London and such inland centers of population and commerce as Hartford, Middletown, and Wallingford. The smallest lodge towns were Guilford, with slightly less than 3,000 residents, and Waterbury, population 3,500; the largest were Norwich with 7,300 citizens and New Haven with 8,300. Fifteen years later in 1787, there were only three new lodges: in Colchester, Derby, and Farmington. By 1797, however, Connecticut's Masons had dotted the entire state with lodges, more than forty of them as well as seven encampments and chapters for Masons of higher degrees.[6] Most lodges still clustered in centers of trade, population, and government, but a few had been established in such tiny and isolated communities as Warren, a town of 1,100 in central Litchfield County, and Norfolk, population 1,650, in the extreme northwest corner of the state.[7] After 1800, Connecticut's Freemasons continued to organize new lodges, but at a less rapid pace; in 1817 there were fifty-three of them as well as twenty chapters and encampments for elevated Masons.[8]

To the north in Maine, New Hampshire, and Vermont, masonic lodges followed closely in the wake of the pioneers who were expanding New England's frontier. In 1817, lodges served southern New Hampshire, southwestern and coastal Maine, and almost all of Vermont except Essex County in the state's northeastern corner. A few lodges even reached into northern New Hampshire in the towns of Lancaster and Bath and into central Maine in such communities as Farmington, Bangor, Eastport, and Machias.[9]

At the same time that mutualism in general and Freemasonry in particular were entering their most vigorous period of growth in the 1790s, New Englanders began to establish the humanitarian and missionary associations that eventually supplanted the fraternities in the public spotlight. Before long, most new organizations were devoted entirely to humanitarianism or evangelism.

Prior to the Revolution, humanitarian activities were the province of a small number of societies, which augmented their basic mutual programs with relief to non-subscribers.[10] During and immediately following the war other mutual institutions also aided needy neighbors without regard to membership status. Boston Masons took up a public collection in 1778,[11] a practice that Rhode Island Masons followed several times in the late 1780s and 1790.[12] A number of organizations founded in the early 1790s, notably the Humane Society of Bath, Maine, formed in 1793, and the Roxbury Charitable Society, established the following year, relieved members on a mutual basis and nonmembers as funds allowed.[13]

Such hybrid institutions tried to serve more than one objective; the humanitarian organizations that became common by the 1790s defined their aims more narrowly. Most early humanitarian associations were established to cope with sudden personal crises. In the early nineteenth century, additional New England organizations also began to organize to relieve chronic sufferers.

The Massachusetts Charitable Fire Society, organized in 1792, and the Boston Dispensary, founded in 1796, were typical of New England's earliest humanitarian institutions. Both served critical but temporary needs. The Charitable Fire Society made emergency grants to Massachusetts families that had been burned out of their homes;[14] the Dispensary offered home care and medicine to worthy but poor Bostonians.[15] Neither institution contemplated providing long-term assistance, nor did such other organizations as the Massachusetts Humane Society, the Merrimack Humane Society, founded in Newburyport in 1802, and the Immigration Society, set up in Boston in 1793 to provide useful information to Europeans thinking of emigrating to New England.[16] Of the institutions organized before 1800, only the Hartford Charitable Society, established in 1792 to provide the town's poor with food and fuel, ran any real risk of having to take care of a beneficiary over a long period of time.[17] New Englanders continued to institute critical-care associations occasionally after 1800, often on an emergency basis. Such an organization was the Boston Fuel Society, established in 1812 to supply firewood to those out of work due to the economic dislocation caused by the War of 1812.[18]

The short-term commitments of New England's first humanitarian societies contrasted with the obligations that many organizations accepted after 1800. Women's associations were the first to deal routinely with chronic problems. Each female charitable society defined its own program, choosing its own objectives, but in the relief of persistent difficulties the institutions shared a common ambition. In Boston, Salem, Newburyport, and Portsmouth the local association ran an asylum for female orphans. In Providence, Wiscasset, Cambridge, Concord, Massachusetts, and Concord, New Hampshire, as well as in Salem, the local society relieved destitute women, often elderly widows, who were unable to care for themselves.[19] Eventually, after 1810, New Englanders set up a variety of chronic-care facilities, including the Massachusetts General Hospital, instituted in 1811 and opened in 1821, and the Connecticut Asylum for the Deaf and Dumb, founded in 1816.[20]

Like the first mutual benefit societies, early humanitarian organizations were urban institutions. Cities and towns like Boston, Salem, Newport, and Hartford were the first to support such organizations; smaller communities followed suit only gradually. In 1805 the smallest town to support its own humanitarian society was Wiscasset, an active seaport, population about 2,000, northeast of Portland. The rest of New England's eighteen active humanitarian institutions were still clustered in larger commercial centers. A dozen years later, in 1817, most of New England's approximately sixty humanitarian organizations were still located in major cities and towns, but residents of a few middle-size communities like Concord, New Hampshire, and Deerfield, Massachusetts, also maintained such associations.

The gradual spread of organized humanitarianism stood in contrast to the rapid diffusion across New England of organized evangelism. By the end of 1817 New Englanders had established at least 933 Bible, tract, education, home missionary, foreign missionary, and Sunday school societies. Most of these were auxiliaries and female cent societies located in small towns and designed to support such larger institutions as the ABCFM and the American Bible Society. Organized evangelism could now be found in tiny and isolated communities in every corner of New England except the leading edge of the frontier of Maine and New Hampshire.

The period from 1787 to 1816 was one of extraordinary growth and change for organized evangelism. Still, the movement was slow to take root in New England. The first successful missionary organization was the Society for Propagating the Gospel among the Indians and Others in North America (SPGNA), founded in Boston in 1787. Eleven years elapsed, however, before the formation in 1798 of the next two organizations, the Missionary Society of Connecticut and the Congregational Missionary Society of Berkshire and Columbia Counties. Nevertheless, by 1807 there was a statewide missionary society in each of the five states, as well as independent societies in many of the most populous counties. Meanwhile, from the first few female cent societies and auxiliaries, established around 1800, a geographically comprehensive network of more than 900 local associations had grown up by 1817.

The early missionary societies were only a prelude. Organizations like the SPGNA and the Missionary Society of Connecticut sent evangelists out to minister to American Indians and pioneers; to distribute Bibles, testaments, and tracts; and to promote morality on the frontier. In the early nineteenth century, specialized associations began to perform many of these functions. By the mid-1810s, for instance, ten tract societies had taken over much of the responsibility for distributing small and inexpensive religious pamphlets.[21] Following the examples of the British and Foreign Bible Society and the Philadelphia Bible Society, New Englanders organized forty-three societies to distribute the gospel by the end of 1817. Meanwhile, beginning in 1803 with the establishment in Salem of the Society for Promoting the Education of

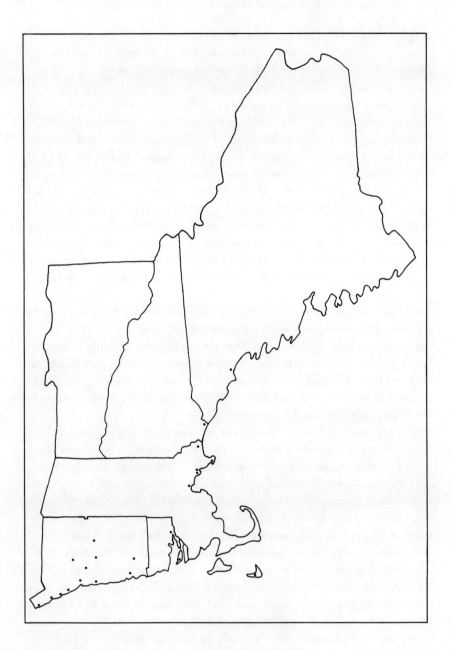

Localities Having Charitable Organizations by 1772

Religious Young Men, the first of about two dozen such associations set up by 1817, New Englanders started to form education societies to subsidize the training of impoverished students interested in the ministry.

The formation of national and regional associations after 1810 offered the greatest encouragement to the spread of small, local missionary, tract, education, and Bible societies. The Auxiliary Foreign Mission Society of Middlesex, Connecticut, was typical of hundreds of similar associations, each affiliated with a larger, "parent" institution. In this case, the parent was the ABCFM. The Board, and such other institutions as the New England Tract Society, the American Education Society, and the American Bible Society, advanced their causes by urging local clergymen and lay leaders to establish affiliates and by drafting model constitutions for their auxiliaries. Eventually, in the 1820s, they also sent out paid agents to help organize local societies in parishes across New England and the nation. In Middlesex County, Connecticut, the local ministerial association took the lead, holding a gathering of the friends of foreign missions. The conclusion of this meeting, which began with a missionary sermon by the Reverend Joseph Vaill of East Haddam, was the adoption of a constitution that committed the auxiliary to raise money exclusively for the ABCFM. Thereafter, the Society met annually in September to elect its officers, listen to a mission sermon, and take up a collection. Between these meetings, the auxiliary's officers were empowered to conduct routine business, but they had little to do. Important decisions were made by the Board's own Prudential Committee.[22]

By 1817, the ABCFM, the most wide-reaching of the regional and national organizations in early-nineteenth-century New England, drew support from 287 local affiliates. Sixty-five were auxiliaries established specifically to support the Board's work; most of the remainder were independent female cent societies and ladies' prayer circles, which contributed to the cause from their discretionary funds.[23] The Board maintained contact with its extensive network of supporters, who must have numbered in the tens of thousands each year, through its published annual reports and its magazine, the *Panoplist*. No other organization had yet spread its nets as wide as the Board's, but by 1819 the American Bible Society had secured the affiliation of most of New England's existing state, county, and local Bible societies and had begun to encourage the establishment of additional affiliates.[24]

Reform institutions would eventually become as numerous, widespread, and specialized as those for evangelism. As late as 1820, however, the outlines of organized reform were still blurred and many institutions battled for survival. The movement would not mature until the 1830s.

One may date the introduction of organized reform in New England from

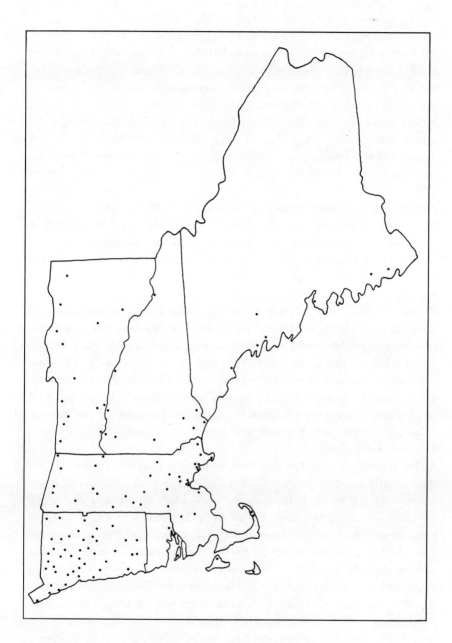

Localities Having Charitable Organizations by 1797

the establishment, in 1812 by the Reverend Joseph Tuckerman of Chelsea, of the Boston Society for the Religious and Moral Improvement of Seamen, and in the following year, of two more associations, the Massachusetts Society for the Suppression of Intemperance and the Connecticut Society for the Promotion of Good Morals. Thereafter, New England was never without active and important reform associations. Nevertheless, in a sense the roots of organized reform extended back more than a century to the measures taken by Cotton Mather shortly before 1700. Three other organizations formed after the Revolution—the Providence Society for Abolishing the Slave Trade, established in 1789; the Connecticut Society for the Promotion of Freedom, organized in 1791; and a reform association in Franklin, Massachusetts, set up by Nathaniel Emmons, a disciple of Jonathan Edwards, established in 1795—were also antecedents to organized reform in the nineteenth century.[25]

The reform organizations established by New Englanders after 1810, however, owed at least as much to a variety of institutions founded primarily for purposes other than reform as they did to those seventeenth- and eighteenth-century initiatives. Almost every successful mutual benefit, humanitarian, and missionary association established in colonial, revolutionary, and postrevolutionary New England included reform among its stated goals and activities. Masonic lodges oversaw the behavior of members, encouraging them to drink with moderation and foreswear gambling. Asylums for female orphans monitored the moral growth of their charges. Domestic missionary societies tried to eliminate drunkenness, Sabbath-breaking, and profanity on the frontier. After 1812 when New Englanders organized to suppress vice, they were following familiar paths.

The reform organizations that New Englanders established after 1812 fall conveniently into two categories: institutions for individual regeneration and associations for social reconstruction. Both kinds of organizations relied primarily on pamphlets to draw the public to their causes. Of the societies for personal reform, historians have paid special attention to two associations. One, the Massachusetts Society for the Suppression of Intemperance, tried to prevent alcoholism and, to a lesser extent, to convince confirmed alcoholics to moderate their drinking habits.[26] The second, the Connecticut Society for the Promotion of Good Morals, worked to prevent swearing and Sabbath-breaking as well as intemperance.[27] Other institutions, for example, the Society for Discountenancing and Suppressing Public Vices in Bath, Maine, and the Society for Discountenancing Vice and Immorality in Concord, New Hampshire, promoted similar causes.[28] Of the institutions to reform society, the Massachusetts Peace Society, established in 1816, and the American Colonization Society, of which an auxiliary was set up in Vermont in 1819,

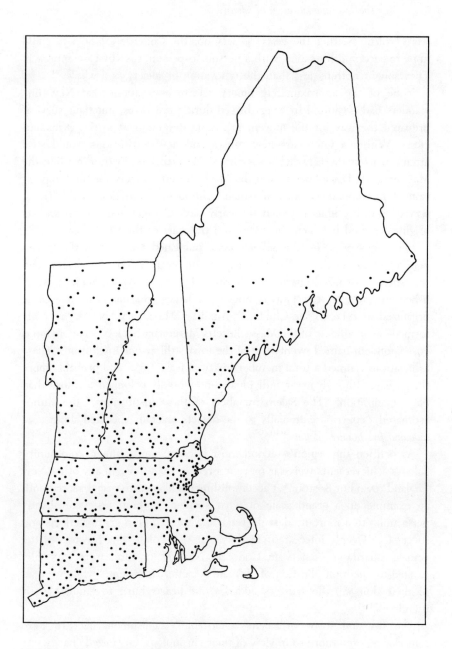

Localities Having Charitable Organizations by 1817

were typical. Neither the Peace Society nor the Colonization Society could hope to accomplish its aims with a person-to-person, case-by-case approach. They sought nothing less than the renovation of society as a whole.[29]

None of the approximately ninety reform associations that New Englanders had organized by 1817 thrived during the 1810s, but their survival prepared the way for the movement's rapid development in the 1820s and 1830s. Within a few years new causes and new institutions would steal attention from these earlier associations. Nevertheless, institutions like the Massachusetts Peace Society and the Massachusetts Society for the Suppression of Intemperance, both of which continued to function in the 1820s, served as direct links between the early days of organized reform and its brightest period between the 1820s and the start of the Civil War.

On August 2, 1816, the *Salem Gazette* published a census of the town's benevolent associations. The newspaper's survey revealed how diverse and widespread organized charity had become. From the Marine Society, established in 1766, to the Dorcas Society, a ladies' charitable sewing circle organized in 1811, to the Children's Auxiliary Missionary Society, "recently formed" as an affiliate of the Massachusetts Missionary Society, an anonymous correspondent named twenty-five of the town's thirty-one institutions. These associations claimed a total membership of at least 1,500, and probably more than 2,000, although many individuals undoubtedly belonged to more than one organization. "The Salem members of these institutions," the author estimated, "contribute annually to the objects severally specified about *three thousand five hundred dollars*."[30]

As befitted the region's second most populous and affluent community, Salem's achievements were far more impressive than those of any other New England town but Boston. Yet accomplishments like Salem's represented both an example on a grand scale of what smaller communities were already performing to a more modest degree and a spur to even greater efforts and successes. "Deeply interested" in the *Gazette*'s account, the directors of the Female Charitable Society in Concord, New Hampshire, were especially excited by the multiplication of "Female Societies" in Salem: "while we read of their doings," the trustees added, "our hearts burn to emulate their usefulness."[31]

The size and scope of Salem's charitable establishment in 1816 were remarkable, even more so in view of their chronology. Organized charity was a relative newcomer in Salem. In 1766 the Marine Society had been the town's first charitable institution. More than three decades later in 1798 Salem still possessed only two charitable associations, a masonic lodge having been organized in 1779 and reestablished after a hiatus in 1791. As recently

Charitable Institutions—Founding Dates Through 1817

	To 1772	1773– 1787	1788– 1797	1798– 1807	1808– 1817	Total
Connecticut						
Mutual	12	10	34	9	18	83
Humanitarian	0	0	1	0	9	10
Missionary	0	0	0	7	198	205
Reform	0	0	1	0	32	33
Total	12	10	36	16	257	331
Maine						
Mutual	1	1	7	15	11	35
Humanitarian	0	0	0	2	2	4
Missionary	0	0	0	3	84	87
Reform	0	0	0	0	7	7
Total	1	1	7	20	104	133
Massachusetts						
Mutual	19	14	33	41	18	125
Humanitarian	4	3	5	3	23	38
Missionary	0	1	1	15	395	412
Reform	1	0	0	0	38	39
Total	24	18	39	59	474	614
New Hampshire						
Mutual	2	3	9	13	12	39
Humanitarian	0	0	0	2	3	5
Missionary	0	0	0	9	116	125
Reform	0	0	0	0	7	7
Total	2	3	9	24	138	176
Rhode Island						
Mutual	3	2	8	12	7	32
Humanitarian	0	0	0	2	2	4
Missionary	0	0	0	4	8	12
Reform	0	0	1	0	0	1
Total	3	2	9	18	17	49
Vermont						
Mutual	0	2	12	17	19	50
Humanitarian	0	0	0	0	0	0
Missionary	0	0	0	4	89	93
Reform	0	0	0	0	3	3
Total	0	2	12	21	111	146
New England						
Mutual	37	32	103	107	85	364
Humanitarian	4	3	6	9	39	61
Missionary	0	1	1	42	890	934
Reform	1	0	2	0	87	90
Total	42	36	112	158	1,101	1,449

SOURCE: Appendix 3

as 1804, the town could count only three more charitable institutions, a second marine society, a female charitable society, and an education society. Salem's first strong wave of beneficent institutions had not come until recently—within the previous twelve years.

Although by 1816 Salem had proceeded farther along the path of institutionalization than any other community but Boston, in most respects the town had followed a typical course. Commercial centers like Newburyport, Portland, Portsmouth, and Providence each claimed at least fifteen charitable institutions in 1817, and even small and isolated Montpelier, Vermont, was home to at least eight local and state associations. By the mid 1810s, a mounting wave of organized charity had swept over New England, affecting small towns and large ones, pioneer outposts and coastal communities. Hardly a hamlet was free from its influence (see table).

"The Importance of Acting in Concert"

Compassion had often been "unavailing," according to President Jesse Appleton of Bowdoin College, "while the methods most suitable to be adopted . . . were unknown." But now associations had been formed, "a system adopted, and benevolent feelings concentrated." As New Englanders realized "The importance of acting in concert,"[32] they began to see its implications for a corner of their lives they had rarely examined. Organized charity formalized relationships that had once been informal and encouraged new relationships where none before had existed. Moreover, its distinguishing marks—often including annual collections and invested endowments, elected officers and salaried employees, corporate charters and written by-laws—ensured unions more permanent and cooperation more effectual than the well-meant but haphazard efforts of individuals.[33] There could be no doubt by the early nineteenth century that charity had been fundamentally transformed by its institutionalization.

The changes brought about by institutionalization differed from one kind of association to the next; fraternalism was not the same sharp break with the past that organized humanitarianism, evangelism, and reform were. Even within mutual associations, though, institutionalization led to structured and enduring relationships among members who would otherwise have dealt with each other informally and in passing.

When Barnabas Webb wrote to his brothers of the Massachusetts Charitable Society on September 4, 1786, to express "his grateful Acknowledgment to this Society for their kind and generous Relief"[34] he inadvertently revealed many of the principles underlying organized mutualism. Webb was one of those nearly anonymous men who leave only the slightest scratch on the historical record. A retailer and liquor seller, he had been a charter member of the Massachusetts Society (the adjective "Charitable" was inserted in 1779 when the organization applied for incorporation) at its establishment twenty-four years before, almost to the day, on September 6, 1762. Before the Revolution Webb had accumulated merchandise and real property worth more than £400.[35] But now unspecified "misfortunes" had forced him to apply for aid, and the Society had responded.[36]

Organizations like the Massachusetts Charitable Society functioned as non-profit cooperative insurance companies to provide for participants and their survivors, but to members like Webb, admission to the organization meant much more than the purchase of a policy. Persuaded "that We are not born for Ourselves, but as Social Beings," Webb and his friends had associated "for the generous Purpose of promoting the happiness of civil Society, and the welfare of each other."[37] The Massachusetts Charitable Society, the various marine and mechanic organizations, and the Freemasons were fraternities—lodges composed, at least in theory, of "good men and true"[38] whose induction formalized the unstated ties of affection and obligation that already joined them as neighbors and friends. When Webb wrote to acknowledge the assistance of the members of the Massachusetts Charitable Society he was thanking them as friends and lodge brothers, not as partners in a joint insurance venture.

The central premise underlying mutual organizations like the Massachusetts Charitable Society was freedom of choice in association. Charity could never be compelled. Without voluntarism, almsgiving was public poor relief, not charity. Mutualists chose their own brethren, looking to make certain of both the congeniality and financial stability of potential members, and they decided whom to refuse admission. Through the by-laws they adopted they also fixed the terms of their union. In September 1762 Barnabas Webb associated with six other men. In succeeding months and years the Massachusetts Society grew; by 1786, 118 men had belonged at one time or another, and about 80 remained active participants.[39] Each had been admitted by vote of the entire membership.

There was one choice that mutualists almost always made: to keep their fraternities compact and uncomplicated. A decade after its establishment, a census of Webb's Massachusetts Society would have revealed sixty-eight members, almost all of them comfortable but not affluent shopkeepers and master craftsmen. According to the 1771 tax valuation list for Boston, an average member held £219 in merchandise and real estate, a figure that placed him in approximately the town's seventy-fifth percentile of tax-payers.[40] Twenty-seven years later in 1798, when the United States Direct

Tax produced a real property valuation for the town of Boston, the average member held land and buildings worth $6,442, placing him in the eighty-fifth percentile of real property owners. Although a few of the fraternities, notably the marine societies (and before the Revolution such urban masonic lodges as First Lodge in Boston and St. John's Lodge in New Haven)[41] were composed largely of the wealthy and influential, most others drew their membership from the middle ranks of New England society. Rural masonic lodges were for the most part composed of men of local importance, but of no wider influence.[42]

Most mutual societies were small enough for every member to know each of his lodge brothers. With more than 200 members in 1790, the Providence Association of Mechanics and Manufacturers was unusual; like the Massachusetts Charitable Society, lodges more typically admitted between 30 and 80 brothers. And with the significant exception of the Freemasons, most of these small fellowships had only limited use for officers: marine societies each named a master to preside at meetings, a deputy master to take the chair in the master's absence, a treasurer, and a clerk; each mechanic society also selected a steering committee to correspond with sister organizations and administer emergency relief between meetings of the full membership.

Freedom of choice in association allowed mutualists to set their own regulations. Barnabas Webb was eligible for relief from the Massachusetts Charitable Society because he had followed its rules during his twenty-four years of membership. He had paid his dues faithfully, attended meetings periodically, behaved with decorum at quarterly convocations, and served a term in office as the association's treasurer. In fact, above all it was the existence of stated regulations such as those Webb observed that distinguished organized mutualism from the occasional charity of friends and neighbors.

There was little difference among the rules adopted by masonic lodges, marine societies, mechanic associations, and independent mutual institutions like the Massachusetts Charitable Society—with good reason, since their regulations, which were often borrowed from British fraternities, were little more than attempts to codify common assumptions about charity. Barnabas Webb had done all that most mutual societies asked of their members. Dues assured the funds to relieve members, their widows, and orphans. Monthly or quarterly meetings, which everyone had to attend on penalty of fine, refreshed brotherly affections. To the extent prohibitions worked, regulations against gambling, profanity, and intoxication during meetings ensured that sessions did not become rowdy or vituperative. Proper conduct presumably came as second nature to anyone who already lived in charity.

The same codes that helped to make organized mutualism more durable than individual charity, however, also robbed the fraternities of their flexibility. New England mutualists responded vigorously when regulations were broken, often expelling the violators. The two most common infractions were habitual absence from meetings and failure to pay dues and fines. Early in the history of every mutual benefit association there came a time, usually after several years of inaction, when the members in good standing decided to compel those who were in arrears to pay up on penalty of losing their fraternal rights. In Providence, the craftsmen of the mechanic association reached this conclusion in 1792, three years after their organization's establishment.[43] More serious violations were less common. During the Revolution, however, several organizations, including the Newburyport Marine Society and the Massachusetts Charitable Society, expelled Tories for their politics.[44] Fraternities also found it necessary occasionally to punish members for other forms of misbehavior: in 1813, for example, the Newport Marine Society expelled two members whose intemperance threatened to be a public embarrassment for the association.[45]

Small and homogeneous, mutual benefit organizations assured their members and survivors of compassionate relief in time of need. These were simple organizations, fraternities whose primary purpose was to cement the one-to-one bonds that joined their lodge brothers. Mutualists did not deny their wider social obligations. Yet as long as they believed that "our powers are limitted" it was easy for them to explain their fraternities' practical constraints. If they wanted to spread their charity more widely, they would have to turn to humanitarianism, evangelism, or reform.

The complex relationships common to fiduciary organizations were in evidence at 3:15 in the afternoon of September 25, 1801, when "an enraptured assembly"[46] observed the first anniversary of the Boston Female Asylum. From the pulpit of the First Baptist Church, the Reverend Samuel Stillman, the congregation's pastor, slight of frame but erect and dignified, instructed his listeners in the merits of their "*new-born charity.*" On a raised platform at the front of the meetinghouse sat a dozen young residents of the orphanage. The Asylum's officers and subscribers, women who had contributed at least three dollars during the previous year in exchange for the right to participate in the organization's governance, occupied pews on either side of the broad main aisle of the meetinghouse. Other well-wishers, both women and men, filled much of the rest of the hall. Somewhere in the auditorium—probably toward the front near the platform, although surviving records are silent on the subject—Mrs. Susanna Draper, the children's governess, almost certainly kept a close eye on her charges.[47]

The meetinghouse of the First Baptist Church held representatives of all the major parties to fiduciary charity in postrevolutionary New England. Humanitarianism, evangelism, and reform provided for many more roles than mutualism did, positions that were more carefully differentiated and less readily interchangeable than those within fraternities. Each association was its own little drama with as many as half a dozen parts to cast, linked to each other by relationships formal and informal. Every fiduciary organization had officers, members or subscribers, and "objects" or beneficiaries. Many also relied on salaried employees—governesses for orphans' asylums, evangelists for missionary societies—supportive laymen, and well-disposed local clergymen.

The Asylum's constitution, by-laws, and rules, supplemented in 1803 by its charter of incorporation, described the most formal of the relationships the institution encompassed and defined the roles of its officers, subscribers, employees, and charges. The managers of the Asylum, a board of twelve prominent women, controlled the organization. They met monthly to set policies, accept orphans, supervise the girls' care and education, and bind each child to a suitable family when she reached the age of ten. As secretary, Mary Lynde Smith, the wife of a local physician, recorded proceedings and notified the managers and subscribers of meetings. Widow Elizabeth Perkins, the treasurer, maintained financial records, paid bills on the orders of the managers, and rendered accounts periodically. Hannah Stillman, Samuel's wife and the first directress, presided over meetings and held the casting vote when the managers divided evenly on an issue. The second directress, Elizabeth Dorr, whose husband Ebenezer was a merchant, was responsible for the same functions in Mrs. Stillman's absence.[48]

At their periodic meetings, Hannah Stillman, Elizabeth Dorr, Mary Lynde Smith, Elizabeth Perkins, and the Asylum's other officers served as proxies for its 300 subscribers; between sessions, Susanna Draper served in turn as their proxy. The governess's obligations were clearly defined and set down in the compacts that governed the institution; each member's rights and responsibilities, which were carefully limited, were similarly prescribed.

Susanna Draper and the women who succeeded her at intervals of two or three years as governess held a peculiar position, a job that was at once a combination of mother and hired help. The governess was a surrogate parent to the girls in her care; in the words of the Reverend Thaddeus Mason Harris of Dorchester, "To her belongs the important duty of watching over them with maternal solicitude, of forming them to habits of industry and order, imparting to them the elements of knowledge, inspiring them with the love of goodness, and training them in the practice of virtue and piety."[49] But she was also an employee, subject to periodic review by a committee of the managers and bound by a set of rules so precise that they required her to attend divine worship each Sunday with her charges at a church chosen by the managers, specified menus and daily schedules, and even obliged her to "visit the Childrens'-Room every night before she goes to bed."[50]

The women who held such an anomalous post often found that the tensions it incorporated pulled them in competing directions. For Susanna Draper, the primary concern seems always to have been money. Between her appointment as governess in October 1800 and her angry resignation in February 1802, she engaged in a running argument with the managers over compensation. Within a month of her selection, Mrs. Draper was arguing with the trustees; when she presented a bill on November 25 "for Board and tuition of the Children at two Dollars per week," the managers deferred payment, considering the charges "as contrary to agreement," and threatened to place the girls in the care of another governess. By December, Mrs. Draper "had reconsidered the price of the Children's Board and had consented to take the sum of nine Shillings per week for each Child." In January 1802, however, when the managers pressured the governess once again to reduce her rates, this time to one dollar per child per week, she refused and her relationship with the Asylum was terminated.[51] By contrast, in Ann Baker, Mrs. Draper's successor, the managers found a selfless women whose "unremitted care and affectionate attention" toward Harriet Westcomb, a chronically ill orphan, so moved them that they rewarded her with a twenty-dollar bonus "as an expression of their approbation."[52]

The Asylum's subscribers remained in the background and raised only an occasional voice in its proceedings. For most, the Asylum was an annual obligation, their contacts with it largely monetary.

The women who subscribed to the Asylum could afford their participation. Although not all were wealthy, most lived in very comfortable circumstances. The subscribers fall conveniently into three groups: housewives; dependent daughters, sisters, or widowed mothers of local men; and the self-supporting. Of the 299 subscribers, at least 132 were married to men listed in the Boston town directories of 1798 or 1800: 50 to merchants; 17 to physicians; 14 to attorneys, judges, or public officeholders; 11 to ships' captains; 7 to clergymen; and 26 to a miscellany of retailers both large and small, manufacturers, and minor professionals. Only 7 were married to master craftsmen. At least 14 provided for themselves: 5 as retailers, 5 as innkeepers, and 1 each as a milliner, printer, huckster, and school mistress. One hundred five subscribers or their husbands held real property in Boston in 1798 according to the United States Direct Tax; their mean holding,

$10,571, placed these members on average in the ninety-third percentile of real estate holders in Boston.[53]

Anniversary day was the yearly occasion for the members to fulfill their duties. The day began with a meeting for the selection of managers and the presentation of reports on the previous year's activities. In 1802, 69 members, about one-sixth of the Asylum's now 421 subscribers, attended this session to vote unanimously for a slate of trustees, approve the expenditure of $1,095.04, and hear that a subscription for a permanent asylum house had resulted in $8,990 in contributions from the men of Boston.[54] At the anniversary service that followed, the Reverend Joseph Eckley of Old South Church reminded them of their primary role in the life of the Asylum: "the maintenance of the orphans, is almost wholly dependent on the *subscribers* to the institution," Eckley instructed. Unlike the "*Directresses,* with the other *Managers* and . . . the *Governess*" to whom the members owed a debt of thanks "for their unremitted attention" to the "support, comfort and improvement" of the orphans,[55] the subscribers' contributions were in coin, their only perquisites the gratitude of the orphans and preference should one wish to take in one of the girls as a domestic.

However intermittent the contacts were between most members and the Asylum, the informal connections that joined other friends, both interested clergy and wealthy laymen, were even more infrequent. The nature of their ties with the institution was never well defined, but the Asylum's officers and charges depended on the leading men of Boston for a number of important services. Ministers like Stillman and Eckley publicized the organization, certifying it in the process as a worthwhile cause; laymen like Samuel Smith, a merchant, and William Jackson, a physician, volunteered their time and skills to meet many of its most pressing needs.

Anniversary celebrations were the best opportunities for the Asylum to appeal to the public at large, and clergymen were almost always the central figures at these events. Associations like the Asylum relied on ministers to make the case for supporting the institution, both to those in attendance and to the readers of their discourses, which were usually published as pamphlets. In 1801, four clergymen officiated at the Asylum's anniversary; in addition to Stillman, whose discourse the *Boston Gazette* described as "engaging and pathetic," Joseph Eckley and Jedidiah Morse each offered a prayer and Thaddeus Mason Harris contributed an ode and a hymn, both written especially for the occasion.[56] The resulting publication included both Stillman's discourse and Harris's pieces, as well as an occasional ode by Charles P. Sumner, a Boston lawyer.[57]

Most interested laymen made contributions to the Asylum that were less public than Sumner's. Samuel Smith initiated the subscription for a permanent asylum building among the leading men of Boston and advised on the institution's investments; William Jackson offered his professional services gratis between 1801 and 1806.[58]

The beneficiaries of these efforts—the "objects" of the charity—were the girls of the Asylum. Seated in 1801 on the stage at the front of the meeting-house in the First Baptist Church, they probably seemed to the audience a distant and anonymous little band; as Samuel Stillman reminded his listeners, however, their own daughters, "the children of those who now possess wealth and competency, may, through a change of condition at some future time, need this charity."[59] This was an overstatement of the case, but there was no denying that the institution's inmates were the innocent victims of terrible misfortune. The girls of the Asylum had never shared the social circumstances of most of its subscribers. They were the daughters of artisans and laborers, both native-born and immigrant. Many had lost both parents; some, including two of the girls on the stage, Lydia Clark and Eliza Vaughn, had a living father, mother, or even both, but had been thrust into such perilous circumstances that their surviving parents were unable to provide for their support.

"Very poor, but with prospects as promising as attend the greater part of poor but industrious People," the parents of Lydia Clark, age four, had been "Industrious and frugal" and had done "all in their power to support a Family of young and helpless Children." Their efforts had been unavailing, though, and "a want of fortitude" had "subjected them to accumulated distress from which they could not extricate themselves; a state of despondency but too soon succeeded, and they were not only reduced to a state of poverty past all hope of recovery but in part *to a state of debility of Body and Insanity of Mind* which rendered them incapable of the care and government of their family and wholly dependent on their Friends for support." Both of Lydia's parents survived, but in such deplorable circumstances that they could never take care of her.[60] On March 31, 1801, the managers admitted Lydia to the Asylum. Three years later they bound her out as a domestic to Mrs. Henry Higginson, the wife of a Boston hardware merchant.[61]

On April 28, 1801, when "A Mrs. Vaughn presented her little Daughter by the name of Eliza," age seven, for admission,[62] her request was a final act of desperation. "Mrs. Vaughn represented her situation as a Widow with four Children and expecting soon to be confined with another." Her husband had died several months before, "leaving her destitute of support . . . a Stranger and a Foreigner" with only "an unblemished reputation . . . to sooth her sorrow and soften her unhappy lot." An investigation by a committee of managers revealed "that her situation was even more distressing than what had been represented," and Eliza was admitted on May 1. Nine months later, the managers bound Eliza out as a domestic to Mrs. Mary L. Smith, their secretary and the wife of a physician.[63]

Under the supervision of the governess, and following the instructions of the managers, Lydia, Eliza, and their friends lived a structured existence. From mid-April to mid-October, the children rose at six, said their prayers, washed with cold water, and cleaned their rooms. After breakfast they could play until nine, when they began classes until noon. Classes resumed at two, following lunch and recreation, and lasted until five. Between five o'clock and bedtime at eight they had time for supper, an hour of play, and prayer. Three times each week they washed their feet, and they bathed "all over" on Saturday night. Between mid-October and the middle of April, the schedule was similar, but the girls arose at seven, went to bed at six, washed their feet only twice each week, and did without baths.[64]

This was a relatively spartan regimen, but Eliza Vaughn and Nabby Peterson, who was also admitted to the Asylum during its first year of operation, remembered their days there gratefully. Before her bond had expired, each girl received an unexpected inheritance. In appreciation, each subscribed to the Asylum as soon as she fulfilled her indenture.[65] Thaddeus Mason Harris considered this "noble oblation on the altar of charity" the strongest endorsement the institution could receive.[66] Certainly, the Asylum's subscribers and well-wishers took satisfaction in the rescue of such girls and in the thanks they received in return.

Such expressions of gratitude may have done as much to reinforce New England's growing reliance on organized charity as any other single factor. Whatever the case, by the start of the nineteenth century the region was clearly becoming dependent on institutional beneficence. As more and more New Englanders took part in the work of orphans' asylums, missionary societies, temperance associations, masonic lodges, and the other institutions that New Englanders were introducing, organized charity fed on its own successes.

Organized Charity and the Maturing of New England

A great change was taking place, and New Englanders were pleasantly astonished to find themselves alive during such an eventful period. No one had foreseen this "age of wonders,"[67] but "The institution of public societies for charitable purposes" had become one of the day's "distinguishing characteristics."[68]

Such "unusual exertions among Christians to do good"[69] seemed to require some sort of explanation, and contemporaries were quick to comply. Speaking in Newburyport in 1807 to the members of the Merrimack Humane Society, the Reverend Samuel Spring felt "happily constrained to remark and record the recent goodness of God, both to the souls and bodies of men."[70] As James Richardson, a Dedham lawyer, added in an address before the Massachusetts Charitable Fire Society in 1810, "for extending and enlivening the charities of life, and establishing humane and benevolent institutions, we are principally indebted to the mild and benignant spirit of the gospel, and to the example of him, 'who went around doing good.'"[71] With hardly an exception, Richardson's contemporaries came to the same conclusion. It is difficult to find anyone at the time who questioned either the desirability of the rise of organized charity or its divine inspiration.[72]

Even before the turn of the century, though, a few observers began to recognize that the institutionalization of charity also belonged to a broader pattern of social and structural change which they did not necessarily attribute to divine intervention. "We see societies *religious, scientific, commercial, military, political, humane,* &c.," the Reverend William Walter of Boston's Episcopal Christ Church pointed out to an audience of Freemasons in Charlestown in 1793: "all of them useful, commendable and meritorious."[73] A comprehensive roster of the profit-making and non-profit institutions established in New England between the 1780s and the 1820s would include thousands of entries: cultural organizations such as the American Academy of Arts and Sciences, the Massachusetts Historical Society, and the Connecticut Academy of Arts and Sciences; such professional associations as the Massachusetts Medical Society and the New Hampshire Medical Society; commercial concerns, for example, the Massachusetts Turnpike Company, the Rhode Island Mutual Fire Insurance Company, and the Nantucket Bank; new state governments; and a further grab bag that included fire clubs, singing societies, tontines, political fraternities, and associations for the detection of horse thieves, to mention only some of many.[74]

It was no coincidence that all these institutions took shape within a few years. Many of the considerations that gave rise to the spread of missionary societies and mutual associations, for example, also encouraged the development of historical societies and turnpike corporations. Independence forced New Englanders to rely on themselves—not on British governors, investors, and benefactors—to manage their own affairs and solve their own problems. New domestic insurance companies, for example, often handled business previously transacted in London.[75] Indeed, independence made self-reliance easier. When corporate charters were desired it was no longer necessary to apply to the king and to the Privy Council, as the organizers of Boston's aborted missionary society did without success in 1762. Although there were periodic fluctuations, the region's economy boomed throughout most of the years between the end of the Revolution and Thomas Jefferson's first embargo in 1807.[76] Good times encouraged both private, profit-making ventures and civic institutions, each of which benefited from the injection of capital.[77] And the geographic and demographic growth of New England—the extension of settlement into frontier areas of Maine, New Hampshire, Vermont, and even Rhode Island—created new settlement and investment opportunities at the same time that it opened new communities both to missionaries and to Freemasons. New England was maturing and New Englanders were learning how to take care of themselves.

In 1798, eleven years after the founding of the Society for Propagating the Gospel among the Indians and Others in North America, the Reverend Peter Thacher of Boston, the association's secretary, recalled the sequence of events that led to its establishment. Thacher's story revealed how New Englanders took responsibility for one form of charity, evangelism. The outbreak of the Revolution cut off the missionary subsidies on which colonial New Englanders had depended. At war's end, after more than a century of financing evangelism in Massachusetts, the New England Company resolved to divert its energies to missions in Canada. The Society in Scotland for Propagating Christian Knowledge followed a different course, however. "In the year 1787," Thacher wrote in a brief account of his organization's origins, "a commision from the society in Scotland, for propagating christian knowledge, was received by a number of gentlemen in Boston and its vicinity, to superintend the funds of the society which were devoted to christianizing the aboriginal natives of America." The New Englanders approved the objective, but not the method. "Ashamed that more solicitude for this object should be discovered by foreigners than by themselves," they revived the 1762 plan for a local missionary organization "and associated for the purpose of forming a society similar to that in Scotland."[78]

Like the SPGNA, many of New England's other early charitable institutions were initially expressions of independence and even of patriotism. As a matter of national honor, New Englanders, like adolescents breaking away from the control of their parents, had to show that they could stand on their own.[79] As a matter of civic pride and boosterism, New Englanders in every major city and town had to demonstrate that they were in no way deficient in community spirit, compassion, or social polish. As a practical matter, independence had reduced the flow of support from Great Britain to New England to a trickle. Now that they had broken away from the mother country, New Englanders had no choice but to see to their own needs.

It was in the region's major cities and towns that New Englanders worried most about matters like national honor, civic pride, and social polish. These communities were in the closest communication with the British Isles, the European continent, and the leading commercial centers of the Atlantic coast, where experiments with profit-making and non-profit corporations were also underway. They also contained New England's greatest concentrations of the wealth necessary to underwrite expensive institutions like charity schools, dispensaries, and missionary societies. Banks, insurance companies, and other corporations issuing stock were located in Boston, Providence, Newport, Hartford, New Haven, and other principal centers; their organizers and investors were often the same men who established the new temperance societies and education associations and whose wives formed the female asylums.[80] Profit-making corporations were also financial opportunities for charitable institutions, whose directors invested the funds entrusted to them in shares of stock. When New England's publicly held corporations grew and profited during the boom times that preceded the first embargo act, the organizations that put their money in these companies benefited as well.

As they undertook the establishment of regional and statewide organizations, New Englanders found that wartime and postwar military, political, and governmental experiences aided them. During the war, the British occupations of Boston and Newport had each necessitated widespread relief efforts which served New Englanders in good stead after the war both by developing networks of contacts and by providing examples of charity that inspired further efforts. After the war, the need to organize and administer state governments further strengthened contacts among leading citizens and encouraged them to think in terms of statewide enterprises rather than strictly local ones. In Newport, Samuel Hopkins, an ardent opponent of slavery, was troubled that the Providence Society for Abolishing the Slave-Trade was organized on "too confined" a basis. Hopkins urged Moses Brown to rename the institution so that it could "be extended to the whole state."[81] State and national organizations combining politics and charity—notably the Society of the Cincinnati, the Jeffersonian Tammany societies, and the Federalist Washington Benevolent societies—also provided experience in establishing and administering large and geographically dispersed institutions.

New England's early charitable institutions were noteworthy successes, at least as far as their members were concerned, and their accomplishments attracted emulators. The Maine Missionary Society, established in 1807, was a direct outgrowth of the SPGNA, which had been supporting missionary work in the District of Maine for years. New England's Bible societies, which took shape almost overnight shortly before and after 1810, were copied directly from the Connecticut Bible Society and the Massachusetts Bible Society and indirectly from the British and Foreign Bible Society and the Philadelphia Bible Society.

With each institution's establishment, the organization of further associations became easier. As more and more New Englanders grew accustomed to formal organizations, they came to expect them. On the frontier, as New Englanders settled new areas they brought with them their developing assumptions about the desirability, and even necessity, of charitable institutions.[82] The rapid growth of masonic lodges on the frontier, for example, was due in large measure to the migration of active members of the fraternity to the wilds of northern New England. In Middle Hero, Vermont, in 1799, for instance, Masons who had belonged to the fraternity in southern New England settled, conferred among themselves, determined to organize a lodge, interested neighbors in the brotherhood, and petitioned the Vermont Grand Lodge for a charter.[83] By the early nineteenth century most institutions that actively sought affiliates in small-town New England—the ABCFM, for instance—found, as Ward Stafford learned during his tour on behalf of marine Bible societies, that it was relatively easy to interest potential supporters because they already knew about organized charity and recognized its advantages.

Chapter Three

Denominations and the Rise of Organized Charity

THERE IS, unfortunately, no simple way to characterize the relationship between changes in religion and changes in charity in New England following the American Revolution. That there was a connection, and an important one, is clear enough. Historians have often attributed the development of organized evangelism, humanitarianism, and reform to the religious revival of the period, the so-called Second Great Awakening.[1] No doubt many saints drank deeply of the revival and found that it nourished their charitable impulses. Both the evidence of membership records and of chronology, however, undermine attempts to anchor the roots of organized charity in the Awakening. Organized charity found support across New England's religious spectrum, drawing on rational liberals no less than on friends of the revival. And as we shall see in Chapter Five, organized missionary activity began before, not after, the start of the wave of apocalyptic enthusiasm that swept across New England in the early nineteenth century. When hopes began to rise, contemporaries even pointed to organized evangelism as one of the principal signs of the impending millennium.

As important as it was, the Awakening was not New England's only noteworthy religious event during the early years of the new republic, nor was it the most significant where the emergence of organized charity was concerned. Instead, it was the rise of denominations. Between the 1780s and the 1820s Americans established the first of the formal denominations that have characterized the nation's church polity ever since. New Englanders were active participants in this development, and their missionary, tract, and education societies played a vital role in it. In return, the introduction of denominations stimulated the growth of some forms of charity. The ultimate configuration of organized charity was strongly influenced by its interaction with the new ecclesiastical order.

New England Denominationalism

"America is the classic land of sects, where in perfect freedom from civil disqualification, they can develop themselves without restraint. . . . In America, there is, in fact, no national or established church; therefore no dissenter. There all religious associations, which do not outrage the general Christian sentiment and the public morality . . . enjoy the same protection and the same rights."[2] By 1854, when Philip Schaff, an immigrant Swiss theologian living in Pennsylvania, offered this assessment, the ecclesiastical transformation that made it valid for New England was long since over and the structure of religious institutions that resulted had been allowed to harden and settle. As Schaff, himself, realized, though, the United States had not always been a safe haven either for sects and splinter groups or for mature denominations.[3]

On the eve of the Revolution New Englanders did not yet possess any formal denominations, but important preconditions for their development were in place. The doctrinal disputes that would play a central role in the emergence of these institutions had already figured in the formation of factions within the Standing Order.[4] Meanwhile, thanks in part to organized charity, groups on the outside, especially the Baptists, were becoming increasingly institutionalized and assertive. Between 1780 and 1820 informal clusters of like-minded men and women united to establish formal denominations.

Denominations were the culmination of a process that proceeded incrementally along various paths through several steps. Small and specialized institutions of like-minded clergymen and laymen—missionary societies, tract societies, and education societies, as well as ministerial associations and seminaries—were the building blocks from which New Englanders constructed their denominations. By the 1820s new denominational organizations such as the Baptist Triennial Convention and the American Unitarian Association were bringing together laymen and ministers who had already joined with each other for decades in smaller institutions.

Because of their second-class legal status, dissenting sects were early to institutionalize. In 1767, after several false starts, a group of clergymen established an association to discuss theology, resolve disputes, and promote Baptist interests in Warren, Rhode Island. By 1804 thirteen Baptist conferences covered most of New England.[5] These societies were vital centers for many activities and were catalysts in the emergence of the Baptist denomination. Most important, before the establishment of formal missionary societies the associations supported evangelism by ordaining itinerants, underwriting proselytizing, and publicizing successes.[6]

The Baptists had many successes to publicize. Between 1734 and 1795 the movement in New England (excluding Rhode Island) grew from 6 churches and approximately 200 members to 198 churches and more than 15,000 members. One historian has estimated that by the late 1790s, Baptists constituted twelve percent of the population of Massachusetts, compared to less than one percent in 1740. Meanwhile, their leaders began to establish a variety of institutions to serve their growing needs. The Massachusetts Baptist Missionary Society, formed in 1803 on the model of the British Baptist Foreign Missionary Society, promoted home missions until 1812 and then divided its work between domestic and foreign evangelism. The society's journal, the *Massachusetts Baptist Missionary Magazine,* was the sect's strongest public voice. After 1812 specialized associations also provided tracts and Sunday schools for laymen and educated candidates for the ministry.[7]

It is impossible to say when New England's Baptists crossed the line from sect to denomination. By the late 1810s, though, they had most if not all the necessary accoutrements. New England's Anglicans passed through a different series of steps, but the result was the same.

The passage from Anglican to Episcopal required the resolution of a relatively simple problem, but one that had festered since the late seventeenth century. Colonial Anglicans labored under a crippling disability: they had no American bishops. According to church law, bishops consecrated in the apostolic succession served many important functions, including ordaining clergymen and confirming the laity. In the absence of bishops on American soil, commissaries appointed by the Bishop of London served as agents; theirs were hybrid roles that made them both ambassadors to members in the New World and administrators over the colonial church's property and personnel. Commissaries, however, lacked apostolic authority to ordain and confirm. Under such circumstances, the Anglican church in America was an incomplete institution, a body without a head. Persistent efforts to persuade the authorities in London to create American bishoprics fell afoul of the lobbying efforts of English dissenters protecting the interests of American Congregationalists and Presbyterians.

The defeat of the king's forces in 1783 had the paradoxical effect of freeing American Anglicans, among whose number had been many of the Crown's most loyal supporters, from these disabilities. As the Episcopal clergy of Connecticut pointed out, "however dangerous bishops formerly might have been thought to the civil rights of these states, this danger has now vanished, for such superiors will have no civil authority. They will be purely ecclesiastics." With the consecration in Scotland in 1784 of Samuel Seabury as bishop of Connecticut, American Anglicans, now Episcopalians, took their most significant step toward the creation of a national denomination. By 1789, three American bishops had been consecrated. The establishment in the same year of a triennial convention marked the achievement of a permanent, national denominational organization.[8]

After the Revolution the relative speed with which New England's Anglicans accommodated themselves to the new order contrasted with the more gradual and fitful disintegration of the Standing Order into competing Congregationalist and Unitarian denominations. New England's religious establishment became increasingly fractured after the First Great Awakening, but as late as the 1820s many clergymen still tried to span the opposing camps. The decision of orthodox clergymen in the Boston area, beginning with John Codman of Dorchester in 1812, to refuse to exchange pulpits with their Unitarian counterparts, however, sounded a death knell for all hopes of cooperation between the two parties.[9] By the end of 1833, every New England state had disestablished religion, thus confirming the dissolution of the Standing Order.

Although theological disputes were at the heart of the division between the orthodox and liberal wings of the Standing Order, institutions—presbyteries, seminaries, and certain kinds of charitable societies—made a fundamental difference in the nature of this competition and marked unmistakable lines of combat. The institutionalization of conflict was at first the incidental result of measures undertaken with different purposes in mind, those of effectively screening and training young candidates for the ministry. By the start of the nineteenth century, however, an "orthodox" group of clergymen made up of moderate Calvinists and New Divinity representatives was organizing in Massachusetts explicitly to stem the rising tide of liberal Christianity or Unitarianism. Within a few years, the Unitarians responded with institutions of their own.

The institutionalization of divisions within the Standing Order followed different courses in Connecticut and Massachusetts. In Connecticut, where Arminians never achieved more than an insecure toehold, presbyteries effectively excluded liberals, blocking them at the Massachusetts border or inducing them to turn Episcopal; practices for training the clergy meanwhile assured a steady flow of reliable preachers, ministers whose standards for ordination and installation would ensure the orthodoxy of the Standing Order. In Massachusetts, by contrast, competing liberal and orthodox ministerial associations and seminaries grew up within the Standing Order.

With the establishment in Northampton in 1802 of the General Association of Massachusetts, an organization limited to clergymen who accepted the

Shorter Catechism of the Westminster Assembly, the Commonwealth's orthodox ministers began to isolate themselves from the liberals. By 1809 the Association had begun to exchange delegates with the general associations of Connecticut and New Hampshire, measures that reflected its general acceptance as the voice of the orthodox clergy of Massachusetts. The following year, the Association gave birth to the American Board of Commissioners for Foreign Missions. Seven years later in 1817 it also established a domestic missionary society.[10]

Liberal ministers were slower to organize, although they predominated in many of the regional ministerial associations of eastern Massachusetts. Their eventual segregation from the orthodox had a number of elements, including the founding of periodicals and missionary societies. But the establishment in the early nineteenth century by the orthodox and by the liberals of competing theological schools was both central to the process and typical of most of its other component parts.

The event that led to the founding of the first divinity schools was the appointment in 1805 of an avowed liberal, the Reverend Henry Ware of Hingham, as Harvard's Hollis Professor of Divinity. The Hollis Professorship, the oldest and most prestigious chair in American academia, had been held by David Tappan, a Calvinist of moderate views, until his death in 1803. In the process of selecting Tappan's successor, the liberals and the orthodox each proposed candidates. When Ware received the appointment in 1805 and that choice was followed a short time later by the selection of Samuel Webber, another liberal, as the university's new president, orthodox leaders dismissed the institution as a lost cause. Professor Eliphalet Pearson, an orthodox Calvinist who had coveted the presidency, resigned his position and joined with other moderate Calvinists and with adherents to the New Divinity to set up a more acceptable school in Andover.[11] To preserve the purity of the new Andover Theological Seminary, faculty members had to attest to their orthodoxy at the time of their appointment and thereafter at five-year intervals. The orthodox followed this first institution with another, Bangor Theological Seminary in 1816, and a third, the divinity school at Yale in 1822. The liberals meanwhile established their own divinity school at Harvard in 1816.

From the establishment of these seminaries it was only a few short steps to the creation of formal denominations. Liberals marked off their first pace in Boston in 1820 with the establishment of the Berry Street Conference, an annual meeting where like-minded preachers could air theological ideas. A year later, they set up the Publishing Fund Society, a tract society to subsidize the circulation of approved devotional literature. By 1824, young liberal ministers had begun to discuss the establishment of a denominational association. Their efforts resulted in the formation in 1825 of the American Unitarian Association.[12]

As great fissures formed within the religious leadership of New England, similar cracks appeared on the parish level, especially in eastern Massachusetts. Churches and parishes had begun to divide over theological matters during the First Great Awakening; this process accelerated in the early nineteenth century and the growing differences between Unitarians and the orthodox formed the wedge that finally drove the two sides apart. Outside their stronghold in Boston and its immediate environs, the liberals never seriously threatened orthodox control, but by the 1830s they held about one-third of the churches of the Standing Order in Massachusetts.[13]

Meanwhile, on New England's northern fringe in the new frontier towns of Maine, New Hampshire, and Vermont, where orthodox clergymen had never been settled, dissenting groups also gained strength. New England's backcountry was a religious vacuum, one that Baptists, Universalists, and Shakers, among others, rushed to fill. Even though the Standing Order retained dominion in these regions, in the early nineteenth century its rights were observed only in the breach. Where the Standing Order had never existed, there was nothing to dismantle. From the first, New England's frontier was the scene of intense religious competition.[14]

By 1833, when Massachusetts became the last state to disestablish religion, the Commonwealth brought the law into line with reality. As early as 1800, more than thirty percent of the churches of Massachusetts stood outside the Standing Order.[15] Following the examples of Vermont, Connecticut, and New Hampshire, Massachusetts now recognized that in a democracy where there were many competing denominations, a state church was an anachronism.

Denominationalism, Revivalism, and Charity

The alignment of denominations with missionary, tract, and education societies was made possible by striking changes in the nature of the missionary enterprise itself. What were the aims of evangelism? To whom should missionaries minister? As religious conflict grew after 1810, most New Englanders offered different answers to these questions than anyone had before 1790, answers that led them to emphasize potentially divisive theological doctrines. In the early nineteenth century, evangelism, now dramatically transformed, and New England's denominations converged to reinforce each other.

Throughout the colonial period, New Englanders who differed vehemently over theological matters agreed nevertheless that evangelists had to wield two-edged swords: one edge to win converts to Christianity, the other to enforce appropriate standards of social and moral conduct both on Indians and on pioneers. Agreement over the significance of evangelism's cultural role allowed men like Eleazar Wheelock and the younger Charles Chauncy, who disagreed with each other over almost every other matter of religious importance, to join forces in the missionary movement for a time, Wheelock as the head of Moor's Charity School, Chauncy as the secretary of a committee overseeing some of the contributions on which the educator-evangelist relied.[16]

Doctrinal differences might nevertheless have separated orthodox from liberal supporters of evangelism had everyone not agreed that the peculiar circumstances of the mission field made theological hairsplitting out of place. David Brainerd, a disciple of Edwards, explained in the mid-1740s how he simplified his teachings among the Indians of Pennsylvania and New Jersey to meet their needs and abilities: "In my labours with them, in order 'to turn them from darkness to light,' I studied what was most *plain* and *easy,* and best suited to their capacities; and endeavoured to set before them from time to time, as they were able to receive them, the most *important* and *necessary* truths of Christianity." Brainerd chose to emphasize "the *sinfulness* and *misery*" of the human condition and the "*fullness, all-sufficiency,* and *freeness* of that redemption,* which the Son of God has wrought out by his obedience and sufferings,"[17] doctrines which almost any New Englander in the 1740s could have accepted although not ones that all would have stressed. Whether ministering to Indians or to isolated pioneers, colonial missionaries believed that their listeners were so theologically unsophisticated as to be capable of comprehending only the most basic teachings.

As long as they remained committed to the traditional aims of evangelism, New Englanders could still cooperate with each other, no matter what their views on controversial theological subjects. Gradually, however, New Englanders began to concentrate on "home missions" among white pioneers instead of reaching out to the natives. Before long, the orthodox friends of evangelism also began to favor the cause of conversion at the expense of cultural goals. As a growing number of missionaries made winning converts to orthodoxy their paramount objective, theological differences became more important than shared charitable intentions and the two sides drew apart.

In arriving at this outcome, the institutional history of organized evangelism followed two distinct paths. In Connecticut, the focus was always on the needs of the pioneers. The members of the General Association, the province's ministerial convention, began on the eve of the Revolution to enlist support for frontier missions. When the General Association formed the Missionary Society of Connecticut in 1798, it was the result of twenty-four years of effort.[18] More instructive of the general course of evangelism in New England, however, are the histories of two other organizations, the Society for Propagating the Gospel among the Indians and Others in North America and the New Hampshire Missionary Society. Each association followed the route that Eleazar Wheelock first traced in the 1760s when he diverted his attention from the Indian scholars of Moor's Charity School to the white students of Dartmouth College.

At first, the members of the SPGNA followed the priorities established in 1787 in their corporate charter: "to 'propagate the Gospel among the Indians, in such a manner, as they shall judge most conducive to answer the design of their institution; and also, among other people who, through poverty or other circumstances, are destitute of the means of religious instruction.'"[19] Within two years a bequest encouraged their efforts. In his last will and testament, John Alford of Charlestown, who had died in 1761, had directed his executor to maintain a trust "to extend the knowledge of the gospel among the indians in North America if *practicable.*" By the mid-1780s, Alford's agent, Richard Cary of Charlestown, had spent a quarter of a century investigating ways to meet this provision of the will; perhaps the most promising, a mission to the Indians at Norridgwock, Maine, by the Reverend Daniel Little, ended in failure when the natives expressed a preference for Roman Catholicism. Convinced in 1789 that the new association met the terms of the legacy, Cary turned the Alford bequest over to the Society, which used it to support three existing missionary stations.[20]

Ironically, the Alford bequest, so useful in supporting services to the Indians, allowed the Society to ignore them after 1790. Using the Alford money, it continued to support going enterprises among the natives, but it concentrated its major new efforts on white settlers. Even John Alford had recognized that home missions might serve as an acceptable outlet for his charity if Indian evangelism were thwarted; he had provided as an alternative that his bequest might be used "to assist in the education of some pious young men of good natural abilitys, for the express purpose of preaching the gospel of Jesus Christ,"[21] presumably among white New Englanders. Starting with a modest donation from Samuel Dexter in 1789, the Society began to shift its attention to the pioneers. Dexter provided about fifty pounds "to purchase bibles for the use of the societys in the eastern parts of this commonwealth," or, in other words, in the District of Maine. Soon thereafter the Society added the receipts of its own solicitations to Dexter's donation.[22]

In 1786 Cary had instructed Daniel Little to devote some of his time to the white residents of the Norridgwock area. Little had been well received. After Cary transferred the Alford funds to the SPGNA the pioneers petitioned the organization directly in 1789, "setting forth that they are now destitute of a preached gospel and are unable to procure it for themselves, and praying the society to afford them some assistance." In 1789 and 1790, lacking adequate funds to prosecute the cause, the Society sent shipments of Bibles and other religious books rather than sending preachers. By 1791, though, aided by a grant from the Commonwealth of Massachusetts, the Society was able to name Little to a mission of five months throughout the backcountry of the District. Fifteen years later in 1806 the Society supported seven summer circuits, for which it hired three ordained clergymen and four candidates for the ministry.[23]

The members of the New Hampshire Missionary Society took even less time to follow a similar course. In 1801, in a sermon preached at the formation of the organization, the Reverend Elihu Thayer of Kingston urged them to follow the examples set by the most noted evangelists to the Indians, such "predecessors, [as] Elliot, Brainard, and others."[24] The New Hampshire Missionary Society, however, was no more successful at this work than other associations had been. By 1802 it was concentrating its attentions "chiefly among the infant settlements in the northern parts of this State."[25]

An important demographic development—the rapid growth of New England's frontier—underlay this redefinition of the missionary movement. Great Britain's defeat of the French in the Seven Years' War had reduced the dangers of wilderness life and opened up enormous tracts of land in Maine, New Hampshire, and Vermont, as well as in New York, Pennsylvania, and Nova Scotia. Censuses soon revealed dramatic changes in settlement patterns. Between 1759 and 1775, for example, the population of New Hampshire grew from about 40,000 to more than 82,000.[26] The settlers had "come from Towns Below" where they had "injoyed appreached Gosple and the ordinances of the same,"[27] but their new communities were poorly served by religious institutions. They were eager to welcome missionaries, and parts of the northern frontier even experienced their own "Great Stir" between 1776 and 1783.[28] In view of the Indians' indifference to evangelizing, it is hardly surprising that the missionaries and their sponsors turned to a new and more fertile field.

Frontier towns demanded missions unlike those that served the reluctant Indian population. Missionaries like John Sergeant, David Brainerd, and Samuel Kirkland lived in or near Indian villages, where they ministered to the natives; so many frontier towns now clamored for evangelizing, however, that missionaries were spread thin, traveling from one hamlet to the next to care for as many settlers as possible. The pioneers, moreover, were theologically more sophisticated than the Indians, better able to distinguish between competing expressions of reformed Protestantism.

At first, frontier conditions encouraged missionaries to continue preaching a simplified, theologically uncontroversial message. For evangelists most missionary societies sought experienced ministers, each of whom could afford only a few weeks or months away from his own congregation on the roads and trails of the backcountry. As these itinerants attempted to meet the needs of hundreds of towns and hamlets, there was never enough time to stay in a settlement for more than a few days. Baptisms, home visits, catechism classes, and weddings occupied the greatest portion of most days, leaving only enough time at each stop for one or two sermons. There was so much to say and so brief a time to say it that most evangelists concentrated, as David Brainerd had in the 1740s, on the central truths of Christianity rather than on fine points of exegesis and doctrine. It is not surprising that Boston's first female cent society, founded in 1800 to support domestic missions, had both Baptist and Congregationalist members. Frontier life seemed so disordered and pioneers so susceptible to the blandishments of sectaries that through the early years of the nineteenth century the officers of most missionary societies encouraged their itinerants to "dwell mainly upon . . . cardinal subjects in preaching and conversion . . . rather than to produce unprofitable disputations."[29]

"Unprofitable disputations," however, could not be averted for long. At the same time that factional warfare in the great towns of New England was resulting in formal denominations, missionaries began to report the disruptive effects of religious division on the frontier. By 1802 the Baptists had their own society which sent out evangelists, and regional Baptist associations also hired itinerants. Methodist circuit riders started to evangelize the backcountry by 1790. Universalists and Shakers made inroads as well. During several missionary tours of Maine, undertaken for the SPGNA between 1796 and 1798, Paul Coffin, the Arminian minister of Buxton, Maine, grew concerned over the religious friction he found on the frontier. Coffin believed that religious institutions should unify communities, but he was appalled that doctrinal disputes had left many towns "much divided." In Livermore he found "many Baptists, and two of them ministers, and one Methodistical preacher." They were, he noted, "superstitious, ignorant and predestinarian."[30]

By 1810, growing denominational conflict in New England's major communities and increasingly bitter religious feuding on the frontier combined to confront the officers of most missionary societies with doctrinal differences.

In response, in 1798 the Congregational Missionary Society of the Counties of Berkshire and Columbia included a standard of faith for potential supporters. The test limited membership to trinitarian Calvinists.[31] Other missionary organizations gradually adopted tests of faith for members and missionaries or issued summaries of Christian doctrine that expressed party views on such controversial issues as the trinity and regeneration by faith alone.[32]

Most of New England's missionary societies aligned themselves with the orthodox coalition. As state and local missionary societies were established in Connecticut, New Hampshire, Vermont, and Maine, it was inevitable that they would serve the orthodox; there were not enough liberals to have an effect on missionary affairs anywhere but in and around the large commercial towns on the Atlantic coast between Portland and Newport. A few organizations nevertheless remained outside the orthodox orbit. For several years the Hampshire Missionary Society did not publicly take sides; the SPGNA remained a cooperative project of orthodox and liberal members, officers, and agents throughout the period.[33] Another organization, ironically named the Evangelical Missionary Society, formed in eastern Massachusetts in 1807, served the liberals; it eventually became affiliated with the American Unitarian Association.[34]

More than any other factor, it was the new character of evangelism that led the members of the missionary societies to choose sides in the day's ecclesiastical wars. As long as colonial missionaries agreed on the crucial importance of Anglicizing the natives, cooperation across the religious spectrum was possible. Conversion was a controversial issue, however, one over which liberal Christians and orthodox Calvinists were very much at odds not only in the mission field but also in the pulpit and in the seminary. These divisions did not carry over into the activities of Bible societies, but they did extend into the work of two other, related kinds of organizations—tract and education societies.

There was nothing controversial about the work of Bible societies after the establishment of the Connecticut Bible Society—New England's first—in 1808, until the 1830s, when the need to translate the scriptures into foreign tongues led Baptists to argue with other denominations over whether to render "baptism" in terms implying full immersion. Until then, New Englanders, like the supporters of Bible societies around the world, believed that theirs was "a design, in which all can meet, whatever be their private interpretations of Scripture."[35] The function of each society was simple: "The distribution of the holy Scriptures among the needy and destitute" was to "be the only object." The text selected was "the version . . . in common use, without note or comment."[36] Where the only activity was the spreading of

God's revealed word, there seemed to be no room for the "human prejudices"[37] that were becoming more apparent elsewhere. As long as the members of every denomination—Baptist and Episcopalian, orthodox Congregationalist and Unitarian—accepted the authority of the Bible and used the
same version, there was no basis for disagreement.

A similar consensus was not possible where tract and education societies
were concerned. In each case the specific cause was too divisive for cooperation. Religious tracts grew increasingly partisan during the early nineteenth
century, and New Englanders of every theological leaning believed that the
training of seminarians was too important to allow a role in the process to
anyone who was religiously suspect.

Before 1800 the early missionary societies made the distribution of uncontroversial religious books, tracts, and testaments one of their principal tasks.
A number of them, notably the SPGNA and the Hampshire Missionary
Society, devoted their book budgets to Bibles and volumes like *The Rise and
Progress of Religion* by Philip Doddridge, an early-eighteenth-century English
dissenter whose views were so bland as to be inoffensive. As the SPGNA
noted in 1798, the Society never distributed "Books of controversy."[38] In the
early nineteenth century the organizers of New England's first tract societies
similarly promised "to adopt no measures in our associated capacity, which
will favour one denomination of Christians in preference to another."[39]
Nevertheless, most of these societies soon became the tools of religious
parties. Such prominent orthodox figures as Jedidiah Morse and Eliphalet
Pearson led the founders of the Massachusetts Society for Promoting Christian Knowledge. United for "the purpose of promoting *evangelical truth and
piety*" through the distribution of religious books and tracts, the Society
limited its membership to men who shared its founders' "piety, benevolence,
prudence, activity, integrity, firmness, zeal, and perseverance," and who could
pass a searching examination of their suitability for admission.[40] Liberals
responded in 1805 with their own organization, the Society for Promoting
Christian Knowledge, Piety, and Charity.[41] By 1814, when a group of men
affiliated with Andover Theological Seminary established the New England
Tract Society, the predecessor of the American Tract Society, the little pamphlets the associations distributed had become weapons in denominational
warfare.

Early education societies were characteristically founded by the members
of individual churches, aware of the needs of impoverished young neighbors
who wished to enter the ministry.[42] The combination of origins in individual
congregations and the theological concerns of the founders of divinity schools

ensured that these organizations would promote specific doctrinal view-points. In Salem, where the Society for Promoting the Education of Religious Young Men for the Ministry, organized in 1803, was one of New England's first such organizations, only a "public professor of the religion of Jesus Christ"[43] could become a trustee, a restriction that eliminated liberal Christians, most of whom no longer made public confessions of faith. When a group of orthodox laymen and ministers associated with Andover Theological Seminary organized the American Education Society in 1815 its founders dedicated it to the nationwide promotion of Congregational and Presbyterian Calvinism in the face of challenges from Baptists, Methodists, and Roman Catholics, as well as from Unitarians.[44] Local boards of examiners set up around the country made certain that successful applicants for educational loans from the Society's treasury were suitably moral and orthodox.[45] Liberals, led by John T. Kirkland, replied in kind in 1816 with the establishment of the Society for Promoting Theological Education, an association to support divinity students at Harvard.[46]

A symbiotic relationship had developed by the early 1810s between most missionary, tract, and education societies on one side and the orthodox wing of the Standing Order on the other. Similar bonds also linked the liberal wing with such organizations as the Evangelical Missionary Society and the Society for Promoting Christian Knowledge, Piety, and Charity, and linked the Baptists with the Massachusetts Baptist Missionary Society. Orthodox Calvinists comprised so much of the region's population, however, that the union that developed between them and their voluntary associations had unusually powerful repercussions.

In the early nineteenth century, the simultaneous development of organized evangelism and the organization of orthodox Congregationalism resulted in a religious revival more intense than either could have produced alone. Outpourings in individual parishes had long been common; Solomon Stoddard, Jonathan Edwards's grandfather, oversaw five harvest seasons during his long ministry in Northampton, and a scattering of towns in Connecticut experienced stirrings between 1767 and 1792.[47] Isolated, local revivals led to Great Awakenings, however, only when one town could communicate its excitement to others. In the 1740s, itinerant evangelists like George Whitefield, Gilbert Tennent, and James Davenport carried this sense of anticipation with them as they traveled by foot or on horseback. At the start of the nineteenth century, organizations fulfilled much the same role.

The first stirrings of New England's Second Great Awakening shook Connecticut in 1797. The center of upheaval was Litchfield County in the northwest corner of the state, where the Reverend Edward Dorr Griffin, at the time the pastor of the church in New Hartford, reported that he "could stand at my door . . . and number fifty or sixty contiguous congregations laid down in one field of divine wonders."[48] By 1801 the level of excitement began to wane, but it renewed periodically until as late as the mid-1820s. Yale felt a stirring in 1802, which resulted in the conversion of one-third of the 230-member student body. An historian has marked five later peaks in the state's religious temperature between 1807 and 1826.[49]

The Missionary Society of Connecticut, established in 1798, took the lead promoting the revival in two ways; other missionary associations followed suit as they were founded. Their evangelists worked the mission fields, seeking to recreate Litchfield's harvest in hamlets on the frontiers of Maine, New Hampshire, and Vermont, in the sparsely settled hill country of western Rhode Island, and throughout such territories as New York's Burned-Over District and Ohio's Western Reserve, where New Englanders were moving in search of new land and new opportunities. The societies then reported on their triumphs. Their published annual reports carried word of missionary tours throughout the backcountry and described the eagerness with which the settlers were greeting the evangelists. Periodicals that many of the societies published bimonthly or quarterly—such journals as the *Connecticut Evangelical Magazine,* the *Massachusetts Missionary Magazine,* and the *Piscataqua Evangelical Magazine*—carried stories about revivals at home, on the frontier, and around the world in Great Britain, India, and everywhere else that missionaries were carrying God's word.

The cumulative effect of these accounts was a sense of expectancy in whoever read them, much as the oral reports of Whitefield, Tennent, Davenport, and the other itinerants fired the hopes of the New Lights during the First Great Awakening. As more and more optimistic accounts streamed in, many orthodox New Englanders concluded that "The revivals of religion which have taken place in different sections of our country, and in some of the new settlements, the formation of Missionary and Bible Societies, of Charitable and Theological Institutions, the concern which is felt for the moral and religious welfare of the community, these are all tokens for good. In these we trust the Spirit of the Lord is lifting up a standard, while the enemy is coming in like a flood."[50]

The simultaneous emergence of denominations and missionary, tract, and education societies nourished each kind of institution, encouraging spiritual awakening in the process. Their common concern for doctrinal purity brought them together and strengthened each movement. In other circles, however, doctrinal considerations still seemed unduly divisive.

Secular Charity and the Bible Societies:
The Relevance and Irrelevance of Denominationalism

If the activities of most missionary, tract, and education societies complemented those of New England's new denominations, the interests of the rest of the region's charitable associations usually ran in another direction. Addressing the members of Newburyport's Merrimack Humane Society in 1804, the Reverend Joseph Dana of Ipswich considered it a "pleasant circumstance of this establishment, that it knows no distinction of parties, civil or religious. . . . [I]t aims to combine those of every denomination who are disposed to do good. And its *benefits are to extend* without discrimination."[51] The example of the good Samaritan required that charity comprehend everyone, orthodox and liberal, Episcopalian and Baptist, even Roman Catholic and Jew. It was a challenge, however, to maintain a spirit of universal love at a time of increasing denominational division.

Although the development of denominations did not ordinarily affect other forms of organized charity as directly as it touched missionary, tract, and education societies, none entirely escaped its influence. Before the Revolution, Freemasons, troubled by "the melancholly divisions" that seemed rife, emphasized that their charity was not limited "to them particularly who are of the same Church or Opinion with us."[52] St. John's Lodge of Newport even admitted members of the town's Jewish merchant community.[53] By the early nineteenth century, denominations were such an important feature of the institutional landscape that they were impossible to ignore. Charitable institutions that did not align themselves with specific denominations often had to struggle to span religious divisions. At the very least, their members had to make their catholic intentions explicit and public.

There were two common ways to think of the proper relationship between denominations and such institutions as masonic lodges, humane societies, temperance organizations, and Bible associations—one passive, the other active. Some commentators suggested that since denominational affiliations were irrelevant to the work of such organizations, they could simply be ignored. John Sylvester John Gardiner, the rector of Boston's Trinity Church, Episcopal, remarked in 1803 that one of the great virtues of most New Englanders was their ability to set aside their "speculative tenets, and external forms" and "harmonize, in the true spirit of evangelical charity." Elsewhere, "graceless zealots" might disrupt society, but in New England "the utmost liberality of sentiment is united with moral practice."[54] Gardiner assumed that the rise of denominations posed few if any direct problems for most forms of organized charity.

A growing number of New Englanders, though, agreed with Joseph Dana that organized charity had a more active role to play. Concerned about growing theological and ecclesiastical divisions, observers like Dana believed that dispensaries, marine societies, masonic lodges, and the like could weld New England back together. An association like the Merrimack Humane Society that drew its support from members of all denominations and dispersed its relief impartially could "do away [with] that disesteem and distrust which too often divide those who ought to be united."[55] Much as common moral principles reunited Christians who disagreed over theological specifics, cooperation in nondenominational charitable organizations could unite New Englanders whose religious differences sometimes brought them to blows.

Whether one spoke nostalgically like Gardiner of a society without significant denominational divisions or more practically like Dana of the overarching principles that united men and women of competing religious communions, such words related a basic truth: aside from most missionary, tract, and education societies and a few reform associations, throughout the postrevolutionary period the membership of New England's charitable organizations reflected society's religious heterogeneity.[56]

On July 6, 1809, when thirty-two clergymen and seventy-five laymen met in Boston to establish the Massachusetts Bible Society, the religious diversity of the gathering indicated the concern for the cause of New Englanders of many shades of opinion. Edward Dorr Griffin, the fiery evangelical preacher of the town's new Park Street Church, was there, along with such orthodox friends as Joseph Eckley of Old South and Jedidiah Morse of Charlestown. But so was a contingent of Unitarians, including Joseph Stevens Buckminster, the promising young pastor of Boston's Brattle Street Church, John T. Kirkland of New South Church, soon to become president of Harvard, and Henry Ware, the Hollis Professor whose appointment had so incensed Eliphalet Pearson, also a subscriber. Abiel Holmes, a close friend of the Hopkinsians, stood in for that wing. Among the laymen were such notable names as John Quincy Adams, a liberal, and William Phillips, of a wealthy family accustomed to benefiting orthodox causes.[57] In Providence four years later on August 10, 1813, when many of the state's most respected citizens convened to establish the Rhode Island Bible Society, the moderator was Moses Brown, the Quaker merchant, politician, and public benefactor. The society's first slate of officers included the Reverend William Patten of Newport's Second Congregational Church, first vice president, and Rt. Rev. Alexander Griswold, Episcopal bishop of Rhode Island, second vice president.[58] Among the founding members of the Massachusetts Society for the Suppression of Intemperance the majority was orthodox but a sizable minority, forty percent, was Unitarian.[59] And among the subscribers to the Humane Society of the Commonwealth of Massachusetts was Jean-Louis Cheverus, New England's first Roman Catholic bishop.[60]

As long as they avoided controversial issues and programs, the officers and members of postrevolutionary New England's fraternal, humanitarian, Bible, and reform organizations were able to work together notwithstanding the variety of their theological views. It was not always possible to skirt controversy, however, nor did everyone seek to do so. As the temperature of denominational discord rose, a few isolated incidents let New Englanders know that their charitable institutions were not completely sheltered from the winds of religious contention that swirled around them.

In Salem, William Bentley recognized a problem in the making in 1810 when Lucius Bolles, the pastor of the town's Baptist church, had his turn to preach the anniversary sermon for the local female charitable society. Bolles's sermon on Luke 16:9 emphasized the role of divine grace in the practice of true charity. "And I say unto you," the text read, "make to yourselves Friends of the Mammon of Unrighteousness, that when ye fail, they may receive you into Everlasting Habitations." Bolles explained that the characters in this story had "been under the influence of *grace,* and by manifesting their title to, is said to procure for them everlasting habitations."[61] He went on to endorse not only the work of the Salem Female Charitable Society, but the civic activities of other organizations, especially the missionary societies. Bentley believed that Bolles had unfairly taken advantage of the opportunity to speak before the society to expound sectarian views. "It has been usual to print the Sermons delivered before the female Asylum," Bentley noted in his diary: "The Sectaries, who by virtue of the rotation have their opportunity to preach, associate the subject with their Theology and so have a new vehicle of their opinions by the aid of those who would never willingly contribute to them."[62]

Opportunism like Bolles's might rankle others for a moment, but there was greater potential for disruption when the religious convictions of an organization's members led them to incompatible ideas on policy. Female asylums were especially susceptible to denominational division, since the members recognized an obligation to oversee the religious education of the girls in their charge. But what would be the nature of this religious education? In part, it would consist of the catechism lessons an asylum's governess taught the orphans and of the bedtime prayers she instructed them to say. These could be denominationally neutral, but another obligation, the duty to attend Sunday worship services, seemed to compel an asylum's officers to express their religious preferences.

Both in Salem and in Boston, differences of opinion arose between the overseers of the orphanage and its governess as to where the girls should attend church. The two disputes were almost identical. In Salem, the trustees voted on December 2, 1801, "that the children shall attend publick worship, at the meeting house of the Reverend Dr. Barnard; in case it should be agreeable to Mrs. Elson; their Governess." Mrs. Elson objected immediately that Barnard's meetinghouse was unsuitable because she and the girls would have to travel a distance to it unaccompanied, but the trustees insisted that the orphanage's party worship there, where good seats had already been provided.[63]

Within two months it became clear that Mrs. Elson had not fairly stated the nature of her objections to attendance at Barnard's meetinghouse. Thomas Barnard, Jr., was a prominent Arminian minister; Mrs. Elson was partial to the New Divinity exercises at Salem's Third Church conducted by Daniel Hopkins, the younger brother of Samuel Hopkins of Newport. On the first day of the following February the trustees discussed Mrs. Elson's failure to bring the girls to Barnard's Sunday services, and they appointed a committee "to call on Mrs. Elson, represent to her the impropriety" of keeping the girls at home, "and enjoin it on her, to send them the next Sabbath to the place agreed on for their attendance." Mrs. Elson still had not complied by March 3, when the trustees met again. Through inquiries at the Third Church, the overseers determined that Hopkins's society had no pews to accommodate the orphanage's party. They repeated their order to Mrs. Elson, and on March 11 they received a report that the girls had attended divine worship at Barnard's meetinghouse the previous Sunday.[64]

In Boston the establishment of Park Street Church, Edward Dorr Griffin pastor, led to a similar contretemps. As in Salem, the governess and the orphan girls had been worshipping under the guidance of a liberal minister, in this case John T. Kirkland of New North Church. The founding of a new church in liberal Boston, however, organized to spread a warmer version of the gospel than the town's Unitarian ministers disseminated, provided the Asylum's governess and her assistant with an opportunity to express their dissatisfaction with existing arrangements.

Before the August 1810 meeting of the trustees of the Asylum, a member of the board received a letter from Miss Susannah Bacon, the governess, and her assistant, a Miss Whittier. "As the professed disciples of Christ," they wrote, "we wish to attend where the Gospel is preached in its purity; believing that the pure doctrines contained therein will support us in the hour of death." "We do not conceive," they added, "that morality alone constitutes a christian, nor that the Gospel is preached by any who do not believe in regeneration, election, and decrees."[65]

The governesses' request received an unsympathetic hearing. In a letter to Miss Bacon the board members explained their views: "When you entered on the trust which you have so well fulfilled . . . No confession of the peculiar doctrines in which you believed was then required, nor was it wished. That you were a christian, implied that you were bound by the moral obligations of the gospel, and the distinguishing tenets of any sect to which you might belong were disregarded." Compliance with the request, the board feared, "would establish a precedent which would continually expose them to solicitations for a change."[66] Miss Bacon and her assistant could take turns, one attending the Park Street Church, the other caring for the children, but the board voted unanimously that the girls, themselves, would continue at New North.

The board of directors had expressed the beliefs of most New Englanders in 1810: where humanitarianism was concerned, not to mention fraternalism and reform, sectarian distinctions were not germane. It is a measure of the wide acceptance of this view that through 1820 further sectarian differences of opinion very rarely disturbed the work of fraternal, humanitarian, and reform organizations. By 1810 New Englanders almost never denied that missionary, tract, and education societies acted properly when they aligned themselves with congenial denominations. As for the rest of New England's charitable institutions, they acted appropriately when they stood as far apart as possible from the religious disputes of the day. After all, why look for new problems when every association already faced a fundamental one? It had to accommodate its services to the needs of its community.

Chapter Four

Experimenting in Charity

ONCE ORGANIZED CHARITY became commonplace, it slipped most people's minds how tentative its first years had been. By Ward Stafford's time, years of practice made the steps for starting a new organization seem routine and obvious: identify a need, rally support, agree on a constitution and by-laws, and begin to take action. Familiarity rendered the complexity of this process invisible and its potential pitfalls harmless. Earlier in the century, however, New Englanders could still appreciate how difficult it was. Above all, they could still remember how hard it had been before the 1810s to decide what they wanted to accomplish.

Voluntary association was a powerful tool, but for what ends? The answer was not obvious. Institutionalization raised new questions. As long as charity remained primarily individual, each would-be benefactor needed only to consider his or her own opportunities and resources when playing the Samaritan. Association fundamentally changed the nature of charity, however. It expanded horizons at the same time that it magnified abilities, and it allowed compassionate men and women for the first time to try to accommodate their efforts to community rather than individual requirements.

But what were these needs? Everyone had heard moving stories of people in trouble, but before there were social scientists, before there were statistics to report society's problems, no one really knew the truth. No one doubted the existence of deprivation and suffering or the duty to ameliorate them, but who and where were the "children of adversity and want"[1] and how should they be relieved?

If consensus on such issues is always difficult to achieve, it was especially elusive before the 1810s. It demanded new perceptions, a new way of thinking about need, one that took into account the requirements of communities, not individuals, and the abilities of institutions, not private benefactors. The associations themselves were New England's best tutors. Understanding came with experience—experience gained by working with the institutions. Until New Englanders attained a sophisticated new level of awareness, their uncertain, incomplete, and anecdotal understanding of their own social, moral, and spiritual circumstances shaped the practice of organized charity.

Charity and Society

In an open letter to the citizens of Massachusetts in 1814, the trustees of the Massachusetts General Hospital made a curious, third-person confession. "Antecedent to their appointment," they revealed of themselves, they "had but faint impressions of the nature and necessity of such an establishment. They had, previously, no conception of the loss occasioned the community and the suffering inflicted on individuals by the want of it." Ignorance rather than apathy explained the failure of a town "proverbial for its charity" to provide a hospital for its destitute, they believed: "Such is the condition of social life, and the classes of men are necessarily so far removed from one another, that the cry of distress will often never reach the ear of the able or willing." Service on the hospital's board, however, had opened the trustees' eyes to hidden needs.[2]

Theirs was a familiar story before 1820. A clear and precise understanding of socioeconomic, spiritual, and moral conditions was almost never the cause of early charitable initiatives. Instead, New Englanders learned important lessons only after they became involved in organized charity. Fraternalism, humanitarianism, evangelism, and reform provided an education in the sociology of poverty, disease, irreligion, and depravity. What participants learned shaped the subsequent courses of their institutions. With time, New Englanders identified such problems and organized effectively to relieve them. At first, though, they lacked the experience that would one day serve them well, and their efforts often bore little relation to the circumstances of those they intended to serve.

The history of organized charity in New England has its share of ironies. Of these, among the most remarkable is its curious chronology. Although the revolutionary war years produced economic dislocation that persisted through the 1780s, between the early 1790s and 1807 organized charity's first years of rapid growth coincided not with a time of increasing squalor and desperate need but of unparalleled affluence. Strangely, as New England's standard of living rose to unprecedented heights, its leading citizens discovered more want rather than less. The extent of their awareness of community and regional needs had little in common with New England's changing circumstances. At least at first, awareness of need was more the consequence of the growth of organized charity than it was a reflection of actual conditions.

The period of growth and prosperity that New England entered in the early 1790s had more than one source. Ambitious New Englanders could find opportunities both on the frontier and in the region's commercial centers. If in each case economic expansion was a legacy of the Revolution, frontier and urban conditions were otherwise largely independent of each other.

From the District of Maine to the Western Reserve the lure of the frontier, the most important reason for its rapid settlement, was the opportunity it offered for economic betterment. The defeat of the French in the Seven Years' War began to open this land in the early 1760s; independence two decades later removed the pioneers' last significant obstacles. The first settlers knew that for a few years their lives would be difficult, their willpower and endurance tested as they tried to turn forests into farms. The reward they sought, though, land for the taking, was enough to persuade tens of thousands of men, women, and children between 1780 and 1820 to settle in the New England wilderness.

Commercial centers like Boston, Salem, and Portsmouth benefited, meanwhile, from the entrance of the United States into foreign trade. As long as they remained subjects of the British Crown, New Englanders were denied direct access to most international markets thanks to the provisions of the Navigation Acts. With the signing of the Treaty of Paris in 1783, however, American political independence resulted as well in commercial freedom. For some established merchants, the freedom to compete was the freedom to fail; in Newburyport, for example, the most prominent colonial merchants who survived the war were unable to adapt to the postwar trading environment, and they gave way to a new generation of commercial leaders. For many more New Englanders, however, direct trade with western Europe, the East Indies, and China, now possible for the first time, led to unprecedented wealth. The merchants, captains, and seamen who were most fully involved gained the greatest profits from international commerce, but its effects spread throughout most New England seaports, lifting almost everyone to new levels of affluence. In Newburyport, for instance, between 1793 and 1807 the median value of the assets of male residents rose from $440 to $1,600 and almost everyone in town "had a share in the extraordinary prosperity of the period."[3]

Notwithstanding such promising developments, New England communities continued to encounter situations that called for charity. On the frontier, opportunity came at the cost of a religious isolation that left many new towns without a preached gospel. As letters home from new settlements to Eleazar Wheelock and other educators had indicated for decades, many pioneers, lacking the benefits of regular religious services, hungrily welcomed the missionaries, Bibles, and tracts they received from such centers of civilization as Boston, Hartford, and Northampton.[4] In these and other established communities, meanwhile, a few residents continued to rely on friends, neighbors, or the town for subsistence. The most depressed of these commercial centers was Newport, which prosperity bypassed at the end of the Revolution in favor of Providence.[5] Yet even in Boston and Salem, enough widows, orphans, and invalids required assistance for their relief to constitute a continuing concern. In such seaports, the number of public wards and private charges actually grew as urban populations became more and more concentrated. Boston's almshouse had twice the number of inmates in 1790 that it held in an average year before the Revolution.[6] New England's increasing dependence on foreign trade, which could be chancy and erratic, moreover, opened the region to cyclical recessions as certainly as it presented the possibility of periods of prosperity. Meanwhile, by loosening traditional community ties, geographical mobility seemed to encourage moral decay both on the frontier and in commercial entrepôts; by the early nineteenth century, most contemporaries were convinced that drunkenness and depravity posed a growing threat to the social order.

With experience, New Englanders eventually learned to identify want in the midst of plenty, then address it systematically and effectively. This process seems simpler in retrospect, however, than it was at the time. There was no automatic or immediate correlation between needs and programs. If it was easy enough to recognize a catastrophic event—a massive fire, epidemic, or commercial collapse[7]—and try to ameliorate it, in many New England communities civic leaders found themselves facing more subtle and puzzling conditions.

January 24, 1809, was a noteworthy date for the Wiscasset Female Charitable Society, the day when the "Asylum," as it was sometimes called, at last became an active force in its community. In important respects, Wiscasset's peculiar history leading up to this day epitomizes postrevolutionary New England's early experience with organized charity.

Founded during the autumn of 1805 at a gathering of thirty-three women, the organization had left its affairs largely untended for the next three years. At its first meeting the Society's subscribers, members of many of the seaport's most prominent families, pledged $86.25 and chose a slate of officers. Over the following weeks and months they recruited another sixteen subscribers and received an additional $24.00 in contributions, but neither the

Society as a whole nor its directresses convened regularly to conduct business. Between its establishment and January 1809 there were only three meetings of any kind, the last in 1806. The January 1809 session was consequently the first in more than two years. It was also the first at which the Society authorized a charitable contribution. By a vote of the fifteen members in attendance, the Asylum appropriated $30.00 to charitable uses, a small portion for designated causes, the rest to be expended at the discretion of the directresses.[8]

For its first three years the Asylum set a remarkably languid pace, but if its inactivity betrayed no sense of urgency it is almost certainly because prior to 1808 its supporters felt none. Like the members of most other contemporary charitable societies, they associated for a variety of reasons, none of which clearly dictated their course of action or their organization's objectives. If they expected to play the part of the Samaritan, they were by no means certain what that role entailed.

Their uncertainty was an ironic consequence of Wiscasset's unprecedented prosperity. In Wiscasset, as everywhere else in New England, a few unfortunate widows, orphans, and invalids depended for support on relatives, friends, neighbors, and the town. For the rest of the community's residents, however, the years before 1808 were the best of times, a period so good that the Society's friends found it hard to settle on appropriate outlets for their charitable impulses. They associated, like public-spirited women in similar towns across New England, with nothing more specific in mind than a general desire to assist females in need. In Boston, the organizers of the local asylum vaguely proposed at first to establish a female humane society, a women's counterpart to the Massachusetts Humane Society, before settling on an orphanage.[9] Elsewhere, similar women's groups eventually fastened on widows as the proper objects of their attention. In Wiscasset, however, times were so flush that the association languished, its members uncertain what useful work there might possibly be for them to do. Coastal Maine's economy boomed between the early 1790s and 1807, and Wiscasset thrived thanks to the expansion of the local timber, shipping, and shipbuilding industries. As long as the demand for its exports held firm, Wiscasset's prospects seemed bright and its charitable needs modest.[10]

Diplomatic rather than commercial developments finally brought the port's prosperity to an end, opening a window of opportunity for the Asylum and its supporters. The Embargo Act, passed at Thomas Jefferson's urging in 1807, and over the opposition of most New Englanders, devastated seaports like Wiscasset. Ships lay idle at their moorings, and residents who depended directly or indirectly on the sea for their livelihoods turned to their neighbors for help as unemployment reached as high as sixty percent in the coastal communities between Eastport and Kittery.[11]

Painful as it was, the crisis nevertheless clarified the objectives of the supporters of the Society. Finding a growing number of destitute girls and women to help, they sprang into action, defining their goals in terms of the circumstances of their new dependents. Thanks to the embargo, Wiscasset's needs finally suited the services the Asylum could provide.

Organization proceeded without reference to local conditions in Wiscasset, a circumstance that explains the delays in bringing the Asylum's programs to life but calls for an explanation in its own right. Expectations rather than solid evidence of adversity almost certainly led to the establishment of the Society. Similar institutions had proven useful elsewhere, and the Asylum's founders took it for granted that their association would find someone to serve in Wiscasset. They modeled their institutions on similar ventures in Boston, Salem, Portsmouth, and a number of other towns along the Atlantic coast. Until the crisis of 1808, though, prosperity upset their assumptions, providing all but the few local residents on the town dole with good livings. The Asylum's own exogenous origins dictated its inactivity.

If the Asylum's supporters were especially out of touch with their community's needs before 1808, the general problem they faced was nonetheless quite common. No matter what means compassionate New Englanders chose to channel their charity, experience taught that all too often their institutional solutions were utterly unsuited to the problems they encountered. The obvious course of action was organizational reform.

The Domestication of Organized Charity

The history of almost every charitable society in New England prior to 1820 is one of imitation and adaptation. Because voluntary association was not a domestic innovation, every program patterned itself to a greater or lesser degree on at least one established institution. There were practical limits to this course of action, however. Nothing guaranteed that what had worked well in London, Edinburgh, or Philadelphia could be transplanted successfully to Boston, New Haven, or Portsmouth. Trial and error eventually taught how difficult it was to conform borrowed practices to the special demands of local conditions. As domestic circumstances changed with time, moreover, the friends of many organizations learned that adaptation was an unending process.

The imitation of existing charitable programs took not one but two distinct forms, one considerably more limited than the other. Occasionally, men and women who had acted unsuccessfully as individuals or in coalitions, sometimes for years, turned to voluntary associations to provide the coordination and continuity their previous efforts lacked. Such benefactors had already begun to educate themselves about the social, spiritual, and moral conditions they proposed to relieve, and in institutionalization they primarily sought new ways to make their continuing efforts more productive. More often, however, relevant experience did not precede the establishment of new associations because the problems they targeted were themselves poorly understood or only recently recognized. The founding members of most of New England's charitable ventures consequently began their education in earnest only when they set up their institutions. Many of them learned not only new institutional practices from those they copied, but the very nature of the problems they hoped to resolve.

Of the earliest postwar charitable institutions, the missionary societies drew on the greatest store of practical experience. In Boston in 1787, the organizers of the Society for Propagating the Gospel among the Indians and Others in North America built on nearly a century and a half of work with the native tribes of Massachusetts as well as on home missionary activities that dated from the beginning of the century. In Hartford in 1798, the founding members of the Missionary Society of Connecticut had a record of nearly a quarter of a century of intermittent domestic evangelizing. Missionary needs were old news both in Boston and Hartford. It is hard to imagine that anyone in either community was surprised by what spokesmen for each cause had to say.

No doubt, it was the lure of a proven formula, tested by years of experience in London and Edinburgh, that eventually led the founders of the SPGNA and the Missionary Society of Connecticut to model their programs on established ones. Concerned to "devise some measures to perpetuate the missions in the new settlements,"[12] they found their answers in the work of such institutions as the New England Company and the Society in Scotland for Promoting Christian Knowledge.

In contrast, the founders of the earliest humanitarian and reform associations ordinarily had less direct and relevant experience on which to draw. To be sure, neither death by drowning nor chronic intoxication, to take two examples, was a new problem when the organizers of the Massachusetts Humane Society and the Connecticut Society for the Promotion of Good Morals established their programs. Yet in the absence of outside encouragement, none of these issues had inspired persistent or systematic responses.

The Boston Dispensary, set up in 1796, traced a course that many other institutions also followed. The Dispensary was not one person's doing, but if a single individual were to receive the credit it would not be a Bostonian but

Dr. Benjamin Rush of Philadelphia. It was Rush who first brought dispensaries to the attention of Bostonians, and the success of the Philadelphia Dispensary, in which he played an active part, seemed to demonstrate both the medical needs of the worthy poor and the efficacy of clinics.

Dr. Rush's own first-hand experience with such clinics dated from 1786, when he helped to organize the Philadelphia Dispensary. The plans that Rush and other leading Philadelphians used came from a pamphlet entitled *Medical Memoirs of the General Dispensary in London,* written in 1774 by John Coakley Lettsom, an English humanitarian. Using Lettsom's model, the Philadelphians established a clinic under the supervision of an apothecary, who served as administrator. Its staff included both attending and consulting physicians and surgeons, each of whom donated his time. Philadelphia's city government had always taken care of the sick poor in small numbers, and since 1751 the Pennsylvania Hospital had provided for them as in-patients. The dispensary, however, immediately revealed unsuspected health needs, serving more than 1,500 patients in 1787, its first full year of operation, and 16,855 between its founding and 1800.[13] By the winter of 1790, New York had followed suit, quite possibly under Rush's prodding, and set up its own City Dispensary, which took care of 310 patients in 1791, its first full year in service.[14]

Rush first introduced Lettsom's plan to Bostonians in 1788. In two letters to the Reverend Jeremy Belknap he described the structure and benefits of clinics, and he urged Bostonians to form a similar program.[15] They demurred at first, but eight years later a group followed Rush's suggestion, then immediately acknowledged their debt to the dispensaries that had preceded theirs "both in Europe and in several of the capital towns in America."[16]

Belknap and his neighbors were not entirely unaware of the sick poor when Rush reminded them of the problem, but the situation was not one to which anyone had devoted himself, nor was anyone well informed about it. Rush's principal contributions to the establishment of the Boston Dispensary were to draw attention to the cause and to provide a model to follow. Time and again, New Englanders drew similar lessons from the programs they copied.

Neither the best of intentions nor a proven formula can insure success. Some organizations—notably the Indian missionary societies—were stymied in their efforts, although no one questioned that the needs they served were real and pressing. Others discovered that their causes were less acute than they had imagined: only fifty-nine patients sought the help of the Boston Dispensary in 1797, its first full year of operation, for instance, less than one-fifth the number the City Dispensary served during the comparable year and less than four percent of the number the Philadelphia Dispensary cared for at the same point in its existence.[17] Whether it was lack of success or of need, or perhaps merely changing conditions, that led them to reassess their activities, sooner or later most charitable organizations found it necessary to reform their programs to respond to local circumstances.

If they learned too much from successful programs elsewhere, if they imitated others too faithfully, New Englanders eventually learned from their failures and successes that their own circumstances were never completely like anyone else's. There were limits to what they could copy from others. As a rule, the general practice of voluntary association translated well from one community to another. The broad principles of organization—whether fiduciary or fraternal—that worked well in Amsterdam and New York also functioned in Salem and Providence. Specific programs, however, often seemed out of place when someone tried to prefabricate them for use in new communities.

The founders of the Massachusetts Congregational Charitable Society learned as much between its incorporation in 1786 and 1801. None of postwar New England's early charitable associations relied more heavily on borrowed models and expert advice than did the Congregational Charitable Society. And none found the methods it appropriated less suited to its purposes.

The Massachusetts Congregational Charitable Society was unlike anything New Englanders had ever seen, but its origins were obvious. The Society succeeded the Massachusetts Convention of Congregational Ministers in 1786 as the principal agency for relieving needy clergymen, their families, and heirs, and at its founding the Convention transferred the assets of its orphans' fund, £571, to the new association. The Society's methods, however, were very different from those of the Convention. Correspondence between its organizers and Dr. Richard Price, an English clergyman and statistician, resulted in an association that was unique, at least in New England. Although the Society appealed to the public for support, its regulations limited its benefits to paying members and their heirs. Price was well known for his actuarial calculations and his published essay *Observations on Reversionary Payments.* Instead of providing generally for destitute ministers, their dependents, and heirs, thanks to their consultation with Price the clergy of Massachusetts established an annuity society for paying participants. Working with the model Price suggested, the officers of the Society set out to serve a constituency far narrower than the ministerial association relieved before the Revolution.[18]

Price's advice showed the Society how to maintain its solvency, but in adopting the annuity approach it set aside the needs of everyone who could not keep up a regular schedule of payments. The Society continued on an annuity basis for its first fifteen years, but at the same time it solicited public donations, which the treasurer pooled with the premiums he received. In 1801, however, the Society abruptly reverted to the Convention's practice of relieving the relicts of clergymen regardless of their husband's participation in the fund. Although the members of the Society never publicly explained themselves, their reasons for abandoning the original scheme were clear enough. The more experience they had with Price's actuarial approach, the more they recognized the failure of these methods to meet an important part of the job they had taken over from the Convention. An attempt by trustee Theophilus Parsons, a lawyer, to separate annuity funds from public contributions led briefly to the segregation of assets into two different accounts, but by 1811 the Society was drawing on both funds at once to relieve a widow.[19]

Much as the members of the Society learned the shortcomings of borrowed practices through experience, those of most other charitable associations in New England learned with time that they, too, had to reform their programs to meet their objectives. Once New Englanders began to try to suit their activities to local conditions, moreover, they ensured that institutional reform would never end. No organization was free from pressures to adapt to social, spiritual, or moral needs. Because these needs were never static, in pursuing moving targets programs and practices had to change constantly as well.

Even mutual associations felt these pressures. Of all the charitable organizations in postrevolutionary New England, the fraternities were the most removed from their own communities. By limiting enrollment and by ordinarily restricting relief to members in good standing, the mutualists shut themselves off from many of their communities' worst problems. Yet no fraternity was able to isolate itself completely. Domestic poverty occasionally stirred lodges to extend relief to non-members, especially in the 1780s and early 1790s. More often, the mutualists enlarged and reorganized their associations to meet the challenges of urban growth and frontier expansion.

The Freemasons were New England's largest fraternity, and their transformation following the Revolution reveals how even the most cloistered of organizations reformed borrowed practices in response to changing external conditions. Small "private" or "secular" lodges were the local building blocks of Freemasonry in colonial New England, and they remained its foundation after the Revolution. As the brotherhood expanded following the war, however, its leaders began to centralize it. The result was a major restructuring at the turn of the century.

In theory, Freemasonry was always centralized. Each private lodge always accepted the oversight of its grand lodge. In practice, however, the two grand lodges in colonial New England, St. John's Grand Lodge and Massachusetts Grand Lodge, both located in Boston, bickered with each other constantly and maintained loose supervision over the lodges each had chartered. It was this chaotic state of affairs, exacerbated by rapid growth in the number of secular lodges, that the Masons sought to correct through reorganization.

Restructuring took more than two decades, 1783 through 1805, and it encompassed five reforms. First, between 1783 and 1794, conventions established state grand lodges in Connecticut, Rhode Island, New Hampshire, and Vermont. Meanwhile, in 1792 the two competing grand lodges in Massachusetts merged. Each grand lodge now assumed ultimate control of almost all its state's masonic activities.[20] Second, to relieve traditional regional rivalries the grand lodges in Rhode Island, Connecticut, and Vermont adopted plans in the early 1790s to alternate semi-annual meetings between competing communities. Rhode Island and Connecticut Masons also agreed to divide grand lodge offices equally by region.[21] Third, to confirm their authority over each private lodge, between 1789 and 1797 masonic leaders instituted "visitations" or inspections for the "purpose of establishing a uniformity of working" or ritual from lodge to lodge.[22] Fourth, to supplement regular visitations the grand lodges of Vermont and Massachusetts appointed part-time circuit riders in the early nineteenth century "to lecture the several secular lodges" on the principles of masonry.[23] Finally, between 1801 and 1804, Masons in Massachusetts, New Hampshire, and Vermont established systems of geographical districts, each under the supervision of a District Deputy Grand Master.[24]

By the early 1800s, New England's Masons had responded to urban and frontier growth by restructuring their fraternity. Through reorganization, masonic leaders assured better lines of communication than ever before, notwithstanding the difficulties of great distances and great numbers. Not everyone agreed on the desirability of centralization; in Salem, William Bentley, an active member, deplored the reforms, worrying that the measures would serve only to "enrich the Grand Lodge!" and that "District Deputies" would act as its "spies."[25] Whether or not members like Bentley approved of centralization, the future course of Freemasonry was set. The fraternity's leadership would reform the brotherhood whenever it recognized the need.

New Englanders might imitate others at first, but no program could go on for long if it did not conform to domestic conditions. The more New Englanders learned about their own needs, the more responsive to them their institutions became.

On the Learning Curve

The institutionalization of charity began a learning process. First, public-spirited New Englanders learned how to organize; then they learned how to organize effectively. The crucial ingredient in their success was experience, because with it both institutional officers and the general public attained a new perception of need, an awareness of the community as well as of the individual.

The early years of almost every charitable association were ones of discovery, as officers and members came to recognize how little they knew about their own communities and took steps to remedy this ignorance. Their new awareness of their social, spiritual, and moral circumstances led them inexorably to set new goals for their institutions and to search for new ways to carry out their missions.

In Salem, the officers and members of the local Bible society followed a typical course. At its organization in 1810, the trustees of the Bible Society of Salem and Vicinity intended to devote their attention briefly to seeing that every local family had a copy of the scriptures before undertaking what they conceived to be their ultimate mission, supplying the gospel to pioneers lacking it. Two years of experience, however, brought the board's members to the realization that a surprisingly large number of their own neighbors needed their services. "It already appears," the trustees commented in 1812, that within Salem and its neighboring towns before 1810 "the number of persons destitute of the Bible was not small." Once they started to look seriously at the needs of their communities, the Society's officers began to realize that they had previously harbored no idea of the magnitude of the problem. "As inquiry continues to be made," they now believed, the "melancholy fact" of their neighbors' needs would "more and more appear."[26] At least for the present, the Society would have to set aside its thoughts of the frontier in favor of more immediate problems.

It was no coincidence that in towns like Salem public awareness of local circumstances developed at the same time that the first charitable institutions were established. Not merely a response to need, the associations provided better means for assessing actual social, spiritual, and moral conditions than New Englanders had ever previously possessed. It was not that New Englanders had never given thought to society and its shortcomings. To the contrary, more than a century and a half of jeremiads undergirded their concerns. Yet institutionalization brought New Englanders into contact with various forms of need more constantly than ever before and forced them to ask new questions about want's causes and remedies. New Englanders now had access to more and better information about local, regional, and national conditions than ever in the past; they had better means to gather and digest data than at any previous time; and they had a new responsibility to think systematically about the causes they served. The eventual result was a systematic self-portrait that differed fundamentally from prerevolutionary New England's hazy understanding of itself and its obligations.

It was the opportunity that organized charity afforded to learn from experience that allowed the evolution of systematic, coordinated, and informed practices in place of what seemed in comparison the stasis, haphazardness, and discontinuity of efforts before the Revolution. Organizations retained corporate memories of their successes, failures, and observations, and these institutional recollections outlasted individuals, permitting associations to develop as long as their understanding of society's circumstances grew increasingly refined.

At first, New England's growing awareness of its own social, spiritual, and moral conditions was itself largely accidental, an unintended by-product of the day-to-day operation of charitable organizations. In Portsmouth, for example, a female charity school gave way in 1804 to an orphans' asylum when the leading women of the town concluded after a year's operation that a residential institution would better serve local needs.[27] By the early nineteenth century, however, as New Englanders became more and more adept as administrators, they increasingly came to depend on information they gathered intentionally. Once they grew to recognize the value of narrative reports and statistical data, they began to demand and circulate them.

The first such reports came from Indian missionaries in the field. As early as the middle of the seventeenth century, New England evangelists had written occasionally to their benefactors, the officers of the New England Company in London. Both the New England Company and the Society in Scotland for Propagating Christian Knowledge required their agents to render accounts to local committees of leading citizens, who relayed them to the parent organization.[28] Returns from the frontier were few in number, though, and fragmentary and impressionistic at best as long as New England supported only a small number of missionaries. With the growth of home evangelism, however, the contemporary understanding of spiritual conditions in the backcountry grew increasingly cohesive. By the early nineteenth century, a dozen or more itinerants made reports each year. Meanwhile, as civic-minded New Englanders grew increasingly involved in organized humanitarianism, many of them came in direct and sustained contact with destitute neighbors. A provision in the by-laws of the Boston Dispensary requiring each patient to be recommended for relief by a donor in good standing, for example, meant that community leaders who might otherwise have ignored sufferers in their midst had to pay attention to the sick poor.[29] Similarly, the managers of the Providence Female Charitable Society informed themselves of local conditions through regular visits to each of the widowed families on their list of beneficiaries.[30]

Fiduciary considerations were the initial reasons for these early reports from the field. The trustees of missionary societies required accounts from their itinerants as evidence of the satisfactory performance of their duties; meanwhile, to ensure the accuracy of claims, the managers of humanitarian institutions personally investigated candidates for assistance. In each case, the account served as an internal institutional control, assuring contributors that their money was well spent. The information that New Englanders collected, though, proved to have far wider uses than anyone originally envisaged.

In the hands of narrow circles of institutional officers and trustees, manuscript reports from the field could reshape programs and revise priorities. Such accounts revealing the failures of Indian mission work led to its eclipse by domestic evangelism. Similarly, a survey of local conditions authorized at the first regular meeting of the New Haven Moral Society in 1814 persuaded the association to dissolve itself because it had no useful purpose to serve. At its next gathering less than two weeks later the investigating committee observed "with entire oprobation and great satisfaction the measures lately adopted by the Tithingmen." The second meeting adjourned sine die, and as someone noted later in the organization's record book, "This was the end of the Moral Society." The New Haven Moral Society was not unique; most of the other local auxiliaries to the Connecticut Society for the Promotion of Good Morals also disappeared within a few years of their founding— presumably for want of work to do.[31]

Circulated more widely, printed reports began by the early nineteenth century to increase significantly public knowledge and awareness of the causes the associations served. As early as the 1750s, the published returns of Boston's Society for Encouraging Industry and Employing the Poor seemed to shed light on the plight of the town's jobless.[32] Between 1763 and 1775, Eleazar Wheelock's open letters to his supporters both in Great Britain and in the colonies similarly afforded the public apparent insight into the religious circumstances of Indians and white settlers on the frontier.[33] After the Revolution, as each passing year brought more and more charitable institutions, a growing volume of published sermons, annual reports, charters, acts of incorporation, and periodicals, including quarterly or even monthly magazines, the favorite tools of many missionary societies, addressed supporters.

By 1820, New England's charitable organizations were issuing more than one hundred publications of various descriptions each year.[34] Such a deluge of reports could provide anyone who was interested with all the data he or she could absorb about local social, spiritual, and moral conditions.

By the standards of a later day, the data that charitable institutions supplied their officers and friends were crude at best, and were often strongly influenced by the values and assumptions of the compilers. Early reports were ordinarily entirely anecdotal, and the first statistics printed, in the 1790s, gave raw accounts to the friends of missionary societies of how many baptisms, sermons, and other services their itinerants had provided, and to humane-society and dispensary supporters of how many sufferers their institutions had assisted, without in any case attempting extended analysis. By the standards of the times, however, both qualitative and quantitative accounts provided the bases for further action, the baseline against which to measure further discoveries.

Organized charity took root and flowered at the same time that New Englanders, no longer dependent on a European power but citizens of an independent nation, eagerly began to examine themselves and all their peculiarities, triggering, in the words of one historian, "a fad for 'statistics' and 'authentic facts' in the 1790s."[35] Although such inquiries sometimes took an antiquarian turn, resulting in nothing more than compilations of curiosities and trivia, investigations as early as the census of 1790 and Alexander Hamilton's 1791 "Report on the Subject of Manufactures" revealed how data intelligently gathered could profitably serve as the basis for public policies. By the early 1810s, Americans were beginning to fill gazetteers, almanacs, and magazines with tables of data. With a growing belief in the utility of objective information, and especially of statistics, many New Englanders began consciously to turn to empirical methods to assist in planning charitable activities.[36]

Dr. Mason F. Cogswell showed the way. The father of schools for the deaf and dumb in the United States, Cogswell was also the first New Englander to make systematic use of an objective survey and of quantitative data for charitable purposes. In 1811, Cogswell, whose two-year-old daughter Alice was deaf, wrote Connecticut's General Association to ask its help in conducting an inquiry into the extent of the problems of deaf children. When the association's report was ready the following year, it revealed seventy-four deaf and mute children in Connecticut, more than anyone had guessed and enough to convince Cogswell, the Reverend Thomas Gallaudet, whom the doctor recruited to learn the latest European techniques for instructing such victims, and many of Cogswell's friends of the magnitude of the problem. The

Connecticut Asylum for the Educational Instruction of the Deaf and Dumb, the first such American institution, established in 1817, was a direct consequence of Alice Cogswell's handicap and of her father's survey.[37]

Within a few years of Cogswell's initiative, New Englanders were making regular use of statistics and surveys both to inform and to influence. In 1814, the officers of the year-old Massachusetts Society for the Suppression of Intemperance prepared and circulated a pamphlet that statistically detailed the extent of American alcohol consumption and intemperance. Samuel Dexter, the pamphlet's author and the Society's president, used census data and marshals' returns on the domestic manufacture of spirits to estimate that American consumption per capita had been nearly five gallons in 1810. He further extrapolated that spirits had cost the American public $20 million that year, a figure, he pointedly noted, that did not take into account the value of labor lost through the misuse of alcohol. To refine their knowledge of the problem, the officers of the Society appended to Dexter's essay a questionnaire in which they asked readers to report on such matters as the extent of drinking in their neighborhoods, its increase or decrease, the number of chronic alcoholics, and the worst observed consequences of substance abuse.[38] Meanwhile, in 1816 peace reformers, led by Noah Worcester, attempted to calculate the costs of war—in military expenditures, destroyed property, death, and disease—in order to demonstrate its folly.[39]

Notwithstanding their new familiarity and comfort with "statisticks" and other measures of their social, spiritual, and moral climate, New Englanders still had a great deal to learn about themselves in the late 1810s. Many years would pass before their grandchildren could legitimately claim to practice "scientific philanthropy."[40] In the 1810s, doubts still enveloped the conclusions that the more ardent partisans of some causes tried to extract from their allegedly objective data. Certainly, the reform lessons that Dexter and Worcester drew were not to everyone's liking.

Yet thanks to their organized charitable activities, New Englanders had learned some valuable lessons, and almost everybody agreed that their experience had led to undeniable progress. Who could doubt that their charity was more effective now than ever before, that it was more congruent with the causes to be served, that it was reaching more people genuinely in need than at any previous time? New Englanders knew more about themselves than ever before, and with every passing day they learned more and more about how to serve their neighbors in need. The more experience they had with organized charity, the more most New Englanders began to realize that something important was happening, a revolution in the nature and practice of charity.

PART THREE

The Acceptance of Organized Charity

****

Curtius

IT IS NOT difficult to guess why "Curtius" adopted a pen name. Although purveyors in print of even the blandest ideas routinely adopted pseudonyms in the eighteenth and early nineteenth centuries, the generations-old custom was at its most useful when it served to protect commentators like Curtius whose views might prove controversial. The letter on the incorporation of the Boston Female Asylum that he addressed to the *National Aegis* of Worcester in 1803, and which the newspaper published in three installments between September 14 and October 19, was uncompromising, strident, bitter, even sarcastic in tone. Curtius could not abide this novel institution, and its incorporation drew him into wild speculations about its origins and likely consequences. Nowhere but in the "bold and Masculine imagination of Mary Wolstoncraft" could such an institution have been devised, Curtius frothed. It was "absolutely incomprehensible," he added, "that among the highest rank, by the most respectable part of her sex, *any* should be met with, actually adopting the most crazy of her schemes." No good could come from an institution proposed by the "Mistress of Godwin," and if Curtius shielded his identity behind a pseudonym, he had no intention of concealing his opinions.[1]

The immediate reason for the address by Curtius was the adoption by the Massachusetts legislature on February 26, 1803, of an act of incorporation for the asylum. "I impeach not the *personal* delicacy of those who solicited, nor the *general* wisdom of those who granted incorporation," Curtius maintained, "but I assert, that the one discovered less discernment than indifference, and the other *'far out step'd the modesty' of sex!*"[2]

Curtius outlined three objections to the asylum and the charter: first, 'That the Incorporation of the BOSTON FEMALE ASYLUM was unnecessary and *inconsistent* with the purposes of *charity*"; second, "That the consequences, which will naturally result from it, must be hostile to the peace of society, and to the regularity and harmony of families"; and third, "That similar institutions are opposed to the spirit of a republican government." The asylum had operated between 1801 and 1803 without a corporate charter, proving to Curtius's satisfaction that the act was unnecessary. In fact, before the establishment of the institution its organizers had carried on satisfactorily, extending their charity as individuals, not as a corporate body. Furthermore, the founding of the asylum provided contributors with an excuse to reject mendicants who called on them as individuals for relief. Unless the institution relieved everyone who might need its assistance, it risked stigmatizing as unworthy those it could not help.[3] Finally, the power consolidated in such an organization threatened good government. Incorporated institutions attracted political power and financial resources, each of which when "thrown into the political balance" might "preponderate the scale" filled only with individuals.[4]

There was some basis for Curtius's analysis. Certainly, women's charitable associations drew their members out of the domestic sphere and into the public arena. Such corporations were restructuring society. Still, Curtius did not carry the day—in fact, he seems to have been the asylum's only public critic. His fulminations, though, were part of a broader pattern.

At the turn of the century, New Englanders began to come to terms with organized charity—to recognize its effects on their lives and speculate on its potential effects in years to come. This accommodation took two different forms: sweeping reconsiderations of the nature of charity and narrow, precise, and incremental responses to specific circumstances. If the rare dissident like Curtius had the greatest adjustments to make, no one was immune from the effects of the institutionalization of charity. For the rise of organized charity jarred everyone's unspoken assumptions. It fundamentally transformed both the virtue, itself, and the way people thought about it. Charity would never again seem the same.

Chapter Five

"The Advantages of Association"

Happy Columbia, on whose Shores these valuable Institutions have
thus early found a place! for you they shall erect a Barrier more stu-
pendous than Alps or Apennines; for you they shall secure the Protection of that Providence which is a Refuge from every Blast, a safe
Shelter from every Storm.
— William Walter, *A Discourse Delivered before the Humane Society*
(Boston, 1798)

THE ORGANIZATION of charity had come as a surprise to everyone, partisans no less than the rare detractor. Instead of questioning the
development, or aspects of it, as Curtius did, however, most contemporaries
considered it an unalloyed sign of progress. The great transformation was
carrying New England into a "polished age," a time when, as Dr. John
Bartlett of Roxbury commented in 1796, "the arts and sciences are rapidly
advancing towards the point of perfection." "Ignorance and error" were now
put to flight by "charity, with all its pleasing train."[1] Voluntary association
allowed New Englanders to make their charity "more extensive and permanently useful." The parable of the good Samaritan and similar scriptural
passages had set colonial New Englanders a universal standard for their
charity. More and more it now seemed possible that this objective was within
their reach. "By increasing the number of institutions, and varying the descriptions of persons to be relieved by them," Bishop Samuel Seabury of New
London noted, "all the poor who are not provided for by public law, may be
brought within the reach of relief."[2]

Such a development, most New Englanders reasoned, had to have some
meaning, some underlying pattern and cause. Convinced that "The increase
of charitable Institutions among us, is an undoubted evidence of the im-

proved state of society, and a delightful exemplification of the benevolent affections, which the ever blessed God have implanted in our nature,"[3] exhilarated contemporaries found teleological significance in the events they were witnessing. If they were reading the signs correctly, a divine hand must be at work.

"The Dawn of Philanthropy"

A full appreciation of New England's delight in the rise of organized charity requires an act of historical imagination, a willingness to think back to a day before the end of the eighteenth century when such institutions were not yet commonplace but apologies still were. Once parents started to encourage their children to join juvenile cent societies, to contribute their pennies and nickels to orphans' asylums and missionary societies, they ensured that organized charity would eventually be taken for granted by a generation of young adults who had never known a time without it. At the close of the eighteenth century, however, charitable associations were still new and exciting, full of potential although the extent of their promise remained unknown. When most New Englanders could still recall a time before the "great movements of the present day," when the Christian world was still rousing itself from "the slumber of the ages,"[4] it was difficult not to be swept up in the tide of enthusiasm.

Compared with what they had known all their lives, it was the power and the permanence, the ambition and the achievement, of organized charity that captured the attention of New Englanders at the turn of the century. Nothing in their previous experience could approach what they were witnessing now. Colonial New Englanders had understood the "Advantages of Unity,"[5] of course, and in Great Britain the humanitarian age had antedated developments in America by several decades. But New England's prerevolutionary accomplishments paled when set beside postwar developments, and most of those New Englanders who were aware of humanitarian activities in the British Isles knew of them through hearsay rather than personal experience. What a difference it made to see at first hand the rapid establishment of one benevolent institution after another, to take part in the creation and operation of these organizations!

By the end of the eighteenth century, organization had made it possible for Samaritans to extend their charity nearly to the limits of their imaginations. "Much has been effected by the exertions of benevolent and enterprising individuals," Daniel Appleton White, a Newburyport lawyer, remarked in 1805, "But the exertions of individuals are unequal to the accomplishment of designs, which require great diversity of powers, or abundance of resources;

which demand the combined energies of wealth, of science, and of labor." Associations of men or women could do far more than an equal number of individuals could ever hope to accomplish alone. "The institution of societies, therefore for the promotion of important objects," White continued, "has received the sanction of the wisest and best men, especially of modern times."[6]

With the passage of time, New Englanders became increasingly accustomed to organized charity. Eventually, familiarity bred apathy, at least for some. Between the late 1780s and the early 1800s, however, there were new discoveries to make, new reasons for delight in the associations' emergence.

By 1805, when William Patten, the pastor of the Second Congregational Church in Newport, addressed the annual meeting of the town's Female Benevolent Society, two decades of discussion had resulted in a consensus about the "Advantages of Association." One tally might differ slightly from the next, but almost everyone concurred in Patten's general conclusions. There was a litany of good reasons for taking part in the work of a charitable society.[7]

The advantages of association were both functional and spiritual. The text that Patten expounded—"Two are better than one; for they have a good reward for their labour"[8]—spoke directly to the more practical considerations. Effective organization facilitated the sharing of resources and the coordination of efforts. "Whilst unassociated for these merciful and beneficial ends, we may still be humane," the Reverend Thomas Barnard of Salem commented in 1794, "Yet, it is by no means likely, that we shall know of so many objects who deserve our compassion and assistance, nor that we shall so regularly exert ourselves for their relief."[9] An association could find the needy and certify their worthiness more readily than individuals, who often "have not the leisure nor the opportunities to search out the circumstances of the poor," Professor Andrew Yates of Union College added in 1812.[10]

Such practical considerations were not the only benefits of organized charity. Association could also encourage the lazy to be charitable, shield the poor from embarrassment, and deflect criticism. In his first epistle to the Corinthians, the apostle Paul warned that "charity vaunteth not itself." It was bad form to boast of compassion, but New Englanders recognized that the public activities of charitable organizations could stir potential contributors from their lethargy. Association was "conducive to the accomplishment of useful purposes, as it animates persons to the performance of their duty."[11] One reason that Christians traditionally discouraged self-congratulation for acts of charity was the embarrassment that such public attention often brought to beneficiaries. As Luther Baker, Warren, Rhode Island's Baptist minister, told an audience there in 1806, "Societies established for . . . useful and benevolent purposes . . . render such a disclosure unnecessary."[12] When charity was institutionalized it allowed a welcome measure of anonymity that was impossible for someone who had to beg for aid in public. If an association could prevent embarrassment by shaping the climate of opinion, through social pressures it could also silence critics like Curtius. Even the best of plans, Patten noted, "are by some condemned." "A Society state is conducive to the accomplishment of useful purposes," he added, "because it is formidable to opposers."[13]

If an association did its work well, New Englanders concluded, there would be rewards in this world and in the next. Charity brought pleasure both to benefactors and beneficiaries, and organized charity made "the joy of doing good work more diffusive, and therefore increases the sum of happiness." The Lord rewarded the charitable, Patten added, "in proportion to the usefulness of an object." Because organized charity had broader consequences than the work of isolated individuals, Patten maintained, it was "a more extensive subject of the divine blessing, and the ground of an increased reward."[14]

Association produced more than the sum of the good deeds of individual participants. A critical mass of good will could generate its own energy, enthusiasm, and accomplishments. Moreover, as many observers began to comment by the turn of the century, the benefits that resulted when individuals cooperated were multiplied once again when associations worked with each other.

New England's recognition of the benefits of institutional cooperation developed gradually over the better part of a decade. As they grew more and more accustomed to organized charity, anniversary-day orators became increasingly sophisticated in their understanding of the relationships among their associations. Before long they were basing predictions on the optimistic belief that organized charity had become so comprehensive that "Every form of distress finds its appropriate relief; every calamity, its remedy, or alleviation."[15]

The seed of this refined awareness was a form of civic boosterism. The rise of organized charity was a reason for public pride, New Englanders agreed. "The public institutions of a community may be justly considered as the strongest features of its character," Charles Paine, a Boston lawyer, maintained in 1808: "In them, as in a mirror, we may behold the principles, habits, and manners, of a nation truly represented."[16]

When the Reverend John Lathrop of Boston addressed the Massachusetts Charitable Fire Society in 1796, he recognized Paine's sort of virtue in that institution, along with a dozen other incorporated charitable and cultural institutions ranging from Harvard College and the American Academy of Arts and Sciences to the Massachusetts Humane Society, the Boston Marine Society, and the Society for Propagating the Gospel among the Indians and Others in North America. "This Commonwealth," Lathrop asserted, "hath honoured itself by the encouragement it hath given to literary and charitable institutions." Such an institution was "a powerful motive to . . . works of charity and beneficence," Lathrop judged, a reason to wish organized charity well.[17]

From general valedictions it was only a short step to the recognition that these institutions were collectively in position to render unprecedented service to society. By the early 1800s New Englanders were beginning to describe an informal federation of charitable institutions sharing "one general design, even to relieve the distressed, while they differ as to the particular objects of their beneficence."[18] Through cooperation, New Englanders began to believe, organized charity had become so effective that "No species of misery is abandoned or neglected. No state of human depression is so desperate, that it might not find in some benevolent institution a refuge from contempt, or the means of being useful."[19] "Scarcely any project is proposed," the trustees of the American Education Society added in 1814, "which does not find patrons, or objects patronised, which fails of accomplishment."[20]

Although they still believed in the prior claims of "the members of our families, who are more immediately under our eye, and whom GOD has committed to our care," New Englanders began to minimize the practical considerations that had once discouraged them from venturing farther to "love others also."[21] The merciful, Jedidiah Morse exhorted in 1801, "confine not their beneficent acts to their kindred, friends, neighbours or countrymen, nor yet to the human species, but extend their compassionate feelings and aid to every thing that has life and sensibility, to all creatures in misery."[22] New Englanders had long believed that the "arm of benevolence embraces the stranger, the remotest relation among human beings." Now they could cheer that "Many, whom [they] never saw, and never will have knowledge of" might "experience the happy effects of [their] Liberality."[23]

Horizons had begun to appear nearly limitless to men and women who had grown up believing in the duty of comprehensive charity but apologizing for their shortcomings. The good Samaritan's universal compassion was almost within reach. As Luther Baker reminded in 1806, the parable's closing admonition, "'go thou and do likewise' is solemn, forcible and instructive." Unlike the priest and the Levite, the compassionate Christian encountering need was not to "pass by without affording the desired and necessary relief"; instead, "Samaritan like," he was to "pour the oil of joy and the wine of consolation into the bosom of the afflicted sufferer."[24]

No development better reflected the hopes that the rise of organized charity engendered than a growing vogue for the word "philanthropy." The term's acceptance into common daily usage, first hinted at while the Revolution was still in progress and very clear by the late 1780s, was hardly accidental. New Englanders adopted the word because it described relationships that were, for them at least, almost without precedent. "Philanthropy" expressed comprehensive love, much as "charity" usually implied a more limited spirit.

"Philanthropy" was derived from the Greek words "philos," meaning "love," and "anthropos," meaning "man" or "mankind." New Englanders took the broad implications of the word seriously. "Philanthropy" was an expression of universal brotherhood and love.

Although "philanthropy" had not been completely unknown to colonial New Englanders, they had used the word sparingly. In 1742 when he discoursed on the second commandment, Joseph Sewall spoke of "a general *Philanthropy*, or a Love of Men," which was, he explained, "a Duty that extends to all."[25] A dozen years later in 1754 at the ordination of Joseph Roberts in the Massachusetts town of Leicester, Andrew Eliot urged on the new pastor "that benevolence of the soul; that divine philanthropy, which Christianity was designed to produce."[26] Anonymous political pamphleteers sometimes styled themselves "Philanthropos."[27] Throughout the colonial period, however, most New Englanders found that terms like "charity," "compassion," and "kindness" sufficed.

By the late 1770s and 1780s, though, the popular adoption of "philanthropy" reflected recent accomplishments and embodied a new understanding of New England's charitable abilities. "Philanthropy" became a shorthand notation for universal love. As one local orator now reminded his neighbors: "remember . . . our benevolence is not confined. It is philanthropy."[28]

It is probably impossible to determine who first seized on the term in Revolutionary New England and when, but it is clear that it was coming into fashion by the end of the war, even before the rapid rise of organized charity. By the 1780s, the spread of Freemasonry accelerated the word's acceptance. Masons were among the first New Englanders regularly to hear the praises of philanthropy. As early as 1778, the Reverend Zabdiel Adams of Lunenburg asked the Masons of Lancaster, Massachusetts, whether any virtue was "more excellent, more divine . . . more productive of our own happiness, or productive of the well-being of the world around us, than . . . *Philanthropy?*"[29]

Although it seems likely that Freemasons were leaders in the populariza-tion of "philanthropy" in New England, its use soon spread beyond the fraternity. A few associations like the Philanthropic Society in Warren, Rhode Island, incorporated the word in their names; dozens more simply assumed their purposes to be philanthropic. Spokesmen for fraternal organizations, including the Masons, of course, often tried to relate their mutualism to universal expressions of the sentiment. Addressing fellow members of the Providence Association of Mechanics and Manufacturers in 1796, George Burrell lauded his club's "Motives of universal Philanthropy, and . . . general Advantage."[30] Speakers before fiduciary institutions emphasized that they were philanthropically engaged in a work of universal benevolence.[31]

Convinced of the significance of their advances, New Englanders believed that a golden day had broken for charity. When they saw their achievements against the background of apologies and hesitations that had marked colonial charity, they felt a thrill. In 1800 when Zechariah Eddy, a young school-teacher recently graduated from Rhode Island College, addressed an audience in the small town of Raynham, Massachusetts, he captured the sentiments of the age; the day's advances, Eddy believed, portended the "dawn of philan-thropy."[32]

The dawn of philanthropy marked the fulfillment of generations of dreams. New Englanders had aspired to philanthropy as the epitome of Christian moral conduct. Now, thanks to organized charity they could achieve it. There was another dream, though, one even more exciting, that New Englanders also shared—the second coming of Christ. As philanthropy rose over the horizon, some New Englanders believed that they also saw the apocalypse in the distance.

In Search of the Millennium

The millennium, like philanthropy, had often seemed beyond reach. A graph of colonial New England's hopes for the second coming would reveal a sharply spiked pattern of peaks and valleys. Between 1649 and 1660, for example, New Englanders like John Eliot, the "Apostle to the Indians," believed fervently that the millennium was almost at hand. During the 1740s, friends of the Great Awakening considered the revival an encouraging devel-opment. And from the mid-1750s through the early 1760s the Seven Years' War raised the hopes of many observers.[33] Between such bursts of optimism, however, there were extended periods of lassitude and discouragement when there seemed little reason for hope.

Periods of optimism had always depended on signs that the Lord might be stirring. Any major deviation from the norm might contain a divine message.

Good news—especially missionary accomplishments—suggested that the Lord was extending His mercy to humanity. But there might even be advantages in affliction. War, pestilence, famine, or political conflicts might announce the Bible's time of troubles, a necessary preparatory step before the millennium.

Between the mid-1790s and the early 1800s, as New Englanders surveyed the events of the day their hopes surged then fell. Then in much the same way that they read the dawn of philanthropy into the great changes of the revolutionary era, many of them began to interpret the establishment of missionary, tract, Bible, and education societies as a precursor of the apocalypse. Never a popular interpretation in Episcopal and Arminian or Unitarian circles, this idea nevertheless won a devoted following among orthodox Calvinists by 1810, as well as among the more evangelical sects, notably the Baptists. The support of these groups fueled New England's growing excitement over the rise of organized charity.

The emergence of home missionary societies forced orthodox and sectarian New Englanders to reexamine their assumptions concerning the second coming. The same frustrating failures that drew them away from Indian missions in favor of work among white pioneers encouraged them to keep watch for the unexpected. Properly interpreted, the development of organized charity was the promise of the coming day of judgment.

Like their colonial forebears, New Englanders in the early nineteenth century peeled their eyes in search of divine messages. As early as 1798 a few of them, confident that they lived "in an age, replete with remarkable occurrences of divine Providence," pointed to the Revolution in France and to political battles at home between Federalists and Jeffersonians— "Convulsions" that were "shaking the civil kingdoms of this world to their centre"—as evidence that the scriptural time of troubles had commenced.[34] In Berkshire County, the trustees of the Congregational Missionary Society placed more stock in these events than the officers of any other, similar institution. Dismissing the skepticism of contemporaries who believed that "the time is not yet come to build the visible kingdom of the Redeemer," the trustees believed they were "called to action." Buoyed by the disorders around them, they asserted that "the present day appears to be more extraordinary, on some accounts, than ages past." Through His prophets, they maintained, the Lord had "foretold that the time should come, when he would arise, and shake terribly the earth." This, they believed, "he is doing now." In view of these disorders, would "it be suggested," the trustees asked, "that the objects of this and our sister Societies are impracticable?" The time was ripe: "these, and every other objection, when weighed in the balance with eternity, appear lighter than vanity."[35]

Many of their contemporaries felt insecure in this judgment in 1798, but like the managers of the Congregational Missionary Society they maintained their vigilance. When he addressed the Massachusetts Missionary Society in 1801, the Reverend Samuel Niles of Abington cast his entire sermon in prophetic terms. Niles offered no hope, however, that the time was near.[36] The following year, speaking to the same organization, Samuel Spring similarly examined "the fulfillment of prophecy." Much like Niles, Spring saw no proof that the millennium was imminent. He counseled trust in God: "we devoutly pray, confidently expect and patiently wait for better times." "The Lord has promised," Spring urged, "that his church shall embrace the nations; and while we suppress all unwarrantable confidence respecting the universal triumph of grace, the Prophets impel us to hail the approaching day when the temple of Christ will be commensurate with the habitable globe."[37]

Between 1801 and 1806 orthodox New Englanders, joined by a few liberal Christians, searched expectantly for further signs of the final times. By 1805, though, their hopes spent, the officers of the Congregational Missionary Society brooded that New Englanders had slipped into a "period of general languor in religion, *when iniquity aboundeth, and the love of many waxeth cold.*"[38] Other observers expressed similar fears. Using a text from Haggai—"Go up to the mountain and bring wood, and build the house; and I will take pleasure in it, and I will be glorified, saith the Lord"—the Reverend Paul Litchfield of Carlisle told the Massachusetts Missionary Society that "the work of building the church is so great and arduous, the trials so various, the enemies so numerous, of such diversity in appearance, so artful and formidable, that little will be effected without a spirit of perseverance, patience, wisdom, holy fortitude and zeal."[39] The next year, despite his reluctant conclusion that there did "not appear to be in mankind an inclination to embrace the true religion, or to worship and reverence the true God," the Reverend Joseph Barker of Middleborough urged the same society to persevere.[40] As Joseph Eckley reported in 1806 to the SPGNA, in the absence of more encouraging signs, only one conclusion made sense: that "these events are in a state of postponement."[41]

The speed with which these gloomy assessments gave way to optimism, at least in orthodox and certain sectarian circles, surprised everyone, as did the astonishing reason for the transformation. By the end of 1806 many friends of evangelism began to recognize in their own work a reason for hope. Within a year or two, most orthodox New Englanders were persuaded that missionary societies themselves were precursors of the millennium. If this interpretation were correct, then the imminence of the apocalypse presaged an unprecedented explosion of evangelism. Conversely, an extraordinary increase in evangelistic activity almost certainly had to mean that the millennium was nearly at hand.

Expressing pleasure at "the zeal with which so many of God's people appear to be animated in the present day," the trustees of the Missionary Society of Connecticut voiced the first words of renewed confidence in 1806. Revived by the apparent success of their recent activities, the trustees predicted "that some glorious events in favor of the Church are about to take place."[42] The following year, the Reverend Elijah Parish of Byfield, using the same text from Haggai that Paul Litchfield had employed to counsel patience, proclaimed to the Massachusetts Missionary Society that the time had come. "Of late peculiar light has been thrown on the volume of Revelation," Parish instructed, "the means of undertaking it are increased; it is, therefore, a good time, to spread the gospel of Jesus Christ."[43]

Parish and Timothy Cooley, who delivered the same message in 1808 to the members of the Hampshire Missionary Society, set out a line of thought that orthodox New Englanders grasped eagerly, although most liberals, mistrustful of the interpretation, rejected it. In order to demonstrate the imminence of the apocalypse, Parish and Cooley turned to a section of the book of Revelation to which New Englanders had previously paid little attention.

Unlike many colonial millennialists who depended for their optimism on an uncertain identification of the American Indians with the ten lost tribes of Israel, Parish and Cooley had other reasons for confidence. They turned instead to Revelation 14:6, where John of Patmos recorded:

> And I saw another angel fly in the midst of heaven, having the everlasting gospel to preach unto them that dwell on the earth, and to every nation, and kindred, and tongue, and people.

By common consent, Protestant commentators agreed that this vision foretold a time when the gospel, for "many centuries . . . confined to a very small part of the inhabited earth," would be ". . . preached to every kindred, and tongue, and people."[44] As they examined the exciting growth of missions around the world, Parish and Cooley urged that the time was now, and that their missionary societies, in cooperation with Old World institutions, were the angels of the prophet's dream.

As Parish and Cooley pointed out, the preceding two decades had witnessed dramatic advances. Reports from around the world gave them every reason to believe that missionaries had been gratefully received: "Of late the minds of men have felt new conviction," Parish noted, "that *christianity* is necessary to their happiness."[45] Even though the "missionary cause" was still "in its infancy," Cooley commented, already "thousands . . . have been brought into the kingdom of Christ, by the means of missionary labors."[46] As Parish added, it was "a good time to send Missionaries to every nation to extend the Redeemer's kingdom." Missionary successes were proof that the Lord's time had nearly come; missionary societies could hasten events even more rapidly to their inevitable conclusion. They were incontrovertible evidence, Parish asserted, of the "zeal, to spread the gospel, which now so generally prevails."[47]

This interpretation of recent events received rapid, enthusiastic, and undoubtedly relieved support from orthodox New Englanders wearied by their wait. To be sure, in 1808 Abiel Holmes, for one, still harbored some reservations and found it difficult to agree that the apocalypse was actually coming into view. Nevertheless, the Cambridge pastor was pleased that through missionary and Bible societies Christianity was "spreading at this moment among pagan nations, with a rapidity scarcely paralleled since the apostolic age." Missionary progress gave him hope that through "these means it is unquestionably the divine purpose to propagate [the gospel] until *all the ends of the earth* shall have *seen the salvation of God.*"[48] Other orthodox and sectarian observers abandoned even a hint of caution. In 1809 the Reverend John Emerson of Conway told the Hampshire Missionary Society that one of the most important signs of the impending millennium was

> that very remarkable spirit . . . of christian zeal and philanthropy
> which has pervaded the hearts of christians in various parts of
> christendom, to select and send missionaries to remote corners of
> the globe to announce the glad tidings of salvation to the wretched
> inhabitants, immersed in heathenism, darkness and barbarianism.

The efforts of Bible societies and "female associations" also gave Emerson hope for the near future, as did advances actually centuries old in printing, navigation, and exploration. Emerson believed that when the Lord was ready "to spread his gospel in the world, he will doubtless furnish means adequate to the glorious object." The development of missionary and Bible associations gave him "ground of encouragement."[49] In 1810 the trustees assured the friends of the Maine Missionary Society that their work would be "one great mean[s] of introducing the glories of the millennial period."[50] And in 1815 the overseers of the Bible Society of Salem and Vicinity, gratified with the

progress of such organizations around the world, suggested that their activities were a means with which "God [was] fast preparing the world for the
millennial reign of his Son."[51]

Caught up in the enthusiasm, trying to prove the merits of the societies
that had called on their services, a scattering of spokesmen for humanitarian
and fraternal organizations even tried to draw these organizations under the
millennial blanket. Although contemporaries did not, for the most part,
follow his lead, when he addressed the Merrimack Humane Society in 1807
Samuel Spring, happily impressed by "the recent goodness of God," asserted
that the development of humanitarian as well as missionary organizations
proved that God was "now doing great things for the information and
reformation of man." Spring compared "the missionary spirit, which has
lately pervaded Christendom, and already explored some of the dark reaches
of the earth" to the "humane spirit [which] within a few years [had] erected
its hallowed tabernacles and houses of reception for the children of distress,
in every section of the globe." The "confluence of these limpid streams of
living water" demonstrated the exciting future that awaited Christians
around the world. They evinced, Spring claimed, "that God, agreeably to his
covenant, is preparing the mind of man for the glorious display of his grace."
The "dark period, which has long enveloped the world and the church" had
nearly come to an end; "Both humane and missionary establishments are
harbingers of the day."[52] In similar terms, somewhat atypical for a liberal
Christian, Thaddeus Mason Harris, a Unitarian, also recognized the apocalyptic implications of the flowering of organized charity. Speaking for world
peace on behalf of the Freemasons, Harris noted that "Prophecy has foretold
this gladsome event as the result of an universal diffusion of Christianity, and
the unrestrained operation of its conciliation and pacific influences."[53] Like
Spring, Harris recognized in the dramatic growth of evangelism reason to
hope that the pacifists' millennium was at hand.

Liberal Christians were not immune to eschatological appeals, as Harris's
masonic statement showed, but between 1806 and 1810 they rarely embraced
them with the enthusiasm of the Calvinists. It was not that the liberals had no
interest in the apocalypse. As late as the Civil War, prominent Unitarians
occasionally couched sermons, essays, and hymns in millennial terms; Julia
Ward Howe's "Battle Hymn of the Republic" is a powerful example of
Unitarian apocalypticism. Nevertheless, they did not join in the fervent
expressions of their neighbors. All too often, such appeals focused on the
doctrines that most isolated the liberals from other New Englanders. Cooley,
for example, emphasized "the necessity of regeneration" for redemption on
Judgment Day.[54] Old Calvinists and friends of the New Divinity could agree

with this view; in fact, their urgent desire to convert as many sinners as possible before the second coming probably helped them to set aside the theological disagreements that still divided the two orthodox factions. Liberals, however, seeking to avoid the doctrinal controversy that they deplored, tried to deflate the newly aroused expectations of their contemporaries.

In Salem, William Bentley noted privately in his diary that the "Missionary Sermon by Mr. Parish was a compilation of all the extravagancies which would disgrace the dark ages. We have nothing to promise ourselves from the devotees who compose the Massachusetts Missionary Society."[55] More circumspect in their comments for public consumption, the Unitarian and Episcopal editors of the *Monthly Anthology and Boston Review* muted their remarks. Reporting on an apocalyptic sermon preached by the Reverend Edward Dorr Griffin at the dedication of the Park Street Church, one reviewer concurred with the speaker in his desire for a revival of religion but added that the editors did not share Griffin's optimism for the immediate future, since they believed that "those appearances, which the preacher ventures to parallel with the extraordinary operations of the spirit on the day of Pentecost, *may be* the effect of natural causes, and sometimes even of 'enthusiasm' itself, and not of supernatural interposition, or the fruits of that spirit which is meekness, joy, peace and love."[56] In 1810 most liberal Christians continued to understand the rise of missions in philanthropic rather than in eschatological terms.

Millennial expectations gave added force to orthodox and sectarian forecasts that liberals could not match. For all their excitement at the emergence of philanthropy, most liberal Christians believed they were witnessing a secular millennium; the scriptural apocalypse, in contrast, was the end which Christians had anticipated for close to two thousand years. Liberal or orthodox, though, New Englanders could agree on at least one conclusion: there was no "more decided evidence . . . of the improved state of society, than the increase of liberal and charitable institutions."[57]

"Every Thing Here is Progressive"

Whether they looked back only a few years or to ancient times, as they surveyed the course of world history New Englanders in the early nineteenth century were struck by the superiority of their own age. No one doubted that urban poverty, frontier irreligion, increasing political factionalism, and a variety of other contemporary ills were worrisome, yet the tools on hand to cope with these problems were far more powerful than anything previously available. Technologically, morally, and spiritually, contemporary accomplishments surpassed all of mankind's previous achievements. When the Reverend

Manasseh Cutler of Hamilton addressed the members of the Bible Society of Salem and Vicinity in 1813 he exuded delight over the present and optimism for the future. War with Great Britain had broken out the year before, but its destruction and commercial dislocation were not enough to cause Cutler to lose heart. "Every thing here is progressive," he determined;[58] most New Englanders agreed.

The conviction that life was growing better and better and civilization more refined was not unique to New England, nor did the view owe its growing acceptance in the region after the Revolution solely to the emergence of organized charity. The establishment of democratic state governments, economic growth, and the obvious opportunities that the frontier offered anyone sufficiently strong and courageous to accept its challenges all undoubtedly encouraged optimism about the future. The writings of some of the eighteenth century's leading political economists, furthermore, encouraged the surge of optimism and helped shape the form it took.

It is possible to find expressions of the idea of progress in writings as early as those of the ancient Greeks, but New Englanders at the turn of the century owed a far more substantial debt to a number of more recent French and Scottish thinkers.[59] By the second half of the eighteenth century, such philosophers as Helvétius, Turgot, Adam Ferguson, and Adam Smith had come to a rough consensus over the evolutionary process that societies naturally followed. Occupied primarily by economic concerns, these writers ordinarily described social development in terms of modes of production. Society had passed through four stages, political economists often instructed: hunting, pasturage, agriculture, and commerce.[60] Where charity rather than the economy was the focus of attention, the precise characteristics of the various phases were not necessarily of great interest. Nevertheless, New Englanders translated the basic structure of these teachings into charitable thought. When they proposed that the emergence of missionary societies, orphans' asylums, and temperance associations, for example, announced the start of a new day they were speaking the language of eighteenth-century political economics as well as that of moral philosophy and eschatology.

In keeping with the teachings of the leading political economists, New Englanders in the early nineteenth century thought of social evolution in terms of an ascending sequence of plateaus. Each succeeding stage represented a quantum advance in social organization. The new order was invariably more structured, refined, and cosmopolitan than its predecessor. The day's institutional changes were a flight from provincialism and rudeness toward a "happy and enlightened age."[61]

Writers on charity at the turn of the century adopted two different ways to describe this graduated pattern of social evolution, one essentially secular, the other largely spiritual. At times they appropriated some of the actual categories of political philosophy and economics. In 1797 when Arnold Welles, a Boston merchant, addressed the Massachusetts Charitable Fire Society he traced the evolution of civilization "from rudeness to the polished scenes" of the contemporary day. Following John Locke, Welles stressed the acceptance of a "social compact," with which men and women "Pressed . . . by . . . wants and imbecilities" common to a "state of nature" found security in "mutual aid and support."[62] Like many of the physiocrats and the eighteenth-century Scottish philosophers, Welles was concerned with the rise of civility out of savagery. More often, however, New Englanders devoted the greater share of their attention to the triumph of faith over infidelity; "from the savage, through the civilized, to the christian state of society," many speakers instructed, " . . . the principle of benevolence [had] gradually expanded." It was the light that "the gospel diffused upon man," Benjamin Whitwell, a Boston attorney, told the Charitable Fire Society in 1814, that distinguished the Christian era from an earlier age governed by natural religion and uninspired reason.[63] According to each schema, the outcome was the same. The emergence of organized charity helped to signal the start of a new and better time, one characterized in part by the increase and promotion of benevolence.

What would this new age be like? No one could be certain, but the common belief that they stood at its inception had a powerful stimulus on charitable New Englanders. There were, to be sure, curmudgeons like Curtius who doubted that anything useful would come from the developments of the day. More often, though, New Englanders entered this new era fortified by an unusual openness to change, a willingness to test new ideas, institutions, and procedures. Persuaded that unprecedented accomplishments would characterize the new age, New Englanders took on challenges that had previously seemed to be beyond them.

Humanitarianism, evangelism, and reform all benefited from the stimulus of New England's willingness to experiment and to undertake increasingly difficult challenges. Growing efforts after 1800 to serve the chronic needs of orphans, and after 1815 to educate the deaf, for example, each expressed rising humanitarian aspirations in an age marked by unusual achievements. By the same token, the optimism of the men who established the ABCFM and sent missionaries as far away as India and Hawaii contrasted sharply with the resignation of John Sergeant and Eleazar Wheelock after years of unsuccessfully ministering to the American Indians, as well as with the more parochial concentration on home missions of most of their contemporaries before 1810. New England's most productive institutional experimenters, though, were the organizers of the region's early reform societies. By the early 1810s the zeal of many moralists was leading them to attempt activities—the end of intemperance, swearing, and sabbath-breaking—that a more apologetic age had once rejected as impossible. A few years later at the conclusion of the War of 1812, a smaller group, this one composed of "friends of peace," sought an even more ambitious objective, the end of war.

Decades later when Lyman Beecher recalled the origins of reform in New England, he pointed to 1812 as the crucial year.[64] Both in Connecticut and Massachusetts, 1812 was the year when New Englanders began to believe that they could rehabilitate at least a portion of the degenerates in their midst.

What could reform accomplish? Who could be saved from vice? New England's revolution in reform depended on the development of ambitious new answers to these perennial questions.

Before the early 1810s the consensus was clear. "Childhood is the most promising season to introduce useful knowledge into our minds," the Reverend Thomas Barnard instructed a Salem audience in 1803.[65] The malleability of youth made this a crucial time, New Englanders believed. Susceptible to virtuous examples or to evil ones, boys and girls were balanced on the point of a fulcrum, able to rise or fall as those around them dictated. The flexibility of youth soon gave way, however, to settled habits. Because they believed "that it is easier to prevent disease, than after it is seated, to effect its cure,"[66] New Englanders assumed that the prospects were poor for recovering anyone who had slipped into dissolute ways.

New Englanders never questioned the importance of moral education for young children,[67] but after 1810 as they became more and more aware of the impressive achievements of their day they increasingly grew to question the common assumption that there was little likelihood of curing vicious habits. Hardened sinners still seemed beyond help; they almost always defeated the best efforts of even the most persistent reformers. But somewhere between the occasional inebriate, swearer, or sabbath-breaker and the confirmed reprobate reformers began to recognize a middle range of wrong-doers.

It was their recognition of a class of men and women whose vicious ways were still unsettled enough to permit the possibility of reclamation that gave New Englanders hope. This discovery owed less to objective inquiry than to the reformers' profound desire for reasons to believe their efforts might be productive. As early as 1803, Lyman Beecher began to urge "the practicability of suppressing vice, by means of societies instituted for that purpose."[68] Over the course of the next decade, the more they examined the subject, the more most reformers became convinced they could distinguish "those whose habits . . . are confirmed, from those who may not be so far gone, as to preclude all hope of reformation" and assist the latter.[69] "It should be distinctly kept in mind," the officers of the Massachusetts Society for the Suppression of Intemperance admonished in 1814, "that the concern of the society is not wholly nor chiefly with those unhappy individuals who are too far gone into intemperance."[70] "Will you say habits of intemperance have become so deeply rooted," Professor Parker Cleaveland of Bowdoin College asked an audience in Brunswick, Maine, the same year, "that reformation is impracticable?" This might sometimes be the case, Cleaveland admitted, "especially among the more advanced in life," but instance after instance when reprobates were rescued gave hope to every friend of reform.[71]

The first indications of this more aggressive approach toward reform took shape in 1811 at the annual meetings of two groups of clergymen, the General Association of Ministers in Connecticut and its orthodox counterpart to the north, the General Association of Massachusetts. Within the space of a month, each organization appointed a committee to propose remedies for the moral problems that were plaguing their states. When the committee in Connecticut reported in 1812, it confessed that its members had no solution, but the next day a hastily established panel chaired by Lyman Beecher brought in a recommendation urging public addresses in opposition to intemperance, the worst of the abuses, abstinence from alcohol at public functions, moderation in the use of spirits on other occasions, and the establishment of a voluntary society to promote temperance and good conduct in general. New Englanders had always resigned themselves to failure when they talked about reform, but Beecher recognized that "melancholy apprehension" could result in self-fulfilling prophecies "eminently calculated to paralyze exertion."[72]

The following year when the Massachusetts Society for the Suppression of Intemperance and the Connecticut Society for the Promotion of Good Morals were both founded their organizers shared the conviction, as Beecher urged, that the "Reformation of Morals [was] Practicable and Indispensable."[73] The Massachusetts reformers recognized "that vices, when prevalent and inveterate, are not easily suppressed." Yet they felt that there was good reason for hope: "experience testifies," they added, "that by suitable endeavours, they may be counteracted and checked." Association was the answer to the problem of immorality: "From such an association in this Commonwealth, calculated to act upon an extensive scale, great and lasting utility may reasonably be expected."[74] "Immense evils . . . afflict communities," Beecher remarked in retrospect, "not because they are incurable, but because they are tolerated; and great good remains often unaccomplished merely because it is not attempted."[75]

In hindsight, the most striking characteristic of New England's early moral societies was the naive and hopeful simplicity of their formula for reform. Historians have sometimes tried to portray the founders of these institutions as the members of a social elite, terrified by the turmoil of the day, whose recipe for restoring order emphasized close oversight by sheriffs, tythingmen, and other public officials charged with keeping miscreants in line.[76] There is some basis for this view, since reformers, especially along the Connecticut River valley in the early 1810s, devoted their energies in part to encouraging law keepers in the performance of their duties.[77] Throughout New England, though, most activists made clear their belief that "in the reformation of morals more is to be expected from example, than from precept or compulsion."[78] "Advice and persuasion" were the tools at their command.[79] It was through education, sermons, tracts, words of encouragement, and examples of personal rectitude that most reformers hoped to reform their neighbors, not through measures for social control.[80] The members of the Moral Society of Goshen, Connecticut, were typical in their approach to their work. Although they urged local officials to suppress "indicencies," the focus of their activities was their encouragement of "strict morality in the conduct of the members of this society."[81] In Massachusetts, the members of the Society for the Suppression of Intemperance did not even make provisions for the kind of direct civic oversight that their counterparts in Connecticut encouraged but made it their object instead "to discountenance and prevent as far as may be by his own example and influence, every kind of vice and immorality."[82]

The prime targets of reform campaigns, those who were dissolute but not beyond redemption, could be won back "by admonition and persuasion, and by promoting a faithful execution of the laws."[83] By definition, this group was composed of drunkards, swearers, and Sabbath-breakers who were susceptible to the appeal of common sense and compassion. Confident reformers had no doubt that the great majority of reprobates would repent if only they were shown the error of their ways.

The moralists' faith in the potential of reason and good examples rather than compulsion to effect reform carried over into the work of New England's peace activists after 1815. There was, of course, no way for average citizens to compel the governments of the world to foreswear war. Peace societies disclaimed any intention of forcibly imposing their will on government officials or fellow citizens. Instead, their plan was "to exhibit in a clear and distinct manner, the pacific nature of the Gospel, and to diffuse a spirit of love and harmony, and an enlightened philanthropy and benevolence through the world."[84] "News papers, tracts and periodical works, adapted to the pacific designs of the societies"[85] would be their only tools: in 1820 the officers of the Portsmouth Peace Society noted with some embarrassment that the nature of the institution precluded the kind of spectacular "achievements calculated to show off in Reports."[86] Yet "pacific tracts," through the case they made against warfare, had the potential, peace activists believed, to provide "a more efficacious and permanent security against war, than all the fleets and armies on which nations rely for their safety."[87]

Such faith in the powers of reason and revelation would have seemed preposterous if New Englanders had not experienced the extraordinary run of success that had accompanied the rise of organized charity. Not so long before, it had been easy enough to excuse all sorts of shortcomings with apologies. Now, though, in "an era of great events,"[88] all things seemed possible. Nevertheless, in less exhilarating moments New Englanders could still recall the bounds to their charity. Could a finite number of human institutions produce universal charity? The day-to-day administration of these organizations and the problems it presented had a way of reminding most New Englanders of their limits.

Chapter Six

Corporate Compassion

On EASTER SUNDAY, March 25, 1788, Bishop Samuel Seabury addressed the annual meeting of the Boston Episcopal Charitable Society. Less than five years after the signing of the Treaty of Paris those in Seabury's audience could easily recall recent hard times for the sixty-four-year-old institution. The outbreak of the American Revolution had cost it many of its most affluent supporters, prominent Anglicans whose ties to the British provincial administration had made them unwelcome in revolutionary Massachusetts. Wartime dislocation had forced the organization to suspend operations between 1775 and 1779 and again between 1780 and 1783.[1] Inflation, meanwhile, had devastated the Society's investments and produced a nasty confrontation with John Rowe, a leading Boston merchant and for two decades the association's treasurer, over who should bear the portfolio's losses.[2] During much of its history, the Society had helped impoverished Anglicans throughout the province. In 1784, however, its limited resources had forced it to restrict its assistance for the most part to the churchmen of Boston, reaching beyond the town's boundaries only to aid active subscribers who resided in surrounding communities.[3]

Notwithstanding the association's weakened condition, Seabury praised it for its years of service and urged Bostonians of all faiths to follow its members' lead. What would be the result if dozens or hundreds of similar groups took their cue from the Episcopalians? "May their example inspire, their zeal warm, and their prudence direct others to form and conduct similar Societies," Seabury encouraged, "till every class and denomination of distressed poor are, as far as human infirmity will permit, rescued from their sufferings."[4]

Bishop Seabury was making the best of an unfortunate train of events, but before long neither the association's course of action nor the speaker's exhortations would seem anything but commonplace. New Englanders like Seabury were progressing toward a new, "liberal" understanding of charity, one that had much in common with political and economic theories that were also beginning to win popular acceptance.[5] Most colonial New Englanders had used the idea of a virtuous self-love to explain how faithful Christians, limited in their means, could set priorities and still follow the example of the good Samaritan; as New Englanders reappraised their social relationships following the war, they agreed that a well-tempered self-interest retained a critical role in the practice of charity. Without denying the importance of altruism, they concluded that the community would benefit if individuals honorably pursued their own agendas.

The Episcopalians possessed limited resources and pursued limited objectives, but by exhibiting their association as a prototype Seabury was showing how through cooperation such organizations could serve their own ends and still promote the cause of universal love. Just as many contemporary political economists and political philosophers taught that the public benefits of free enterprise and democracy grew out of private economic and political aspirations, most postwar commentators on charity maintained that in concert with a pure spirit of selflessness, individual interests properly pursued might lead to philanthropy.

To arrive at this result, New Englanders needed a new way of looking at charity, one that acknowledged the constraints on individuals and organizations but showed how to overcome them. Mutualists were quick to trace one path from limited charity to philanthropy. Most New Englanders eventually came to prefer a second alternative, however, one suggested by the success of fiduciary organizations.

"Artificial Persons"

Before the Revolution, generations of New Englanders had readily admitted their own individual charitable shortcomings, usually taking their imperfections so much for granted that challenges to their assumptions (like those of Jonathan Edwards and his followers) seemed little more than fantasies. The development of organized charity, so unexpected and so inexplicable in traditional terms, forced New Englanders to reconsider their abilities and obligations. Experience with organized charity taught that more was possible than ever before. But were there limits to what organized charity could accomplish?

The greater their experience, the more certain most New Englanders became of organized charity's role in the achievement of philanthropy. Universal charity was no more within the reach of a single institution than of a single individual, but together tens or hundreds or even thousands of associations could serve every human need. What aspiring philanthropists needed to learn was how to coordinate their informal federation of associations. This objective required New Englanders to take into consideration both the abilities of individual institutions and their capacity to work together.

If ever there were a time when anyone toyed with the notion that a single institution might try to approximate philanthropy, it was a brief moment shortly after the Revolution when New England's benevolent associations, still few in number, faced an imposing array of social problems. John Clarke, a Boston clergyman, offered the day's most optimistic vision of the potential of a lone association in 1793 when he addressed the annual meeting of the Massachusetts Humane Society. Clarke had no doubts about the importance of the Society's primary mission, the rescue of potential drowning victims and others at risk of "sudden death," but he was concerned nonetheless about other, untended forms of misery. "What a pleasing reflection it would afford," he mused, "could our funds permit us to extend a charitable aid to a numerous class of sufferers in this town?" Perhaps the Society could also assist the elderly, poor, sick, lame, and homeless citizens of Boston. "The same principle, which has led us to provide a temporary shelter for the shipwrecked seaman," Clarke noted, "would render us ambitious of doing good in every form."[6]

Almost as he spoke, would-be philanthropists in several other New England towns—including Hartford, Bath, and Roxbury—were establishing goals nearly as ambitious as those Clarke envisioned for the Humane Society. In Hartford, the local charitable association's organizers proposed in 1792 "to provide and dispense charitable relief to all inhabitants of every class and description within the limits of the first and second societies [i.e., parishes] . . . who need the aid of the benevolent, for whom the poor laws of the state do not provide the relief suitable to their condition and circumstances or adequate to their necessities." Among the prime candidates for aid were "the widow, the orphan, the aged, laboring people depressed by sickness or inevitable misfortunes, [and] persons or families of decayed fortune." Poor children whose parents could not afford to educate them would also receive assistance.[7] In Bath, the members of the local humane society resolved in 1793 both to assist each other and to appropriate funds "to any other purpose which this Society shall think proper."[8] And in Roxbury, the founders of the town's charitable society promised at its founding in 1794 to assist everyone who merited their relief, while giving preference to their own members.[9]

Even brief experience taught a sobering lesson, however: such aspirations were impossibly ambitious. Clarke conceded to the Humane Society in 1793 that "till we can alleviate human affliction to the extent of our wishes, we must be satisfied with doing it to the extent of our ability." As Thomas Barnard added the following year, organizations like the Society were of a "confined nature." There were some who asked, Barnard noted, why the Society lavished "so much expense of time and property upon *particular* objects of charity" instead of devoting itself "to the *whole* number of the miserable?" Human institutions, Barnard replied, had limited resources. No less than individuals, associations had to make choices among worthwhile causes. It was enough if the Society's chosen goal was "an object worthy our anxious concern, and spirited exertion."[10]

Occasional misadventures reinforced this lesson. Organizations that tried radically to expand their spheres of activities—for example, the mutualists of the Massachusetts Charitable Society, who briefly provided blankets for inmates in Boston's town jail in the 1780s and also tried to organize a charity school[11]—almost always found their efforts short-lived and ineffectual. Most New Englanders had no wish to risk such failures.

By the late 1790s, no one even suggested that an individual institution might attempt what Clarke had proposed, then rejected. The only hope for universal charity lay in institutional coordination. Then, each association could set narrower goals in keeping with its resources.

Sooner or later, the members of every mutual benefit association and fiduciary institution encountered a common question. Modern management consultants often encourage their clients to begin their strategic planning by asking: "What business am I in?" Eighteenth- and nineteenth-century New Englanders faced a similar issue; they had to agree on their organizational objectives.

Mutualists usually found this a relatively easy matter to resolve. Because their options were restricted by the extent of their resources, the members of fraternities always knew they had to monitor and to check institutional ambitions. Although a few associations like the Massachusetts Charitable Society and the masonic grand lodges of Massachusetts and Rhode Island experimented occasionally with public assistance,[12] most mutual societies strictly limited their aid to members and dependents.

The most difficult problem mutual societies ordinarily faced was determining the eligibility for assistance of marginal applicants. Did the spinster daughter of a deceased member qualify for relief? If she did, how long was the fraternity obliged to help her? If she never married, was the organization responsible for her for the rest of her life? Did the messenger who notified members of upcoming meetings, a part-time employee, have a claim on the fraternity's treasury? If he did, how much could he expect and for how long?[13] In most cases, once the members of a fraternity agreed to provide support, within their abilities they would provide whatever seemed appropriate—food, fuel, clothing, shelter, medical care, moral supervision, and education.

Unlike the mutualists, the organizers of many fiduciary organizations had no clear and unalterable objectives, at least at first. If their institutions had developed in response to specific social or spiritual problems, New Englanders would have found it easy to define their purposes. The British origins of these institutions, however, tended to blur their goals. The constant tinkering that New Englanders engaged in, adapting foreign organizations to domestic circumstances, was in part an attempt to define and limit each association's sphere of activities. As they redirected associations and redefined purposes, New Englanders had to keep in mind three considerations: local needs, announced goals, and the activities of other, potentially competing, associations.

Eventually, the proliferation of organizations reduced the range of available options, easing the definitional problems facing many institutions. As late as the turn of the century, however, the circumstances that encouraged John Clarke in 1793 to consider an expanded role for the Massachusetts Humane Society existed in towns across New England. In the 1790s and early 1800s, many organizations encountered an institutional vacuum. Problems were many, resources were small. Civic-minded New Englanders had to choose their causes carefully; given their limited means, they could hope to remedy only a few.

The early years of the Massachusetts Humane Society provide a useful example of a common sight in turn-of-the-century New England, a charitable institution in search of its objectives. What was the function of a humane society? If eighteenth-century presidents James Bowdoin, Thomas Russell, Jonathan Mason, John Warren, and the Society's other officers had remained true to the example of the Royal Humane Society, they would never have needed to consider this question. They could have emulated the British institution and limited their work largely to the dissemination of information on resuscitation techniques. In 1787, however, the Society's officers started to diversify into other, related activities. First, they began to erect huts, each filled with food and clothing, along isolated stretches of beach, three in 1787, three more in 1789, another in 1792, and a total of sixteen by 1806. Shipwrecked sailors could take shelter in these structures and await help. In 1788, the year after the erection of the first hut, the Society began to consider a second initiative, a program to station rescuers to assist the victims of shipping disasters. The plan was to establish a small community on the Isle of Sables near a particularly treacherous passage. Lobbying efforts with local and federal authorities failed to secure the support necessary to establish such a settlement, but in 1797 similar petitioning led to success for a third project, the erection of a lighthouse on Cape Cod. By 1807, the Society was involved in an additional enterprise, stationing a lifeboat at Cohasset. Meanwhile, in 1800 it also provided funds to build a secure bathing facility in Cambridge for Harvard students.[14]

There was a logic to this institutional odyssey. Although they never retreated from their announced purposes, the officers of the Massachusetts Humane Society steered it in directions unimagined by its founders. In organizing the Society in 1786, Henry Moyes, James Freeman, Aaron Dexter, and Royall Tyler called it an association "for the recovery of such persons who meet with such accidents as produce in them the appearance of death."[15] As it added program after program, the Society gave up its exclusive concentration on informing the public about artificial resuscitation, but as far as its officers were concerned its new activities were logical outgrowths of those undertaken at its establishment, ones consistent with its announced purposes.

There were important reasons—both practical and legal—for keeping this mission firmly in mind. As a practical matter, an organization risked alienating potential supporters who felt they could not count on it to apply their donations to the purposes they had intended to underwrite. Where capital gifts were involved, this was an especially serious concern.

Institutions like the Humane Society depended on their friends for two kinds of support, annual dues and capital gifts. Annual dues underwrote current expenses; other gifts were earmarked for endowment. Ordinarily, dues were spent as they were received or within a short time thereafter; members could rest assured that their yearly payments were supporting ongoing projects of which they approved. Members who began to differ with the activities of an association could register their dissent by declining to renew. Capital gifts, in contrast, supported an institution in perpetuity. Some of these contributions were special donations or bequests; others were large, one-time payments in exchange for life membership. In either case, endowment funds were beyond the reach of donors, who relied on the assurances of the trustees that their gifts would be used wisely and only for the purposes specified at the time of donation. The implied or explicit promises trustees made when they accepted capital contributions obligated their successors in office, ensuring that each institution would remain true to its original objectives.

Legal considerations reinforced the promises of officers. With the exception of masonic lodges, almost all of New England's charitable institutions were either corporations or, in the case of such associations as cent societies, affiliates of corporations. The laws that governed their operation restricted the activities of their officers, assuring that each organization confined itself to a well-defined program about which its supporters were in agreement.

When New Englanders wanted to learn about the legal rights and responsibilities of charitable corporations and the fiduciary role of trustees, they turned to the writings of a number of scholars of the Anglo-American legal tradition, the most notable of whom was William Blackstone.[16] The four-volume *Commentaries on the Laws of England* that Sir William first published between 1765 and 1769 set the terms of postwar New England's understanding of the legal status of these institutions. Corporations, charitable or otherwise, were "artificial persons," associations recognized by the courts and granted many of the legal powers of individuals, including the right to a name; to sue and be sued; to acquire, hold, and dispose of personal and real property; to establish by-laws; and to transact business endorsed by an official seal. Their "general *duties,*" Blackstone summarized, "may . . . be reduced to this single one; that of acting up to the end or design, whatever it be, for which they were created by their founder."[17] Between 1795 and 1835, prominent American commentators like Zephaniah Swift of Connecticut, Nathan Dane and Francis Hilliard of Massachusetts, and James Kent of New York amplified and refined Blackstone's summary of the legal status of corporations but never materially contradicted it.[18]

By its very nature, a corporation is subject to limitations of various sorts. Its principal advantages are its ability to combine the investments or contributions of a large number of shareholders or members and, if granted a perpetual charter, to enjoy, in Blackstone's words, "a kind of legal immortality."[19] In other respects, however, a corporation's officers have to contend with checks on their institution and their powers.

As Blackstone taught, there were many kinds of corporations—sole and aggregate, ecclesiastical and lay. Chartered charitable institutions were all of the same legal genus, however, "eleemosynary," a variety of lay corporation. Eleemosynary corporations shared most of the characteristics of all chartered organizations, but their objectives distinguished them from other establishments. As a group, chartered institutions of the "eleemosynary sort" were "constituted for the perpetual distribution of the free alms, or bounty, of the founder of them to such persons as he has directed." The intentions of the founder or founders consequently fixed boundaries that trustees transgressed at their peril.[20]

Every corporate charter contained an article expressing its founders' objectives. This statement might be narrowly restrictive, specifying very limited purposes. In most cases, though, it defined a broad area of concern within which the trustees could use their discretion. The latitude contained in the charters granted to the SPGNA and to the New Hampshire Missionary Society, for example, allowed the trustees of each institution to seize the most productive proselytic opportunities open to them and to favor domestic over Indian missions. In each case, however, it prevented them from considering activities that did not directly promote the spread of the gospel.[21]

If a corporation were an "artificial person," established for a clearly defined purpose, then its stated objectives rather than its membership distinguished it from every other chartered institution. Early in their histories, before shifting interests added and subtracted supporters, in a few places several organizations seem to have shared common rosters of members, who convened seriatim as each association.[22] It was even possible, as Swift remarked, for "a great variety of corporations [to] be composed of the same persons, with perfect consistency, all . . . capable of suing each other."[23] As fiduciaries, trustees were expected to pursue the best interests of their associations, divorcing themselves in this capacity from personal considerations and other institutional affiliations.

There is no way to know for certain what would have happened to trustees who failed in their fiduciary roles, although James Kent noted the possibilities in the late 1820s. New England trustees were uniformly faithful in adhering to the terms of their charters, recognizing with Kent that "The modern doctrine is, to consider corporations as having such powers as are specifically granted by the act of incorporation, or are necessary for the purpose of carrying into effect the powers expressly granted, and as not having any other."[24] Trustees, as Kent instructed, were personally liable for their official misdeeds and were subject to lawsuits by members and state attorneys general if they abused their positions. Perhaps this sanction accounts for the fact that there is no record, at least through 1820, of any serious charge that a board had misused its powers.[25]

Custom, common sense, and legal sanction kept every charitable institution in New England true to its announced objectives through 1820. Mutualists, humanitarians, evangelists, and moral reformers agreed, however, that these constraints were no barrier to philanthropy. Although they differed over specifics, mutualists and the friends of corporate charity each developed explanations of the philanthropic roles of self-interested individuals and organizations. The key to reconciling institutional limits and philanthropic objectives lay in the ease with which civic-minded men and women could organize. As long as they could establish new institutions whenever needed, universal charity seemed within reach.

Fraternal Philanthropy

The philanthropic vision that stirred New England's mutualists in the late eighteenth and early nineteenth centuries has grown faint and indistinct over the decades that have since intervened. Simple in the extreme, mutualism's solution to the quest for universal charity began before long to seem too simple-minded to take seriously, a verdict that experience supported. As mutualism lost its central place in the practice of charity, fraternal aspirations in the early nineteenth century fell from most New Englanders' priorities. Before 1800, however, thousands of brothers in lodges of various sorts across New England still saw in the combined altruism and self-love of mutualism the most obvious path to philanthropy.

Although they differed over details, Freemasons on the one hand and merchants, sea captains, and mechanics on the other shared a common approach to the achievement of universal charity. Self-interest played no less critical a role in the lodge than in town meeting or in the marketplace. Philanthropy would result, they agreed, when every worthy citizen could turn to his friends and neighbors, confident of their help. Mutual benefit societies could assure this assistance, but only if everyone recognized his best interests and became properly affiliated. The worldwide federation of lodges that Freemasons envisioned followed different membership policies from those that mariners and mechanics adhered to, but their wish for a comprehensive network of such associations was common to all mutualists.

With the introduction of grand lodges for each state and the adoption of such expedients as visitations, lectures, and regional districts, New England's Freemasons had reorganized their brotherhood by the middle of the first decade of the nineteenth century. These innovations were structural, but their significance was not solely institutional. At the same time that they were reorganizing their fraternities, New England's Masons were developing related theories about philanthropy. Although their society remained private, its most cherished secrets and rituals hidden from public view, lodge members began to recognize that as their brotherhood grew, it came closer and closer to their vision of universal charity.

By the early 1790s, many Freemasons began to believe that philanthropy was more than a passing dream. Hopeful Masons started to understand their fraternity's possibilities in a different light. Freemasonry and philanthropy could be one. With diligence and perseverance, they could eventually enroll in their lodges "Every good man and true, whatever be his country, kindred, language or religion," who was willing to "conform to the principles . . . of this Ancient and Honourable Society." They would continue to exclude the "*stupid Atheist* or *irreligious Libertine*" who applied for admission, but the "virtuous and pious man, guilty of no mean action; not of a doubtful character, but naturally benevolent, industrious, temperate, and economical," would receive a warm welcome. Indeed, good Masons would actively recruit such men for their association. Their fraternity could truly become the embodiment of universal love, or so they hoped.[26]

Colonial Freemasons had frequently pledged to unite all "good men and true,"[27] but the aim had always appeared far beyond their grasp. Now, as new lodges formed almost daily, it seemed well within reach. Masons theorized that their fraternity could form a universal honeycomb of cells, the framework of a compassionate, harmonious world order. Thousands of lodges, each granted an exclusive franchise to a specific geographic region, could take shape in towns and villages across New England and wherever else moral men were found. They could unite brothers in a close personal communion. More impersonal bonds of love could cement individual lodges to their neighbors, to their own grand lodges, and to distant members of the order around the world.

Grand lodges across New England legislated with this end in view. Rules promulgated in Connecticut in 1791 and in Vermont in 1798 gave each lodge an exclusive regional franchise.[28] Other laws prohibited each lodge from admitting members who lived closer to a sister society without the second lodge's explicit approval.[29]

By 1800, the masonic ideal, an integrated network of lodges tying worthy men everywhere together in a single, vast, nucleated brotherhood, seemed almost at hand. When they achieved it, as they felt sure they would, they could provide for the needs—physical, moral, and emotional—of every honest, decent man in New England, and through him those of the members of his household.

The ideal was easier to announce than to achieve. Race posed one obstacle. During the occupation of Boston between 1774 and 1776, British soldiers belonging to a military or "traveling" lodge had organized a society of black Masons. Despite this group's persistent demands for recognition, white Masons in Massachusetts assumed that race made this association, the Prince Hall Lodge, unsuitable for affiliation.[30]

Women also presented a problem. Despite their pretensions to include all the worthy within their ranks, the Masons refused to admit their "*amiable female friends.*" A few apologists for this sometimes embarrassing situation cited tradition. Abraham Lynson Clarke, the rector of the Episcopal church in Providence, reminded women who protested their exclusion that "the *institution* is derived from *practical Masonry,* and still retains . . . many ancient ceremonies and laborious rites."[31] Josiah Dunham, a recent Dartmouth College graduate, added in 1796 that woman, "the last and best work of GOD . . . was formed for the less extensive though equally important sphere of Domestic life." According to Dunham, in fitting women for the home, God had not prepared them to cope with the abstract philosophy to which Masons adhered. They could no more become Masons, he admonished, than attend universities, counsel the nation's leaders, or preach in churches.[32] In general, Masons agreed, women were too delicate for admission to their fraternity. "Theirs are milder virtues,"[33] one brother noted, too fragile, in the view of another, to risk "promiscuously" mixing with men.[34] Besides, the needs of virtuous women would be met through their husbands, fathers, and sons, who, as worthy men, would belong to the fraternity.

Masonic leaders knew that even without admitting blacks and women their task was formidable. They could hardly fail to recognize how much more difficult it would be to supervise thousands of Masons scattered over entire states than it had been to superintend a few dozen within a single lodge.

Masonic orators responded to this problem by giving a new focus to their addresses. In the years before the Revolution, speakers had stressed the importance of the unifying force of charity within each lodge. In the early 1790s, however, they shifted their emphasis to questions of morality. If Masons were to make their organization inclusive, they would need an active campaign to persuade their neighbors to "enter our temple and share our blessings."[35] One unfortunate result, they feared, might be the admission of marginal applicants. After 1790, a growing masonic concern for morality aimed to nudge members who were tottering on the edge of iniquity away from wrong and in the direction of a proper way of life. Successful efforts to encourage proper conduct would reduce the number of hopeless cases who required expulsion. And, of course, the smaller the number of men barred from the brotherhood, the closer the fraternity came to philanthropy.

Freemasonry's rapid growth showed the attractiveness of mutualism's methods, but there were other ways to achieve the same end. New England's craftsmen, merchants, and sea captains pressed a clear alternative to the masonic approach. Drawing on the writings of Francis Hutcheson for justification, the mechanics and mariners envisioned a society of "interests" or "classes."[36]

Because the meanings of "interest" and "class" have changed since the end of the eighteenth century, it is important to understand what these terms meant to the men who used them. By the middle of the nineteenth century, Americans would regularly describe society in terms of antagonistic social and economic strata, but in theory, at least, the interests to which the mechanics and mariners referred were neither competing nor horizontally defined social groups. The members of the Providence Association of Mechanics and Manufacturers observed that their community consisted of "three great Classes . . . the Agricultural, the Commercial, and the Mechanical and Manufacturing." Each of these groups contained rich men as well as poor, and each placed the public good ahead of its own special needs. The three interests, or classes, were vertically ordered occupational groups. As workers in related trades, the members of each interest, bound by sentimental attachments, shared common experiences and training, but they all presumably recognized that "the true Interest of one [class] cannot be opposed to the real Interest of either of the others."[37] Later observers might charge them with naivety, but until the early years of the nineteenth century advocates of the "interest" description of society firmly believed that in the long run New Englanders would advance or retreat together, and not at each other's expense.

Through the network of occupational societies that appeared between the end of the Revolution and the early nineteenth century, New England's merchants, sea captains, and master mechanics attempted to institutionalize their vision of society. Like the Masons, they wanted to establish a comprehensive network of charitable associations. Except for the idle and a few professionals—ministers, doctors, and lawyers—who were already forming their own occupational societies, most adult male household heads fitted one of the three categories. Many others, for example journeymen craftsmen and farmhands, might receive assistance as dependents of their masters. By recognizing common occupational bonds and organizing around them, mariners and mechanics saw a way to provide for everyone's charitable needs.

The key to the "interest" approach, like the masonic alternative, was inclusivity. Merchant and mechanic leaders recognized that if their institutions were effectively to represent the groups for which they hoped to speak, every man had to join the appropriate association. This goal was never easy to achieve. The members of older, prerevolutionary and newer, postwar fraternities faced slightly different problems. Newburyport's mariners, like the members of many other colonial associations, had intended theirs to be a small, intimate society. At the war's end, therefore, they had to stretch their institution to admit unaffiliated merchants and captains. In 1783, through revisions in their by-laws they began to draw away from their original course.

By gradual increments the brotherhood authorized increases in its member-ship to accommodate eligible outsiders. Between 1783 and 1808 the society grew—first to forty-five, then to sixty, and finally to seventy members.[38]

Newer institutions adopted similar objectives but lacked existing, inhibit-ing precedents like those facing Newburyport's mariners. In Providence, the mechanics organized a membership drive almost as soon as they established their society. On November 23, 1789, they voted to create a committee "to wait on such of the Mechanics and Manufacturers of this Town as have not yet joined the Association, to lay before them the Necessity and Importance of an immediate Union." By the following May they were able to report that their association contained "rather more than Two Hundred Members,—among which we reckon nearly all the Mechanics of Reputation in the Town."[39]

Despite these promising advances, by the turn of the century mariners and mechanics had begun to recognize the inadequacies of their approach both as a description of society and as a basis for charitable organization. Efforts to cooperate notwithstanding, the members of different interests increasingly found their aims in conflict. Boston's mechanics were shocked in 1795 when the "principal merchants of the town," fearing the economic and political strength of the artisans, refused to endorse their petition to the legislature for a charter of incorporation. Repeated applications for incorporation met re-buffs until 1806; even then, the Great and General Court expressed its concerns in the warrant it granted. Boston's craftsmen had first sought an act in the name of the "Associated Mechanics and Manufacturers of the Com-monwealth of Massachusetts" and then on behalf of "The Massachusetts Mechanic Association." In 1806 when the legislature finally acceded to the petition of the artisans, it named the institution it incorporated "The Massa-chusetts Charitable Mechanic Association." The General Court added the word "charitable" to emphasize that the organization's goals were beneficent rather than commercial or political.[40] Moreover, when the Providence me-chanics attempted to lobby in Congress for a tariff to protect American manufacturing, they ran into stiff opposition from southern agricultural inter-ests. Debates over the question led one Providence craftsman in 1799 to charge bitterly that the "prejudices and narrow policies of the great Land-holders in the Middle and Southern States" were unfairly obstructing the erection of a protective tariff wall, a barrier that he considered to be unques-tionably in the public interest.[41] By the turn of the century, many careful observers had begun to believe that conflicts between interests were inevi-table.

At about the same time, it became apparent that occupational societies would never include every eligible individual. Although a group of men interested in agronomy organized the Massachusetts Society for Promoting Agriculture in 1793,[42] it never developed into a fraternity for farmers comparable to the marine and mechanic associations, nor did any other institution fulfill this role. Mariners and mechanics soon began to notice, moreover, that many of their own brethren were balking at participating in their institutions. Some refused to join at all; despite its claims, the Providence Association of Mechanics and Manufacturers never enrolled more than half the town's eligible craftsmen.[43] Other artisans accepted admission but declined to attend meetings, heed admonitions, or pay the dues that made assistance possible. The mechanics and manufacturers of Providence had hoped to mediate disputes between members through their society, but by 1798 their attempts were failing regularly and members had begun to confront one another in court. And delinquency in paying dues had proven a problem as early as 1792. By 1798, the association was dismissing members for non-payment.[44]

Notwithstanding all these problems, throughout the late eighteenth and early nineteenth centuries members continued to turn to their fraternities when need arose, and to believe that their brotherhoods, however imperfect for the moment, could be the agents of philanthropy. But what if a problem were relatively unusual? What if a problem afflicted men and women who otherwise shared no community of interests? What if needs were so widespread that they exhausted the resources of a mutual association and its members? As New Englanders began to recognize, fiduciary organizations, by virtue of the nature of the relationships that they encompassed, could offer an alternative path to philanthropy.

The Charitable Christian in an Age of Institutions

Fiduciary charity has been so common for so long—the dominant form of almsgiving in the United States since the early 1800s—that its underlying principles no longer seem novel or curious. Success and longevity have transformed these tenets into unspoken beliefs and even clichés. In the early nineteenth century, however, many observations that would eventually become tacit assumptions were still new and were examined at length because of their novelty.

Because fiduciary charity seemed surprising and different, New Englanders in the early nineteenth century discussed it with a measure of explicitness, detail, concern, and clarity that they have never since approached. A commonsense assessment of its attributes was at the foundation of this discussion, but contemporary appraisals were not entirely empirical. No less than for mutualism, scripture set the standard for fiduciary charity. Although twentieth-century Americans rarely still worry about their inability to measure up to the Bible's teachings about divine charity, modern secular attitudes and practices are nonetheless in good measure the consequences of these early-nineteenth-century inquiries and initiatives.

Much as fraternities institutionalized the mutual responsibilities of friends and acquaintances, fiduciary organizations formalized those of strangers for each other. As they thought about fiduciary charity, New Englanders gradually developed a sense of the compassionate Christian's place during a time of organized philanthropy. Real philanthropy seemed possible, but only under certain conditions. Organized charity had to be comprehensive, serving every need, and individuals had not only to recognize but to fulfill their personal responsibilities. In theory, at least, the first condition seemed to pose no difficulties. If would-be philanthropists organized whenever they recognized a new problem—social, spiritual, or moral—none would be without a potential means of resolution. Orphans and inebriates, castaways and unchurched pioneers, could each find assistance through the appropriate institution. For these associations to function successfully, however, they needed supporters and resources sufficient to meet the demands placed on them.

What each association needed were limited commitments from scores or hundreds or even thousands of supporters, who responded as well to other appeals as they arose. This kind of relationship between institutions and their friends had few local precedents—certainly it was unlike a fraternal bond— so most New Englanders learned about it through a process of trial and error. Events like a dispute in 1812 and 1813 over the proposed baptism of the orphans in the care of the Salem Female Charitable Society consequently taught important lessons.

The baptism was next-to-last in the order of service, following an "Occasional Ode" and preceding the concluding "Magdalene Ode."[45] Reverend Thomas Barnard of Salem's North Church, a kindly, corpulent man with a nose slightly too long for the rest of his double-chinned face, offered a "fervent and impressive" baptismal prayer,[46] and soon twelve small girls between the ages of five and twelve were securely in the religious care of the Salem Female Charitable Society.[47]

Baptism, of course, was a traditional ordinance in Puritan New England, and had long been the subject of discussion, debate, and discord among local theologians. Barnard's baptism of the Female Charitable Society's young charges on August 4, 1813, however, culminated a controversy on the issue the likes of which New Englanders had never before encountered.

Like other religious ordinances, baptism defines and formalizes relationships—in this case, relationships both between those baptized and God and between them and their families. As Elizabeth G. Dabney, the maiden secretary of the Society, observed, "to be solemnly dedicated to Heaven was . . . a great priviledge," not in the least because "the children thus dedicated . . . thereby acquire a claim upon those, who offer them up, to attend particularly to their moral and religeous education."[48] The decision to baptize the children consequently posed an intriguing and troublesome question: who would stand in loco parentis? The situation was complicated, moreover, by the presence of a number of antipaedobaptists in the membership of the Society.

One kind of formal relationship already joined the Society and the girls in its charge. The corporation was each child's legal guardian. Many of the girls were "true orphans," without close surviving relatives, but in some instances, children proposed for admission to the orphanage still had living parents whose other family obligations and straitened circumstances precluded them from providing their daughters with adequate support. Before the Society would accept such candidates, it required the parents in writing to waive all rights to bring up their offspring. Parents promised not even to try to see their daughters without the permission of the Society's officers.

The subject of baptizing these charges had first come up on September 24, 1812, at a meeting of the Society's Board of Managers. An officer of the organization had suggested the need for the ordinance. After a discussion, the board had voted unanimously to ask Barnard to perform the ceremony at the next annual meeting a few days later. The failure to act would obviously violate one of the Bible's "most solemn engagements." One officer in attendance had initially objected that "those who manage the concerns of this Society, are chosen but for one year" and could not be expected "to take on themselves vows, which they must depend on others to have fulfilled." The board determined, however, that this responsibility was not personal, but corporate: "the Ladies, comprising this Society," Elizabeth Dabney noted, "are a corporation or body politick. . . . [C]onsequently all the authorised acts of the Directresses and Managers, who are merely the representatives and agents of the Society, are equally binding on their successors in office."[49]

The board's action satisfied most members of the Society, although Hopkinsians among them may have felt uncomfortable that Barnard, an Arminian, was to dedicate the children.[50] Salem's Baptists, however, disturbed that the ceremony would include girls who were unconverted, protested that the board had exceeded its authority. Lucius Bolles, the pastor of the local Baptist church, called first on Barnard and then on the Society's first directress and on one of its managers to insist on a postponement. Although the board members "had no doubt of their authority to act," they determined to call the Society together to discuss the subject.[51]

At this meeting, held on October 15, the twenty-four members in attendance debated whether a religiously heterodox association, that is one with both regenerate and carnal members, could offer children for baptism "consistently with the laws . . . contained in the New and Old Testament," and alternatively, whether the Society would be negligent if it failed to attend to the ordinance. By a vote of twenty-two to two, the members decided to carry on with the sacrament, but to postpone it to a later date and to withhold it from girls of Baptist backgrounds. As far as the Female Charitable Society was concerned, Barnard's ceremony at the annual meeting in 1813 resolved the issue once and for all.[52]

The Female Charitable Society's members had answered three basic questions. First, they had affirmed their right to baptize the children. Second, they had recognized their officers' obligation, in their corporate roles, to see to the girls' baptism. Third, they had determined the various corporate relationships that united everyone involved—orphans, officers, and members. To reach this last verdict, they had decided that an officer's or a member's spiritual health and denominational affiliation, as personal rather than institutional matters, were not relevant considerations. At the same time, the members had also prescribed their charges' role, specifying the assistance they could expect.

These determinations led the members to important conclusions about the nature of the Salem Female Charitable Society and the relationships it encompassed. In early-nineteenth-century New England, no charitable institutions offered their beneficiaries a wider range of services than the female asylums provided the girls in their care. Food, shelter, clothing, schooling, domestic education, religious training, moral guidance, companionship, and love were all within their purview. Nevertheless, even within these institutions, affiliations were neither as flexible nor as comprehensive as family relationships. The charter and by-laws that governed an asylum outlined the specific duties and rights of its officers, members, employees, and inmates more rigidly than custom or the common law had ever determined kinship roles. Moreover, annual elections and dues were recurring reminders that voluntary relationships were impermanent. In a charitable institution, no matter what its objectives, the Reverend Charles Stearns of Lincoln told a Concord audience in 1815, each participant's "connexion" with the society was "perfectly voluntary, and no one remains a member longer than he pleases."[53] In Salem and across New England, fiduciary organizations promoted a new kind of social affiliation—voluntary, formal, and limited.

Although such relationships were without precedent in the practice of charity, they were not unique to organized beneficence. Formal institutions—corporations and parties—were assuming ever greater roles in commerce and politics. As the influence of these organizations grew, New Englanders became increasingly accustomed to the temporary, voluntary, limited, and self-interested relationships each encompassed.

Because fiduciary affiliations were circumscribed, in most instances requiring only a small commitment of money or time, it was ordinarily possible for an individual to support a variety of institutions, much as an investor might hold shares in many corporations. Throughout the first two decades of the nineteenth century, practical experience encouraged New Englanders to speculate on how such limited participation in a large number of institutions could lead to philanthropy. Their most important conclusion was that individuals needed to make choices. Although institutionalization had transformed the practice of charity, in important respects it had left the aspiring philanthropist's predicament unchanged. William Godwin, the radical English philosopher, revealed the folly of his ideas, New Englanders believed, through his rejection of priorities resulting from "benevolent feelings to our personal relations."[54] No one could answer every appeal or "love all mankind equally."[55] In fact, the proliferation of charitable institutions had multiplied the number of requests for relief many times over. In setting their priorities, New Englanders had always weighed the importance in their own lives of each candidate for assistance. Somehow, they now believed, philanthropy would be the outcome of countless individual—and to some extent self-interested—decisions.

No one except a few New Divinity clergymen and laymen, believers in the need for uncompromising altruism, took issue with the basic order of priorities New Englanders had embraced for generations; "the social and relative duties of life were sanctioned by the great author of Christianity."[56] "To take from your own families the necessaries of life, for the sake of contributing to societies, however well established," Alden Bradford, a Boston merchant and politician, instructed a Wiscasset audience in 1811, "is neither required by christianity, nor approved by reason."[57] Once they had taken care of their families, though, good Christians still had to do whatever they could to provide for the rest of humanity. As late as the 1790s, New Englanders had only a general idea of the appropriate priorities for charity among strangers; by the early 1810s they had arrived at a consensus.

To choose among Sunday schools and dispensaries, peace societies and immigrant aid associations, potential donors had to examine their own values and circumstances. If each institution addressed only a portion of the region's needs, in order to rank their loyalties contributors had to segment their lives. This was, in effect, a process of self-definition, the end result of which was a reasoned and ordered set of personal priorities and aspirations.

Once New Englanders began in the 1790s to examine their options, they depended on two distinct but mutually reinforcing considerations—empathy and duty. There were times when it was impossible to find a point of contact between a cause and a potential contributor; on some occasions there seemed to be no good reason to favor one institution over all the others clamoring for support. Prospects were more promising, however, if a donor identified with a cause or acknowledged some unusual personal ability to promote its work. Charitable New Englanders looked both for the will to act and for a way to proceed.

The will to act was seated in the heart. Compassionate men and women were "obligated to the exercise of mercy by those principles of sympathy which Heaven has implanted in the human bosom." These were "the delicate cords which unite man to man; which powerfully attract us to the distresses and griefs of our fellow-creatures, and which almost irresistibly engage us to mitigate and relieve them."[58] Empathy closed the distance between strangers, allowing potential contributors to imagine themselves, or those close to them, in need. It acknowledged the fragility of life, health, and fortune, and it demonstrated the self-interest inherent in philanthropy, charity's practical benefits to benefactors as well as beneficiaries. Between the late 1780s and the start of the nineteenth century, appeals to empathy grew more and more emotional. As the number and variety of institutions grew, New Englanders adopted increasingly impassioned means of soliciting attention and support.

Early philanthropic organizations like the humane societies and the Massachusetts Charitable Fire Society aided the victims of accidents from which no one was completely secure. Their advocates minced no words about the benefits of contributing to such institutions. As the Reverend Chandler Robbins of Plymouth reminded the members of the Massachusetts Humane Society in 1796, "no class of men are exempted—no situation in life, however elevated by prosperity, is secure against the strokes of adversity and various woes."[59] It was possible, as the Reverend Samuel Cary of Boston pointed out at the annual meeting of the Merrimack Humane Society in 1806, "that some individuals of this assembly, who now bestow of the wealth which God has given them, for the service of this institution, may present themselves at our next anniversary, the living monuments of its value."[60] "Imagine the feelings of him, who in an instant has lost every thing," Alexander Townsend, a Boston lawyer, urged his audience at the 1809 annual meeting of the Charitable Fire Society;[61] there was no way to ensure oneself against a similar fate.

It was easy to identify with a cause if one might suffer a similar tragedy. Such a self-interested sentiment amounted to a distended form of mutualism, fraternalism on a grand and impersonal scale. It was almost as easy to respond to similar potential threats to relatives and friends. In 1803, Episcopal clergyman Edward Bass of Newburyport asked members of the Merrimack Humane Society to place themselves in the shoes of the relatives of an apparent drowning victim. As rescuers attempted resuscitation, he wondered,

> what must be the feelings of those, who are most nearly interested! During the operation, with what doubts, hopes and fears must they be at different times agitated! To what dismal apprehensions are they subjected! What anxiety appears in every gesture! What despair is depicted on every countenance! But when the operation begins to produce the desired effect, when it first appears, that vital warmth is restored to the cold body, and respiration to the breathless corps— their transports are beyond the powers of description.—Who can express the rapture of those to whom, in this manner, have been restored an affectionate husband, a kind brother, a dear and intimate friend, or a beloved child.[62]

Parents could identify both with the plight of a helpless father or mother and with that of an orphaned child. For the benefit of the Boston Female Asylum, in 1807 Jedidiah Morse imagined the dying words of a parent, concerned for the fate of a helpless daughter:

> "Alas," may have said the pious, affectionate father, or mother, languishing under misfortune and disease, "alas what will become of my poor, destitute, perishing offspring, cast upon the wide world, without a protector, guide or friend, exposed to a thousand snares and temptations, and to the ruin both of soul and body forever."[63]

The emotional distance between benefactors and beneficiaries narrowed even more when they came face to face. Many asylums therefore exhibited their inmates at annual meetings. In New England, the practice began with Samuel Stillman's first address in 1801 to the Boston Female Asylum. A footnote to his printed sermon indicates that "The children were present, neatly dressed in blue, and placed in an elevated situation, that the friends of the Institution might see the *first fruits* of their bounty." To ensure that even the myopic noticed the girls' presence, Stillman asked to "be permitted to call the immediate attention of this benevolent assembly, to those children." The girls "address you in silent, but persuasive eloquence," he assured his audience: "The little supplicants ask your assistance."[64] The public display of orphans soon became a regular part of the annual meeting of every female asylum in New England. A few orators simply acknowledged the girls' presence, but others used it for dramatic effect. John Lathrop added the final touch in Boston in 1804, when at his sign, "the Children of the Asylum, 27 in number, neatly dressed in blue uniform, rose, and presented themselves before the Congregation." Lathrop urged the audience to "let them plead for themselves: their language will be more impressive than any that I can use: it will reach your heart."[65]

A special bond connected benefactors and beneficiaries, a shared realization of their common humanity. Every large town had its full measure of "decent, reputable persons, living with straitened economy on the wreck of former sufficiency."[66] "No age, station, or condition of life" could exempt one from "the afflictions of . . . life."[67] In fact, far from insulating them from suffering, their skills and resources placed many men and women under additional obligations. Seventeenth-century New Englanders had turned to Petrus Ramus to explain the responsibilities inherent in the "affirmative contraries" he described, and throughout the eighteenth century many had found in Cotton Mather's *Bonifacius* a convenient introduction to such mutual relationships as those of pastors and their parishioners, rich men and the poor, and Christians and the unconverted. Drawing on this centuries-old heritage, New Englanders began in the late 1780s to describe similar special duties in an age of institutions.

There was little either novel or obscure in New England's analysis of these special obligations; to their contemporaries, their understanding seemed little more than common sense. "The social body consists of a variety of parts, or members," the Reverend John Prince reminded a Salem audience in 1806:

> It is composed of persons of different characters, in various and opposite conditions in life. We see in society the high and the low, the rich and the poor, the strong and the weak, the wise and the simple, the virtuous and the vicious.

No one was blessed with every virtue, but "by the union of these powers in the social body, the several members of it are enabled to make the best use of her other gifts for promoting the general happiness."[68] New Englanders had

always believed that "the fruits of our compassion must be diversified according to the different circumstances of the objects";[69] every benefactor had an
obligation "to consider what relief will be most effectual."[70] By the same
token, it seemed only reasonable to expect "Good Stewards [to] choose the
most *efficient method* of accomplishing the Lord's design." As Lucius Bolles
instructed, "Such a method . . . [would] relieve the most and do it effec-
tually."[71]

This doctrine had many applications. In Boston in 1812 the Society for the
Religious and Moral Improvement of Seamen made a special appeal to sea
captains:

> Perhaps, gentlemen, there is not a class of men in society, who might
> more essentially aid the cause of religion and virtue than yourselves.
> Your authority and influence are very great, and a captain well prin-
> cipled, and determined to do all the good in his power to sailors,
> might not only preserve, but rescue many from degradation and
> wretchedness.[72]

Doctors could contribute their services to humane societies and dispensaries.[73] The residents of long-settled, religiously enlightened areas like Connecticut were under peculiar obligation to relieve former neighbors who had
removed to the frontier.[74] And because their wealth was their most useful
attribute, the affluent had a special duty to serve as "*almoners* of the poor."[75]
As the Reverend James Wilson instructed a Providence audience, "the rich
and affluent are . . . especially called to the exercise of compassionate liberality in banishing want from the door, and sorrow from the hearts of the
suffering sons and daughters of poverty."[76]

Although it is possible to distinguish between appeals to empathy and to
duty, New Englanders assumed that they ordinarily worked in unison, pulling
and pushing philanthropists toward acts of charity. There is no better example of their cumulative effect than in the doctrine of woman's separate
sphere, to which New Englanders turned to justify and promote the cause of
female charitable societies. Freemasons had excused the exclusion of women
from their lodges with the explanation that females were too delicate to
participate in the brotherhood's coarse and masculine fellowship,[77] but there
was a corollary to this thesis: women were particularly suited to provide for
each other.

As late as 1815, there were still skeptics who maintained that women were
invariably too fragile, inexperienced, and frivolous to manage the affairs of a

charitable corporation.[78] The cast of mind that made them so appealingly feminine, doubters argued, disqualified them from accepting significant responsibilities. Most New Englanders disagreed, however, seeing in women both the will and the means to serve the needy. Women were blessed with "*superior sensibilities*";[79] they were "possessed of . . . finer feelings" than men.[80] "The God of heaven," the Reverend Daniel Dana told the friends of the Female Charitable Society of Newburyport in 1804, "has more exquisitely attuned their souls to love, to sympathy and compassion" than he had men's hearts.[81] Perhaps it was possible, as critics warned, to be too sensitive to the needs of the deprived, and consequently both too affected by the brutal realities of poverty and too susceptible to scams. Most New Englanders believed, however, that charity was "the *natural* province of the gentler sex."[82]

In theory, it was possible for women, no less than men, to be drawn to a wide assortment of charitable causes. In practice, however, only missionary work competed with the needs of widows and female orphans for their attention. A "separate world of women" who paid special attention to each other's needs had been apparent in New England as early as the seventeenth century;[83] with the organization of charity, women's groups institutionalized activities that had dated from New England's earliest days. Generations of experience taught that it was only natural for females to "sympathize especially with the sufferings of their own sex."[84] What could be easier for women in comfortable circumstances than to identify with the plight of little girls who had lost their parents or with widows whose husbands and children were gone, leaving them without reliable means of support? Common sense instructed, moreover, that it was "essential to the hopes of civil society, that female virtue will be the fond guardian of its own sex."[85] Who is it, William Bentley asked, "who watch over our beds of sickness, and cheerfully perform the tender offices which alleviate despondency and distress?"[86] Who knew the needs of suffering orphan girls and widows better than their compassionate female neighbors? Opportunity and empathy seemed to compel compassionate women to the side of their afflicted sisters.

If New Englanders everywhere followed the example that the members of female charitable societies were setting, then the odds for philanthropy seemed good. Optimism still required several leaps of faith. Philanthropy as New Englanders understood it was impossible if society's needs outstripped its resources, or if maldistribution produced pockets of insufficiency, or if well-tempered self-love gave way to inordinate self-interest. Without any evidence to support their assumptions, though, New Englanders brushed away their doubts. Aside from the occasional vagrant unworthy of assistance, it was hard to think of anyone in trouble without a claim on some potential benefactor—family or friend, coworker or countryman. Perhaps there was no conclusive proof that fiduciary institutions would produce universal charity, but all the signs were encouraging. New Englanders could take philanthropy for granted, they began to believe, confident that it was at hand.

Chapter Seven

"A Habit of Doing Good"

IN THE LATE WINTER OF 1822, a correspondent to the *Christian Spectator,* a religious monthly published in New Haven, tried to explain *"the peculiar characteristics of the benevolent efforts of our age."* That these efforts were *"entirely different* from those of any former age," there could be no doubt. Compared with the *"exertions of the apostolic age"* or those of "the corrupted Greek and Roman churches," the initiatives, he believed, especially the missionary initiatives, of the "new era" were marked by "UNITED, VIGOROUS, SYSTEMATIC efforts" so strenuous and persistent that they seemed to warrant the millennial belief "that they will be *finally successful."* It was hard to deny, the correspondent concluded, that he and his contemporaries were witnessing "the dawning of an everlasting day—a day without storms—a day whose radiance shall never be clouded."

Missionary and humanitarian accomplishments had often provided opportunities to express confidence in the future, but it was not to such singular events that "L.," as the correspondent styled himself, pointed to bolster his conclusion. Christians had frequently seen reasons for optimism in the signs of the times only to find their hopes dashed, replaced by the somber fog of lethargy. But now L. saw greater reason for encouragement. Earlier observers had fastened their hopes to unique events and charismatic individuals, anxiously expecting that the Lord would pursue great ends through such evanescent means. Eventually, disappointments had revealed the danger of placing too much reliance on the exertions of transient agents. "To complete the argument for the final success of these operations," L. knew he had " . . . to show that they can suffer no permanent decline."

L. based his conclusions not on practical accomplishments, but on an intangible change apparent wherever he looked, the development of a new temper, a new cast of mind, that seemed to foretell the durability of the dawning age. Modern benevolence was habitual, and this quality was an encouraging indication that a radical and permanent transformation had taken place. "When an individual has once formed a habit of doing good," L. noted, "we of course consider it probable that he will continue to do good." The same principle, multiplied thousands of times over, prompted the conclusion "that the public is forming a *habit* of benevolent exertion." The propagation of the gospel, for example, was now attracting contributions across the United States of "not less than two hundred thousand dollars annually." It seemed reasonable to conclude that "each of the individuals who contribute towards this sum, has formed a habit of doing good." "The certainty that he will continue to do good," L. added, arose ". . . not merely from the force of his own individual habit" but from ". . . the habits of all the individuals who go to form the mass of the public." "The public habit," L. contended, was "not merely the sum, but . . . the product of all these individual habits." Indeed, as the generations passed, "each successive one growing up under the influence of the preceding," one could only feel delight for those to come, "accustomed from infancy, to every species of benevolent enterprise":

> Thirty years hence . . . will not the habit of benevolence be much stronger . . . than in the present generation with whom that habit originated? The next succeeding generation will be still more extensively educated in the same habits. . . . Thus the great operations of benevolence will acquire new strength as ages roll away. . . . They will be like the waves of a rising tempest, when each successive one is larger and larger, till what was at first only a gentle undulation, comes sweeping along with irresistible and overwhelming power.[1]

The *Christian Spectator*'s correspondent had recognized a fundamental feature of the transformation of charity: it was, in the final analysis, a transformation of the mind. When New Englanders learned to accept organized charity, to take it for granted, to practice it habitually, then their charitable revolution was at an end, its objectives accomplished. Organized beneficence had insinuated itself into the fabric of New England life, transforming the very assumptions of compassionate men and women and redefining the meaning of charity.

Identifying Organized Charity

By the early 1820s, as L. recognized, most New Englanders no longer gave the infant struggles of organized charity a second thought, accepting instead the mature institutions as a matter of course. Before organized charity became second nature to New Englanders, however, there were questions to answer and problems to resolve. As voluntary associations spread across the region, New Englanders were forced to learn how to pick out those that were truly benevolent and then to make room for them both in their formal definitions and in their informal assumptions about charity and its practice. The product of this process was a partial redefinition of charity.

New Englanders could hardly have become used to organized charity without learning first to identify it. But amid the welter of new associations that were established after the Revolution, recognizing those that were authentically benevolent could be a problem. There were fire societies and singing societies, tontines and lotteries, banks and turnpike companies, all of them formally organized, many holding state charters of incorporation that attested to legislative determination that their purposes were in the public interest. But which of these institutions were truly charitable? Where was the dividing line between charitable and non-charitable organizations?

If New Englanders had denied a well-tempered self-love a role in charity, then drawing this line would have been simple. As long as would-be philanthropists operated from pristine motives, lacking all thought of personal benefit, then their activities and institutions could meet the most exacting standards. Yet practical-minded men and women routinely denied the possibility of such purity of motivations, and most New Englanders regularly conceded private, personal considerations a part in charitable initiatives.

Once they admitted the place of self-interest in the practice of charity, New Englanders had to judge shades of gray. Some of their decisions remained easy. The promoters of commercial banks and turnpikes, for example, might make a persuasive case for the public economic benefits of their corporations, but no one could mistake profit-seeking investors for philanthropists. The primarily altruistic nature of most non-profit fiduciary associations was equally clear. Notwithstanding potential personal benefits, no reasonable review of their activities could demonstrate that their contributors' calculations were principally selfish. But what of the mutual societies that New Englanders organized between the 1770s and 1820? What was it that made one charitable but disqualified another?

New Englanders never offered a single, clear answer to this question, but their actions in specific cases suggest their calculations. Personal ends might be interwoven with civic goals, but a charitable institution had to devote itself primarily to public objectives. In the absence of acute personal need the direct benefits to supporters had to be limited to psychic gratification, not to financial or political gain.

Between the late 1790s and the late 1810s questions arose over the benevolent qualities of four different initiatives: mutual insurance programs, political clubs, savings banks, and the Freemasons. Of these, only the last named survived the scrutiny of contemporaries. Throughout much of the period even the Masons were often suspected of devoting more energy to their own entertainment and to private political advancement than to public purposes.

Boston insurance offices, organized as individual agencies and small partnerships, began to make fire and marine coverage available by the 1720s, but the advent of large mutual-protection schemes was part of the revolutionary era's general transformation of American business practices. At the same time that merchants in Boston, Providence, Newport, and other commercial towns began to establish banks and turnpike companies, many also formed New England's first chartered insurance institutions.[2]

Postwar fire and life insurance ventures took two forms: joint-stock companies and mutual partnerships. There is no sign that contemporaries ever regarded joint-stock companies—for example, such profit-making concerns as the Newport Insurance Company, chartered in 1799, and the Hartford Insurance Company, incorporated in 1803—as philanthropic organizations, however useful they might be both to investors and to policy-holders. Profits were so obviously the investor's central concern that community benefits were incidental. As for the policy-holder, his only interest was to protect the value of his property or secure the financial future of his heirs.[3] Mutual insurance programs were another matter, however. They bore enough similarity to benevolent fraternities that it was reasonable to ask whether mutual insurance was philanthropic.

Like fraternity members, subscribers to mutual insurance plans pooled their dues to provide a fund for relieving needy participants. Unlike the lodges, though, the insurance programs narrowly circumscribed their stated purposes. While the members of fraternal orders tried to oversee each other's morals and to maintain loving communities of lodge brothers, mutual fire insurance societies confined themselves to protecting property and mutual life insurance programs limited themselves to providing annuities. In each instance, the company invested its premiums. If the resulting income exceeded what was needed to relieve subscribers, everyone shared in the profits in proportion to the amount invested. Because their services were entirely financial and involved none of the close interpersonal relationships of traditional fraternities, the organizations could enroll hundreds, or even thousands, of members.

New England's first contact with mutual insurance on a large, impersonal scale came through a proposal by the Reverend William Gordon of Jamaica Plain. Gordon's *Plan of a Society for Making Provision for Widows, by Annuities for the Remainder of Life,* published in 1772, a life-insurance scheme based on principles set out by Richard Price,[4] was never consummated. In 1786, however, when the Massachusetts Ministerial Convention established its Congregational Charitable Society, the organizers' reliance on the same actuarial guidelines revealed the haziness of the distinction in many minds between mutual insurance and mutual charity.[5]

The Congregational Charitable Society's eventual conversion from an annuity association to a fiduciary charity coincided with the establishment in Boston and across New England of dozens of humanitarian institutions. In fact, the members' dissatisfaction with their original practices may have resulted in part from their growing recognition that mutual insurance was not as selfless as other endeavors. At about the same time that the Society's members were reforming their practices, the founders of the Massachusetts Mutual Fire Insurance Company, established in Boston in 1798, also tried briefly to promote their organization as "incorporated for the benevolent purpose of guarding its associates against losses of Buildings by Fire."[6] Such language disappeared quickly from the records and publications of mutual insurance organizations, however. By 1818, when the board of trustees of the Massachusetts General Hospital played a leading role in the establishment of the Massachusetts Hospital Life Insurance Company, the place of insurance corporations in organized charity was clear. They were investment opportunities, not philanthropic organizations.[7]

Experience also quickly persuaded New Englanders that political societies were beyond the line that divided charity from self-service. The clubs that New Englanders founded in the early nineteenth century—principally chapters of the Washington Benevolent Society—were precursors of an organized party system. Even at the time it was well known that its members were almost exclusively Federalists. Yet between 1811 and 1815, when New Englanders established more than 150 of these societies, there seemed to be some reason to accept the organizers' claims to benevolence.[8]

Federalists across New England established the Washington Benevolent societies in response to a Jeffersonian challenge, the rise of the Tammany Society, or Columbian Order. Strongest in the middle-Atlantic states, the Tammany Society boasted only eight affiliates in New England, four in Rhode Island and four in Massachusetts. Disgruntled Rhode Island Federalists, however, credited the Tammany lodges in Providence, Newport, Warwick, and Bristol with coordinating a sweeping Jeffersonian victory in the 1810 statewide elections. Although clearly a partisan tool by then, the Tammany Society was originally a mutual benefit organization much like the Masons, and in its rhetoric, if not in its day-to-day political activities, it retained vestiges of its fraternal character.[9] The Federalists' Washington Benevolent societies were partisan political associations no less than the lodges of the Tammany Society, but like their rival, they maintained a philanthropic facade.

Notwithstanding their obvious partisan ties, the Washington Benevolent societies undertook enough charitable work to establish at least the pretense that they were authentically philanthropic. The Washington Benevolent Society of Massachusetts, for example, located in Boston, responded to occasional pleas for assistance from members.[10] To the west, the Washington Benevolent Society for the County of Worcester made five donations of between $10 and $150, most of them to victims of fires, from February 1814 to March 1815. In Stockbridge, meanwhile, a meeting of the "Benevolents" collected $73 to assist a subscriber who had lost his property to a fire.[11]

Even these activities raised doubts, though, especially in the Jeffersonian press. Almsgiving was a ruse by the Society's Federalist leadership, critics contended, designed to deceive members about the true nature of their fraternity. "The credulous are made to believe that benevolence is the grand object," one skeptic remarked, but he knew differently: "Some acts of charity are undoubtedly performed to blind the eyes of their deluded followers and to stimulate others to become members."[12]

Federalist spokesmen bridled at these charges and defended the integrity of their associations. There were ways to portray even the political activities of the Benevolents as charitable deeds. Instead of depicting themselves as political partisans, eager for power and patronage, many Benevolents described themselves as concerned citizens, selflessly promoting policies that advanced the welfare of the nation. It seems likely that many or most of those who made this claim actually believed it, but so many non-members hooted in skepticism that the organization's preferred public image never had a chance of widespread acceptance. "Their leaders have denied that their object is political," one doubter noted in 1814, but this self-characterization was impossible to accept: "It is as evident as the sun at midday that their objects are not only political, but intended to overthrow the present republican administration."[13] Indeed, in their private communications, even some members of the Society admitted that their public posture was disingenuous: at its dissolution in the early 1820s, the members of the Washington Benevolent Society of Massachusetts consoled themselves with the thought "that the political purposes for which the society was instituted had been fully accomplished."[14] Partisan gain, as almost everyone recognized, was rarely compatible with selfless ends, nor was political association a convincing form of organized charity.

In contrast to the Benevolents and their protestations of selflessness, no one denied that savings-bank depositors stood to profit by their investments. The institutions were founded to assure them a fair return on their money. The banks' philanthropic claims, however, had little to do with passbook holders. It was the initial investors and officers, not the depositors, who hoped to use these institutions charitably.[15] Until the organizations grew so large that they needed professional management, savings banks actually offered philanthropists an opportunity to assist their neighbors.

The objective of the founders of New England's first savings banks—the Provident Institution for Savings in the Town of Boston (1816), the Salem Savings Bank (1818), the Society for Savings of Hartford (1819), the Savings Bank of Newport (1819), and the Providence Institution for Savings (1819)—was to provide the working poor an opportunity to save and earn interest. Men and women with only a few dollars left over after paying for necessities lacked sufficient capital to invest in commercial merchandise or stocks, and all too often, it seemed, they squandered what they had on high living. The establishment in the 1760s of the first savings banks in Germany and in the early 1810s of similar banks in Great Britain, however, provided New England merchants with model institutions for encouraging thrift among the worthy poor. To organize and administer such banks, men like the Provident's James Savage, a Boston lawyer, volunteered their services part-time for free—in Savage's case, for forty-five years, almost all of them unpaid.[16]

Notwithstanding such examples, most of the banks' early officers fell away after a few years, replaced by full-time, paid managers. By the late 1820s the demands of overseeing hundreds of thousands of dollars in invested assets proved too great for part-time volunteers. Although the banks continued to provide small-scale depositors the same investment opportunities that they had at their inception, with the replacement of the founders by salaried employees the original philanthropic goals bore less and less relationship to the institutions' activities. After all, once the founders departed, everyone who was left—officers and depositors alike—received some sort of compensation in wages or interest.[17]

Scrutiny led New Englanders after a time to agree that mutual insurance societies, political clubs, and savings banks were too self-serving to be philanthropic. The same concern, expressed through doubts about fraternal secrecy, confronted the Freemasons in the late 1790s. In this case, however, it led to a more uncertain conclusion. At the turn of the century, Freemasons found themselves in the awkward position of trying to prove that their closed-mouth, private association really had the public's best interests at heart.

What kind of charitable institution swears its members to secrecy? Masonic spokesmen never questioned that their customs were innocent and their order a benefit to the community at large, but public worries that had festered for decades led to trouble in 1798. At their core were doubts whether the Masons really served their communities, as they claimed, or used their meetings behind closed doors to promote their own advantage.

Masonic secrecy was a logical consequence of the mutualist form of organization. Unlike fiduciary institutions, which publicize their activities both to solicit support and to inform potential beneficiaries of their services, mutual associations ordinarily have no reason to announce their accomplishments. Indeed, organizations that only serve their own members' needs have an incentive for silence; publicity may result in unsolicited, and unwanted, appeals for assistance. The Masons consequently had every reason to maintain their privacy and none to breach it. When they joined the order, new members swore to guard the "Essential Secrets of masonry." These included the "Common private transactions" of individual lodges relieving and disciplining their members as well as fraternal rituals so mystical they could "never be understood by Such as are unenlightened."[18]

In its silence the fraternity was not alone, although it was New England's most visible secret society and probably the only one subjected to criticism for its clandestine practices. Many other mutual organizations also used passwords and signs to preserve their privacy and draw the boundary between members and outsiders. Only Masonry, however, the largest, most prominent, and most widespread mutual society seemed potentially powerful enough to pose a threat to the freedom and security of non-members. Between the 1730s and 1750s, outsiders subjected the fraternity to periodic attacks, often musing on the nature of the Masons' "brotherly love" for each other. At their harshest, colonial anti-Masonic attacks took the form of salacious poetry and what may have been New England's first obscene cartoon in print.[19]

As long as mutualism was New England's predominant form of organized charity, the Masons were able to deflect questions about their secrecy. It was no coincidence, however, that the first serious challenge to Freemasonry arose as New Englanders were actively engaged in spreading organized evangelism and humanitarianism. As fiduciary institutions became increasingly common, masonic philanthropy began to seem hollow and unsatisfying to critics who believed they knew a more effective—and more selfless—way to organize.

Jedidiah Morse, the minister of the Congregational church in Charlestown, was the instigator of antimasonic activities in the late 1790s. From reading a book entitled *Proofs of a Conspiracy against all the Religions and Governments of Europe* by John Robison, an eccentric Scotsman, Morse picked up the idea that subversive activities by the Bavarian Illuminati, supposedly a renegade faction of the Freemasons, had produced the French Revolution. Afraid that similar treachery was possible at home, the preacher revealed his fears in a public Fast Day sermon on May 9, 1798. Morse published his address, which went through two editions, and followed it up with a series of newspaper articles.[20]

It would be misleading to suggest that Morse's warnings stirred up a powerful antimasonic groundswell across New England.[21] Even in Connecticut, where President Timothy Dwight of Yale echoed Morse's words two months later in a Fourth of July address, little surviving evidence indicates public concern at Masonry's political threat.[22] In Massachusetts, however, the fraternity and its skeptics alike took Morse's admonitions seriously.

Secrecy was the key to Morse's attack and to the masonic rejoinder. Morse attacked the Bavarian order, and by implication its alleged masonic collaborators, for its mysterious ways. He charged that the "society, under various names and forms . . . [had] secretly extended its branches through a great part of Europe, and even into America." Operating covertly through Europe, the fraternity had tried to subvert religion, to dominate public education and the newspapers, and to gain control of the governments. It seemed likely to Morse that the brotherhood would extend its nefarious activities to the United States as well.[23]

Morse's concerns might equally have applied to New England's other mutual associations were it not for two considerations. First, Morse's theory made sense only if one assumed a massive international conspiracy. The Masons were not the only society potentially open to question, but unlike the members of marine and mechanic associations, for example, initiates of the ancient and honorable fraternity proclaimed that formal bonds of brotherhood united their lodges around the world. Second, unlike marine and mechanic societies, which began to define limited but visible and unexceptionable roles in the public service between the early 1780s and the mid-1790s, the Masons were unsuccessful in spelling out the community benefits they provided.

The public activities of marine and mechanic societies took a number of different forms. As the generally recognized voices of the maritime and artisanal sectors of the community respectively, both occasionally advised state and federal officials on public matters. The governor of Massachusetts regularly relied on the Commonwealth's marine societies to nominate qualified men as port surveyors and harbor and river pilots, and in 1790 the Boston Marine Society consulted with the Commonwealth on the construction of a vessel to protect coastal trade.[24] Meanwhile, in 1792 at the behest of Alexander Hamilton the Providence Association of Mechanics and Manufacturers conducted a survey of the local economy for use in establishing tariffs.[25] Moreover, the members of many marine societies also acted independently of the government to serve the public interest by collecting and publicizing navigation information as well as by certifying the accuracy and efficacy of nautical charts and inventions. It is clear that the associations took their civic duties seriously. In fact, in 1783 the Newburyport Marine Society refused to certify a wood preservative without further testing, and in 1789 the Boston Marine Society declined to approve a collection of charts without proof from the cartographer of their accuracy.[26]

Marine and mechanic societies continued to follow traditional mutualist practices where financial relief was concerned, but in other respects they became public institutions by the mid-1790s. As the Masons answered the charges of Morse and others in the late 1790s they recognized that their critics' bill of particulars required them to define Freemasonry's civic role and demonstrate its public service.

Although the masonic response to Morse and the order's other critics took a number of forms, the brotherhood's principle rejoinder was an attempt to show that the fraternity served the nation by producing and nurturing its leading citizens, men whose probity and honor were beyond question. Since public charges required public responses, the Masons mounted a campaign to convince their neighbors of the order's selfless, civic merits. To this end the members of the Massachusetts Grand Lodge solicited a letter of endorsement from President John Adams. They probably found the reply of the president, who did not belong to the fraternity, mildly disappointing, but he did reveal the comforting information that "many of my best friends have been Masons." More to the point were public orations in which masonic speakers reminded their listeners that such patriots as Paul Revere, Benjamin Franklin, and George Washington belonged, or had belonged, to the order.[27]

President Washington's fortuitously timed death on December 14, 1799, clinched the Masons' argument. Washington's passing triggered an orgy of lamentation throughout New England and the nation. For good reasons, the Masons were among the most lachrymose of the mourners. As one orator reminded the members of the fraternity, "You were attached to your illustrious brother, by uncommon bonds." The public would not be allowed to forget this affiliation.[28]

Masons throughout New England held public services to memorialize their brother. In many towns they joined community-wide ceremonies and processions. In Boston, however, to emphasize its special links to Washington the fraternity held a separate service the day before his birthday in 1800. The ceremonies, which attracted "upwards of sixteen hundred Brethren," commenced with a funeral procession. In a letter of condolences to the president's widow the officers of the Grand Lodge of Massachusetts had requested "a lock of her deceased husband's hair." These strands they placed in a golden urn, which six former grand masters, among them Paul Revere, attended in the cortege. Prayers, odes, a eulogy, and a "Masonic dirge" followed a parade through the streets of the town from the Old State House to Old South Church. After a second procession, a funeral service at the Stone Chapel concluded the ceremonies.[29]

In 1826, doubts about the fraternity and its clandestine ways would recur, leading many New Englanders to join anti-Masons across the northeast. For the moment, though, the Masons had succeeded in persuading their neighbors of their good intentions. In the early nineteenth century, whenever New Englanders drew a line dividing public-spirited from self-serving institutions, they counted the Masons among the philanthropic. There were limits to this acceptance; by the early 1800s, comparison with more modern forms of charity led some commentators to conclude that "in this age of light and general improvement, masonic institutions were of little use." With the spread of fiduciary charity, such reservations about mutualism grew, regardless of the form it took. Yet until the 1820s even skeptics of the fraternity conceded that "the most earnest defenders of the christian faith would have nothing to fear from the triumphs of Masonry."[30]

Exposure to mutual insurance companies, political associations, mutual savings banks, and the Freemasons helped New Englanders in a new era to clarify what it was to be charitable. Because these institutions teetered precariously on the dividing line between self-serving and public-spirited activities, they tested important assumptions about the virtue. Unlike the Massachusetts Mutual Fire Insurance Company, the Washington Benevolent Society, the Provident Institution for Savings, and the Massachusetts Grand Lodge, most local associations never had to face critical consideration of their programs. Such thought-provoking cases, however, helped to point out the need to reconsider the meaning of charity.

Redefining "Charity"

Because "charity" is a noun, its meaning is susceptible to revision with changes in whatever it denotes. Both Samuel Clarke and Jonathan Ashley recognized as much when they remarked on their contemporaries' apparent willingness to equate the word with almsgiving. New Englanders redefined the virtue after 1800 as they made increasing use of organizations. Received traditions retarded this transformation, however, leaving it incomplete in the 1820s.

The redefinition of "charity" was an involved process, as complicated as New England's understanding of the virtue itself. Because this understanding drew on many sources, the word was rich with connotations. New Englanders thought of "charity" systematically, in the terms that theology, moral philosophy, and jurisprudence dictated, but they also thought of it informally and unsystematically, relying on their own experience. "Charity" denoted private and intimate relationships, but it also signified public and formal ones.

A comparison between the English lexicographer Samuel Johnson on "charity" and Noah Webster of Hartford on the same subject reveals the scope of New England's redefinition of the word. Johnson's description of "charity" in 1755 in the first edition of his famous *Dictionary of the English Language* was one that most New Englanders of the day also espoused. Nearly three-quarters of a century later in 1828, Webster updated Johnson in the first edition of the *American Dictionary of the English Language*. In each case, "charity" was rich in meanings. Johnson offered five separate definitions. "Charity" was "Tenderness; kindness; love." It was also "Good will; benevolence," and a "disposition to think well of others." Further, it was the "theological virtue of universal love." Under certain conditions the term might denote "Liberality to the poor"; in the same vein, it might mean "Alms," or the "relief given to the poor."[31] Webster repeated the earlier definitions almost verbatim in 1828. Aware as well of the word's changing usage, however, the American lexicographer added three more definitions. At times "charity" also was "liberality in gifts and services to promote public objects of utility" as practiced by "bible societies, missionary societies, and others," at other times it was an "act of kindness or benevolence," and on still other occasions it was "a charitable institution."[32]

Webster's description of "charity" epitomized New England's response to the need to expand its meaning. He made room for new definitions at the same time that he preserved the word's original sense. Gradually, New Englanders as a group were following the same conservative path.

There were good reasons why New Englanders held onto much of their inherited understanding of "charity." The practical consequences of the rise of organized charity were considerable but circumscribed. Institutionalization's effects on New England's understanding of the virtue were similarly substantial but limited. New Englanders typically attended the needs of acquaintances through mutual benefit societies, and those of strangers through fiduciary associations, but cared for their closest friends and relatives more privately and informally. It is not surprising, therefore, that institutionalization's greatest effect on the popular understanding of "charity" concerned impersonal and formal relationships, largely sparing those involving families and intimate friends.

If New Englanders were loath to dismiss their received understanding of "charity," the spread of philanthropic organizations was nevertheless altering the balance among the various relationships that the term signified. As scores of associations flooded the region, they gave New Englanders increasing opportunity to talk about their accomplishments. Once public philanthropies became commonplace, distributing tracts and topcoats, sermons and salt cod, their work often overshadowed private and personal acts of kindness. If postrevolutionary New Englanders seemed at times almost to equate "charity" with institutional almsgiving, it was because they now had so many opportunities to talk about organized activities.

In fact, the institutionalization of charity encouraged New Englanders to talk more about the virtue than ever before. The apostle Paul had warned in his first epistle to the Corinthians that charity "vaunteth not itself," but this was hardly suitable advice to men and women whose good works depended on their ability to raise money. In anniversary sermons, pamphlets, newspapers, and magazines, as New Englanders promoted their activities they sped the identification of charity with formal programs.

The incompleteness of the redefinition of "charity" was due, in the end, to the conservative effects of the systematic theological, moral, and jurisprudential teachings that New Englanders read as students and referred to throughout their lives. Drawing on centuries of scholarship, the authors of the texts that New Englanders considered definitive focused on individual rather than corporate responsibilities and intimate rather than public situations. In so doing, they found it easy to preserve the vocabulary that had sufficed before there were any charitable institutions to take into account. As long as institutionalization presented no overt contradictions to their teachings, New England's theologians, moral philosophers, and legal theorists were able to accommodate their systems to whatever novelties organized charity presented.

For moral philosophers and theologians, the emergence of organized charity was, in fact, more a solution than a problem. Speculative thinkers who had wrestled for generations with the practical puzzles imposed by utopian ideas about philanthropy could now explain that institutions made their schemes possible. Thanks to organized humanitarianism, fraternalism, and reform, limited men and women could practice limitless charity; thanks to organized evangelism sinful men and women could spread God's message wherever there was an audience to listen to it.

Because the new institutions seemed for the most part to confirm rather than to challenge traditional teachings, moral philosophers and theologians prior to the 1830s saw no need to address the problems and prospects of organized charity. Jasper Adams, a New Englander transplanted to South Carolina, may have been the first writer to take notice of the subject in a formal treatise in 1837; however, his *Elements of Moral Philosophy* was quite consciously an essay on *"practical* morals" rather than on the theory of morals, and his list of "Five special rules given to direct charitable societies and individuals dispensing alms" provided prudent advice, not a theoretical analysis of the philosophical consequences of the emergence of organized charity.[33]

Of New England's systematic thinkers, only the writers of state constitutions, whose work forced them to address practical problems that philosophers and theologians could ignore, noticed organized charity and made explicit provision for it. The constitutions of Massachusetts, New Hampshire, and Vermont literally made room for organized charity through clauses that provided for the promotion of civic institutions, among them philanthropic organizations. In Massachusetts, sometime between 1778, when the citizenry rejected a draft frame of government, and 1780, when it adopted a new version largely authored by John Adams, civic leaders agreed to include a section providing for "The Encouragement of Literature, &c." The clause called on legislators and magistrates "to encourage private societies and public institutions," and it also enjoined them "to countenance and inculcate the principles of humanity and general benevolence, public and private charity . . . in their dealings."[34] Three years later, New Hampshire's constitutional convention adopted substantially the same wording.[35] In Vermont, meanwhile, between 1777 and 1793 successive draft constitutions routinely contained similar provisions for encouraging civic organizations, including philanthropic institutions.[36]

Although the redefinition of "charity" remained incomplete as late as the 1820s, New Englanders had taken into account the spread of philanthropic organizations by expanding their understanding of the virtue. Once they made room in their definition for organized charity, they could turn to other concerns. Organized charity became second nature to them.

Taking Organized Charity for Granted

In the September 1807 issue of the *Monthly Anthology* a weary critic launched his review of an anniversary discourse before the Portsmouth Female Asylum with an extended speculation:

> We have often puzzled ourselves in conjecturing the motive, which may be supposed to influence a man of sense to publish an occasion-

al sermon. It cannot be the hope of fame, one would think, for who ever reads a charity sermon, except his nerves are so out of order as to require an anodyne? And yet we can hardly ascribe it to the nobler motive of a hope of usefulness, for even the self complacency of an author cannot conceal from himself that on such a topick, he is adding nothing to what all the world already knows, and that every thing he can say has been at least as well said a thousand times before.[37]

Curiously, in expressing this view the reviewer was dispensing a cliché of his own. Commentators in the *Anthology,* itself, had often remarked on the near impossibility of saying anything fresh about charity. "Discourses upon charity have been so frequent," one correspondent observed, "that novelty is scarcely to be expected." By 1806 bored reviewers could already "find no original thought to engage us" in the charity sermons they read: "no artful combination of old ones to amuse or surprise." Wrote a critic of one discourse: "There is little to censure; much to approve; but nothing to admire." It was something to celebrate when a speaker escaped "the proverbial dulness of charitable discourses."[38]

As early as the start of the century, years of discussion were making the fundamental premises of organized charity unexceptional—common knowledge never questioned by anyone alert to the events of the day. Its universal aspirations and practical limitations were generally recognized, as was the brew of selfless and self-interested motivations that fueled its supporters. New Englanders still paid attention whenever someone discovered a "flower by the way to embellish his discourse,"[39] and something new or controversial, whether an institution with novel objectives or a development as momentous as a glimpse of the distant millennium or the dawn of philanthropy, could still seize the popular imagination. Repetition, however, was making the recounting of basic teachings tedious.

The achievement of such a consensus is difficult to trace. Once most New Englanders discovered themselves in agreement about the nature and purposes of organized charity, far from proclaiming these fundamental truths they rarely needed to recur to them. Although anniversary speakers continued occasionally to offer brief explications of organized charity, these were usually delivered in passing as orators pursued more original and entertaining subjects; two addresses—*The Advantages of Association* (1805) by William Patten of Newport and *Charity Recommended from the Social State* (1806) by John Prince of Salem—mark the conclusion of New England's extended consideration of the premises underlying organized charity.

The general failure after 1806 to talk systematically about organized charity, however, masked the fact that the precepts that New Englanders had outlined repeatedly a few years earlier continued to underlie their every philanthropic initiative. In fact, the absence from anniversary sermons of extended discussion of the nature of organized charity and its connection to philanthropy is a reliable sign that New Englanders no longer felt the need to justify themselves or their practices. The principles that Patten and Prince expounded at length were now in no sense unusual or controversial. They had joined the stock of unspoken assumptions that everyone shared.

If these assumptions ordinarily went unsaid after 1806, they continued nonetheless to influence New England thought about organized charity. These beliefs constituted the conventions common to all organized charitable activities. In the rare instances when they emerged from the silent obscurity that is usually the lot of tacit assumptions, these presuppositions revealed their continuing ability to shape popular beliefs. But the mounting clamor of institutions, each competing for attention as associations proliferated after 1800, insured that eventually New England's basic charitable premises would again reveal themselves.

Competition was, in fact, the dark side of the rapid rise and spread of organized charity, candid observers admitted after 1805. Whether associations vied with each other for supporters or for monopoly over specific charitable causes, mutualists and the friends of fiduciary charity alike agreed that competition wasted resources that might otherwise find more efficient use. Even as associations tested each other, however, in conceding the threat they posed to one another they also tacitly confirmed their acceptance of common principles and ends. These precepts set the standards for measuring every charitable activity. In their quest for support, associations competed with each other to persuade potential friends that each was the perfect embodiment of charity.

Civic boosters had emphasized the necessity of institutional cooperation for more than a decade, but no matter how strongly they agreed in theory, on a practical level New Englanders admitted that sooner or later sister organizations would compete for the same limited sources of support. The prospect of competition already cast a shadow in 1806 when Thaddeus Mason Harris addressed the Massachusetts Humane Society:

> God forbid that what is meant to excite charity [Harris pleaded]
> should create a jealousy of interest, or an interference of claims
> among Institutions which have one common object in view, the suc-
> cour of distress, the alleviation of human misery in whatever shape it
> appears!

Having recognized the problem, Harris pledged to avoid "detracting from the necessity or importance of other charitable institutions." This was a difficult standard to uphold, though, and even Harris challenged other organizations to measure up to the humane society. After all, he asserted, the humane society performed "A DEED OF MATCHLESS CONSEQUENCE."[40]

The proliferation of calls for contributions had an unintended consequence: those making the appeals were forced to compete to distinguish their causes from all the rest. Spokesmen for benevolent institutions quickly realized that there was no reason to belabor the obvious desirability of organized charity in general, since by the early nineteenth century everyone took it for granted, but every reason to set their programs apart from the others if they hoped to attract support. In the philanthropic marketplace, each cause was a product to differentiate from its competitors and its survival depended on the marketing ability of its promoters.

In making the case for dispensaries and orphanages, Sunday schools and tract societies, everyone followed the same course, no matter what the cause. The need was acute, its advocates contended, and the service that an organization provided was an especially pure expression of the charity that all Christians owed their fellow human beings.

In terms that were strikingly similar to the earlier general appeals for organized charity, the advocates of individual causes competed with each other after 1805. Their success varied significantly from one sector of the growing benevolent empire to another, but none did better than organized evangelism.

As they promoted their projects in the early nineteenth century, spokesmen for evangelism agreed on one central point. Organized charity was laudable no matter what ends it served, but evangelism's goals were the most important of all. If the altruism of mutual insurance programs, political fraternities, and savings banks were open to question, no one could doubt the motives underlying organized evangelism. Compared with humanitarianism and mutualism, evangelism's objectives were peculiarly disinterested, or so the argument went.

In 1806 when Joseph Eckley addressed the annual meeting of the Society for Propagating the Gospel among the Indians and Others in North America he explained the superior merit of evangelism. Speaking on behalf of "a cause, confessedly of the highest importance," Eckley attempted to demonstrate why it deserved priority. "You often assemble," Eckley reminded his listeners, "that you may minister to the temporal wants of your afflicted and poor brethren." Today, however, they were "convened, in the sanctuary of the Lord, to enjoy the satisfaction, and participate in the honour of ministering to the necessities of their *souls,*—of sending the message of salvation among a people who have not the means of providing for it themselves; making 'the wilderness and the solitary place glad for them, and the desert rejoice, and blossom as the rose.'" What task could be more important, more deserving?[41]

It was not that humanitarianism and mutualism were undeserving or unfit to be called charity. Rather, evangelism was so important, serving a need so basic to anyone with an unclean soul, that nothing should stand in its way.

By the end of the decade, Eckley's message was commonplace. Missionary sermons were incomplete without this truism. As the charitable field grew increasingly crowded, public spokesmen emphasized evangelism's selfless, spiritual merits with growing urgency. Comparisons became explicit. When the officers of the new Connecticut Bible Society trumpeted the significance of their institution in 1808 they made clear its peculiar virtues. "Are not charities, in things pertaining to the body," they asked, "though often necessary, utterly worthless, in comparison" with programs that promised to save human souls?[42] Spokesmen for the Bible Society of Maine agreed. "How frequently," they wondered in 1809, "does the book of God enjoin it upon us to minister to the temporal wants of the necessitous? But how much more important is the charity, which supplies the spiritual need of our fellow men? If a famine of bread is dreadful, how much more so a famine of the word of God."[43]

Such arguments concerned the friends of temporal causes. Many of their spokesmen reacted to the efforts of missionary groups with a counteroffensive designed to show that other organizations also did God's work.

Humane societies and female asylums were the most active on this score. When Jedidiah Morse addressed the Massachusetts Humane Society in 1801 he tried to explain the organization's divine ends. Arguing that "the restoration of the present life" gave near victims of drowning more time to serve both God and man, Morse pointed out that by "prolonging the lives of our fellow-men, the good have a further opportunity of being useful, and the bad a space for repentance." Through their donations, Morse urged, Christians who were "concerned for the spiritual welfare of [their] fellow-men" acted "to save their souls from everlasting perdition."[44] The following year Eliphalet Porter delivered the same society a similar message. Convinced that Christians passed through the "present life" to prepare themselves for "a future state of existence," Porter also placed importance on the "prevention of its sudden and premature close" for spiritual as well as temporal reasons.[45]

Orphanages provided a different set of services, but their supporters were equally convinced that they, too, met eternal as well as temporal needs. In

1804, when he spoke on behalf of the Boston Female Asylum, John Lathrop praised the institution's moral instruction for "saving many poor creatures from ruin" and for "preparing them, not only for usefulness in this life, but for happiness in the world to come."[46] Three years later in 1807 when Morse addressed the same society he made a point to prove that it was "designed to promote not only the temporal, but the spiritual and eternal welfare of its subjects." Because they provided moral guidance in addition to physical assistance, such associations could "be instrumental in recovering a sinner from the error of his ways, or in preserving him from vice." Beneficence that "saves a soul from death," Morse insisted, was "charity to the soul, as well as to the body."[47]

Such appeals would have been unthinkable a decade or more earlier, not because New Englanders would have doubted their truth but because they took for granted assumptions that had only recently become second nature. Once Eckley, Morse, Lathrop, and their contemporaries began to debate which of their programs was the most valuable, New Englanders passed beyond explaining and defending organized charity in general. By the middle of the decade this point appeared self-evident. Indeed, so accustomed to one form of organized charity—the fiduciary variety—had New Englanders become by the early nineteenth century, that it began quietly to shape their understanding of their relationships to one another.

Since cash contributions were the lifeblood of every fiduciary association, sustained exposure encouraged supporters to define each society's activities in terms of economic conditions and relationships. John Winthrop had believed in 1630 that charity was everyone's obligation, the poor person's no less than the rich,[48] but the more its practice became the province of fiduciary organizations, the easier it became to equate the virtue with almsgiving and to assign special responsibility for it to the wealthy.

Some activities lent themselves to this conclusion more readily than others, but by the early nineteenth century assumptions about economic relationships began to infuse the popular understanding of almost every form of organized charity. It was a simple matter for the supporters of impoverished widows and orphans, for example, to describe themselves as the wealthy friends of the worthy poor, but what about the friends of other causes? Organized charity's ability to shape the language—even the perceptions and patterns of thought—of philanthropic men and women, revealed itself between 1800 and 1810 in the transformation of New England's understanding of domestic missions. In the missionary literature of New England, frontiersmen and frontierswomen passed from pagans to paupers.

Throughout the seventeenth and eighteenth centuries evangelism had primarily meant Indian missions, and New Englanders had evangelized the natives both to convert and to civilize them. These concerns had carried over to popular perceptions of the condition of pioneers on the frontier.[49] Until the early 1800s, most coastal New Englanders believed that life in the wilderness was best characterized by its "barbarism";[50] according to Nathan Perkins, a missionary who toured the northern reaches of New England in 1789, life in cultured Connecticut was "a paradise compared to Vermont."[51]

What attributes of society did pioneers lack? At first, it seemed, almost all of them. The absence of established churches and of a regular ministry was the most serious deficiency. The trustees of the Missionary Society of Connecticut reported in 1801 that "GREAT dissoluteness of morals prevails in many places" on the frontier where "all religious institutions [were] neglected." Frequently, they added, "the sabbath is profaned." And "children are suffered to grow up in intire ignorance of the first principles of religion."[52] The managers of the Hampshire Missionary Society reassured, however, that if a frontier community "let it be a leading object to produce able and faithful gospel ministers to settle" with them, "substantial advantages to [its] civil and temporal interests" would result.[53]

Educational deficiencies also troubled the managers of the missionary societies. In 1790 the overseers of the Society for Propagating the Gospel among the Indians and Others in North America worried that few frontier children were being "taught to read, and those who have been taught, cannot now procure books." The residents of established communities further feared that civil anarchy might prevail where children were "educated not only in an ignorance of religion, but also without human learning, or even the arts of civilization." Already, they reported, "crimes of the most attrocious nature . . . have encreased among them, and furnished large, but disagreeable business to the courts of law." The managers of the SPGNA warned that unless steps were taken "to establish schools and other institutions there, it is the opinion of the most intelligent persons" on the frontier "that consequences fatal to the peace, and possibly to the existence of the government will ensue."[54]

Although this description of frontier life undoubtedly had some basis in fact, it did not grow out of a careful, empirical appraisal of conditions on the fringes of white settlement. When New Englanders transferred their attentions from the Indians to the white pioneers, they continued to assume that effective evangelists had to civilize the objects of their missions.

Between the turn of the century and 1810, though, New Englanders exchanged their traditional description of evangelism for a new one. By 1808 when the trustees reported to the Hampshire Missionary Society, their portrait of its beneficiaries as "poor and destitute brethren" was becoming commonplace.[55]

The backcountry itself had changed between 1760 and the end of the century. The inhabitants of many wilderness communities had taken great strides toward the standards of civility that New Englanders in older settlements prescribed, though one further step usually remained. Most of these thriving inland villages still lacked the crowning symbol of civilization, the settled ministry. Many towns contained "a sufficient number of inhabitants to settle stated ministers," and were "desirous of procuring candidates for the purpose."[56] The situation in others, though, was less encouraging.

To their dismay, the members of New England's missionary societies recognized continuing problems in many frontier settlements. In 1802, in answer to objections that their missionaries were spending "too much of their time in large towns where the inhabitants are sufficiently numerous and wealthy to settle ministers," the trustees of the Missionary Society of Connecticut responded that even in many communities "which have been several years in settling, the greater part of the people from having been so long unaccustomed to religious worship, have become loose in their sentiments and morals."[57]

Reports of religious controversy in the backcountry offered further reason for the failure of many frontier villages to release their grasp on the missionary societies. In some towns, like Bartlett, New Hampshire, where "the people were very attentive to meeting, But much divided in sentiment," it was unlikely that the residents could muster the consensus to call, or the money to pay, a regular clergyman. In others, like Eaton, New Hampshire, where the members of two competing Baptist factions had each named a pastor, the settlers had made, from the standpoint of Congregationalist missionary societies, wrong choices.[58]

Notwithstanding occasional fears about the degenerative effects of life on the frontier, by the early 1800s most New Englanders began to believe that the inhabitants of the first towns settled after 1763 no longer fit the profile of the uncouth pioneer. As the line of settlement expanded to the west into Ohio and to the north into the upper reaches of Maine, New Hampshire, and Vermont, new settlers still faced a period of isolation and social turbulence. Experience showed that the crises of these early years soon passed, but other problems clearly remained.

The Reverend Peter Thacher of Boston was New England's first missionary spokesman to call the beneficiaries of evangelistic assistance "the poor." In 1798, describing the activities of the SPGNA, Thacher noted that in at least one missionary field it had paid special attention to the needs of impoverished settlers. By 1798 many religious books had "been distributed among the poor" in Maine. Thacher still maintained that the Society's primary purpose was to civilize the frontier,[59] but gradually, within the next few years, other observers also recognized what Thacher had noted and concentrated their resources on a portion of the pioneers.

Peter Thacher had identified what would become the redefined clientele of the missionary societies, and he had pointed out the problems they now faced. As long as many frontier towns still lacked permanent clergymen, their residents could meet their religious needs at least in part through edifying books and tracts. In 1802 the trustees of the Hampshire Missionary Society instructed the pioneers that "when destitute of a preached gospel" they should "carefully and punctually . . . assemble on the Lord's day for public worship: and unite in social prayer and thanksgiving, in singing God's praises and in reading and hearing the holy scriptures and such pious tracts and discourses as may be in your possession."[60] Affluent settlers could provide themselves with the necessary texts; the impoverished required assistance. By about 1805 the managers of New England's missionary associations began to recognize that the "poor and destitute are the objects of [our] mission."[61] In 1812 this idea was so thoroughly accepted by New England missionaries that Ephraim Abbott, touring rural Rhode Island for the Massachusetts Missionary Society, refused the persistent requests for a copy of the scriptures of an innkeeper who had given him free lodging. For as Abbott noted, his host was "able to buy a Bible if he wanted one."[62] Evangelism had truly become the gift of the rich to the poor. Missionaries had begun to apply means tests.

Although missionary-society trustees still insisted occasionally that their success did not depend on "the rich alone,"[63] it was increasingly difficult to ignore wealth's role. Perceptive observers agreed with the spokesman for one organization that it would fail "without the aid of the rich, the activity of the good, and the general approbation and concurrence of the community."[64] To be sure, most organizations promised to make use of every volunteer, no matter what his station in life. The structure of fiduciary institutions, however, placed a premium on wealth. Money was the one kind of contribution that an organization could always use.

The maturation of the frontier further encouraged New Englanders to adopt an economically based description of charitable relationships. One result of the frontier's development was the emergence of a stratum of settlers financially able to meet not only their own needs, but those of many of their neighbors as well. By 1804 an itinerant for the Hampshire Missionary Society was using the phrase "the better part" to refer to a segment of the population of Maine.[65] The following year, encouraged by the SPGNA, residents of the district initiated plans for an auxiliary to the Boston society.[66] No later than the same year, residents of two coastal counties in Maine established the Lincoln and Kennebec Tract Society.[67] Two years later in 1807, ministers and laymen in the district formed the Maine Missionary Society.[68] At the same time, the General Convention of Ministers in the State of Vermont founded their own missionary society.[69]

Missionary societies in Maine and Vermont could hardly claim to be serving distant barbarians. Although northern contributors joined with societies in Massachusetts, Connecticut, and New Hampshire to send evangelists on tours of remote settlements, New Englanders clearly regarded these activities as a species of local self-help. Assuming that the members of the Maine Missionary Society had current knowledge of conditions in their region, the officers of the SPGNA requested the new organization in 1808 to act as its agent "to direct their charitable efforts for the benefit of the destitute inhabitants of this District." In the eyes of the trustees of the parent society, the Maine Missionary Society existed to provide relief to its neighbors.[70]

With the development of Bible societies after 1808, an important evolutionary process in New England's understanding of evangelism was complete. Bible societies fed the spiritual needs of impoverished neighbors much as soup kitchens fed their bellies; they brought the mission field home. New Englanders now provided the urban poor with religious services on a regular basis through formal, incorporated societies. Whether donors and recipients lived hundreds of miles apart or across the street, their relationship was the same. Indeed, it was the same relationship that obtained within any fiduciary charitable organization. And it was one that New Englanders could now take for granted.

PART FOUR

The Charitable World of Antebellum New England

══

Anniversary Week

LYMAN BEECHER and his wife, Harriet, planned a relaxing week in New York. Setting out from their home in Litchfield, Connecticut, early in May 1820, they passed through New Haven, where they rested a few days to allow Mrs. Beecher to recover from a heavy chest cold, and reached their destination on May 9, "a beautiful morning, when everything looked fair and bright." Beecher had come to New York to address the fourth annual meeting of the American Bible Society. Mrs. Beecher found the sessions "very interesting" and noted in a letter to Harriet Foote, the sister of Beecher's late first wife, Roxana, that her husband's talk was "a good one." On arrival, Beecher was also solicited to address 2,000 children as part of the annual meeting of the New-York Sunday-School Union, an event held in conjunction with the Bible Society's convention. Two other organizations, the Union Foreign Missionary Society and the Society for the Conversion of the Jews, had also scheduled meetings during the week which was, according to an informed observer, "peculiarly appropriated to the Christian charity and duties in this city." A pleasant round of visiting took up the rest of the stay, and then the Beechers hurried home, arriving barely in time to avoid a storm which lasted for more than three weeks and made the weather feel "almost as cold as winter."[1]

Fourteen years after the Beechers' visit to New York, Andrew Reed and

James Matheson, in the city representing the Congregational Union of England and Wales, had little time for social calls. The coordinated meetings held in 1820 had proven to be the germ of "Anniversary Week." By 1834 more than a dozen local and national societies, meeting in New York in twenty-two sessions, now scheduled their annual conventions for the first full week of May. Among the cooperating associations, in addition to the American Bible Society and the Sunday-School Union, were the American Peace Society, the American Anti-Slavery Society, the American Tract Society, the American Home Missionary Society, the New York Colonization Society, and the New York City Temperance Society.[2]

In New England, by design or by accident, other times of year were busy seasons. January was an active time in Salem, as William Bentley noted in his diary. As early as 1814, during the first full week of the month residents of Salem were asked to take part in three charitable collections: for the American Board of Commissioners for Foreign Missions, for the local Bible society, and an ad hoc offering for the victims of a recent fire in Portsmouth. By the middle of the month the town's Baptists had also been solicited to support their missionaries.[3] In Boston, the third week in May was set aside for conventions; after their visit to New York in 1834 and a brief detour to take in Philadelphia's "Ecclesiastical Week," Reed and Matheson hurried on to the capital of the Bay State, where they attended the annual meetings of a local missionary society, the pastoral association of the Commonwealth's orthodox clergy, the Society for Promoting Christian Knowledge, the ABCFM, and the Massachusetts Congregational Charitable Society.[4]

In antebellum America, observers both domestic and foreign, impressed by the symbolism of such festivals as "Anniversary Week," recognized how central voluntary institutions had become to the conduct of charity in New England and across the entire nation. "It may be said, without much exaggeration," William Ellery Channing commented in Boston in 1829, "that every thing is now done by societies. Men have learned what wonders can be accomplished in certain cases by union, and seem to think that union is competent to every thing. You can scarcely name an object for which some institution has not been formed."[5] After visiting Beecher, Channing, and Joseph Tuckerman in 1831 during his tour of the new nation, Alexis de Tocqueville remarked: "As soon as several inhabitants of the United States have taken up an opinion or feeling which they wish to promote in the world, they look out for mutual assistance; and as soon as they have found one another they combine. From that moment on," Tocqueville added, "they are no longer isolated men, but a power seen from afar, whose actions serve for an example and whose language is listened to."[6] By the next decade according to Domingo Faustino Sarmiento, an Argentinian educator, journalist, philosopher, and statesman who traveled across the United States in 1847, association was "the soul and basis of the individual and national identity" of the American people.[7]

By the time of the Beechers' journey to New York in 1820, Americans had effected the institutionalization of charitable principles and practices. Organized charity was woven into the fabric of their lives. In important ways, its presence governed their thoughts and actions. For New England's rising generation it was difficult to imagine being without organized philanthropy.

Chapter Eight

Organized Charity and the "Spirit of Liberality"

LITCHFIELD, CONNECTICUT, is less than forty miles southeast of Stockbridge, Massachusetts, and both towns lie within a range of hills that gradually steepens as it becomes the Green Mountains of Vermont. The parsonage to which Lyman and Harriet Beecher fled in 1820, however, stood in a different time, and in nearly a different world, from the isolated home of Jonathan Edwards that Gideon Hawley fled in 1757. Lyman Beecher was a country preacher in 1820—Litchfield's population was about 4,600[1]—but his ministry stretched far beyond the middle-size community he served. Active in reform and missionary organizations, a prominent figure throughout New England and the northeast, Beecher was helping to lead not only his own parishioners but thousands more men, women, and children into a moral and Christian era. Gideon Hawley tried to do much the same when he undertook his mission among the Iroquois on the New York frontier, but he set out at a time of limitations, frustrations, and apologies. Hawley soon determined that his efforts were doomed to failure. Beecher's age, in contrast, seemed filled with possibilities. In 1820 he was primed and ready to conquer religious apathy, intemperance, dueling, and any other spiritual, moral, or social problem that came to his attention.

The difference was organization. Thanks to association, by the 1820s civic-minded New Englanders were able to do so much that they found it increasingly difficult to accept any of life's imperfections. If their faith enjoined philanthropy, and if their institutions brought that previously unattainable virtue within reach, how could conscientious men and women accept anything less? Success bred ambition, just as it undermined excuses. The more that charitable New Englanders achieved, the more they were ready to undertake.

The Achievement

Four months after Boston's anniversary week in 1830, on September 29 the city celebrated another occasion, the two-hundredth anniversary of its founding. To deliver the principal address the city fathers prevailed upon Josiah Quincy, Boston's second mayor after its incorporation in 1822 and now Harvard's fifteenth president. Quincy's oration was filled with the predictable superlatives that such events call for, paeans to the piety and patriotism of the city's residents. If the recollections of an observer can be trusted, though, when Quincy's address reached print a few weeks later one passage caused a stir. In his spoken remarks Quincy had uttered an unremarkable platitude about the benevolence of two centuries of Bostonians: "To no city has Boston ever been second in its spirit of liberality." The printed version, however, included an appendix to substantiate this routine claim. Since 1800, Quincy calculated, Bostonians had contributed at least $1,801,273 for charitable purposes, and almost certainly considerably more.[2] As Samuel A. Eliot remarked in the *North American Review* some years later, "The amount of money shown by this catalogue to have been given away . . . excited some surprise, and was very gratifying to those who from birth, personal relations, or other circumstances, took an interest in the character and reputation of the city."[3]

Josiah Quincy's catalogue provides a convenient introduction to postrevolutionary New England's charitable accomplishment. It was a substantial and durable achievement. Organized charity was well established and seasoned when Quincy wrote, and its basic outlines had been clear since the 1810s. Decades to come would bring innovations and refinements, new institutions and new approaches to philanthropy as yet unimagined. But until the New Deal and its alphabet agencies turned attention away from charity to relief and made relief primarily a public concern in the 1930s,[4] every significant initiative would be built on the private, voluntaristic foundation that was now firmly in place.

In compiling his account, Josiah Quincy took into consideration every expression of charity about which he could conveniently find information. The twenty-three organizations for which he had data had received a combined total of $1,155,986. Quincy listed the institutions by name, and beside each entry he indicated the amount the association claimed in contributions. Four canvasses for the victims of man-made disasters—fires in Newburyport, St. John's, Augusta, and Wiscasset—resulted in donations of another $67,462. To these sums Quincy added $108,400 in assorted contributions "for the patronizing of distinguishing merit, or for the relief of men eminent for their public services." Finally, he included $469,425 that the churches of

Boston had "collected for objects of general charity, or for the promotion of literary, moral, or religious purposes."[5]

Despite Quincy's attempt at inclusiveness, his catalogue was actually quite incomplete. Although he noted such prominent institutions as the Massachusetts Humane Society, Massachusetts General Hospital, and the Boston Female Asylum, he omitted many others—for instance, the Massachusetts Charitable Fire Society, the Boston Episcopal Charitable Society, and the Scots' Charitable Society. His list included such mutual benefit organizations as the Massachusetts Charitable Society and the Massachusetts Charitable Mechanic Association, but it failed to record the Freemasons or the Boston Marine Society. It contained the Boston Society for the Moral and Religious Instruction of the Poor but omitted the Massachusetts Society for the Suppression of Intemperance. It recognized the Massachusetts Bible Society and the American Education Society but not the Society for Propagating the Gospel among the Indians and Others in North America, or the short-lived Society for the Promotion of Christianity in India, organized by Joseph Tuckerman, the Unitarian missionary to the city's poor. All told, Bostonians actually supported at least eighty-six locally based charitable organizations when Quincy wrote, and probably many more.[6]

If Quincy overlooked many of the programs that Bostonians supported between 1800 and 1830, his account nonetheless revealed the range of charitable organizations that were now in existence. There were humanitarian, evangelistic, reform, and fraternal associations, some for women and others for men, and within each category there were many new varieties. Where once the Boston Female Asylum had provided only for orphaned girls, for example, a counterpart, the Boston Asylum for Indigent Boys, now took care of their brothers. Although the Massachusetts General Hospital could provide for most of the medical needs of the poor, a specialized clinic, the Boston Eye and Ear Infirmary, now ministered to ophthalmological and otolaryngological problems.

One obvious conclusion to draw from Quincy's account was that organized charity had become a highly specialized enterprise in Boston. A second was that if such associations coordinated their work they could raise substantial sums of money with which to do a great deal of good.

Outside Boston, no other city or town in New England could boast as complete or as diversified a roster of charitable organizations, but the course of every community's institutional evolution was clearly in the same direction. Between 1820 and 1829 alone, one modern historian has conservatively calculated, the residents of Massachusetts and Maine organized at least 200 charitable societies of various sorts.[7] If a full tally were possible, it would undoubtedly add, at a minimum, scores more associations, and probably hundreds.

As charitable organizations grew both more numerous and more wealthy, the task of administering them became increasingly complicated. To the extent that the institutions of Quincy's day differed significantly from earlier associations the changes were responses to growing complexity.

One important development was the introduction of full-time, salaried secretaries to direct the larger and more ambitious agencies. New Englanders who grew up before the rise of organized charity sometimes found this innovation difficult to accept, feeling that payment for such services compromised the charitable spirit of the salaried staff. As late as 1819, Noah Worcester, who as secretary of the Massachusetts Peace Society was among the first New Englanders to draw on his charitable work for his own support, expressed the dilemma in which he found himself thanks to his reliance on such compensation: "Ever since I began to write on the subject of war it has been to me a source of anxiety that I have been dependent on my labors in the benevolent cause for my daily bread. It exposes me to the suspicion of acting from sordid motives. Had I been in circumstances to relinquish all claim to pecuniary compensation, it would have added to my happiness."[8]

Notwithstanding such delicate feelings—with which most other paid staff members seem to have coped more successfully than Worcester—salaried employees became common by the 1820s. Medical institutions like the Massachusetts General Hospital relied on paid doctors and nurses to care for their patients,[9] and many of the largest missionary and reform societies depended on compensated administrators, often men with clerical training like Elias Cornelius of the American Education Society and Rufus Anderson of the American Board of Commissioners for Foreign Missions.[10]

The associations administered by such paid secretaries as Cornelius and Anderson were complicated both in their programs and in the networks of affiliates on which they relied for support. Evangelists under the sponsorship of the American Home Missionary Society, for example, now served nearly 400 impoverished communities in 21 states as well as both Upper and Lower Canada,[11] and from its headquarters in Boston the American Education Society supported 524 scholars between May 1829 and May 1830.[12]

To support their ambitious programs, the American Home Missionary Society, the American Board of Commissioners, the American Education Society, and a host of other missionary and reform organizations had built national networks of auxiliaries. The most successful and extensive of these systems was the American Bible Society's. From its home in New York City, the Society began at its establishment in 1816 to forge a nationwide chain of affiliates. First it persuaded existing state and local organizations—for example, the New Hampshire Bible Society and the Bible Society of Salem and Vicinity—to associate with it and to pledge some or all of their revenues to the national society. Then it sent out agents like Ward Stafford to establish new local branches organized according to model constitutions and by-laws provided by the parent association. By the late 1810s, the national society was already putting into place a three- or four-tiered structure of auxiliaries: local societies reported to county or state societies, which dealt in turn with the headquarters in New York City. The systematic organization of the American Bible Society's supporters led by 1830 to an annual income of more than $170,000.[13] Other national organizations, including the American Temperance Society, the American Sunday-School Union, and the American Home Missionary Society, followed similar plans. So extensive had many of these networks of men's, ladies', and juvenile societies become by the 1820s that no one would hazard to guess their size.

New England's role in some of the national missionary and reform associations was severely circumscribed, especially in societies that established their headquarters outside the region. Distance, and the active participation of supporters from other sections of the country, diluted New England's influence in such organizations as the American Colonization Society, which met in Washington, and the American Sunday-School Union, located in Philadelphia. Indeed, local and regional humanitarian, missionary, and reform associations were also common across the country now, in the south, the west, and the middle Atlantic states as well as in New England.[14] Nevertheless, because they believed that every organization contributed to the universal cause of philanthropy, New Englanders could take pride and satisfaction in the accomplishments of all charitable associations, whether or not they had a hand in their activities.

The network of charitable institutions that was in place was remarkable now for what it might plausibly attempt as well as for what it could actually do. The supporters of missions might reasonably maintain that no non-believer, domestic or foreign, was beyond their reach, nor was any inebriate outside the range of the friends of temperance, nor any statesman or general out of earshot of the advocates of peace. Orphans and widows, the deaf and the lame, sinners and sufferers of every kind now had benefactors, actual or would-be.

New groups could readily make room for themselves within this federation. As the region's Irish population grew, for example, Catholic Bostonians began to organize themselves in the late 1820s; Catholics elsewhere in New England similarly associated as the century progressed.[15] On the other hand, nativists, who believed the promotion of Protestantism was no less a civic cause than the crusade for temperance, reacted quickly to the apparent Catholic peril. As the threat of "Romanism" grew, militant evangelical Protestants responded, first in the early 1830s through such existing organizations as the American Bible Society, the American Education Society, and the Boston Sunday School Union, and then by the late 1830s through such associations as the Society for the Diffusion of Light on the Subject of Romanism, and the Female Protestant Association, both of Reading, Massachusetts, and the American Society to Promote the Principles of the Protestant Reformation.[16]

By Josiah Quincy's day, New Englanders found it hard to imagine a cause for which they could not associate. Time after time, the recognition of another new cause had set off a new round of organizing. Not only had New Englanders taken care of the needs of thousands of men, women, and children less fortunate than they were, they had grown so accustomed to organizing that the practice now came easily to them, ordinarily requiring only a previously unrecognized problem to trigger it once more. Sometime a few years before 1820, organized charity had achieved a critical mass, a level of size, acceptance, and influence that allowed it to fuel itself. As in a chain reaction, each successful institution ignited attempt after attempt to match or exceed its accomplishments. There seemed to be no end in sight.

Self-confidence now shaped most attitudes toward charity much as apologetic self-doubts had molded them not so many years before. An optimistic new spirit had become pervasive, a direct consequence of the rapid and widespread successes that institutionalization had spawned. Individual philanthropists and associations might have to cope with constraints on their capabilities, but no matter. It was the needs and abilities of the community, the nation, and even the world at large that now counted, not those of a single individual. As long as public-spirited men and women could associate for worthy purposes, and as long as their associations could cooperate, there was no practical reason for pessimism and every cause for faith that a philanthropic, even a millennial, new age was at hand.

Compromise versus Constancy

Self-confidence now governed New Englanders' involvement in charity. The limits of their own imaginations were their only constraints. Encouraged by what they were accomplishing, and attracted by the prospect of further successes, New Englanders extended their ambitions to new levels. As they became comfortable with new means to practice charity, social, spiritual, and moral problems that previously appeared insoluble began to seem worth attempting and geographical distances that once appeared impossibly vast began to seem manageable. If only they could organize themselves effectively and motivate right-thinking men and women to join them, many began to believe, they could convert the world, save it from vice, rescue it from misery, and accomplish almost any other act of charity they could wish.

As New Englanders confronted the great issues of the day, in the causes they considered and in the programs they attempted they took for granted the strength and continuity of action that voluntary association afforded them. Only through association was it possible to convert the Chinese and the Africans; end war, slavery, and intemperance; and assist masses of the sick poor, the orphaned, and the hungry. The woman's rights movement as it emerged before the Civil War, for example, was inconceivable without voluntary association. Over several decades women's organizations provided their members with vital experience in investigating the condition of their needy sisters, in articulating issues, and in mobilizing for action.[17] Undertakings of such magnitude required the participation of large numbers of supporters, and particularly where evangelism and reform were involved their need to mobilize their allies forced many leading New Englanders to make a crucial judgment about their prospects for success: were such causes as world missions, the peace crusade, woman's rights, the temperance movement, and the campaign to end slavery best served by organizing thousands of adherents who differed at times on how to proceed, or by developing a smaller core of highly motivated activists who shared a common vision of a problem and agreed on how to resolve it? In other words, many New Englanders asked themselves, were their purposes better promoted by compromise or constancy?

Voluntary association as a tool or technique was sufficiently flexible to accommodate both courses of action. As long as they agreed on the basic purposes of an association, supporters who differed over particulars could often still work together. Such cooperation might exact a price, though, in the form of barely palatable compromises over matters of controversy. These agreements often left all sides only partially satisfied and resulted in coalition movements that promoted the shared aspirations of their participants but glossed over the points of divergence. Alternatively, the friends of a cause who abhorred compromise with their preferred course of action could canvass the country for men and women similarly committed to their version of perfection. This approach assured the purity of a movement but compromised its chances for success by limiting its appeal and its resources. In both cases, voluntary association itself influenced the outcome, since formal constitutions and by-laws forced members to declare their views unambiguously and to stand by them. In antebellum New England, the most noteworthy compromises involved orthodox religious principles and causes; the most rigid fidelity to principle involved reform movements.

Because sophisticated theological lessons were ordinarily out of place in the mission field, New England's evangelists had routinely taught a simplified version of reformed Christianity since the days of John Eliot, the Mayhews, and David Brainerd. When the American Board of Commissioners for Foreign Missions stationed its evangelists in Indian territory and abroad after 1810, it adhered to this custom by not taking positions on most controversial theological issues. The origins and composition of the Board, however, and those positions it did take revealed that in at least one important respect it represented a new development in charitable organizing in New England. For the Board was an outgrowth of a religious coalition, and in its membership, supporters, and teachings it incorporated compromises on both sides.

The coalition united the Old Calvinists and Consistent Calvinists of eastern Massachusetts, and it came about only after several years of negotiation.[18] Although the differences that separated the two orthodox factions were primarily theological, their best route to reunion was through the cooperative administration of a number of organizations. Translating their doctrinal differences into an institutional idiom was no easy matter, however, and the resulting synthesis was deeply influenced by its encounter with formal organizations.

Disturbed by the emergence and the rapid rise of liberal Christianity in Boston and its environs, orthodox leaders from both camps began around 1800 to investigate the possibility of cooperation and joint organization. The establishment in 1802 of the General Association of Ministers in Massachusetts, a professional organization that clearly made no room for the liberals, was the first fruit of efforts initiated by such moderate Calvinists as President Joseph Willard and Professor David Tappen, both of Harvard, to rally the orthodox clergy. The next year, with the formation of a tract society, the Massachusetts Society for Promoting Christian Knowledge, its founder, Jedidiah Morse, further encouraged united action.

By 1805 both Willard and Tappen had died, and Morse and Eliphalet Pearson, Harvard's professor of Hebrew, both Old Calvinists, and Leonard Woods, the minister in West Newbury and a Consistent Calvinist, assumed the lead in negotiations to establish a working relationship between the two groups. Prior to the formation of the mission board the most important product of these discussions was the establishment in 1808 of Andover Theological Seminary. Deep suspicions on both sides prolonged the talks for months,[19] and it frequently appeared that the inability to agree on mechanisms to preserve each group's doctrinal integrity would result in the creation of two separate institutions, an Old Calvinist seminary in Andover and a Consistent Calvinist divinity school in West Newbury. The theological doctrines that distinguished the two parties—including divisions over baptism, communion, and church discipline[20] as well as differences over Edwardsian teachings about disinterested benevolence—persisted in 1808, but early in the year the negotiators agreed to guarantee each group the choice of a portion of the faculty. This accord resolved the major problems that had prevented the school's establishment. By the summer of 1808, orthodox students of both persuasions were sharing a faculty, a library, and other facilities in Andover. Within a few months, the merger of two religious journals, Morse's *Panoplist* and the *Massachusetts Missionary Magazine,* the periodical of the Massachusetts Missionary Society, largely a Consistent Calvinist association, sealed the establishment of the orthodox coalition.[21]

The agreement to allow Old Calvinists and Consistent Calvinists each to control faculty chairs at Andover ensured that, at least at first, neither group would have to yield to the other. Although they would work cooperatively in the General Association, within the tract society, at the seminary, and on the merged periodical, neither faction would have to disavow any of its teachings. The composition of the mission board during its early years reflected its origins in compromise: organizers were careful to include such Consistent Calvinists as Samuel Spring and Samuel Worcester and such Old Calvinists as Morse and Jeremiah Evarts among the officers. The board also incorporated a second coalition: its joint founders were two general ministerial associations, those of Massachusetts and Connecticut.[22]

The benefits to orthodoxy of coalition were undeniable. By almost every measure, the organizations that resulted were successful. In 1830 the mission board's evangelists served in such remote lands as India, Ceylon, Africa, Hawaii, and the Mediterranean; the Seminary boasted more than 450 graduates, most of whom were actively engaged in the ministry; the General Association counted 275 affiliated churches; and in addition to distributing thousands of pamphlets each year the tract society was supporting clergymen in impoverished parishes across New England.[23] Moreover, other organizations were gravitating towards the orthodox coalition. At its establishment at Boston's Park Street Church in 1826, the American Temperance Society limited its membership so strictly to Trinitarians that the *Christian Register,* a Unitarian weekly newspaper, protested "the spirit of sectarianism, which was permitted to pollute a scheme of benevolence."[24] The coalition also moved to exclude the liberals from many existing institutions: in Newburyport, for instance, the majority of the board of the Female Charitable Society voted in 1832 not to permit the Reverend Thomas B. Fox to baptize its orphans when his regular turn arrived, because as a Unitarian he did "not profess to believe in the equality of the Father, Son, and Holy Ghost."[25] Such measures, however, had come at a cost.

The compromises that had produced the orthodox coalition had resulted in a movement that was neither Old Calvinism, nor Consistent Calvinism, nor even the sum of the two, but was instead the highest common denominator. In 1808, as he was attempting to persuade his fellow Consistent Calvinists to accept the compromises that cooperation entailed, Leonard Woods described his own theological stance to Jedidiah Morse. Although he adhered to the Consistent Calvinists' basic principles, Woods noted, "I dwell not on the peculiarities of their system . . . I reject obnoxious terms and phrases . . . and am altogether disposed to shun their imprudences, their party spirit and their excesses."[26] In the interests of unity, Woods vigorously affirmed the doctrines that Old Calvinists as well as Consistent Calvinists could accept, but he avoided discussing those that were likely to lead to disagreement. For his part, Morse similarly tried to build on shared views while minimizing Old Calvinist doubts about the more idiosyncratic of the Consistent Calvinists' teachings.[27]

In order to work together through the ministerial association, tract society, seminary, mission board, and other associations the two orthodox groups agreed on a pared-down faith. Not everyone could accept this outcome: in the late 1820s the Reverend Bennet Tyler of Portland, believing that compromise had gone too far, initiated a resistance movement that led in 1832 to the establishment of a Consistent Calvinist tract society and in 1835 to a new seminary in Hartford committed to Edwardsian principles.[28] The compromise course, though, which sacrificed theological rigor for the sake of wide public acceptability, was the path that most of evangelical Christianity would take. It was certainly the course that most of New England's orthodox missionary, tract, and education societies would promote throughout the rest of the century.

There were counterparts to Bennet Tyler's resistance to coalition within almost all the major reform movements of antebellum New England. Of them, only the Sabbatarian movement of the late 1820s lacked a well-organized perfectionist wing. Like Tyler, opponents of drinking, slavery, the sexual status quo, and war who felt their causes were too important to compromise decided after attempts at cooperation to organize separately from more temperate advocates of the same ends, believing that moderation jeopardized the moral validity of their crusades. No less than the practical-minded men and women who were willing to compromise for the sake of the added support that resulted, perfectionists found in voluntary association an indispensable tool.

Perfectionism was nothing new to New England in the 1820s and 1830s, but organized perfectionism was. Ever since the first years of European settlement in North America, New England had harbored perfectionists of one sort or another, men and women temperamentally unable to compromise their principles in any way. If a report by John Winthrop is to be believed, in the search for ecclesiastical purity, after trying repeatedly and failing to define the community of saints to his own satisfaction, Roger Williams eventually refused to worship with anyone but his own wife. From Williams's step-by-step rejection of all ecclesiastical compromise in the seventeenth century, through the similar efforts of New Light separatists in the mid-eighteenth century to agree on ways to ascertain the elect, to the attempts of twentieth-century campus radicals to enlist universities and other institutions in various causes, perfectionism has been a recurring presence in New England life.[29] The activities of perfectionists within the temperance, antislavery, women's, and peace movements must consequently be seen in the context of a tendency that has reemerged repeatedly over several centuries.

As long as New Englanders such as Williams, whose controversial beliefs carried them beyond the bounds their townsfolk set for acceptable disagreement, found themselves isolated by their own opinions, dissent was likely to be a lonely activity. Organization counteracted this isolation; men and women whose ideas seemed extreme to their neighbors could form a new community of shared beliefs in which geographical boundaries were limitless but ideological limits were rigidly fixed. By twos and threes, tens and twenties, like-minded men and women from towns across New England could come together in organizations pledged not to compromise principles for the sake of expediency.[30]

Compromises that would in time prove unacceptable to such perfectionists were woven directly into the fabric of the temperance, peace, and antislavery movements at their inception in the 1810s, and indirectly into the fabric of the movement for women's rights. Temperance advocates all agreed that the abuse of alcohol was likely to have pernicious consequences, but at first few of them insisted on complete abstinence. Alcohol had legitimate medical uses, most doctors believed, and moderate social drinking appeared to cause few serious problems.[31] Peace activists differed over the legitimacy of "defensive wars"—that is, ones fought exclusively in self-protection—but initially, complete pacifists were able to cooperate with those who opposed only offensive wars.[32] Meanwhile, opponents of slavery worked together, although they quickly began to disagree over the efficacy of African colonization and other approaches that sought only gradual elimination of slavery.[33]

After slightly more than a decade of cooperation, these compromises began to unravel in the late 1820s. Voluntary societies had brought the two wings within each movement together, but by the 1830s new associations permitted the perfectionists to organize on their own, once they no longer found coalition tolerable. In temperance circles, by the mid-1830s teetotal pledges became common in local societies composed of journeymen artisans and other young men. From these associations, complete abstinence spread into many of the older, more established organizations; eventually, much of the movement against the abuse of alcohol was won over to the acceptance of teetotalism.[34] Within the antislavery community, too, a campaign for the immediate abolition of slavery, which began as a cause on the radical fringe, became in time the core of the movement. The establishment in 1832 of William Lloyd Garrison's New England Anti-Slavery Society opened a new chapter in the history of the crusade, which had been theretofore dominated by the proponents of colonization and gradual emancipation. By 1840 the moderates were on the defensive and the abolitionists, organized locally and nationally in such associations as the Massachusetts Anti-Slavery Society and the American Anti-Slavery Society, were in control of the movement. Female abolitionists led by Sarah and Angelina Grimké and Lucy Stone, among others, meanwhile began a new movement, one inherently extreme in the context of the times—the campaign to win women the vote and other civic rights.[35] Only within peace circles were the perfectionists unable to take command: the New England Non-Resistent Society, established in 1838 in reaction to the American Peace Society's acceptance of defensive wars, soon rejected all forms of government activity as inevitably coercive. The nihilism of the non-resistants was too extreme for most peace activists to accept, and their radicalism eventually shattered what was already a fragile movement.

Although the non-resistants failed where their counterparts in the temperance, antislavery, and women's movements succeeded, in each case the reformers had followed identical courses. By 1840, the ability to organize had shaped each cause, allowing coalitions to develop and dissolve, replaced by new associations.

Perfectionists within each reform movement had assumed that their organizational capacities permitted them to eschew coalition. Men and women of less rigid temperament meanwhile believed that their compromises strengthened their movements. In every case, the ability to organize and the prospect of success that association held forth encouraged New Englanders to participate in the work in which institutions were engaged.

Stewards to the World

In the early 1830s, as radical opponents of slavery began to organize, one activist, Samuel E. Sewall, an ardent abolitionist, enthusiastically predicted that "The whole system of slavery will fall to pieces with a rapidity which will astonish."[36] Not everyone shared Sewall's specific prognostication, of course, or his overriding concern for the plight of the bondsman. In their own ways, however, thousands of men and women across New England shared something else with Sewall—a zeal for activism born of recent successes, a confidence that good deeds would be productive.

If hindsight reveals the excessive optimism of Sewall's expectations of immediate success, his enthusiasm and that of dedicated men and women across New England is nonetheless understandable. What were the limits to charitable accomplishment? Where were the boundaries curbing philanthropists and reformers? No one could yet be sure, and as they basked in the glow of unprecedented achievements, charitable New Englanders felt they had every reason to believe that unimaginable accomplishments lay in front of them.

Opportunity was combining with an ingrained sense of obligation to produce a determination in thousands of New Englanders to assist those who were in need, or seemed to be. This determination might grip some who came within its reach much more urgently than others. It might seem disingenuous when combined with self-interested motivations. It might convert some into self-righteous moralists whom later generations would dismiss as bluenoses and busybodies. And it might turn men and women who disagreed over the priority of specific causes and the wisdom of various tactics against each other. Yet whatever the particular form this determination took, it retained one constant characteristic: it stimulated men and women to act. As Dorothea Dix wrote to a friend sometime in the mid-1820s:

> We are not sent into this world mainly to enjoy the loveliness therein; nor to sit us down in passive ease; no, we were sent here for action; the soul that seeks to do the will of God with a pure heart fervently, does not yield to the lethargy of ease.[37]

There had been a time when apologies made sense, but as the founders of a tract society in Rupert, Vermont, proclaimed in 1819, "The present is a day of Societies, and through their instrumentality much good is flowing to mankind."[38] Once institutions provided the chance to accomplish great things, those who acknowledged an obligation to others ignored the opportunity only at their own peril.

This was a message civic-minded New Englanders were ready to hear. Life in all its facets seemed filled with possibilities, not pitfalls. A continent was opening up, and who could doubt that it was America's destiny to conquer it?[39] International markets promised profits, and technological advances, especially in textiles and transportation, offered the means to capitalize on such opportunities.[40] It was even possible to find good news in crises: the Panic of 1819 shook New England's economy severely, but its effects were only temporary, and the economy was expanding again within a year or two.[41] Public-spirited New Englanders had the resources to act and the confidence to accept major charitable undertakings. They believed, moreover, that their good fortune constituted a divine challenge.

"As every man hath received the gift," the apostle Paul had enjoined in his first epistle, "even so minister the same one to another, as good stewards of the manifold grace of God." Ever since John Winthrop's time, New Englanders had recognized this responsibility to be God's "Stewards . . . dispenceing his guifts to man by man."[42] "By the Bible we are taught," Luther Baker instructed in Warren, Rhode Island, in 1806, "that what we possess, is not our own, that we are merely stewards of it, and that a day is unalterably determined on, when we must surrender an account of our stewardship."[43] "Can we claim to be disciples of Christ," Jedidiah Morse asked in 1807, "and yet refuse to bestow a little of that property, which he has entrusted to our management?"[44]

Only the awareness of need and the ability to imagine solutions to problems now limited philanthropy, or so it seemed. Domestic concerns continued to dominate, but nowhere was beyond reach.

At the same time that New Englanders had begun to organize actively in the 1780s to meet their own charitable needs, Americans had begun to claim their place in world affairs, both diplomatic and commercial. Once the new nation's representatives signed the Treaty of Paris in September 1783, thus winning from the British crown an acknowledgment of the former colonies' independence, American diplomats began to build sovereign ties with foreign governments. Meanwhile, American merchants, freed at last from the restraints of the British colonial system, quickly began to construct commercial relationships, primarily with trading houses in western Europe, but also in the Far East. The new nation's emergence as a full partner in world diplomacy and trade, and the development at home of organized charity, spawned a variety of initiatives after 1810 to promote world evangelism and international humanitarian relief.

Encouraged after 1807 by growing confidence in orthodox circles that the millennium was at hand, a small group of divinity students at Andover Theological Seminary pledged in 1810 to go abroad as missionaries. The immediate product of their resolution was the formation in June of that year of the American Board of Commissioners for Foreign Missions; the eventual result was a missionary program that reached out to the American frontier, the Indian subcontinent, the Hawaiian Islands, the Near East, the Far East, and Africa.[45]

Humanitarian activities, as well, began to reach across international boundaries. In the seventeenth century, New Englanders confronted with little poverty at home had sometimes answered more distant appeals for help. In the 1810s and 1820s, New England's interest in such causes was renewed. When a fire in 1816 destroyed much of St. John's, Newfoundland, Boston merchants responded immediately by chartering a ship, loading it with supplies, and sending it out through winter storms within a few days of receiving word of the catastrophe. Nine years later, Bostonians responded once again when a forest fire in New Brunswick destroyed the homes of 1,500 Canadians. New Englanders also cooperated with contributors from New York, Philadelphia, and elsewhere to mount the most sustained such American effort prior to the 1840s, a campaign throughout most of the 1820s to support democratic Greek forces in their rebellion against their Turkish rulers.[46]

There had been a message in the charitable initiatives of the late eighteenth and early nineteenth centuries, a lesson that succeeding generations of New Englanders took to heart. As missionaries carried the gospel thousands of miles from home, as philanthropists gathered contributions for men and women in need both abroad and at home, and as the agents of reform causes tried to persuade their neighbors of the evils of slavery, intemperance, sexual bias, and war, New Englanders told themselves that any charitable cause was possible now that they had the means to realize it. Their ability to organize made the crucial difference.

In the story of the good Samaritan, the extent of the Christian duty of charity had hinged on the definition of the word "neighbor." "Who is my neighbor?" the lawyer had asked, and the parable's admonition had determined the reach of Christian obligation thereafter. Compassionate New Englanders had never been ignorant of their responsibilities to relieve men and women in need, nor had they ever denied that, at least in theory, this neighborly obligation ultimately extended to all humanity. Now that more was possible than ever before, the whole world was New England's neighborhood.

Appendix One

Charitable Motivations and Historical Writing

CHARITY HAS ATTRACTED the attention of historians of colonial, early-national, and antebellum America for generations. Perhaps because surviving primary sources are both plentiful and informative, scores of
scholars have addressed the subject. The resulting literature is substantial and
diverse, comprising hundreds of books, dissertations, and articles. Although
this volume is not primarily intended to be a synthesis of existing scholarship,
it would not have been possible without extensive prior work on the history
of American mutualism, humanitarianism, evangelism, and reform as well as
on such related subjects as the religious life of New England; moral philosophy and the New England mind; commerce, industry, and the economic
development of the region; and public poor relief.

Considering the daunting quantity of this writing, it would be remarkable
not to find conflicting interpretations of the role of charity in American life.
In fact, stormy debates have swept across the literature repeatedly, especially
since the 1950s. If controversy is a sign of historiographical vigor, then the
scholarship on charity is the picture of health.

The quantity and variety of charity's historiography notwithstanding, the
nub of most recent controversies is easy to summarize: motivations. Beginning in the late eighteenth century, why did so many men, women, and
children choose to share their time, energy, and money with needy neighbors
and strangers? Answers to this question have taken many different forms, but
the issue itself has recurred time and again, controlling the scholarly discussion of the history of charity in America before the Civil War at the cost of
ignoring almost every other potentially fruitful line of inquiry.

It is hardly surprising that motivations have commanded so much of the
attention of historians of American charity. Before the Civil War thoughtful
Americans were, themselves, intensely concerned about the subject. Six-
teenth- and seventeenth-century reformed theology and eighteenth-century

moral philosophy alike had called on faithful and informed philanthropists to check their hearts for the sincerity of their compassion. Who could read the systematic writings of John Calvin and William Ames, the Earl of Shaftesbury and Francis Hutcheson, and fail to conclude that charity's efficacy for the benefactor, and even for the beneficiary, depended on the presence of genuine altruism?

Historians who have tried to trace the charitable consequences of selflessness, self-interest, and selfishness have thus followed the lead of the men and women they were studying, reflecting their sources in their scholarship. It is no exaggeration to claim that much writing on charitable motivations since the 1950s unwittingly derives less from modern psychology than from the thought of the theologians and philosophers who set the agenda for colonial, early-national, and antebellum Americans. Certainly, recent scholarly debates over charitable motivations have echoed the somewhat archaic arguments and intellectual categories of these theologians and philosophers.

In the tradition of earlier debates, modern scholarship on charitable motivations has wrestled with two dichotomies: the compassionate versus the selfish and the sacred versus the secular. Although statisticians insist that a small, finite number limits the possible permutations of two pairs, historians subtly shading their interpretations have managed to combine these two antinomies in dozens of ways.

In the introduction to this book I briefly mentioned my reservations with the two most prominent recent explanations for the emergence of organized charity, the "social control" approach and the identification of the development of certain kinds of institutions with evangelical Protestantism. Although each of these schools of interpretation illuminates some aspects of the great postrevolutionary transformation in charitable thought and practice, neither, it seems to me, is able to account for this process in all its complexity.

"Social control" is a slippery term. Some authors use it expansively to describe any movement to buttress the social order against threats to its stability. More strident analysts employ the phrase more narrowly, incorporating in it the specific charge that nineteenth-century philanthropists and reformers were cynical and malevolent oppressors of the poor.

Historiographical discussions of the social-control interpretation ordinarily take up the story in 1954, when John R. Bodo and Charles C. Cole, Jr., each published a monograph on the civic doctrines of antebellum northern Protestantism.[1] Both authors characterized humanitarianism, evangelism, and reform as conservative social activism intended to cure the disorder and instability that religious pluralism, intemperance, migration both foreign and domestic, and other worrisome developments had visited on the United

States. Three years after Bodo and Cole, in 1957 Clifford S. Griffin brought out "Religious Benevolence as Social Control, 1815–1860,"[2] the first important report of his research on "trusteeship" in America. In this article and the subsequent book it heralded, *Their Brothers' Keepers: Moral Stewardship in the United States, 1815–1865,* Griffin painted a sinister picture of the purposes underlying benevolence and reform. The trustees about whom he wrote— that is, the organizers and supporters of the most prominent and powerful American humanitarian and reform associations—had "formed societies to make other people behave."[3] As far as Griffin was concerned, there was nothing selfless or compassionate about antebellum philanthropy or reform. Missionary, temperance, abolition, and other associations served only the selfish interests of their organizers by repressing their beneficiaries.

Since Bodo, Cole, and Griffin, most scholars of every school of interpretation have conceded that the social control thesis contains at least a kernel of truth. Who can deny that temperance, Sabbatarian, and peace societies, for instance, sought to transform the conduct of their clients? Such accounts of nineteenth-century charity ignored important aspects of the story and confused others, however, and they received at best a mixed reception. Although many social-control writers recognized a duty to look at institutional activities, at least in passing, it was easier to focus on public rhetoric than on private conduct. All too often, scholars allowed a selective reading of a limited number of sources to shape their interpretations. This was not surprising, because many charitable activities did not conform readily to social-control analysis. How did the Massachusetts Humane Society, for example, repress its beneficiaries by informing the public about modern resuscitation techniques and stationing lighthouses, lifeboats, and rescue huts along the coastline? Other initiatives that unquestionably aimed to mold behavior—for example, the temperance and peace movements—developed not only to control society's lower orders, as Griffin and others correctly showed, but also to monitor the behavior of the "respectable" classes.

The tendency of many social-control scholars to blur or ignore the distinctions among charitable motivations, purposes, and outcomes has been as troubling as their propensity to overlook inconvenient aspects of their story.[4] Too many writers have assumed, for instance, that the impulses underlying temperance reform must have been as selfish as, in their view, the movement was repressive. In order to make such an argument, historians need to demonstrate that contemporary activists felt that temperance reform (or evangelism, or medical aid to the poor, or other assistance programs) was not in the best interests of their clients. As long as charitable New Englanders genuinely believed that others would benefit from their efforts, then historians must recognize the good intentions of the philanthropists, no matter what they may think of the programs.

By the same token, scholars run a risk whenever they assume that the results of a program necessarily reveal the motivations underlying it. If New England philanthropists had accomplished precisely what they set out to do, their success would have been remarkable. All too often, the consequences of their initiatives were unintended. Scholars need to distinguish between the immediate, conscious purposes of institutional activities and their larger, sometimes accidental social functions. Extrapolating from Karl Marx, some social-control writers have contended, for example, that organized charity dowsed the flames of social and economic dissatisfaction among the poor and oppressed.[5] Perhaps. But even if this analysis is correct, it is important to recognize that by itself such an outcome does not reveal the objectives of contemporary philanthropists, who may or may not have had social pacification in mind.

Since *Their Brothers' Keepers,* no author has expressed skepticism of philanthropists and reformers quite as profound as Griffin's, but other major books and articles, including works by Charles I. Foster, David J. Rothman, Raymond Mohl, John K. Alexander, Gary Nash, and Paul S. Boyer, have rallied with him under the banner of social control.[6] *Render Them Submissive: Responses to Poverty in Philadelphia, 1760–1800,* Alexander's colorfully titled study of the bickering and self-serving philanthropists of the City of Brotherly Love, for example, depicts a developing metropolis increasingly plagued by poverty as well as social cleavages both within the propertied class and between it and the poor. In Alexander's hands, the efforts of the wealthy to control the poor were a reasonable, but profoundly self-serving, response to growing social crisis. Nash's essay, "The Failure of Female Factory Labor in Colonial Boston,"[7] suggests that the charitable rhetoric of the founders of the Society for Encouraging Industry and Employing the Poor concealed a more suspect plan to convert Boston's poor into a proletarian class, one easily exploited by aspiring industrialists eager to pierce the skyline with factory smokestacks.

Such studies probably tell us as much about their authors as about their subjects. Certainly, many of the more strident contributors to the social-control school have been deeply influenced both by the recent misadventures of modern government anti-poverty programs and by the acerbic comments of such harsh critics of these efforts as Richard Cloward and Frances Fox Piven.[8] Social-control analysts have brought a healthy skepticism to the study of charity (in itself, a useful counterbalance to other, more credulous writing on the subject), but too often their dismay, even disgust, with organized philanthropy and those who undertook it has clouded their judgment, leading them to distort the objectives and dismiss the genuine accomplishments of philanthropists and reformers.

The most important contribution of the social-control school has been to direct attention to the self-interest that was undeniably a part of colonial, Revolutionary, and early-national charity. Perhaps the school's greatest shortcoming, however, at least until recently, has been its inability to understand that self-interest played a reasonable, necessary, and indeed desirable role in the practice of charity before the Civil War. It is an encouraging sign that several scholars have recently tried to combine social-control analyses with other explanations for philanthropy. In her study of *Welfare and the Poor in the Nineteenth-Century City: Philadelphia, 1800–1854,* for example, Priscilla Ferguson Clement offered evidence that a "genuine concern for the poor," a fear that these same poor "might take unfair advantage of welfare programs," and parsimony all shaped the development of public relief initiatives.[9] Other scholars who have tried to combine social-control and other theories include M. J. Heale, Carol S. Lasser, and Charles E. Rosenberg.[10] By augmenting social-control theories with other explanations for organized charity, such studies open an important direction for further work.

Studies emphasizing connections between orthodox theology and organized charity did not develop in direct response to the rise of the social-control thesis; their immediate target was an earlier school of interpretation that emphasized humanitarianism's secular, Enlightenment ancestry.[11] It is reasonable to conclude, however, that the pessimistic excesses of Griffin, Bodo, Cole, and other critics of philanthropy gave encouragement to anyone who offered a more optimistic interpretation. Religion was not the only safe harbor for scholars troubled by the cynicism of social control. Perry Miller argued plausibly in *The Life of the Mind in America: From the Revolution to the Civil War* that national pride was the principal value underlying the rise of the missionary movement in the early nineteenth century.[12] Since the 1950s, though, interpretations emphasizing the role of religion, usually with orthodoxy at their center, have mounted the strongest challenge to social control.

The modern era in the religious interpretations of philanthropy began in 1928 with the publication of *The Rise of the Missionary Spirit in America, 1790–1815* by Oliver W. Elsbree. At the heart of the missionary impulse, Elsbree believed, was the doctrine of "disinterested benevolence." Elsbree correctly understood that in the late eighteenth century Samuel Hopkins, building on the theories of his mentor, Jonathan Edwards, had constructed around the idea of "disinterested benevolence" an important justification for good works. Elsbree failed to recognize, however, that neither the term "disinterested benevolence" nor many facets of the complex of the ideas bound up in Hopkins's formulation of the doctrine was unique to the "New Divinity" that the Newport minister and his students propounded. "Disinterested benevolence" was an important concept in eighteenth-century moral philosophy, and although definitions of it varied, writers of most religious persuasions affirmed some form of the belief. One could not safely assume, as Elsbree apparently did, that anyone who employed the term was a follower of Samuel Hopkins.[13]

Writers who have followed in Elsbree's footsteps have generally either misinterpreted, disparaged, or ignored the activities of liberal philanthropists. Alan Heimert's practice of selectively reading "through and beyond" the lines of eighteenth-century tracts and sermons, for example, led him to conclude that Jonathan Edwards's Old Light antagonists could not possibly have been candid when they professed selfless as well as self-interested motives for their charity. In a remarkable series of unguarded moments, according to Heimert's account, religious liberals like Jonathan Mayhew and Charles Chauncy lied about their purported altruism at the same time they publicly conceded their essentially selfish reasons for charity. Heimert went astray because—in keeping with Edwards but in opposition to most other eighteenth-century moral philosophers—he refused to concede that self-interest and altruism might coexist.[14] Gary Nash agreed with Heimert, although he apparently did not read very deeply in contemporary theological and philosophical literature when he wrote about prerevolutionary Boston, New York, and Philadelphia. Heimert's conclusions formed much of the scholarly substructure of Nash's claim that "a naked appeal to the pockets of the affluent" underlay certain important charitable efforts in mid-eighteenth-century Boston.[15]

An accurate account of the role of religious contributions to charitable thought and practice prior to the Civil War needs to begin by recognizing that Americans of all religious persuasions accepted and practiced the virtue. Outside New England, the majority of charitable Americans were evangelicals of some stripe—but so were most Americans, charitable or not. Indeed, even in Rochester, a center of western New York's "Burned-Over District," Unitarians joined with other denominations in many local women's charitable associations.[16] At one time, in recounting the successes of many early philanthropic causes, scholars gave undue credit to unevangelical contributors, especially Unitarians and Quakers.[17] Somehow in recent years the pendulum has swung too far in the other direction. We need only look at the work of such scholars as Daniel T. McColgan, Daniel Walker Howe, Sydney V. James, and Mack Thompson, to name a few examples, to remind ourselves that unevangelical Christians really did play a significant part in the philanthropic life of America before the Civil War.[18]

Selective reading, a primitive use of psychology, and, in an unhappy application of Occam's razor, a fatal failing for simple answers to complex problems—these are the shortcomings of too many accounts of organized charity published since the early 1950s. Curiously, many of the sturdiest additions to the literature on the subject have been the by-products of research in other areas. The most noteworthy of these contributions are the work of ethnic and women's historians.

Because their primary interests lay elsewhere—usually in determining how their subject groups developed a sense of community or cohesiveness— ethnic and women's historians have treated charitable and other voluntary organizations as analytical tools, not as focal points for study. Half a century ago, Oscar Handlin showed in *Boston's Immigrants* how newcomers to the city used a variety of voluntary associations to acclimate themselves to their new surroundings.[19] Ever since, it has been an article of faith among most ethnic historians that the importance of these institutions was largely functional— that is, as agencies around which communities coalesced. In this view, the specific purpose of an organization was of less interest than its larger role as a community focal point. Studies of Germans in Milwaukee, Italians in Chicago, German and eastern European Jewish immigrants to New York City, and a variety of groups in Lawrence, Massachusetts, agree, in consequence, that charitable organizations were important—but no more important for the purpose of acclimatization than such other agencies as newspapers, churches, and burial societies.[20]

Women's historians have similarly attempted to unravel the connection between female associations and the development of the antebellum women's rights movement. Keith Melder and Barbara J. Berg, among others, have argued that early women's benevolent associations were the direct ancestors of the first women's rights organizations.[21] Further work by Nancy Cott, Suzanne Lebsock, and Anne M. Boylan, to name three effective revisionists, has called into question all claims of such a lineal relationship.[22]

Whether or not the suffrage movement emerged from earlier organizations, though, there is no doubt that nineteenth-century women drew strength and experience from their associations. Female organizations of various kinds, including schools, colleges, social clubs, and cultural institutions as well as charitable societies allowed women to serve in management and leadership roles that were ordinarily forbidden them as long as there were men present. And women who gathered together regularly on their own might derive confidence in their abilities as well as an important understanding of the relationship between women as a group and the rest of society. Perhaps because many women's historians believed that the movement for independence and suffrage relied on different and more powerful imperatives than altruism, they often found it easy to ignore or dismiss the motivations that scholars of organized charity typically cited.

What is clear from the work of these ethnic and women's historians is the desirability of putting behind us reductionist arguments over charitable motivations in favor of an examination of institutional processes and their consequences. Ethnic and women's historians felt free to skip over the matter of charitable motivations, or to recognize the variety of purposes underlying association, because the organizations they studied were merely small pieces of other stories they hoped to tell. There is a useful example to follow in the functionalist approach of these scholars to understanding the work of antebellum voluntary associations. Historians unpersuaded by attempts to find the roots of organized charity in one or another single, simple set of motivations should not feel abashed to conclude that the complicated network of institutions that arose following the Revolution had equally involved origins.

Appendix Two

Charitable New Englanders

WHO SUPPORTED charitable organizations in the colonial, revolutionary, and postrevolutionary periods? As central as this question is to
many accounts of the subject, no one has fully answered it. A glance at the
rapid diffusion of organized charity throughout New England after the Revolution may explain scholars' failure to address the issue systematically: by the
late 1810s approximately 1,500 institutions, located in about 500 towns,
relied on the participation of tens of thousands of citizens. Across the United
States as a whole, tens of thousands more Americans subscribed to similar
associations by 1820. Even the task of selecting a truly representative sample
of contributors, institutions, and communities is formidable; it goes without
saying that a comprehensive survey of so vast a group is out of the question.

Incomplete though research is on the subject, it is nevertheless sufficient
to refute the two most common explanations of the origins of organized
charity, at least for New England. While many studies have confirmed, for
example, that charitable New Englanders were ordinarily a bit more affluent
than most of the rest of their neighbors, they have invariably failed to
demonstrate that social-control aspirations underlay their activities. Most
mutualists in such towns as Pomfret, Connecticut, Providence, Rhode Island,
and Salem, Massachusetts, came from their communities' propertied classes,
but within this broad swath associations drew both on local leaders and
residents of very modest means.[1] Indeed, Steven C. Bullock has shown that
wealthy community leaders yielded control of Boston's masonic lodges to
relatively obscure artisans and retailers by the early 1790s.[2] Fiduciary organizations relied more heavily than the mutualists on the affluent and the
prominent, but these associations also turned for support to much more
obscure citizens, men and women of quite limited resources. Peter R. Virgadamo's study of the Scots' Charitable Society between 1740 and 1775

reveals that although wealthy Bostonians led the association, most of its members came from the town's "middle ranks." Their subscriptions, Virgadamo concluded, "represented altruism," not social control.[3] To be sure, some postrevolutionary organizations relied more heavily than the Scots on contributors of means. But even the most prominent associations drew on shopkeepers, innkeepers, and artisans for a share of their supporters. As Robert F. Dalzell, Jr., has concluded, as late as the 1840s wide participation was a hallmark of charity in Boston: "Projects benefiting the community were regularly designed to involve as many people as possible."[4]

Evidence on the religious affiliations of charitable New Englanders offers no more support for the most common alternative thesis: that organized charity grew out of evangelical teachings or the effects of the Second Great Awakening. Once again, eastern Massachusetts provides the most striking refutation. Although a small number of missionary, tract, and education societies here restricted their ranks either to Calvinists or Baptists, each had a liberal Unitarian counterpart. Thus such orthodox or Baptist associations as the Massachusetts Missionary Society, the Massachusetts Baptist Missionary Society,[5] the Massachusetts Society for Promoting Christian Knowledge, and the American Education Society worked at cross-purposes with the Evangelical Missionary Society, the Massachusetts Society for Promoting Christian Knowledge, Piety, and Charity, and the Society for Promoting Theological Education, each made up largely or entirely of Unitarians. Other religious organizations—notably the Society for Propagating the Gospel among the Indians and Others in North America and the Massachusetts Bible Society— drew impartially on the members of various communions, both evangelical and liberal. Meanwhile, reform and humanitarian initiatives found supporters among both the evangelicals and the liberals. In both Concord and Dedham after 1814, for instance, more Calvinists than Unitarians subscribed to local auxiliaries of the Massachusetts Society for the Suppression of Intemperance, but members of both groups joined in force.[6] In Boston, on the other hand, after 1815 the officers of the Boston Female Asylum were predominantly Unitarian.[7] As Anne M. Boylan has remarked, an organization's denominational profile was typically a reflection of local religious circumstances.[8] In fact, it would be surprising if a plurality of the supporters of most humanitarian and reform organizations in Boston were *not* Unitarian, since the liberals made up the town's largest single denomination.[9]

If charitable New Englanders were neither especially wealthy nor notably evangelical, then what were they? Surveys of organized charity in Hartford in 1799 and in Boston in 1754, 1771, 1798, and 1821 reveal who subscribed to organized charity—a virtual cross-section of each community's taxpayers.

A profile of the men who supported the Hartford Charitable Society and St. John's Lodge of Freemasons confirms Boylan's contention that charitable organizations tended to reflect the communities they served. Available records of the four religious societies located in the town's two central precincts are too incomplete for statistical study, but they make it clear that members of each church—two Congregationalist, one Episcopal, and one Baptist—belonged to both charitable organizations.[10] Careful studies of local philanthropists in the late 1790s further reveal that the Charitable Society, in particular, drew a representative sampling of supporters from almost every occupational group and tax-assessment level in Hartford. Only farmers were significantly underrepresented. Surprisingly, the Freemasons drew members more narrowly from the town's leaders than did the Charitable Society. Like the Charitable Society, though, the masonic lodge received significant support from almost every wealth and occupational stratum in Hartford. (See tables 1a and 1b.)

Boston's charitable organizations were less representative individually than Hartford's, but Hub residents established so many organizations so early that as a group their societies encompassed the town's diversity by the start of the nineteenth century. By and large, the colonial era's organizations were peripheral to the lives of most Bostonians; as late as the 1770s, residents rarely turned to voluntary associations unless they questioned whether the town as a whole would serve their needs through public assistance, church-based relief, or private alms. Thus, many of colonial Boston's organized charities served groups—Scotsmen, Irishmen, Episcopalians, mariners—that were clearly distinguished from the community at large by nationality, religion, or occupation. Of these, only the Episcopalians were especially affluent. Tax records for the 1750s have not survived, but a high proportion of the Boston members of the Society for Encouraging Industry and Employing the Poor also followed prominent callings as merchants and professionals.[11]

By the early 1800s, though, hundreds—even thousands—of Bostonians were caught up in the passion for organizing that soon resulted in an extensive network of voluntary associations. Although many associations drew the bulk of their supporters from various narrow segments of the town's populace, as a group they served almost the entire community. African-Americans joined the Prince Hall Lodge and the African Society; Baptists subscribed to the Baptist Auxiliary Education Society; white artisans entered the Massachusetts Charitable Mechanic Association and many of the private masonic lodges; women underwrote the Boston Female Asylum and the Boston Cent Society. Aside from day laborers and transients, it is hard to think of a single significant group without organizational outlets.

It is the diversity of membership, both within individual associations and among them as a group, that undermines the most common theories about their origins. For instance, although a few of postrevolutionary Boston's charitable agencies drew primarily on the richest segment of the community and resembled class-bound associations, at least to a degree, even the wealthiest still relied in part on members of slender means and modest occupations. Nine percent of the members of Boston's most affluent charitable association, the Boston Society for Employing the Poor, were assessed for property worth $500 in 1821 and eighteen percent were artisans or petty proprietors. The Massachusetts Humane Society drew on craftsmen, shopkeepers, and clerks for one-quarter of its subscribers the same year. And more than one-third of the supporters of the Boston Asylum for Indigent Boys were either mechanics or shopkeepers. Other societies bore no resemblance at all to agencies for social control—taxpayers assessed for property worth $500 or less made up between one-third and three-fifths of the participants in such associations as the Howard Benevolent Society, the Auxiliary Education Society, and the Baptist Auxiliary Education Society. (See tables 5a–d and 5f–i.)

Over time, some organizations even changed their composition, drawing their members from different segments of their communities. The Boston Marine Society, for example, largely an association of active sea captains in 1754 and 1771, became much more an organization of settled merchants by 1798. Two decades later in 1821, though, the society had returned to the sea, as sixty percent of its members identified themselves as ships' captains. (See tables 2, 3c, 4c, and 5f.)

It should hardly seem surprising that a large segment of Boston's population participated in organized charity. Voluntary association as a technique was available to everyone. Even cultural institutions, often portrayed as Brahmin enclaves, were remarkably diverse. Although some organizations, notably the Boston Athenaeum, relied largely on wealthy and socially prominent subscribers, others like the Handel and Haydn Society were composed mostly of artisans and shopkeepers lacking in great resources. (See tables 5e and 5j.)

If neither social control nor evangelical piety was at the root of organized charity, then how and why did it develop? The issue is complicated. No one has proposed a thoroughly persuasive alternative, and an appendix is no place to develop a counter-thesis. The early history of the Massachusetts Humane Society, postrevolutionary New England's first charitable association, provides a clue, however. To build the membership, the organizers went from friend to friend to secure subscribers.[12] Acquaintanceship, not class or religion, was the basis of the Society's growth. Although friends might share certain traits—race, class, sex, occupation, or religion—what was most important was that they knew each other, perhaps as neighbors or classmates or cousins.

Tracing networks of acquaintanceship and relating them to the membership rosters of voluntary organizations is much more complicated than surveying class or religious affiliation for the same ends because researchers need to draw on many more types of evidence: church membership rosters, class lists, town directories, neighborhood maps, genealogies, diaries, and correspondence to name only some of the best sources. Even the most ambitious surveys of acquaintanceship undertaken to date have examined only small clusters of people, often the trustees of prominent associations.[13] The key to understanding the development of these institutions may rest, however, in one of the simplest of questions: who knew whom?

Methodological Note

In preparing tables the following conventions have been used:

1) Tables treat only Hartford or Boston members; members residing elsewhere have not been considered.

2) When possible, contemporary membership lists have been employed. Asterisks (*) indicate that a cumulative list of members has been used; members under consideration joined the association within the decade prior to date of table.

3) Figures in each column are based on the percentage of members' names linked to tax or occupational data.

4) For 1798 and 1821 Boston tables, names have not been included if the town directory indicates that more than one person with the same name lived in Boston.

5) Occupation categories are adapted from Peter R. Knights, *The Plain People of Boston, 1830–1860: A Study in City Growth* (New York, 1971), 149–156.

6) For women's organizations, occupations and tax assesments are for the family's primary earner.

7) Percentages have been rounded off and individual columns may not total 100 percent.

The tables employ the following abbreviations:

AAAS　American Academy of Arts and Sciences
AES　Auxiliary Education Society
AS　African Society

BA	Boston Athenaeum
BAES	Baptist Auxiliary Education Society
BBA	Boston Asylum for Indigent Boys
BCS	British Charitable Society
BD	Boston Dispensary
BECS	Boston Episcable Charitable Society
BFA	Boston Female Asylum
BMS	Boston Marine Society
BSEP	Boston Society for Employing the Poor
BSMRIP	Boston Society for the Moral and Religious Instruction of the Poor
CIS	Charitable Irish Society
CL	Columbian Lodge
HBS	Howard Benevolent Society
HCS	Hartford Charitable Society
HH	Handel and Haydn Society
HMS	Humane Society of the Commonwealth of Massachusetts (Massachusetts Humane Society)
MBS	Massachusetts Bible Society
MCCS	Massachusetts Congregational Charitable Society
MCFS	Massachusetts Charitable Fire Society
MCMA	Massachusetts Charitable Mechanic Association
MCS	Massachusetts Charitable Society
MHS	Massachusetts Historical Society
ML	Massachusetts Lodge
MLL	Mount Lebanon Lodge
MMS	Massachusetts Missionary Society
MPS	Massachusetts Peace Society
MSSI	Massachusetts Society for the Suppression of Intemperance
RSL	Rising Sun Lodge
SAL	St. Andrew's Lodge
SARA	St. Andrew's Royal Arch Chapter
SCS	Scots' Charitable Society
SEIEP	Society for Encouraging Industry and Employing the Poor
SJ-B	St. John's Lodge, Boston
SJ-H	St. John's Lodge, Hartford
SPGNA	Society for Propagating the Gospel among the Indians and Others in North America
SPRA	St. Paul's Royal Arch Charter
WEC	Wednesday Evening Club
1797 Tax	Hartford 1797 Tax List

TABLE 1a. Hartford Tax Assessments, 1797

$	HCS (%)	SJ-H* (%)	1797 Tax (%)
1–20	38	5	39
21–40	8	21	12
41–60	17	11	13
61–80	0	5	3
81–100	27	53	24
100–200	6	0	8
201+	4	5	1
N =	82	87	245
% Linked	58	22	100
Average	$60	$77	$57
Median	$50	$84	$40

TABLE 1b. Hartford Occupations, 1799

	HCS (%)	SJ-H* (%)	Residents, 1799 (%)
Unskilled	0	3	1
Semi-skilled	0	0	0
Skilled	42	16	38
Clerk/sales	0	0	3
Petty prop.	13	10	12
Proprietor	29	48	28
Professional	12	3	11
Corp. official	0	3	1
Gvt. official	2	16	5
Mariner	0	0	1
Honorific	0	0	0
N =	82	87	783
% Linked	62	36	53

SOURCES: Frank D. Andrews, comp., *Directory for the City of Hartford for the Year 1799* (Vineland, N.J., 1910); Hartford Charitable Society Papers, 1792–1871, "List of Members of the Charitable Society, 1797," Connecticut Historical Society; Hartford Tax Assessments, 1797, Connecticut Historical Society; *Constitution and By-Laws of the Grand Lodge of Connecticut: and By-Laws of St. John's Lodge, No. 4, Free and Accepted Masons* (Hartford, 1861), 23–24.

TABLE 2. Boston Occupations, 1754

	BMS* (%)	CIS* (%)	BECS* (%)	SCS* (%)	SEIEP (%)
Unskilled	0	0	0	0	0
Semi-skilled	0	0	0	0	0
Skilled	8	0	0	19	10
Clerk/sales	0	25	0	0	0
Petty prop.	2	25	0	3	11
Proprietor	13	0	71	19	50
Professional	5	0	0	6	14
Corp. official	0	0	0	0	0
Gvt. official	0	0	0	8	1
Mariner	56	25	0	36	0
Honorific	15	25	29	8	14
N =	83	12	10	145	172
% Linked	47	33	70	33	82

SOURCES: *The Constitution and By-Laws of the Charitable Irish Society of Boston* (Boston, 1876), 102–129; *The Constitution and By-Laws of the Scots' Charitable Society of Boston* (Cambridge, Mass., 1878), 105–107; William A. Baker, *A History of the Boston Marine Society, 1742–1967* (Boston, 1968), 318–350; *The Original Constitution of the Boston Episcopal Charitable Society* (Boston, 1834), 22–23; *Whereas it is found by Experience. . . .* (Boston, 1754), 7–12; Thwing Index, Massachusetts Historical Society.

TABLE 3a. Boston Tax Assessments, Mutual, 1771

£	BMS* (%)	MCS* (%)	ML* (%)	RSL, 1772 (%)	SAL* (%)	SARA* (%)
0	27	13	23	18	15	20
1–50	0	7	8	9	13	0
51–100	27	17	8	18	12	7
101–150	23	13	23	9	19	27
151–200	0	20	38	0	23	27
201–300	12	9	0	18	6	7
301–400	4	7	0	9	6	7
401–500	0	4	0	9	2	0
501–1000	4	7	0	9	2	7
1001–1500	4	0	0	0	2	0
1501–5000	0	2	0	0	0	0
N =	70	75	14	18	112	25
% Linked	37	61	93	61	46	60
Average	£156	£219	£113	£210	£160	£175
Median	£96	£145	£133	£150	£120	£132

TABLE 3b. Boston Tax Assessments, Fiduciary, 1771

£	BECS* (%)	CIS* (%)	SCS* (%)	Taxpayers, 1771 (%)
0	13	13	15	0
1–50	0	9	12	18
51–100	0	43	23	28
101–150	13	4	8	15
151–200	0	9	0	11
201–300	0	9	12	8
301–400	0	9	12	4
401–500	13	0	0	4
501–1000	33	0	12	7
1001–1500	13	4	4	2
1501–5000	13	0	4	3
N =	29	77	109	1546
% Linked	52	30	24	†
Average	£806	£160	£328	†
Median	£786	£96	£275	†

†These figures are not available

TABLE 3c. Boston Occupations, Mutual, 1771

	BMS* (%)	MCS* (%)	ML* (%)	RSL, 1772 (%)	SAL* (%)	SARA* (%)
Unskilled	0	0	0	0	0	0
Semi-skilled	0	0	0	0	0	0
Skilled	0	52	9	36	41	15
Clerk/sales	0	0	0	0	1	0
Petty prop.	3	16	0	9	8	0
Proprietor	10	25	55	27	15	46
Professional	3	2	9	18	1	8
Corp. officer	0	0	0	0	0	0
Gvt. officer	0	0	0	9	0	0
Mariner	84	0	0	0	28	15
Honorific	0	2	27	0	6	15
N =	70	75	14	18	112	25
% Linked	44	41	79	61	76	52

TABLE 3d. Boston Occupations, Fiduciary, 1771

	BECS* (%)	CIS* (%)	SCS* (%)
Unskilled	0	0	0
Semi-skilled	0	0	6
Skilled	5	24	47
Clerk/sales	0	0	0
Petty prop.	0	8	9
Proprietor	77	12	18
Professional	0	8	3
Corp. official	0	0	0
Gvt. official	5	0	0
Mariner	0	48	12
Honorific	13	0	6
N =	29	77	117
% Linked	76	32	29

SOURCES: William A. Baker, *A History of the Boston Marine Society, 1742–1967* (Boston, 1968), 318–350; *Charter and By-Laws of the Massachusetts Charitable Society of Boston* (Boston, 1907), 27–29; *The History, Charter and By-Laws of Massachusetts Lodge* (Boston, 1863), 24; *History of Saint John's Lodge of Boston* (Boston, 1917), 61; *The Lodge of Saint Andrew and the Massachusetts Grand Lodge* (Boston, 1870), 232–234; *By-Laws of St. Andrew's Royal Arch Chapter* (Boston, 1859), 37–52; *Original Constitution of the Boston Episcopal Charitable Society* (Boston, 1834), 23–24; *The Constitution and By-Laws of the Charitable Irish Society of Boston* (Boston, 1876), 102–129; *The Constitution and By-Laws of the Scots' Charitable Society of Boston* (Cambridge, Mass., 1878), 109–110; Bettye Hobbs Pruitt, ed., *The Massachusetts Tax Valuation List of 1771* (Boston, 1978), 2–46; James A. Henretta, "Economic Development and Social Structure in Colonial Boston," *William and Mary Quarterly* 22:82 (1965); Thwing Index, Massachusetts Historical Society.

TABLE 4a. Boston Tax Assessments, Mutual, 1798

$	AS, 1802 (%)	BMS* (%)	CL* (%)	MCMA, 1800 (%)	MCS* (%)	ML* (%)	SAL* (%)	SARA* (%)
0	0	0	0	0	0	0	0	0
1–500	100	2	0	5	0	7	0	0
501–1,000	0	11	0	15	6	0	15	20
1,001–5,000	0	55	100	59	56	27	69	80
5,001–10,000	0	9	0	16	19	40	7	0
10,001–50,000	0	20	0	4	19	27	7	0
50,001–100,000	0	2	0	0	0	0	0	0
100,000+	0	0	0	0	0	0	0	0
N =	35	134	25	187	28	47	24	44
% Linked	9	33	16	50	57	32	54	34
Average	$367	$6,807	$1,600	$3,463	$6,442	$6,414	$4,008	$2,210
Median	$300	$3,500	$1,550	$2,400	$3,500	$6,000	$2,750	$1,800

TABLE 4b. Boston Tax Assessments, Fiduciary, 1798

$	BD, 1797 (%)	BECS, 1805 (%)	BFA, 1801 (%)	MCFS, 1800 (%)	MCCS, 1798 (%)	HMS, 1798 (%)	MMS, 1799 (%)	SCS, 1800 (%)	SPGNA, 1798 (%)
0	0	0	0	0	0	0	0	0	0
1–500	2	2	1	3	0	1	0	0	0
501–1,000	0	0	5	5	0	2	0	0	0
1,001–5,000	31	40	37	55	22	30	33	43	7
5,001–10,000	27	27	25	19	0	21	67	29	29
10,001–50,000	38	31	31	18	55	44	0	29	57
50,001–100,000	3	0	3	0	22	2	0	0	7
100,000+	0	0	0	0	0	0	0	0	0
$N =$	111	118	299	204	12	226	38	23	36
% Linked	58	38	35	46	75	56	5	30	39
Average	$12,130	$9,007	$10,571	$6,507	$26,780	$10,833	$5,500	$8,221	$18,912
Median	$8,000	$6,000	$6,500	$2,400	$20,000	$10,050	$5,500	$5,700	$14,272

TABLE 4C. Boston Occupations, Mutual, 1798

	AS, 1802 (%)	BMS* (%)	CL* (%)	MCMA, 1800 (%)	MCS* (%)	ML* (%)	SaL* (%)	SARA* (%)
Unskilled	0	0	0	0	0	0	0	0
Semi-skilled	0	1	8	0	0	0	7	3
Skilled	0	8	62	96	53	14	29	40
Clerk/sales	0	1	0	0	0	7	0	0
Petty prop.	0	5	15	2	18	14	29	27
Proprietor	0	32	0	2	12	46	21	23
Professional	0	5	0	0	0	7	7	3
Corp. off.	0	1	0	0	0	4	0	0
Gvt. off.	0	4	0	0	6	4	0	0
Mariner	0	37	15	0	0	4	7	3
Honorific	0	4	0	0	12	0	0	0
N =	35	176	25	177	28	47	17	46
% Linked	0	52	52	99	61	60	82	65

TABLE 4d. Boston Occupations, Fiduciary, 1798

	BD, 1797 (%)	BECS, 1805 (%)	BFA, 1801 (%)	MCFS, 1800 (%)	MCCS, 1798 (%)	HMS, 1798 (%)	MMS, 1799 (%)	SCS, 1800 (%)	SPGNA, 1798 (%)
Unskilled	0	0	0	1	0	0	0	0	0
Semi-skilled	1	0	0	3	0	2	0	8	0
Skilled	10	11	8	29	0	14	33	31	5
Clerk/sales	0	2	2	0	0	0	0	0	0
Petty prop.	14	7	16	26	0	5	67	23	0
Proprietor	51	53	34	21	33	37	0	15	16
Professional	10	15	24	12	42	17	0	0	37
Corp. off.	0	2	1	0	0	1	0	0	0
Gvt. off.	10	0	5	4	17	12	0	8	26
Mariner	4	7	7	1	0	1	0	8	0
Honorific	0	4	4	3	8	10	0	8	16
N =	111	118	299	204	12	228	4	23	21
% Linked	64	47	44	76	100	71	75	43	90

SOURCES: "Particular or Sub-Division List of All Lands, Lots, Buildings, and Wharves, Being within the Town of Boston," A Report of the Record Commissioners of the City of Boston (Boston, 1876–1905), 22:1–442; John West, The Boston Directory (Boston, 1798); Laws of the African Society (Boston, 1802), 7; The Constitution and Laws of the Boston Marine Society (Boston, 1802), 23–42; John T. Heard, A Historical Account of the Columbian Lodge of Free and Accepted Masons of Boston, Mass. (Boston, 1856), 546–576; Constitution of the Associated Mechanics and Manufacturers of Massachusetts (Boston, 1800), 15–24; Charter and By-Laws of the Massachusetts Charitable Society of Boston (Boston, 1907), 31; The History, Charter and By-Laws of Massachusetts Lodge (Boston, 1863), 25; The Lodge of Saint Andrew and the Massachusetts Grand Lodge (Boston, 1870), 237; By-Laws of St. Andrew's Royal Arch Chapter (Boston, 1859), 37–52; Institution of the Boston Dispensary for the Medical Relief of the Poor (Boston, 1797), 10–14; Laws and Regulations of the Boston Episcopal Charitable Society (Boston, 1805), 12–14; The Institution of the Boston Female Asylum (Boston, 1801), 11–15; Act of Incorporation, Laws and Regulations . . . of the Massachusetts Charitable Fire Society (Boston, 1800), 11–18; Account of the Massachusetts Congregational Charitable Society (Boston, 1815), 9–10; William Walter, A Discourse Delivered Before the Humane Society (Boston, 1798), 42–47; To all who are desirous of the Spread of the Gospel of our Lord Jesus Christ . . . (Boston, 1799), 4; Rules and Regulations of the Scots' Charitable Society (Boston, 1800), 8; Peter Thacher, Brief Account of the Society for Propagating the Gospel Among the Indians and Others in North America (Boston, 1798), 7.

TABLE 5a. Boston Tax Assessments, Mutual, 1821

$	BMS* (%)	MCMA* (%)	MCS* (%)	MLL* (%)	SAL* (%)	SARA* (%)	SJ-B* (%)	SPRA* (%)
0	0	9	0	14	0	14	11	3
1–500	41	22	0	41	44	24	44	44
501–1000	9	12	25	27	0	5	11	21
1001–5000	36	44	50	14	33	33	27	28
5001–10,000	0	10	25	4	11	24	4	3
10,001–50,000	9	3	0	0	11	0	2	3
50,001–100,000	4	0	0	0	0	0	0	0
100,000+	0	0	0	0	0	0	0	0
N =	52	289	6	38	15	32	77	64
% Linked	42	72	67	58	60	66	58	61
Average	$7,050	$2,658	$3,450	$882	$4,006	$2,376	$1,447	$1,727
Median	$1,250	$1,500	$3,100	$450	$1,250	$1,400	$500	$600

TABLE 5b. Boston Tax Assessments, Humanitarian, 1821

$	BBA, 1823 (%)	BD, 1817 (%)	BECS, 1818 (%)	BSEP, 1820 (%)	BCS* (%)	CIS* (%)	HBS, 1819 (%)	HMS, 1817 (%)	SCS* (%)
0	4	3	2	4	24	39	10	6	57
1–500	7	6	13	5	30	33	25	7	29
501–1000	8	5	11	4	6	8	10	4	0
1001–5000	33	18	9	20	19	17	32	26	14
5001–10,000	16	13	11	13	8	3	10	16	0
10,001–50,000	28	44	38	42	8	0	11	34	0
50,001–100,000	3	6	13	5	2	0	1	3	0
100,000+	2	6	2	7	2	0	1	3	0
N =	697	263	65	162	233	138	369	355	15
% Linked	80	73	82	60	45	26	75	75	47
Average	$13,526	$25,238	$21,030	$27,241	$6,927	$717	$5,486	$17,422	$286
Median	$3,750	$11,100	$10,400	$10,800	$350	$250	$1,500	$6,500	$0

TABLE 5c. Boston Tax Assessments, Missions, 1821

$	AES, 1822 (%)	BAES, 1819 (%)	BSMRIP, 1817 (%)	MBS, 1821 (%)	MMS, 1818 (%)	SPGNA, 1821 (%)
0	15	25	8	3	20	0
1–500	39	38	11	7	27	0
501–1000	15	15	8	5	7	0
1001–5000	24	17	31	31	27	0
5001–10,000	4	2	12	15	3	0
10,001–50,000	3	2	31	32	17	100
50,001–100,000	0	0	0	4	0	0
100,000+	0	1	0	3	0	0
N =	398	317	81	405	34	7
% Linked	61	54	80	72	88	43
Average	$1,603	$1,707	$7,864	$17,847	$4,463	$18,100
Median	$500	$300	$4,200	$6,500	$650	$16,200

TABLE 5d. Boston Tax Assessments, Reform, 1821

$	MPS, 1819 (%)	MSSI, 1818 (%)
0	7	4
1–500	15	7
501–1000	4	4
1001–5000	35	28
5001–10,000	11	7
10,001–50,000	24	39
50,001–100,000	2	0
100,000+	2	11
N =	161	66
% Linked	76	70
Average	$14,405	$33,432
Median	$3,700	$9,500

TABLE 5e. Boston Tax Assessments, Cultural, 1821

$	AAAS, 1821 (%)	BA, 1821 (%)	HH, 1821 (%)	MHS, 1821 (%)	WEC, 1821 (%)
0	3	1	20	9	14
1–500	3	5	42	5	0
501–1000	10	3	11	5	29
1001–5000	20	18	23	36	0
5001–10,000	3	7	4	5	14
10,001–50,000	50	51	1	36	29
50,001–100,000	10	5	0	5	14
100,000+	0	10	0	0	0
N =	41	118	259	31	18
% Linked	73	77	55	71	39
Average	$16,457	$36,053	$1,398	$11,645	$16,829
Median	$15,050	$17,500	$400	$5,000	$9,000

TABLE 5f. Boston Occupations, Mutual, 1821

	BMS* (%)	MCMA* (%)	MCS* (%)	MLL* (%)	SAL* (%)	SARA* (%)	SJ-B* (%)	SPRA* (%)
Unskilled	0	0	0	0	0	0	0	0
Semi-skilled	0	0	0	0	0	5	2	2
Skilled	7	95	25	33	67	25	20	38
Clerk/sales	0	0	0	4	0	0	0	0
Petty Prop.	0	3	0	25	0	25	14	12
Proprietor	33	1	25	21	0	25	32	15
Professional	0	1	25	8	0	10	23	25
Corp. off.	0	0	0	4	0	5	2	2
Gvt. off.	0	0	25	4	17	0	5	5
Mariner	60	0	0	0	17	5	2	0
Honorific	0	0	0	0	0	0	0	0
N =	52	292	6	38	15	32	77	64
% Linked	29	100	67	63	40	63	57	63

TABLE 5g. Boston Occupations, Humanitarian, 1821

	BBA, 1823 (%)	BD, 1817 (%)	BECS, 1818 (%)	BSEP, 1820 (%)	BCS* (%)	CIS* (%)	HBS, 1819 (%)	HMS, 1817 (%)	SCS* (%)
Unskilled	0	0	0	0	2	26	0	0	0
Semi-skilled	0	0	0	0	0	8 ·	1	0	0
Skilled	19	11	3	6	43	26	24	14	62
Clerk/sales	1	0	0	0	1	3	1	2	0
Petty Prop.	17	15	8	12	12	26	23	9	12
Proprietor	46	50	53	58	21	0	40	45	25
Professional	10	17	21	19	13	10	8	16	0
Corp. off.	2	3	11	4	0	0	0	5	0
Gvt. off.	3	3	5	0	6	3	2	7	0
Mariner	1	0	0	0	1	0	1	1	0
Honorific	0	2	0	0	0	0	0	0	0
N =	697	263	65	162	233	138	369	355	17
% Linked	73	58	58	44	42	28	71	65	47

TABLE 5h. Boston Occupations, Missions, 1821

	AES, 1822 (%)	BAES, 1819 (%)	BSMRIP, 1817 (%)	MBS, 1821 (%)	MMS, 1818 (%)	SPGNA, 1821 (%)
Unskilled	0	1	0	0	4	0
Semi-skilled	1	3	0	0	0	0
Skilled	22	36	8	15	15	0
Clerk/sales	0	1	0	1	0	0
Petty prop.	24	28	21	15	27	0
Proprietor	38	24	63	46	27	38
Professional	12	4	5	15	19	19
Corp. off.	0	0	0	3	0	0
Gvt. off.	1	1	3	3	8	19
Mariner	1	1	0	0	0	0
Honorific	0	0	0	1	0	25
N =	398	317	81	405	31	18
% Linked	52	47	44	66	84	89

TABLE 5i. Boston Occupations, Reform, 1821

	MPS, 1819 (%)	*MSSI, 1818 (%)*
Unskilled	0	0
Semi-skilled	1	0
Skilled	11	9
Clerk/sales	0	0
Petty prop.	17	22
Proprietor	43	27
Professional	22	29
Corp. off.	1	2
Gvt. off.	3	9
Mariner	1	0
Honorific	2	2
$N =$	161	65
% Linked	76	69

TABLE 5j. Boston Occupations, Cultural, 1821

	AAAS, 1821 (%)	BA, 1821 (%)	HH, 1821 (%)	MHS, 1821 (%)	WEC, 1821 (%)
Unskilled	0	0	0	0	0
Semi-skilled	0	0	1	0	0
Skilled	0	1	38	0	7
Clerk/sales	0	1	2	0	0
Petty prop.	4	7	20	0	7
Proprietor	8	54	25	9	0
Professional	88	24	9	65	87
Corp. off.	0	4	2	9	0
Gvt. off.	0	4	2	13	0
Mariner	0	0	1	4	0
Honorific	0	3	0	0	0
N =	43	118	258	30	18
% Linked	56	59	48	77	83

SOURCES: *At a Legal Meeting. . . .* (Boston, 1822); *Boston Directory* (Boston, 1821); William A. Baker, *A History of the Boston Marine Society, 1742–1967* (Boston, 1968), 318–352; Joseph Jenkins, *An Address Delivered Before the Massachusetts Charitable Mechanic Association* (Boston, 1819), 21–24; *Charter and By-Laws of the Massachusetts Charitable Society* (Boston, 1895), 26–32; *By-Laws for the Regulation and Government of Mount Lebanon Lodge* (Boston, 1867), 63–75; *Commemoration of the One Hundred Twenty-Fifth Anniversary of the Lodge of Saint Andrew* (Boston, 1887), 116–119; *By-Laws of St. Andrew's Royal Arch Chapter* (Boston, 1859), 37–53; *History of Saint John's Lodge* (Boston, 1917), 201–232; *Charter and By-Laws of St. Paul's Royal Arch Chapter* (Boston, 1884), 22–69; *An Account of the Boston Asylum for Indigent Boys* (Boston, 1823), 23–32; *Institution of the Boston Dispensary* (Boston, 1817), 15–23; *Act of Incorporation of the Boston Episcopal Charitable Society* (Boston, 1818), 13–24; *Explanation of the Views of the Society for Employing the Poor* (Boston, 1820), 12–13; *Constitution and By-Laws of the British Charitable Society* (Boston, 1880), 13–15; *The Constitution and By-Laws of the Charitable Irish Society* (Boston, 1876), 102–130; *Howard Benevolent Society* (Boston, 1819), 15–19; William Tudor, *A Discourse Delivered before the Humane Society* (Boston, 1817), 57–64; *The Constitution and By-Laws of the Scots' Charitable Society* (Cambridge, Mass., 1878), 111–112; Samuel Farmer Jarvis, *A Sermon, Preached Before the Auxiliary Education Society of the Young Men of Boston* (Boston, 1822), 21–24; *The Constitution of the Baptist Auxiliary Education Society of the Young Men of Boston* (Boston, 1819), 6–11; *Report of the Boston Society for the Moral and Religious Instruction of the Poor* (Boston, 1817), 8–9; *Report of the Bible Society of Massachusetts* (Boston, 1821), 5–10; *The Constitution of the Massachusetts Missionary Society* (Salem, 1818), 6–8; *Report of the Select Committee of the Society for Propagating the Gospel Among the Indians and Others of North America* (Boston, 1856), 123–125; *A Catalogue of the Officers and Members of the Massachusetts Peace Society* (Cambridge, Mass., 1819), 3–4; *The Constitution of the Massachusetts Society for the Suppression of Intemperance* (Boston, 1818), 24–30; *Memoirs of the American Academy of Arts and Sciences,* vol. 11, pt. 1:33–40 (1882); Josiah Quincy, *The History of the Boston Athenaeum* (Cambridge, Mass., 1851), 243–246; Charles C. Perkins and John S. Dwight, *History of the Handel and Haydn Society* (Boston, 1883–1893), 1:appen. 22–27; *Handbook of the Massachusetts Historical Society* (Boston, 1948), 21–93; *The Centennial Celebration of the Wednesday Evening Club* (Boston, 1878), 142–144.

Appendix Three

A Census of Charitable Organizations
in New England, 1657–1817

NEW ENGLANDERS organized more than 1,400 charitable associations between 1657 and 1817. A complete census of these organizations is
almost certainly impossible. Many probably disappeared without leaving a
trace; in other instances, surviving references are so fragmentary and cryptic
that determining whether a single organization went by more than one name,
and distinguishing among several groups with similar names and objectives,
are at best uncertain enterprises.

Despite its inevitable shortcomings, the following list probably approaches
a comprehensive census of charitable associations established in New England
through 1817, when the publishers of some of the more useful sources of
information began to summarize the activities of groups of organizations
instead of reporting on them individually. To compile this survey I have drawn
on the printed reports, accounts, and anniversary addresses of individual
associations as well as on manuscript records, periodicals, almanacs, and town
histories.

Each entry comprises an organization's location, name, type, and earliest
known date as well as a source reference. I have listed county- and statewide
organizations under the county seat and state capital, respectively, except
where I discovered other information indicating that it conducted most of its
operations elsewhere. To save space and avoid repetition, I have ordinarily
omitted town names from the names of organizations. Thus, under Hartford
the Hartford Charitable Society appears simply as "Charitable Society." Many
New England towns divided into more than one community during the
nineteenth and early twentieth centuries, but this list observes town boundaries as they existed during the late 1810s. Thus, North Milford, Connecticut,

appears under Milford, although it is now part of the town of Orange. I have employed the following codes in categorizing the associations: H (humanitarian); M (mutual benefit, including masonic organizations, marine societies, mechanic associations, and independent fraternities); P (proselytizing, including missionary, Bible, tract, education, and Sunday school societies); and R (reform, including antislavery, peace, Sabbatarian, and temperance associations). To determine an organization's primary activities, I consulted its manuscript or printed records, annual reports, by-laws, or anniversary sermons where available. In the absence of such sources, I relied on entries in the annual reports of the many state and national societies (principally proselytizing and reform organizations) that listed affiliated institutions. Reference sources used more than once appear in the following short title list:

ABCFM (1812). *Report of the American Board of Commissioners for Foreign Missions . . . 1812* (Boston, 1812).

ABCFM (1813). *Report of the American Board of Commissioners for Foreign Missions . . . 1813* (Boston, 1813).

ABCFM (1814). *Report of the American Board of Commissioners for Foreign Missions . . . 1814* (Boston, 1814).

ABCFM (1815). *Report of the American Board of Commissioners for Foreign Missions . . . 1815* (Boston, 1815).

ABCFM (1816). *Report of the American Board of Commissioners for Foreign Missions . . . 1816* (Boston, 1816).

ABCFM (1817). *Report of the American Board of Commissioners for Foreign Missions . . . 1817* (Boston, 1817).

ABM. *American Baptist Magazine.*

ABS (1817). *First Annual Report . . . of the American Bible Society . . . 1817* (New York, 1817).

ABS (1818). *Second Report of the American Bible Society* (New York, 1818).

AES (1817). Joseph Chickering, *A Sermon, Preached in Boston, Before the American Society for Educating Pious Youth for the Gospel Ministry* (Dedham, 1817).

ATS (1824). *Proceedings of the First Ten Years of the American Tract Society* (Boston, 1824).

BMNS (1818). *Report of the Third Annual Meeting of the Baptist Missionary Society of Norfolk County and Vicinity* (Boston, 1818).

BR. *Boston Recorder.*

BSCM (1816). *First Report of the Bible Society in the County of Middlesex* (Cambridge, Mass., 1816).

BSCM (1817). *Second Report of the Bible Society in the County of Middlesex* (Cambridge, Mass., 1817).

BSSV (1814). Thomas Barnard, *A Sermon . . . Before the Bible Society of Salem and Vicinity . . . 1814* (Salem, 1814).

BSSV (1816). John Prince, *A Discourse . . . . Before the Bible Society of Salem & Vicinity* (Salem, 1816).

CAAS (1811). Connecticut Academy of Arts and Sciences, *A Statistical Account of the Towns and Parishes in the State of Connecticut* (New Haven, 1811).

CBS (1810). *Report of the . . . Connecticut Bible Society . . . 1810* (Hartford, 1810).

CBS (1811). *Report of the . . . Connecticut Bible Society . . . 1811* (Hartford, 1811).

CBS (1813). *Report of the . . . Connecticut Bible Society . . . 1813* (Hartford, 1813).

CBS (1814). *Report of the . . . Connecticut Bible Society . . . 1814* (Hartford, 1814).

CBS (1815). *Sixth Report of the Connecticut Bible Society* (Hartford, 1815).

CBS (1816). *Report of the . . . Connecticut Bible Society* (Hartford, 1816).

CBS (1817). *Report of the . . . Connecticut Bible Society* (Hartford, 1817).

CEM. *Connecticut Evangelical Magazine.*

CSABB (1816). *Second Report of the Connecticut Society, Auxiliary to the Baptist Board of Foreign Missions* (Hartford, 1816).

CSABB (1817). *Third Report of the Connecticut Society, Auxiliary to the Baptist Board of Foreign Missions . . . 1817* (Hartford, 1818).

CtES (1816). *An Account of the . . . Education Society of Connecticut and of the Female Education Society of New-Haven* (New Haven, 1816).

CtGL. E. G. Storer, *The Records of Freemasonry in the State of Connecticut* (New Haven, 1859).

CtRA. *Records of Capitular Masonry in the State of Connecticut,* comp. Joseph K. Wheeler (Hartford, 1875).

DMSC (1817). *Report of the . . . Domestic Missionary Society, for Connecticut and Its Vicinity . . . 1817* (Hartford, 1817).

EMS (1816). *To the Members of the Evangelical Missionary Society* (n.p., 1816).

ESBN (1816). *Proceedings of the Second Annual Meeting of the Evangelical Society of Bristol and Newport Counties* (n.p., 1816).

GC. *Grand Commandery of Knights Templar, Massachusetts and Rhode Island, 1805–1905* (Boston, 1905).

Keller. Charles Roy Keller, *The Second Great Awakening in Connecticut* (New Haven, 1942).

Mass GL (1857). *The Constitutions of the Grand Lodge of Massachusetts* (Boston, 1857).

Mass RA. *Grand Royal Arch Chapter of Massachusetts, 150th Anniversary, March 7–8–9, 1948* (Boston, 1948).

Mass RA (1819). *Grand Royal Arch Chapter of Massachusetts . . . 1819* (Boston, 1819).

Mass. Reg. (1816). *Massachusetts Register and United States Calendar . . . 1816* (Boston, 1815).

Mass. Reg. (1817). *Massachusetts Register and United States Calendar . . . 1817* (Boston, 1816).

MBMM. *Massachusetts Baptist Missionary Magazine.*

MBMS (1818). *Report of the . . . Massa. Baptist Missionary Society* (n.p., 1818).

MeMS (1810). Eliphalet Gillet, *Sermon Delivered Before the Maine Missionary Society . . . 1810* (Hallowell, 1810).

MeMS (1811). Jonathan Ward, *Sermon Delivered Before the Maine Missionary Society . . . 1811* (Hallowell, 1811).

MeMS (1813). Kiah Bayley, *Sermon Delivered Before the Maine Missionary Society . . . 1813* (Hallowell, 1813).

MeMS (1814). Francis Brown, *Sermon Delivered Before the Maine Missionary Society . . . 1814* (Hallowell, 1814).

MeMs (1815). Asa Rand, *Sermon Delivered . . . Before the Maine Missionary Society* (Hallowell, 1815).

MeMS (1816). David Thurston, *Sermon Delivered . . . Before the Maine Missionary Society* (Hallowell, 1816).

MeMS (1817). John W. Ellingwood, *Nothing Too Precious for Christ* (Hallowell, 1817).

MGL 1. *Proceedings in Masonry* (Boston, 1895).

MMM. *Massachusetts Missionary Magazine.*

Ms. See "Note on Primary Sources," list of records consulted.

MSBC (1813). John Chester, *A Sermon, Delivered Before the Berkshire and Columbia Missionary Society . . . 1813* (Hudson, 1813).

MSBC (1815). *Annual Meeting of the Missionary Society of Berkshire & Columbia* (n.p., 1815).

MSBC (1816). James Bradford, *The Presence of the Lord Sufficient Ground for Encouragement and Execution* (Stockbridge, 1816).

MSC (1805). *A Narrative on the Subject of Missions* (Hartford, 1805).

MSC (1806). *A Narrative on the Subject of Missions* (Hartford, 1806).

MSC (1809). *A Narrative on the Subject of Missions* (Hartford, 1809).

MSC (1813). *A Missionary Address . . . 1812* (Hartford, 1813).

MSC (1816). *Seventeenth Annual Narrative of Missionary Labors* (Hartford, 1816).

MSC (1818). *Nineteenth Annual Narrative of Missionary Service* (Hartford, 1818).

MSPCK (1811). Eliphalet Pearson, *A Sermon, Delivered in Boston . . . 1811* (Cambridge, Mass., 1811).

MSPCK (1813). Thomas Prentiss, *A Sermon Delivered in Boston . . . 1813* (Andover, 1813).

MSPCK (1815). Daniel Chaplin, *A Sermon, Delivered in Boston* (Boston, 1815).

MSPCK (1816). Joshua Bates, *A Sermon, Delivered in Boston . . . 1816* (Dedham, 1816).

MSSI (1814). *Second Annual Report of the Massachusetts Society for Suppressing Intemperance* (Boston, 1814).

MSSI (1815). Abiel Abbot, *An Address, Delivered Before the Massachusetts Society for Suppressing Intemperance* (Cambridge, Mass., 1815).

MSSI (1816). Jesse Appleton, *An Address, Delivered Before the Massachusetts Society for Suppressing Intemperance . . . 1816* (Boston, 1816).

MSSI (1817). Samuel Worcester, *The Drunkard a Destroyer* (Boston, 1817).

MSSI (1818). *The Constitution of the Massachusetts Society for the Suppression of Intemperance* (Boston, 1818).

Myers. Minor Myers, Jr., *Liberty without Authority: A History of the Society of the Cincinnati* (Charlottesville, 1983).

NHBS (1812). *First Report of the New-Hampshire Bible Society . . . 1812* (Concord, N.H., 1812).

NHBS (1813). *Second Report of the New-Hampshire Bible Society . . . 1813* (Concord, N.H., 1813).

NHBS (1815). *Fifth Report of the New-Hampshire Bible Society . . . 1815* (Concord, N.H., 1815).

NHBS (1816). *Sixth Report of the New-Hampshire Bible Society . . . 1816* (Concord, N.H., 1816).

NHCI (1814). *Report on the Concerns of the New-Hampshire Cent Institution, For September, 1814* (Concord, N.H., 1814).

NHCI (1815). *Report on the Concerns of the New-Hampshire Cent Institution, For September, 1815* (Concord, N.H., 1815).

NHCI (1816). *Report on the Concerns of the New-Hampshire Cent Institution for September, 1816* (Concord, N.H., 1816).

NHGL2. *Proceedings of the Grand Lodge of New Hampshire, from June, 5842, to June, 5856, Inclusive* (Manchester, N.H., 1869).

NHMS (1806). *The Funds and Services of the New-Hampshire Missionary Society* (Concord, N.H., 1806).

NHMS (1810). *Report of the Trustees of the New-Hampshire Missionary Society . . . 1810* (Concord, N.H., 1810).

NHMS (1815). *Fourteenth Report of the . . . New-Hampshire Missionary Society* (Concord, N.H., 1815).

NHMS (1816). *Fifteenth Report of the . . . New-Hampshire Missionary Society . . . 1816* (Concord, N.H., 1816).

NHMS (1817). *Sixteenth Report of the . . . New-Hampshire Misionary Society . . . 1817* (Concord, N.H., 1817).

NHRA (1819). *Regulations of the Grand Royal Arch Chapter of the State of New-Hampshire* (Concord, N.H., 1819).

Pan. *Panoplist.*

Pettengill, *Sermon*. Amos Pettengill, *A Call to Help the Lord* (Bennington, 1815).

RIGL. *Reprint of the Proceedings of the M.W. Grand Lodge of Free and Accepted Masons of the State of Rhode Island* (Providence, 1888).

RIRA. *Proceedings of the Grand Royal Arch Chapter of the State of Rhode Island and Providence Plantations, 1982* (Southborough, Mass., 1982).

Voorhis. Harold V. B. Voorhis, *Masonic Organizations and Allied Orders and Degrees: A Cyclopaedic Handbook* (Red Bank, N.J., 1952).

VtBS (1814). *Second Report of the Vermont Bible Society . . . 1814* (Montpelier, 1814).

VtBS (1815). *Third Report of the Vermont Bible Society . . . 1815* (Montpelier, 1815).

VtBS (1816). *Fourth Report of the Vermont Bible Society . . . 1816* (Montpelier, 1816).

VtBS (1817). *Fifth Report of the Vermont Bible Society . . . 1817* (Montpelier, 1817).

VtGL. *Records of the Grand Lodge of Free and Accepted Masons of the State of Vermont, from 1794 to 1846 Inclusive* (Burlington, 1879).

VtMS (1808). *A Circular Letter to the Churches and Congregations of Vermont* (n.p., 1808).

VtMS (1810). *Address to the Churches and Congregations of Vermont* (Middlebury, 1810).

VtMS (1818). *Address to the Churches and Congregations of Vermont* (Middlebury, 1818).

VtRA. *Grand Royal Arch Chapter of Vermont, 1804–1973* (n.p., 1973).

Connecticut

Berlin. Harmony Lodge. M, 1791. CtGL, 65.

　　　　Worthington Cent Society. P, 1816. CtES (1816), 6.

Bolton. Female Charitable Society. P, 1817. CBS (1817), 17.

Branford. Female Charitable Society. P, 1816. CBS (1816), 14.

Bristol. Branch Society for the Reformation of Morals. R, 1814. CEM NS7(1814):307.

Brookfield. Federal Lodge. M, 1797. CtGL, 93.

Brooklyn. Newell Society. P, 1817. ABCFM (1817), 38.

Canaan. Meriden Chapter, Royal Arch Masons. M, 1814. CtRA, 64.
      North Canaan Gentlemen's Association. P, 1816. ABCFM (1817), 41.
      North Canaan Ladies' Association. P, 1816. ABCFM (1817), 41.
      North Canaan Moral Society. R, 1816. BR, July 31, 1816.
      South Canaan Moral Society. R, 1816. BR, July 31, 1816.
      Gentlemen's Association. P, 1817. ABCFM (1817), 45.
      Ladies' Association. P, 1817. ABCFM (1817), 45.
Canterbury. Moriah Lodge. M, 1790. CtGL, 65.
      Ladies' Society. P, 1814. CBS (1814), 17.
      West Parish Female Benevolent Society. P, 1817. MSC (1818), 20.
Canton. Village Lodge. M, by 1794. CtGL, 73.
Chatham. Warren Lodge. M, 1811. CtGL, 233.
Cheshire. Temple Lodge. M, 1791. CtGL, 65.
Colchester. Wooster Lodge. M, 1781. CtGL, 208.
      Vanden Broeck Chapter, Royal Arch Masons. M, 1796. CtRA, 23.
      Washington Encampment, Knights Templar. M, 1796. GC, 87.
      Foreign Mission Society. P, 1812. ABCFM (1813), 39.
      Female Auxiliary Education Society. P, 1816. CtES (1816), 12.
      Female Juvenile Society. P, 1816. ABCFM (1817), 44.
Colebrook. Female Bible Society. P, 1816. CSABB (1816), 10.
      Gentlemen's Association. P, 1816. ABCFM (1817), 41.
      Ladies' Association. P, 1816. ABCFM (1817), 41.
Cornwall. Moral Society. R, 1816. BR, July 31, 1816.
      South Cornwall Gentlemen's Association. P, 1817. ABCFM (1817), 42.
      South Cornwall Ladies' Association. P, 1817. ABCFM (1817), 42.
Coventry. Female Friendly Society. P, 1812. Ms.
      First Parish Branch Society for the Reformation of Morals. R, 1814. CEM
        NS7(1814):308.
      North Coventry Branch Society for the Reformation of Morals. R, 1814.
        CEM NS7(1814):310.
Danbury. Union Lodge. M, 1780. CtGL, 201.
      Fairfield County Bible Society. P, 1814. BR, July 3, 1816.
      Ladies' Society. P, 1814. CBS (1814), 17.
      Female Academy Society. P, 1816. ABCFM (1817), 36.
      Gentlemen's Association. P, 1817. ABCFM (1817), 47.
      Ladies' Association. P, 1817. ABCFM (1817), 47.
Derby. King Hiram Lodge. M, 1783. CtGL, 113.
      Solomon Chapter, Royal Arch Masons. M, 1796. CtRA, 20.
Durham. Female Cent Society. P, 1817. CBS (1817), 17.
East Haddam. Columbia Lodge. M, by 1794. CtGL, 73.
      Hadlyme Branch Society for the Reformation of Morals. R, 1814. CEM
        NS7(1814):310.
      Female Benevolent Society. P, 1815. CBS (1815), 12.
East Hartford. Female Benevolent Society. P, 1816. CtES (1816), 6.
      Female Charitable Society. P, 1816. CBS (1816), 14.

East Haven. Branch Society for the Reformation of Morals. R, 1814. CEM NS7(1814):305.

    Cent Society. P, 1814. ABCFM (1814), 51.

East Windsor. Morning Star Lodge. M, by 1794. CtGL, 73.

    First Parish Branch Society for the Reformation of Morals. R, 1814. CEM NS7(1814):309.

    North Parish Female Benevolent Society. P, 1816. CtES (1816), 12.

    Female Benevolent Society. P, 1817. CBS (1817), 17.

    Female Bible Society. P, 1817. CBS (1817), 17.

    [unnamed association]. P, 1817. ABCFM (1817), 59.

Ellington. Female Beneficent Society. P, 1817. ABCFM (1817), 46.

    Cent Society. P, 1817. ABCFM (1817), 59.

Enfield. Female Auxiliary Bible Society. P, 1816. CBS (1816), 18.

Fairfield. St. John's Lodge. M, 1762. CtGL, 52.

    Ladies' Cent Society. P, 1811. CBS (1811), 16.

    Greenfield Branch Society for the Reformation of Morals. R, 1814. CEM NS7(1814):305.

    Green's Farms Branch Society for the Reformation of Morals. R, 1814. CEM NS7(1814):308.

    Female Foreign Mission Society. P, 1816. ABCFM (1816), 22.

    Green's Farms Bible Society. P, 1817. ABS (1817), 32.

Farmington. Frederick Lodge. M, 1787. CtGL, 205.

    Ladies' Cent Society. P, 1812. *Report of the . . . Connecticut Bible Society . . . 1812* (Hartford, 1812), 25.

    Female Benevolent Society. P, 1813. ABCFM (1813), 23.

    First Parish Branch Society for the Reformation of Morals. R, 1814. CEM NS7(1814):309.

    Northington Female Cent Society. P, 1815. CBS (1815), 12.

Franklin. Female Foreign Mission Society. P, 1813. Pan NS5(1813):380.

Glastonbury. Columbia Lodge. M, by 1794. CtGL, 73.

    Foreign Mission Society. P, 1813. ABCFM (1814), 51.

    Religious Association of Females. P, 1814. ABCFM (1814), 48.

    Cent Society. P, 1817. ABCFM (1817), 37.

Goshen. Moral Society. R, 1813. Ms.

    Female Charitable Society. P, 1816. CtES (1816), 6.

Granby. St. Mark's Lodge. M, 1796. CtGL, 77.

    Branch Society for the Reformation of Morals. R, 1814. CEM NS7(1814):309.

Greenwich. Union Lodge. M, 1764. CtGL, 208.

    Female Charitable Society. H, 1811. Keller, 165.

    King Hiram's Chapter, Royal Arch Masons. M, 1815. Mass RA (1819), 19.

    West Greenwich Female Society. P, 1815. ABCFM (1815), 27.

    Female Foreign Mission Society. P, 1816. ABCFM (1816), 22.

    Ladies' Praying Society. P, 1816. CtES (1816), 12.

    Society of Females in Greenwich formed for the Support of Heathen Schools. P, 1817. ABCFM (1817), 48.

Griswold (North Preston). Female Cent Society. P, 1813. ABCFM (1813), 23.

        Female Benevolent Society. P, 1817. DMSC (1817), 7.

Groton. [unnamed association]. P, 1817. CSABB (1817), 13.

Guilford. Guilford Lodge. M, 1771. MGL1, 483.

        North Guilford Male and Female Cent Society. P, 1811. CBS (1811), 18.

        Foreign Mission Society of the Eastern District of New Haven County. P, 1812. ABCFM (1812), 40.

        East Guilford Cent Society. P, 1813. Pan NS5(1813):475.

        Female Charitable Society. P, 1813. CBS (1813), 10.

        North Guilford Ladies' Cent Society. P, 1813. CBS (1813), 13.

        East Guilford Ladies' Society. P, 1815. CBS (1815), 12.

        Female Benevolent Society. P, 1816. CtES (1816), 6.

        Auxiliary Society for the Promotion of Good Morals. R, 1817. Keller, 149.

Hamden. Day Spring Lodge. M, 1794. CtGL, 71.

Hampton. Cent Society. P, 1808. MSC (1809), 15.

Hartford. St. John's Lodge. M, 1762. MGL, 483.

        Society of the Cincinnati of Connecticut. M, 1783. Myers, 39.

        Connecticut Grand Lodge. M, 1789. CtGL.

        Charitable Society. H, 1792. Ms.

        Connecticut Grand Chapter, Royal Arch Masons. M, 1798. Voorhis, 7.

        Missionary Society of Connecticut. P, 1798. Ms.

        Connecticut Religious Tract Society. P, 1807. ATS (1824), 208.

        Connecticut Bible Society. P, 1809. Ms.

        Female Beneficent Society. H, 1809. *Address* (Hartford, 1813), 3.

        Young Ladies' Cent Society. P, 1810. CBS (1810), 12.

        Connecticut Society for the Promotion of Good Morals. R, 1812. Keller, 144.

        Connecticut Society, Auxiliary to the Baptist Board of Foreign Missions. P, 1814. CSABB (1816).

        Female Cent Society. P, 1814. CBS (1814), 16.

        Auxiliary Bible Society. P, 1816. BR, Sept. 4, 1816.

        Connecticut Asylum. H, 1816. Keller, 166–169.

        Connecticut Domestic Missionary Society. P, 1816. BR, July 3, 1816.

        Female Society. P, 1816. CtES (1816), 7.

        Hartford Evangelical Tract Society. P, 1816. ATS (1824), 208.

        West Hartford Female Society. P, 1816. CtES (1816), 7.

        Connecticut Auxiliary Mission Society. P, 1817. ABM 1(1817):198.

        Pythagoras Chapter, Royal Arch Masons. M, 1817. CtRA, 76.

        West Auxiliary Bible Society. P, 1817. CBS (1817), 17.

Hartland. West Hartland Female Charitable Society. P, 1817. CBS (1817), 17.

Harwinton. Aurora Lodge. M, 1796. CtGL, 77.

        Female Association. P, 1817. ABCFM (1817), 42.

        Gentlemen's Association. P, 1817. ABCFM (1817), 42.

Hebron. Female Association. P, 1804. MSC (1803), 13.

        Warren Lodge. M, 1810. CtGL, 224.

Huntington. Washington Lodge. M, 1791. CtGL, 65.

Kent. St. Luke's Lodge. M, 1806. CtGL, 185.

    Hamilton Chapter, Royal Arch Masons. M, 1813. CtRA, 59.

    Female Association. P, 1817. ABCFM (1817), 46.

    Gentlemen's Association. P, 1817. ABCFM (1817), 46.

Killingly. North Killingly Female Cent Society. P, 1815. CBS (1815), 12.

    Female Mite Society. P, 1817. CSABB (1817), 12.

Killingworth. Trinity Lodge. M, 1797. CtGL, 93.

Lebanon. Female Cent Society. P, 1814. Ms.

    Female Mite Society. P, 1816. CSABB (1816), 8.

    Society of Females. P, 1817. ABCFM (1817), 37.

Lisbon. First Parish Branch Society for the Reformation of Morals. R, 1814. CEM
    NS7(1814):306.

Litchfield. St. Paul's Lodge. M, 1781. CtGL, 203.

    Female Association. P, 1804. MSC (1805), 13.

    Home and Foreign Mission Society of Litchfield County. P, 1812. Ms.

    South Farms Moral Society. R, 1813. Ms.

    Darius Chapter, Royal Arch Masons. M, 1815. CtRA, 69.

    Female Academy Charitable Society. P, 1816. Pan 12(1816):274–276.

    South Farms Gentlemen's Association. P, 1816. ABCFM (1817), 41.

    South Farms Ladies' Association. P, 1816. ABCFM (1817), 41.

    South Farms Charitable Education School. P, 1817. Pan 14(1818):96.

Lyme. Pythagoras Lodge. M, 1800. CtGL, 125.

    Niantic Female Missionary Society. P, 1817. CSABB (1817), 13.

Mansfield. Female Cent Society. P, 1815. MSC (1816), 20.

    Female Charitable Society. P, 1816. CtES (1816), 7.

    Newell Society. P, 1817. ABCFM (1817), 38.

    Northfield Gentlemen's Association. P, 1817. ABCFM (1817), 42.

    Northfield Ladies' Association. P, 1817. ABCFM (1817), 42.

Meriden. Cent Society. P, 1815. ABCFM (1815), 30.

Middlebury. Female Cent Society. P, 1815. CBS (1815), 12.

    Young Ladies' Benevolent Society. P, 1817. ABCFM (1817), 47.

Middletown. St. John's Lodge. M, 1754. CtGL, 50.

    Washington Chapter, Royal Arch Masons. M, 1783. CtRA, 12.

    Female Charitable Society. H, 1809. Keller, 165.

    Foreign Mission Society. P, 1813. ABCFM (1814), 51.

Milford. North Milford Female Society. P, 1816. CtES (1816), 7.

Montville. Female Charitable Society. P, 1814. MBMM 4(1815):177–178.

    Chesterfield Female Mite Society. P, 1817. CSABB (1817), 12.

New Canaan. Female Charitable Association. P, 1812. Pan NS5(1812):242.

    Female Beneficent Society. P, 1813. ABCFM (1813):39.

    Auxiliary Education Society. P, 1816. CtES (1816), 7.

    Mite Society. P, 1817. ABCFM (1817), 38.

New Hartford. Branch Society for the Reformation of Morals. R, 1814. CEM
    NS7(1814):307.

    Gentlemen's Association. P, 1817. ABCFM (1817), 45.

    Ladies' Association. P, 1817. ABCFM (1817), 45.

New Haven. Hiram Lodge. M, 1750. CtGL, 49.

       Connecticut Society for the Promotion of Freedom. R, 1790. James Dana, *The African Slave Trade* (New Haven, 1791).

       Franklin Chapter, Royal Arch Masons. M, 1795. CtRA, 12.

       Society of the Social Tie. M, 1802. *An Oration, Pronounced before the Society of the Social Tie* (New Haven, 1802).

       Ladies' Society. P, 1805. MSC (1806), 16.

       General Society of Mechanics. M, 1807. CAAS (1811), 78.

       Female Charitable Society (#1). H, 1811. CAAS (1811), 77–78.

       Female Charitable Society (#2). H, 1811. CAAS (1811), 77–78.

       Female Charitable Society (#3). H, 1811. CAAS (1811), 77–78.

       Female Foreign Mission Society. P, 1812. ABCFM (1812), 20.

       Foreign Mission Society. P, 1812. ABCFM (1812), 20.

       Tract Society. P, 1812. MSC (1813), 23.

       Education Society of Connecticut. P, 1814. Ms.

       Moral Society. R, 1814. Ms.

       Female Benevolent Society. P, 1814. *Constitution* (New Haven, 1814).

       Female Education Society. P, 1815. CtES (1816), 3.

       West Haven Female Cent Society. P, 1815. CBS (1815), 12.

       Associated Young Ladies. P, 1816. ABCFM (1817), 36.

       Bible and Common Prayer Book Society of the Diocese of Connecticut. P, 1816. BR, Sept. 10, 1816.

       Charitable Society for the Education of Indigent Pious Young Men for the Ministry of the Gospel. P, 1816. BR, Nov. 19, 1816.

       Female Auxiliary Bible Society. P, 1816. Ms.

       Bible Society of Yale College. P, 1817. BR, Sept. 23, 1817.

New London. [unnamed Masonic lodge]. M, 1753. CtGL, 404.

       Union Lodge. M, 1795. CtGL, 73.

       Union Chapter, Royal Arch Masons. M, 1805. CtRA, 32.

       Female Cent Society. H, 1810. Keller, 165.

       Female Foreign Mission Society. P, 1812. ABCFM (1812), 22.

       Foreign Mission Society. P, 1812. ABCFM (1812), 22.

       Branch Society for the Reformation of Morals. R, 1814. CEM NS7(1814):304.

       Female Society. P, 1816. CtES (1816), 7.

New Milford. St. Peter's Lodge. M, 1791. CtGL, 65.

       Charitable Cent Society. P, 1815. CBS (1815), 11.

       Association. P, 1817. ABCFM (1817), 45.

       Female Mite Society. P, 1817. ABCFM (1817), 48.

Newtown. Hiram Lodge. M, 1791. CtGL, 65.

       Hiram Chapter, Royal Arch Masons. M, 1791. CtRA, 9.

Norfolk. Western Star Lodge. M, 1796. CtGL, 77.

       Auxiliary Education Society. P, 1815. BR, Jan. 28, 1817.

       Gentlemen's Association. P, 1816. ABCFM (1817), 41.

       Ladies' Association. P, 1816. ABCFM (1816), 41.

North Haven. Branch Society for the Reformation of Morals. R, 1814. CEM NS7(1814):309.

North Stonington. Widow's Son Lodge. M, 1812. CtGL, 242.

Norwalk. St. John's Lodge. M, 1765. CtGL, 54.

        Cent Society. P, 1813. ABCFM (1813), 24.

        Female Foreign Mission Society. P, 1813. ABCFM (1813), 39.

        Branch Society for the Reformation of Morals. R, 1814. CEM NS7 (1814):304.

Norwich. Norwich Lodge. M, 1766. MGL, 483.

        Columbia Lodge. M, 1785. CtGL, 405–406.

        Franklin Chapter, Royal Arch Masons. M, 1796. CtRA, 16.

        Somerset Lodge. M, 1796. CtGL, 76.

        Ladies' Society. P, 1800. *A Second Address . . . Missionary Society of Connecticut . . . 1800* (Hartford, 1801), 18.

        Foreign Mission Society. P, 1812. ABCFM (1812), 39.

        Female Auxiliary Education Society. P, 1816. CtES (1816), 12.

        Female Benevolent Society. P, 1816. CtES (1816), 12.

        Female [name torn]. P, 1817. CSABB (1817), 13.

        Hanover Female Bible Society. P, 1817. CBS (1817), 17.

Oxford. Morning Star Lodge. M, 1804. CtGL, 169.

Plainfield. Female Foreign Mission Society. P, 1814. ABCFM (1814), 51.

        Cent Society. P, 1816. ABCFM (1817), 36.

Plymouth. Female Association. P, 1817. ABCFM (1817), 42.

        Gentlemen's Association. P, 1817. ABCFM (1817), 42.

Pomfret. Putnam Lodge. M, 1801. CtGL, 134.

        Warren Chapter, Royal Arch Masons. M, 1812. CtRA, 53.

        Female Charitable Society. P, 1816. CtES (1816), 7.

Preston. St. James' Lodge. M, by 1794. CtGL, 73.

        South Preston Female Foreign Mission Society. P, 1814. ABCFM (1814), 51.

Redding. Lynch Chapter, Royal Arch Masons. M, 1808. CtRA, 37.

Ridgefield. Jerusalem Lodge. M, 1808. CtGL, 211.

Salem. Female Union Society. P, 1816. CBS (1816), 14.

Salisbury. Montgomery Lodge. M, 1783. CtGL, 205.

        Branch Society for the Reformation of Morals. R, 1814. CEM NS7(1814):306.

        Female Foreign Mission Society. P, 1816. ABCFM (1816), 22.

        Female Society. P, 1816. CtES (1816), 7.

        Gentlemen's Association for the Education of Heathen Children. P, 1816. ABCFM (1817), 41.

Saybrook. Mount Olive Lodge. M, 1811. CtGL, 237.

        Auxiliary Foreign Mission Society of Middlesex County. P, 1812. Ms.

        Chester Female Benevolent Society. P, 1816. MSC (1816), 21.

Seymour. Humphreyville Female Charitable Society. P, 1817. DMSC (1817), 7.

Sharon. First Parish Branch Society for the Reformation of Morals. R, 1814. CEM NS7(1814):308.

        Female Cent Society. P, 1815. CBS(1815), 12.

        Hamilton Lodge. M, 1815. CtGL, 266.

Sherman. Female Charitable Society. P, 1817. CBS (1817), 17.
Simsbury. Foreign Mission Society of the North Association of Hartford County. P, 1813.
        ABCFM (1813), 39.
           Young Female Society. P, 1816. CBS (1816), 16.
           Female Charitable Society. P, 1817. ABCFM (1817), 38.
Somers. Cent Society. P, 1812. ABCFM (1812), 23.
           Female Foreign Mission Society. P, 1813. ABCFM (1813), 39.
           Branch Society for the Reformation of Morals. R, 1814. CEM
           NS7(1814):310.
           Young Men's Charitable Society. P, 1816. CtES (1816), 7.
Southbury. Female Cent Society. P, 1816. BR, Dec. 9, 1817.
Southington. Friendship Lodge. M, 1796. CtGL, 76.
Stamford. Rittenhouse Chapter, Royal Arch Masons. M, 1810. CtRA, 44–45.
           Foreign Mission Society of the Western District of Fairfield County. P,
           1812. ABCFM (1813), 39.
           Female Benevolent Society. P, 1816. CtES (1816), 12.
Stratford. St. John's Lodge. M, 1766. CtGL, 55.
           Jerusalem Chapter, Royal Arch Masons. M, 1813. CtRA, 59.
           Female Foreign Mission Society. P, 1814. ABCFM (1814), 51.
           Charitable Education Society. P, 1816. BR, Sept. 10, 1816.
           Female Charitable Society. P, 1816. CtES (1816), 7.
           Stratfield Female Mite Society. P, 1816. CSABB (1816), 9.
Tolland. Uriel Lodge. M, by 1794. CtGL, 73.
           Foreign Mission Society. P, 1813. ABCFM (1814), 51.
           Female Cent Society. P, 1817. ABM 1(1817):120.
           United Female Cent Society. P, 1817. ABS (1817), 33.
Torrington. Torringford Female Association. P, 1816. ABCFM (1817), 41.
           Torringford Young Men's Association. P, 1816. ABCFM (1817), 41.
           Gentlemen's Association. P, 1817. ABCFM (1817), 54.
           Ladies' Association. P, 1817. ABCFM (1817), 54.
           Seneca Lodge. M, 1817. CtGL, 284.
Trumbull. Benevolent Society. H, 1811. Keller, 165.
Vernon. Female Charitable Society. P, 1817. CBS (1817), 17.
Wallingford. Compass Lodge. M, 1769. CtGL, 401.
           Cent Society. P, 1815. ABCFM (1815), 30.
Warren. Meridian Sun Lodge. M, 1796. CtGL, 76.
           Female Cent Society. P, 1815. MSC (1816), 20.
           Moral Society. R, 1816. BR, July 31, 1816.
           Female Charitable Society. P, 1817. CBS (1817), 17.
Washington. Rising Sun Lodge. M, by 1794. CtGL, 73.
           Female Association. P, 1810. CBS (1810), 12.
           Gentlemen's Association. P, 1817. ABCFM (1817), 45.
Waterbury. Harmony Lodge. M, 1765. MGL, 1.
Watertown. Federal Lodge. M, 1791. CtGL, 65.
           Female Benevolent Society. P, 1816. CtES (1816), 7.

Weston. Ark Lodge. M, 1797. CtGL, 87.

    Female Cent Society. P, 1817. MSC (1818), 20.

Wethersfield. Cent Society. P, 1809. *A Narrative on the Subject of Missions* (Hartford, 1810), 19.

    Stepney Society. P, 1811. CBS (1811), 21.

    Female Foreign Mission Society. P, 1813. ABCFM (1813), 39.

    Newington Cent Society. P, 1813. Pan NS5(1813):380.

    Stepney Female Foreign Mission Society. P, 1813. ABCFM (1813), 23.

    Rocky Hill Female Cent Society. P, 1814. CBS (1814), 16.

    Third Parish Branch Society for the Reformation of Morals. R, 1814. CEM NS7(1814):309.

    Stepney Ladies' Cent Society. P, 1815. MSC (1816), 20.

    Charitable Female Society. P, 1816. CtES (1816), 7.

Willington. Female Association. P, 1807. *A Narrative on the Subject of Missions . . . 1807* (Hartford, 1808), 15.

Winchester. Gentlemen's Association. P, 1817. ABCFM (1817), 42.

    Ladies' Association. P, 1817. ABCFM (1817), 42.

    Winsted Gentlemen's Association. P, 1817. ABCFM (1817), 42.

    Winsted Ladies' Association. P, 1817. ABCFM (1817), 42.

Windham. Moriah Lodge. M, 1790. CtGL, 65.

    Eastern Star Lodge. M, 1798. CtGL, 111.

    Female Charitable Society. P, 1808. MSC (1809), 15.

    Trinity Chapter, Royal Arch Masons. M, 1808. CtRA, 38.

    Foreign Mission Society of Windham County. P, 1814. ABCFM (1815), 29.

    Female Mite Society. P, 1816. CSABB (1816), 7.

Windsor. Female Benevolent Society. P, 1817. CBS (1817), 17.

Wolcott. Branch Society for the Reformation of Morals. R, 1814. CEM NS7(1814):305.

Woodbridge. Hart's Lodge. M, 1791. CtGL, 65.

    Cent Society. P, 1812. ABCFM (1812), 23.

    Branch Society for the Reformation of Morals. R, 1814. CEM NS7(1814):309.

Woodbury. King Solomon's Lodge. M, by 1783. CtGL, 402.

    Female Benevolent Society. P, 1808. MSC (1809), 15.

    Fidelity Chapter, Royal Arch Masons. M, 1808. CtRA, 39.

Woodstock. First Parish Branch Society for the Reformation of Morals. R, 1814. CEM NS7(1814):304.

    North Woodstock Branch Society for the Reformation of Morals. R, 1814. CEM NS7(1814):305.

    Female Benevolent Society. P, 1816. CSABB (1816), 11.

    Female Cent Society. P, 1816. CSABB (1816), 11–12.

Maine

Albany. Female Cent Society. P, 1816. Joseph Field, *Prosperity Promised to the Lovers of Jerusalem* (Northampton, 1816), 34.

Alna. Female Cent Society. P, 1815. Pan 12(1816):80.

Augusta. Female Religious Society. P, 1814. ABCFM (1814): 48.

      Female Society. P, 1815. Pan 12(1816):80.

      Female Bible Society. P, by 1816. BR, July 3, 1816.

Bangor. Rising Virtue Lodge. M, 1803. *Massachusetts Register . . . 1804* (Boston, 1803), 58.

      Maine Charity School. P, 1815. *Laws* (Bangor, 1815).

Bath. Humane Society. M, 1792. Ms.

      Solar Lodge. M, 1804. Mass GL (1857).

      Female Cent Society (1). P, 1810. MeMS (1810), 27.

      Foreign Mission Society. P, 1812. ABCFM (1812), 20.

      Society for Discountenancing and Suppressing Public Vices. R, 1813. Jesse Appleton, *Discourse* (Boston, 1813).

      Female Cent Society (2). P, 1814. MeMS (1814), 29.

      Female Mite Society. P, 1816. MBMM 4(1816):417.

      Heathen School Society. P, 1816. ABCFM (1816), 24.

Belfast. Belfast Lodge. M, 1816. Mass GL (1857).

Bethel. Cent Society. P, 1816. NHMS (1817), 6.

Biddeford. Cent Society. P, 1813. MeMS (1813), 25.

      Biddeford and Saco Society for Promoting Christianity Among the Heathen and Jews. P, 1817. ABCFM (1817), 38.

Bloomfield. Female Cent Society. P, 1817. MeMS (1817), 39.

Bowdoinham. Village Lodge. M, 1817. Mass GL (1857).

Bridgeton. Oriental Lodge. M, 1804. Mass GL (1857).

Bristol. Broad Cove Cent Society. P, 1816. MeMS (1816), 27.

Brunswick. Foreign Mission Society. P, 1812. ABCFM (1812), 20.

      Brunswick, Topsham, and Harpswell Society for the Suppression of Intemperance. R, 1813. *Constitution* (Portland, 1814).

Bucksport. Female Charitable Society. H, 1815. *Maine Register . . . 1820* (Portland, 1819), 145.

Buxton. Felicity Lodge. M, 1809. Mass GL (1857).

Camden. Amity Lodge. M, 1801. Mass GL (1857).

Caratunk. Cent Society. P, 1813. MeMS (1813), 24.

Castine. Hancock Lodge. M, 1794. Mass GL (1857).

      Hancock County Female Tract Society. P, 1804. ATS (1824), 208.

Columbia. Tuscan Lodge. M, 1797. Mass GL (1857).

Eastport. Eastern Lodge. M, 1801. Mass GL (1857).

      Female Mite Society. P, 1817. ABM 1(1817):149.

Edgecombe. Cent Society. P, 1811. MeMS (1811), 31.

Ellsworth. Female Society. P, 1817. ABM 1(1817), 239.

      Hancock and Penobscot Bible Society. P, 1817. *Massachusetts Register . . . 1817,* 190.

Falmouth. Foreign Mission Society. P, by 1813. ABCFM (1813), 39.

      Female Foreign Mission Society. P, 1813. ABCFM (1813), 39.

      Female Cent Society. P, 1813. ABCFM (1813), 24.

Farmington. Farmington Lodge. M, 1808. Mass GL (1857).

      Female Missionary Society. P, 1817. MeMS (1817), 38.

Frankfurt. Female Assistant Society. P, 1815. MeMS (1815), 31.
    Female Society. P, 1815. Pan 12(1816):80.
Freeport. Freeport Lodge. M, 1814. Mass GL (1857).
    Cent Society. P, 1815. ABCFM (1815), 30.
Fryeburg. Pythagorean Lodge. M, 1803. Mass GL (1857).
    Society for Suppressing Vice. R, 1816. Mass. Reg. (1816), 170.
Gorham. Female Cent Society. P, 1810. MeMS (1810), 27.
    Female Assistant Missionary Society. P, 1813. MeMS (1813), 25.
    Society for the Suppression of Vice. R, 1814. MSSI (1815), 20.
    Female Society. P, 1815. Pan 12(1816):80.
Hallowell. Kennebec Lodge. M, 1796. Mass GL (1857).
    Foreign Mission Society. P, 1812. ABCFM (1812), 20.
    Theological Society for the Education of Pious Young Men for the Ministry.
        P, 1812. Mass. Reg. (1816), 190.
    Female Religious Society. P, 1813. MeMS (1813), 28.
    Female Society. P, 1815. Pan 12(1816):80.
    Kennebec County Bible Society. P, 1816. BR, July 3, 1816.
Hamden. Cent Society. P, 1817. ABCFM (1817), 38.
Limerick. Female Cent Society. P, 1816. MeMS (1817), 36.
Livermore. Oriental Star Lodge. M, 1811. Mass GL (1857).
Machias. Warren Lodge. M, 1778. Mass GL (1857).
Minot. Female Donation Society. P, 1810. MeMS (1810), 27.
    Female Society. P, 1815. Pan 12(1816):80.
New Gloucester. Cumberland Lodge. M, 1803. Mass GL (1857).
    Female Donation Society. P, 1814. MeMS (1814), 31.
    Female Cent Society. P, 1815. MeMS (1815), 31.
Newfield. Female Cent Society. P, 1817. MeMS (1817), 39.
Norridgwock. Cent Society. P, 1810. MeMS (1810), 29.
    Female Tract Society. P, 1817. ABCFM (1817), 39.
North Yarmouth. Female Cent Society (1). P, 1810. MeMS (1810), 27.
    Female Cent Society (2). P, 1810. MeMS (1810), 27.
    Foreign Mission Society. P, 1812. ABCFM (1812), 20.
    Female Missionary Society. P, 1817. MeMS (1817), 38.
Norway. Cent Society. P, 1817. ABCFM (1817), 37.
Otisfield. Praying Society. P, 1817. MeMS (1817), 39.
Paris. Oxford Lodge. M, 1807. Mass GL (1857).
    Oxford County Bible Society. P, 1816. BR, July 3, 1816.
Parsonsfield. Female Cent Society. P, 1817. MeMS (1817), 39.
Portland. Portland Lodge. M, 1762. Mass GL (1857).
    Marine Society. M, 1796. *Laws of the Marine Society* (Portland, 1798).
    Lodge No. 1. M, 1796. Mass GL (1857).
    Benevolent Society. H, 1805. Ms.
    Mount Vernon Chapter, Royal Arch Masons. M, 1805. Mass RA (1819), 19.
    Ancient Landmark Lodge. M, 1806. Mass GL (1857).
    Maine Missionary Society. P, 1807. Ms.

Bible Society of Maine. P, 1809. Ms.

Eastern Society for Promoting the Knowledge of Sacred Scriptures. P, 1809. *Massachusetts Register . . . 1810* (Boston, 1809), 45.

Female Cent Society. P, 1810. MeMS (1810), 27.

Auxiliary Society for Suppressing Intemperance. R, 1812. MSSI (1816), 22.

Foreign Mission Society. P, 1812. ABCFM (1812), 20.

Society for Suppressing Vice and Immorality. R, 1812. Pan NS4(1812):568–569.

Female Missionary Society. P, 1813. MeMS (1813), 25.

Female Donation Society. P, 1814. MeMS (1814), 31.

Society of Young Men. P, 1814. MeMS (1814), 31.

Cent Society. P, 1815. MeMS (1815), 30.

Maine Charitable Mechanic Association. M, 1815. *Constitution* (Portland, 1817).

Maine Baptist Auxiliary Society to Aid Foreign Missions. P, 1816. MBMM 4(1816):417.

Portland Female Charitable Society. H, 1816. Mass. Reg. (1817), 213.

Peace Society of Maine. R, 1817. BR, Apr. 22, 1817.

Readfield. Female Assistant Missionary Society. P, 1815. MeMS (1815), 32.

Female Society. P, 1815. Pan 12(1816):80.

Saco (Pepperelboro). Saco Lodge. M, 1802. Mass GL (1857).

Saco and Biddeford Branch of the Foreign Mission Society. P, 1812. ABCFM (1812), 20.

Saco and Biddeford Society for Promoting Christianity Among the Heathen and Jews. P, 1817. BR, Feb. 10, 1818.

Scarborough. Cent Society. P, 1815. ABCFM (1815), 30.

Sedgwick. Female Mite Society. P, 1816. ABM 1(1817):72.

Steuben. Ionic Lodge. M, 1806. Mass GL (1857).

Sumner. Female Cent Society. P, 1811. MeMS (1811), 31.

Thomaston. Orient Lodge. M, 1805. Mass GL (1857).

Religious Society. P, 1816. MeMS (1816), 28.

Female Missionary Society. P, 1817. MeMS (1817), 38.

Topsham. United Lodge. M, 1801. Mass GL (1857).

Vassalborough. Cent Society. P, 1815. ABCFM (1816), 22.

Waldoborough. Female Cent Society. P, 1811. MeMS (1811), 31.

Warren. St. George Lodge. M, 1806. Mass GL (1857).

Waterford. Cent Society. P, 1816. MeMS (1816), 27.

Wells. York Lodge. M, 1813. Mass GL (1857).

Cent Society. P, 1815. MeMS (1815), 28.

Westbrook. Cent Society. P, 1815. ABCFM (1815), 30.

Foreign Mission Society. P, 1815. ABCFM (1815), 29.

Winthrop. Cent Society. P, 1810. MeMS (1810), 29.

Female Assistant Missionary Society. P, 1815. MeMS (1815), 32.

Female Society. P, 1815. Pan 12(1816):80.

Temple Lodge. M, 1817. Mass GL (1857).

Wiscasset. Lincoln Lodge. M, 1792. Mass GL (1857).

> Lincoln and Kennebec Religious Tract Society. P, 1802. *Tracts* (Wiscasset, 1804), 3.
>
> Female Charitable Society. H, 1805. Ms.
>
> Foreign Mission Society. P, 1815. ABCFM (1815), 29.
>
> Lincoln County Bible Society. P, 1816. BR, Aug. 28, 1816.
>
> Cent Society. P, 1816. MeMS (1816), 27.

York. Cent Society. P, 1815. MeMS (1815), 30.

> Bible Society. P, 1817. Mass. Reg. (1817), 191.

Massachusetts

Abington. Cent Society. P, 1814. Pan 10(1814):332.

Adams. Bible Society. P, 1816. ABS (1818), 29.

Amesbury. Association in First Society. P, 1816. ABCFM (1817), 44.

> Female Association, First Parish. P, 1817. ABCFM (1817), 47.
>
> Female Charitable Association. P, 1817. ABCFM (1817), 47.
>
> Male Association, First Parish. P, 1817. ABCFM (1817), 47.

Andover. Massachusetts Society for Promoting Christian Knowledge. P, 1803. BR, Feb. 21, 1816.

> Society for Promoting Good Morals in Phillips Academy. R, 1812. *Constitution* (Andover, 1814).
>
> New England Tract Society. P, 1814. Pan 10(1814):232–234.
>
> Foreign Mission Society of Phillips Academy. P, 1815. ABCFM (1815), 29.
>
> Moral Society. R, 1815. Ebenezer Porter, *Great Effects Result from Little Causes* (Andover, 1815).
>
> South Parish Female Charitable Society. R, 1815. *Constitution* (Newburyport, 1815).
>
> Essex Auxiliary Society for Educating Pious Youth for the Gospel Ministry. P, 1816. Joseph Dana, *Sermon* (Andover, 1816).
>
> Society for Aiding the Translation of the Scriptures, in Phillips' Academy. P, 1816. ABCFM (1816), 24.
>
> South Parish Charitable Society. P, 1816. ABCFM (1817), 44.
>
> South Parish Juvenile Bible Society. P, 1816. ABCFM (1817), 37.
>
> Ladies Auxiliary Education Society. P, 1817. AES (1817), 37.

Ashburnham. Female Charitable Society. P, 1816. EMS (1816), 9.

Ashby. Social Lodge. M, 1798. Mass GL (1857).

> Auxiliary Education Society. P, 1817. AES (1817), 37.
>
> Female Cent Society. P, 1817. Pan 13(1817):380.

Athol. Harris Lodge. M, 1802. Mass GL (1857).

> Branch, Religious Charitable Society of Worcester. P, 1816. Pan 12(1816): 511.
>
> Female Cent Society. P, 1816. Pan 12(1816):511.

Attleborough. Adoniram Chapter, Royal Arch Masons. M, 1816. Mass RA (1819), 19.

> East Precinct Female Benevolent Society. P, 1817. Pan 13(1817):380.
>
> Female Mite Society. P, 1817. ABM 1(1817), 239.

Barnardston (Florida). Female Benevolent Society. P, 1817. ABCFM (1817), 39.

Barnstable. Fraternal Lodge. M, 1801. Mass GL (1857).

        Auxiliary Bible Society. P, 1817. BR, July 29, 1817.

Becket. Female Charitable Society. P, 1814. MSBC (1815), 9.

Bedford. Cent Society. P, 1811. MSPCK (1811), 33.

Belchertown. Mount Vernon Lodge. M, 1807. Mass GL (1857).

Berkley. Female Cent Society. P, 1816. Pan 12(1816):328.

Berlin. Female Cent Society. P, 1816. Pan 12(1816):511.

Beverly. Amity Lodge. M, 1779. Mass GL (1857).

        Charity School. H, 1814. BSSV (1814), 2.

        Association in Beverly, North Society. P, 1816. ABCFM (1817), 44,

        Cent Society. P, 1816. BSSV (1816), 12.

        Female Mite Society. P, 1817. MBMS (1818), 10.

Billerica. Cent Society. P, 1814. Pan 10(1814):331.

        Branch Bible Society. P, 1817. BSCM (1817), 14.

Blandford. Federal Lodge. M, 1792. Mass GL (1857).

Boston. Scots' Charitable Society. H, 1657. *Constitution and By-Laws of the Scots' Charitable Society at Boston (Instituted 1657)* (Cambridge, Mass., 1878).

        Episcopal Charitable Society. H, 1724. Ms.

        St. John's Grand Lodge. M, 1733. MGL 1.

        First Lodge. M, 1733. Mass GL (1857).

        Charitable Irish Society. H, 1737. Ms.

        Masters' Lodge. M, 1738. Mass GL (1857).

        Boston Marine Society. M, 1742. *Gleanings from the Records of the Boston Marine Society,* comp. Nath'l Spooner (Boston, 1879).

        Society for Encouraging Industry and Employing the Poor. H, c. 1750. Charles Chauncy, *The Idle-Poor Secluded from the Bread of Charity* (Boston, 1752).

        Second Lodge. M, 1750. Mass GL (1857).

        Third Lodge. M, 1750. Mass GL (1857).

        St. Andrew's Lodge. M, 1756. Ms.

        Company for Promoting of Good Order. R, 1761. Ms.

        Massachusetts [Charitable] Society. M, 1762. Ms.

        Massachusetts Grand Lodge. M, 1769. MGL 1.

        St. Andrew's Chapter, Royal Arch Masons. M, 1769. Mass RA, 23.

        Massachusetts Lodge. M, 1770. Mass GL (1857).

        Rising Sun Lodge. M, 1772. Mass GL (1857).

        Prince Hall Lodge. M, 1775. *Proceedings of the One Hundredth Anniversary* (Boston, 1885), 12.

        Friendship Lodge. M, 1779. Mass GL (1857).

        St. John's Lodge. M, 1783. *History of St. John's Lodge of Boston* (Boston, 1917).

        Society of the Cincinnati of Massachusetts. M, 1783. Myers, 38–39.

        Rising States Lodge. M, 1784. Mass GL (1857).

        Massachusetts Congregational Charitable Society. H, 1786. Ms.

Massachusetts Humane Society. H, 1786. M. A. DeWolfe Howe, *The Humane Society of the Commonwealth of Massachusetts* (Boston, 1918).

Society for Propagating the Gospel Among the Indians and Others in North America. P, 1787. Ms.

Grand Lodge of Massachusetts. M, 1792. MGL 1.

Harmonic Lodge. M, 1792. Mass GL (1857).

Massachusetts Charitable Fire Society. H, 1792. Ms.

Massachusetts Society for the Aid of Immigrants. H, 1793. *Information for Immigrants to the New-England States* (Boston, 1795).

Baptist Education Fund. P, 1794. *Massachusetts Register and United States Calendar . . . 1810* (Boston, 1809), 46.

Massachusetts Charitable Mechanic Association. M, 1795. *Annals of the Massachusetts Charitable Mechanic Association,* comp. Joseph Tinker Buckingham (Boston, 1853).

African Society. M, 1796. *Laws* (Boston, 1802).

Columbian Lodge. M, 1796. Mass GL (1857).

Dispensary. H, 1796. Ms.

Massachusetts Grand Chapter, Royal Arch Masons. M, 1798. Voorhis, 7.

Sons of the African Society. M, 1798. *Laws* (Boston, 1802).

Massachusetts Missionary Society. P, 1799. BR, May 15, 1816.

Female Asylum. H, 1800. Ms.

Female Society for Missionary Purposes. P, 1800. Pan 10(1814):334.

Mount Lebanon Lodge. M, 1801. Mass GL (1857).

Boston Encampment, Knights Templar. M, 1802. GC, 91–92.

Female Cent Society. P, 1802. Samuel Austin, *Christians Bound to Spread the Gospel* (Salem, 1803), 25.

Massachusetts Baptist Missionary Society. P, 1802. MBMS (1818).

Massachusetts Society for Promoting Christian Knowledge. P, 1803. *Constitution* (Charlestown, 1803).

Massachusetts Society for Promoting Christian Knowledge, Piety, and Charity. P, 1805. *Massachusetts Register and United States Calendar . . . 1811* (Boston, 1810), 45. Massachusetts Bible Society. P, 1809. Ms.

American Board of Commissioners for Foreign Missions. P, 1810. Ms.

Society of Donations. P, 1810. J. S. J. Gardiner, *Sermon* (Boston, 1813).

Corban Society. P, 1811. BR, Nov. 11, 1817.

Foreign Mission Society. P, 1811. ABCFM (1813), 38.

Howard Benevolent Society. H, 1811. BR, Nov. 5, 1816.

Massachusetts General Hospital. H, 1811. *Report of the Committee of By Laws* (Boston, 1811).

Fragment Society. H, 1812. Ms.

Fuel Society. H, 1812. *Independent Chronicle* (Boston), Dec. 21, 1812.

Society for the Religious and Moral Improvement of Seamen. R, 1812. Pan 10(1814):334.

Evangelical Tract Society. P, 1813. ATS (1824):208.

Massachusetts Society for the Suppression of Intemperance. R, 1813. Ms.

Asylum for Indigent Boys. H, 1814. BR, Apr. 29, 1817.

Female Bible Society. P, 1814. Ms.

Massachusetts Baptist Education Society. P, 1814. ABM 1(1817):238.

New England Tract Society. P, 1814. ATS (1824), 208.

American Society for Educating Pious Youth for the Gospel Ministry (American Education Society). P, 1815. Ms.

Baptist Female Education Society. P, 1815. *Constitution* (Boston, 1815).

Female Education Society. P, 1815. BR, Apr. 1, 1817.

Society for Missionary Purposes. P, 1815. ABCFM (1815), 27.

South Boston Cent Society. P, 1815. Pan 11(1815):329.

Auxiliary Society for the Moral and Religious Instruction of the Poor. R, 1816. Pan 13(1817):509.

Auxiliary Tract Society. P, 1816. ATS (1824), 208.

British Charitable Society. H, 1816. *First Annual Report* (Cambridge, Mass., 1817).

Episcopal Eastern Diocese Tract Society. P, 1816. ATS (1824), 208.

Female Auxiliary Society for the Moral and Religious Instruction of the Poor. P, 1816. *Constitution* (Boston, 1816).

Female Society of Boston and Vicinity for the Promotion of Christianity Among the Jews. P, 1816. Pan 14(1818):285.

Female Tract Society. P, 1816. ATS (1824), 208.

Juvenile Female Society. P, 1816. BR, Dec. 10, 1816.

Warren Association Education Society. P, 1816. ABM 1(1817), 238.

African Sunday School. P, 1817. ABM 1(1817), 277.

American Female Education Society. P, 1817. Pan 13(1817), 179.

Baptist Foreign Mission Society. P, 1817. ABM 1(1817):198.

Children's Cent Society. P, 1817. ABM 1(1817):150.

Education Society for the People of Color in New-England. P, 1817. BR, Dec. 30, 1817.

Graham Society. P, 1817. BR, Feb 10, 1818.

Massachusetts Baptist Evangelical Tract Society. P, 1817. ABM 1(1817):191.

Prayer-Book and Episcopal Tract Society, for the Eastern Diocese. P, 1817. BR, Jan. 21, 1817.

Second Baptist Church Female Sabbath School Society. P, 1817. *Constitution* (Boston, 1817).

Society for the Moral and Religious Instruction of the Poor. P, 1817. BR, Oct. 9, 1817.

Boxford. Moral Society of Boxford and Topsfield. R, 1815. Peter Eaton, *Sermon* (Andover, 1816).

North Parish Charitable Society. P, 1815. MSPCK (1816), 34.

First Society Gentlemen's Association. P, 1816. ABCFM (1817), 44.

First Society Ladies' Association. P, 1816. ABCFM (1817), 44.

Second Society Female Association. P, 1816. ABCFM (1817), 44.

Boylston. Female Charitable Society. P, 1816. ABCFM (1816), 23.

> Female Foreign Mission Society. P, 1816. Reuben Puffer, *The Widow's Mite* (Worcester, 1816).

Bradford (Haverhill, Groveland). Philendian Society. H, 1813. J. D. Kingsbury, *Memorial History of Bradford, Mass.* (Haverhill, 1883), 117–118.

> Society for the Suppression of Intemperance. R, 1814. MSSI (1814), 3.

> Female Charitable Society. P, 1815. Ms.

> Female Cent Society. P, 1816. ABCFM (1816), 28.

> First Society Gentlemen's Association. P, 1816. ABCFM (1817), 44.

> First Society Ladies' Association. P, 1816. ABCFM (1817), 44.

> Second Society Gentlemen's Association. P, 1816. ABCFM (1817), 44.

> Second Society Ladies' Association. P, 1816. ABCFM (1817), 44.

Braintree. Associated Females. P, 1813. ABCFM (1813), 23.

> Female Religious Society. P, 1814. ABCFM (1814), 49.

> Norfolk Auxiliary Society for Educating Pious Youth. P, 1817. AES (1817), 36.

> Union Religious Society. P, 1817. BR, Sept. 23, 1817.

Bridgewater. Fellowship Lodge. M, 1797. Mass GL (1857).

> Society for the Suppression of Intemperance. R, 1814. MSSI (1814), 4.

> Newell Society. P, 1815. ABCFM (1816), 22.

> Evangelical Society. P, 1816. ABCFM (1817), 37.

Brimfield. Female Benevolent Society. P, 1816. Ms.

Brookfield. Meridian Sun Lodge. M, 1797. Mass GL (1857).

> Association to Aid the Massachusetts Society for Suppressing Intemperance. R, 1815. MSSI (1816), 21.

> South Parish Cent Society. P, 1815. MSPCK (1816), 34.

> West Parish Cent Society. P, 1815. *Report of the Executive Committee of the Bible Society of Massachusetts . . . 1815* (Boston, 1815), 22.

Cambridge. Amicable Lodge. M, 1805. Mass GL (1857).

> First Parish Cent Society. P, 1811. MSPCK (1811), 33.

> Second Parish Cent Society. P, 1811. MSPCK (1811), 33.

> Female Humane Society. H, 1814. Ms.

> Humane Society. H, 1814. *Account of the Cambridge Humane Society* (n.p., 1819).

> Cambridgeport Female Cent Society. P, 1815. MSPCK (1816), 34.

> Cambridgeport Female Charitable Society. P, 1815. MSPCK (1816), 34.

> Society for Promoting Theological Education. P, 1816. Ms.

Carlisle. Cent Society. P, 1814. Pan 10(1814):331.

Charlemont. [unnamed association]. P, 1817. ABCFM (1817), 59.

Charlestown. King Solomon's Lodge. M, 1783. Mass GL (1857).

> Female Cent Society. P, 1813. MSPCK (1813), 34.

> Society for the Suppression of Vice and Immorality. R, 1814. MSSI (1814), 4.

Associated Females. P, 1816. ABCFM (1817), 36.

Female Mite Society. P, 1817. ABCFM (1817), 38.

Charlton. Fayette Lodge. M, 1796. Mass GL (1857).

King Solomon's Chapter, Royal Arch Masons. M, 1805. Mass RA (1819), 19.

Female Cent Society. P, 1817. AES (1817), 39.

Chelmsford. Pentucket Lodge. M, 1807. Mass GL (1857).

Female Mite Society. P, 1817. ABM 1(1817), 239.

Chelsea. Winthrop Society for Suppressing Intemperance. R, 1815. MSSI (1816), 21.

Cheshire. Franklin Lodge. M, 1794. Mass GL (1857).

Concord. Charitable [Library] Society. H, 1795. Ms.

Corinthian Lodge. M, 1797. Mass GL (1857).

Auxiliary Society for the Suppression of Intemperance. R, 1814. MSSI (1814), 3.

Bible Society in the County of Middlesex. P, 1814. Pan 10(1814):127.

Female Charitable Society. H, 1814. Ms.

Female Cent Society. P, 1816. EMS (1816), 9.

Female Missionary Mite Society. P, 1817. ABCFM (1817), 56.

Cummington. Female Society. P, 1814. *Report of the Trustees Made to the Hampshire Missionary Society . . . 1814* (Northampton, 1814), 17.

Foreign Mission Society. P, 1814. ABCFM (1815), 29.

[unnamed society]. P, 1814. ABCFM (1814), 49.

Female Society in Cummington, Formed to Aid in the Translations. P, 1815. ABCFM (1815), 26.

Orion Lodge. M, 1815. Mass GL (1857).

Female Foreign Mission Society. P, 1817. ABCFM (1817), 59.

Society in Cummington for the Support of Schools Among the Heathen. P, 1817. ABCFM (1817), 48.

Dalton. Female Cent Society. P, 1815. ABCFM (1815), 30.

Danvers. United States Lodge. M, 1778. Mass GL (1857).

Jordan Lodge. M, 1808. Mass GL (1857).

Auxiliary Society for the Suppression of Intemperance. R, 1814. MSSI (1814), 3.

Cent Society. P, 1814. Pan 10(1814):332.

North Parish Female Reading Society. P, 1815. ABCFM (1815), 26.

Danvers and Middleton Charitable Female Cent Society for Promoting Christian Knowledge. P, 1816. Benjamin Wadsworth, *Female Charity* (Andover, 1817).

Association in North Parish. P, 1817. ABCFM (1817), 46.

Female Association in South Parish. P, 1817. ABCFM (1817), 45.

South Parish Juvenile Society of Females. P, 1817. ABCFM (1817), 45.

Dartmouth. Branch, Female Heathen's Friend Society. P, 1813. ABCFM (1813), 24.

Dedham. Constellation Lodge. M, 1802. Mass GL (1857).

First Parish Cent Society. P, 1811. MSPCK (1811), 33.

Auxiliary Society for the Suppression of Intemperance. R, 1814. MSSI (1814), 4.

Baptist Missionary Society of Norfolk County. P, 1815. BMNS (1818).

South Parish Female Society for Promoting Religious Purposes. P, 1817. BR, Apr. 29, 1817.

Deerfield. Female Benevolent Society. H, 1817. Ms.

Dennis. Sumner Lodge. M, 1801. Mass GL (1857).

Dorchester. Union Lodge. M, 1796. Mass GL (1857).

Female Benevolent Society. P, 1812. BR, Dec 23, 1817.

Cent Society. P, 1814. Pan 10(1814):523.

Dracut. Cent Society. P, 1813. NHBS (1813), 4.

Dracut and Chelmsford Female Cent Society. P, 1815. ABCFM (1815), 30.

Society of Females. P, 1817. ABCFM (1817), 39.

Duxbury. Corner Stone Lodge. M, 1801. Mass GL (1857).

Fairhaven. Female Heathen's Friend Society. P, 1813. ABCFM (1813), 24.

Falmouth. Marine Lodge. M, 1798. Mass GL (1857).

Bible and Missionary Society. P, 1816. BR, July 29, 1817.

Fitchburg. Female Foreign Mission Society. P, 1815. ABCFM (1815), 30.

Branch, Religious Charitable Society of Worcester. P, 1816. Pan 12(1816):511.

Female Charitable Society. P, 1816. Pan 12(1816):511.

Foxboro. Female Tract Society. P, 1816. Pan 13(1817):379.

Framingham. Middlesex Lodge. M, 1795. Mass GL (1857).

Cent Society. P, 1814. MSPCK (1815), 30.

Female Mite Society. P, 1815. BMSN (1818), 10.

Franklin. Montgomery Lodge. M, 1797. Mass GL (1857).

Cent Society. P, 1815. Pan 11(1815):330.

Missionary Society. P, 1817. ABM 1(1817):120.

Gloucester. Tyrian Lodge. M, 1770. Mass GL (1857).

Dorcas Society. H, 1812. Salem Dorcas Society Records, Essex Institute, Sept. 14, 1812.

Female Society for Promoting Christian Knowledge. P, 1814. BSSV (1814), 2.

Female Association in Sandy Bay. P, 1816. ABCFM (1817), 43.

Association of Females. P, 1817. ABCFM (1817), 46.

Association of Males. P, 1817. ABCFM (1817), 46.

Female Mission Cent Society. P, 1817. ABCFM (1817), 37.

Granville. Mount Pleasant Lodge. M, 1808. Mass GL (1857).

Great Barrington. Female Charitable Society. P, 1812. ABCFM (1812), 20.

Branch Bible Society. P, 1817. ABS (1818), 29.

Greenfield. Republican Lodge. M, 1794. Mass GL (1857).

Foreign Mission Society of the County of Franklin. P, 1812. ABCFM (1813), 39.

Auxiliary Society for Suppressing Intemperance. R, 1814. MSSI (1814), 2.

Franklin Association of Ministers Charitable Society. P, 1816. *Constitution* (Greenfield, 1816).

Female Benevolent Society. H, 1817. Records of the Female Benevolent Society of . . . Deerfield, April 1817.

Franklin Chapter, Royal Arch Masons. M, 1817. Mass RA (1819), 19.

Franklin County Bible Society. P, 1817. ABS (1817). ABS (1818), 29.

Groton. St. Paul's Lodge. M, 1797. Mass GL (1857).

St. John's Chapter, Royal Arch Masons. M, 1803. Mass RA (1819), 19.

Charitable Female Society. P, 1814. Daniel Chaplin, *Discourse* (Andover, 1814).

Female Cent Society. P, 1814. Pan 11(1815):431.

Female Auxiliary Education Society. P, 1815. BR, Jan. 28, 1817.

Female Auxiliary Subscription Society. P, 1816. AES (1817), 36.

Hadley. Female Society for Translation. P, 1816. ABCFM (1816), 24.

Charitable Society of Young Men for the Education of Heathen Children in Heathen Lands. P, 1817. ABCFM (1817), 48.

Hamilton. Female Cent Society. P, 1816. BSSV (1816), 12.

Gentlemen's Association. P, 1816. ABCFM (1817), 43.

Ladies' Association. P, 1816. ABCFM (1817), 43.

Hanover. Auxiliary Society for Suppressing Intemperance. R, 1816. MSSI (1817), 22.

Hardwick. Mount Zion Lodge. M, 1800. Mass GL (1857).

Female Cent Society. P, 1814. ABCFM (1814), 51.

Foreign Mission Society. P, 1816. ABCFM (1816), 28.

Religious Charitable Society. P, 1816. ABCFM (1816), 24.

Harvard. Cent Society. P, 1811. MSPCK (1811), 33.

Charitable Female Society. P, 1814. Pan 11(1815):431.

Auxiliary Female Association. P, 1816. ABCFM (1817), 43.

Branch, Religious Charitable Society of Worcester. P, 1816. Pan 12(1816):511.

Female Auxiliary Charitable Society, Religious Charitable Society of Worcester. P, 1816. Pan 12(1816):511.

Religious Tract Society. P, 1816. Pan 12(1816):510.

Haverhill. Merrimack Lodge. M, 1802. Mass GL (1857).

Missionary Society. P, 1814. MSPCK (1815), 30.

Merrimack Missionary Society. P, 1815. *Constitution* (Exeter, 1815).

Association in Haverhill. P, 1816. ABCFM (1817), 44.

Female Cent Society. P, 1816. Pan 12(1816):329.

India and Foreign Mission Society. P, 1816. Mass. Reg. (1817), 144.

First Parish Female Association. P, 1817. ABCFM (1817), 45.

Gentlemen's Association. P, 1817. ABCFM (1817), 45.

Juvenile Association. P, 1817. ABCFM (1817), 45.

Male Juvenile Association. P, 1817. ABCFM (1817), 44.

Hingham. Old Colony Lodge. M, 1792. Mass GL (1857).

Female Religious Society. P, 1815. ABCFM (1815), 25.

Female Cent Society. P, 1817. ABCFM (1817), 59.

Holden. Branch Religious Charitable Society of Worcester. P, 1816. Pan 12(1816):511.

Female Charitable Society. P, 1816. ABCFM (1817), 36.

Holliston. Cent Society. P, 1814. Pan 10 (1814):331.

> Female Charitable Society. P, 1817. AES (1817), 38.

Holmes' Hole (Vineyard Haven). King Solomon in Perfection Lodge. M, 1797. Mass GL (1857).

Hopkinton. Female Cent Society. P, 1816. ABCFM (1816), 28.

Ipswich. Unity Lodge. M, 1779. Mass GL (1857).

> First Parish Female Cent Society. P, 1814. MSPCK (1815), 30.
>
> South Parish Cent Society. P, 1814. MSPCK (1815), 30.
>
> Evangelical Tract Society. P, 1815. MSSI (1815), 23.
>
> Female Cent Society. P, 1815. MSPCK (1811), 33.
>
> First Parish Charitable Society. P, 1815. MSPCK (1816), 34.
>
> Reading Society. P, 1816. ABCFM (1817), 37.
>
> Second Parish Gentlemen's Association. P, 1816. ABCFM (1817), 43.
>
> Association in Second Parish. P, 1817. ABCFM (1817), 46.

Kingston. "Essay to do good Society." P, 1812. ABCFM (1812), 23.

> Female Missionary Society. P, 1817. ABM 1(1817):150.

Lancaster. Trinity Lodge. M, 1778. Mass GL (1857).

Lanesborough. Mystic Lodge. M, 1810. Mass GL (1857).

> Female Cent Society. P, 1814. MSBC (1815), 9.

Lee. Female Cent Society. P, 1815. MSBC (1815), 10.

Leicester. Society for Promoting Good Morals in Leicester Academy. R, 1814. *Constitution* (Leicester, 1814).

Lenox. Evening Star Lodge. M, 1795. Mass GL (1857).

> Berkshire Society for Promoting Good Morals. R, 1814. MSSI (1815), 22.
>
> Female Cent Society. P, 1814. MSBC (1815), 8.

Leominster. Aurora Lodge. M, 1801. Mass GL (1857).

> Female Charitable Society. P, 1816. Pan 12(1816):511.

Lexington. Hiram Lodge. M, 1797. Mass GL (1857).

Longmeadow. Female Association. P, 1815. ABCFM (1815), 27.

Lynn. Mount Carmel Lodge. M, 1805. Mass GL (1857).

> Female Benevolent Society. H, 1814. Ms.
>
> Female Association. P, 1817. ABCFM (1817), 45.
>
> Female Cent Society. P, 1817. MBMS (1818), 10.
>
> Gentlemen's Association. P, 1817. ABCFM (1817), 45.

Malden. Female Mite Society. P, 1817. MBMS (1818), 10.

> Mount Herman Lodge. M, 1817. Mass GL (1817).

Manchester. Society of Females. P, 1816. ABCFM (1816), 24.

> Association of Males. P, 1817. ABCFM (1817), 47.
>
> Female Cent Society. P, 1817. ABCFM (1817), 47.

Marblehead. Philanthropic Lodge. M, 1760. Mass GL (1857).

> Marine Society. M, 1798. *Laws and Regulations* (Boston, 1798).
>
> Gentlemen's Association. P, 1816. ABCFM (1817), 43.
>
> Ladies' Association. P, 1816. ABCFM (1817), 43.
>
> Association for the Education of Heathen Children. P, 1817. ABCFM (1817), 46.
>
> Union Moral Society. R, 1817. MSSI (1817), 22.

Marlborough. Hudson Missionary Society. P, 1814. MSBC (1815), 9.

    East Parish Cent Society. P, 1815. Pan 11(1815):330.

    Foreign Mission Society of Marlborough and Framingham. P, 1815. ABCFM (1815), 29.

Medfield. Female Cent Society. P, 1814. Pan 11(1815):432.

    Female Mite Society. P, 1815. BMSN (1818), 10.

    Female Social Circle. P, 1815. MSPCK (1816), 33.

    Auxiliary Society for Christianity Amongst the Jews. P, 1817. BR, June 10, 1817.

Medway. Cent Society. P, 1814. Pan 10(1814):332.

    West Parish Female Cent Society. P, 1817. Pan 13(1817):380.

Mendon. Charity Lodge. M, 1803. Mass GL (1857).

Methuen. Domestic Female Bible Society. P, 1816. Pan 12(1816):514.

    Female Society. P, 1817. ABM 1(1817):73.

Middleborough. Cent Society. P, 1815. Pan 11(1815):330.

    Female Mite Society. P, 1817. ABM 1(1817):149.

Milford. Cent Society. P, 1814. Pan 10(1814):332.

    Female Mite Society. P, 1816. ABM 1(1816):73.

    Moral and Religious Charitable Society. P, 1816. Pan 12(1816):511.

    Female Missionary Society. P, 1817. ABM 1(1817):120.

Millbury. Branch, Religious Charitable Society of Worcester. P, 1816. Pan 12(1816):511.

Milton. Female Charitable Society. P, 1816. ABCFM (1817), 43.

Monson. Thomas Lodge. M, 1796. Mass GL (1857).

Nantucket. Union Lodge. M, 1771, 1801. Mass GL (1857).

New Bedford. Washington Remembered Lodge. M, 1803. Mass GL (1857).

    Benevolent Society, Instituted for the Purpose of Aiding Pious and Needy Young Men on Acquiring Education. P, 1811. *Constitution* (New Bedford, 1811).

    Female Heathen's Friend Society. P, 1813. ABCFM (1813), 24.

    Auxiliary Society for Suppressing Intemperance. R, 1815. MSSI (1816), 22.

    Branch Bible Society. P, 1817. ABS (1817), 15.

New Braintree. Religious Charitable Society. P, 1814. Pan 11(1815):432.

    Cent Society. P, 1815. Pan 12(1816):479.

New Marlboro. Cincinnatus Lodge. M, 1795. Mass GL (1857).

    Auxiliary Missionary Society. P, 1814. MSBC (1815), 8.

    Female Cent Society. P, 1816. ABCFM (1816), 28.

    Female Foreign Mission Society. P, 1816. ABCFM (1816), 28.

New Salem. Golden Rule Lodge. M, 1815. Mass GL (1857).

Newbury. Byfield Cent Society. P, 1807. MMM 3(1807):114.

    Female Cent Society. P, 1815. Pan 12(1816):79.

    Third Society Ladies' Association. P, 1816. ABCFM (1817), 44.

    Third Society Gentlemen's Association. P, 1816. ABCFM (1817), 44.

Newburyport. St. John's Lodge. M, 1766. Mass GL (1857).

    Marine Society. M, 1772. William H. Bayley and Oliver O. Jones, *History of the Marine Society of Newburyport, Massachusetts* (Newburyport, 1906).

    St. Peter's Lodge. M, 1772. Mass GL (1857).

Society for the Relief of the Industrious Poor. H, 1786. *Essex Journal,* Oct. 11, 1786.

King Cyrus Chapter, Royal Arch Masons. M, 1790. Mass RA, 23.

Newburyport Encampment, Knights Templar. M, 1795. GC, 91.

Merrimack Humane Society. H, 1803. *Institution* (Newburyport, 1803).

St. Mark's Lodge. M, 1803. Mass GL (1857).

Female Charitable Society. H, 1804. Ms.

Mechanic Association. M, 1806. *Constitution* (Newburyport, 1807).

Merrimack Bible Society. P, 1810. BR, July 3, 1816.

Female Cent Society. P, 1811. MSPCK (1811), 33.

Charitable Association, Formed in Newburyport, for the Relief of the Poor. H, 1812. Pan 10(1814):46–47.

Female Missionary Society. P, 1812. Pan 10(1814):186.

Merrimack Branch Foreign Mission Society. P, 1812. ABCFM (1812), 38.

Society for the Suppression of Vice and Immorality. R, 1812. *Articles of Association* (Newburyport, 1813).

Female Benevolent Society. P, 1814. Pan 10(1814):46–47.

Female Auxiliary Education and Mission Society. P, 1815. BR, Jan. 28, 1817.

Cent Society (2). P, 1815. MSPCK (1816), 33.

Second Education Cent Society. P, 1815. BR, Jan. 28, 1817.

Society of Serious Young Men. P, 1815. ABCFM (1815), 26.

Young Men's Auxiliary Education Society. P, 1815. BR, Jan. 28, 1817.

Female Bible and Tract Society. P, 1816. ATS (1824), 208.

Young Men's Auxiliary Society. P, 1816. Pan 13(1817):92.

Auxiliary Society for Educating Pious Youth. P, 1817. AES (1817), 36.

Female Auxiliary Missionary and Evangelical Society. P, 1817. AES (1817), 37.

Female Reading Society. P, 1817. AES (1817), 36.

Female Society in Newburyport for Educating Heathen Children. P, 1817. ABCFM (1817), 47.

Juvenile Society. P, 1817. AES (1817), 36.

Newton. West Parish Cent Society. P, 1815. MSPCK (1816), 34.

Auxiliary to the Massachusetts Baptist Evangelical Tract Society. P, 1817. ABM 1(1817):191–192.

Female Benevolent Society. P, 1817. MBMS (1818), 10.

Northampton. Hampshire Lodge. M, 1784. Mass GL (1857).

Hampshire Missionary Society. P, 1801. *Report of the Trustees* (Northampton, 1802).

Charitable Female Association. P, 1803. *Plan of a Female Association* (Northampton, 1803).

Foreign Mission Society. P, 1812. ABCFM (1812), 39.

Society for the Reformation of Morals. R, 1814. Ms.

Hampshire Charitable Society. P, 1815. *Address* (Northampton, 1815).

Hampshire Bible Society. P, 1816. Ms.

Society in Northampton Which Meets for United Prayer. P, 1817. ABCFM (1817), 38.

Northboro. Fredonia Lodge. M, 1810. Mass GL (1857).

    Cent Society. P, 1814. Pan 10(1814):332.

    Female Auxiliary Cent Society, Religious Charitable Society of Worcester. P, 1816. Pan 12(1816):511.

    Northborough and Berlin Branch, Religious Charitable Society of Worcester. P, 1816. Pan 12(1816):511.

Northbridge. Branch, Religious Charitable Society of Worcester. P, 1816. Pan 12(1816):511.

    Female Cent Society. P, 1816. Pan 12(1816):511.

Northfield. Harmony Lodge. M, 1796. Mass GL (1857).

    Female Society. P, 1812. ABCFM (1812), 23.

    Cent Society. P, 1815. BR, Jan. 28, 1817.

Norton. Bristol Lodge. M, 1797. Mass GL (1857).

Norwich (Huntington). Female Association. P, 1815. MSPCK (1816), 34.

Orange. Perseverance Lodge. M, 1815. Mass GL (1857).

Otis. Charitable Society. P, 1817. AES (1817), 38.

Oxford. Olive Branch Lodge. M, 1797. Mass GL (1857).

Paxton. Branch Religious Charitable Society of Worcester. P, 1816. Pan 12(1816):511.

    Female Cent Society. P, 1816. Pan 12(1816):511.

Pepperell. Cent Society. P, 1815. MSPCK (1816), 34.

    Female Charitable Society. P, 1815. John Bullard, *A Discourse, Delivered at Pepperell* (Amherst, NH, 1815).

Peru. Sincerity Lodge. M, 1801. Mass GL (1857).

    Female Charitable Society. P, 1816. ABCFM (1817), 37.

Pittsfield. Female Charitable Society. P, 1812. ABCFM (1812), 23.

    Berkshire Society for Promoting Good Morals. R, 1814. Pan 11(1815):93.

    Female Cent Society. P, 1815. ABCFM (1815), 30.

    Berkshire Bible Society. P, 1817. BR, Dec. 30, 1817.

Plymouth. Forefathers' Rock Lodge. M, 1801. Mass GL (1857).

    Cent Society. P, 1811. ABCFM (1812), 20.

    Female Foreign Mission Society. P, 1813. ABCFM (1813), 23.

    United Society of Plymouth County and Vicinities, Auxiliary to the Baptist Board of Foreign Missions. P, 1814. *Origination and Constitution* (n.p., 1815).

    Plymouth and Norfolk Bible Society. P, 1816. Henry Colman, *Discourse* (Boston, 1816).

    Plymouth and Bristol Foreign Mission Society. P, 1817. ABM 1(1817):120.

Plympton. Branch of the Heathen's Friend Society. P, 1814. ABCFM (1814), 48.

    Foreign Mission Society. P, 1814. ABCFM (1814), 51.

Princeton. Branch, Religious Charitable Society of Worcester. P, 1816. Pan 12(1816):511.

    Female Charitable Society. P, 1816. Pan 12(1816):511.

Randolph. Cent Society. P, 1814. Pan 10(1814):332.

    Female Mite Society. P, 1817. BMSN (1818), 11.

Raynham. Philandrian Society. M, 1800. Zechariah Eddy, *Philandrianism* (Providence, 1800).

Reading. Mount Moriah Lodge. M, 1798. Mass GL (1857).

Cent Society. P, 1814. Pan 10(1814), 331.

Good Samaritan Lodge. M, 1816. Mass GL (1857).

Heathen School Society. P, 1816. BR, Oct. 8, 1816.

Rehoboth. Evening Star Lodge. M, 1798. Mass GL (1857).

Rural Lodge. M, 1801. Mass GL (1857).

Auxiliary Society for the Suppression of Intemperance. R, 1814. MSSI (1815), 21.

Richmond. Female Cent Society. P, 1812. MSBC (1813), 35.

Rochester. Heathen's Friend Society. P, 1816. ABCFM (1816), 24.

Society Auxiliary to the Principal Society for the Suppression of Intemperance. R, 1817. MSSI (1818), 14.

Rowe. Mountain Lodge. M, 1806. Mass GL (1857).

Rowley. Female Cent Society. P, 1813. ABCFM (1813), 24.

Female Foreign Mission Society. P, 1813. ABCFM (1813), 39.

Moral Society of Rowley and Byfield. R, 1814. *Constitution* (Newburyport, 1814).

Female Auxiliary Education Society. P, 1816. Pan 13(1817):92.

Second Society Female Association. P, 1816. ABCFM (1817), 44.

First Parish Gentlemen's Association. P, 1817. ABCFM (1817), 46.

First Parish Ladies' Association. P, 1817. ABCFM (1817), 46.

Second Parish Gentlemen's Association. P, 1817. ABCFM (1817), 46.

Roxbury. Charitable Society. H, 1794. *Whereas in a State of Civil Society. . . .* (Boston, 1794).

Washington Lodge. M, 1796. Mass GL (1857).

Society for the Suppression of Intemperance. R, 1817. MSSI (1818), 13.

Royalston. Female Cent Society. P, 1811. MSPCK (1811), 33.

Branch, Religious Charitable Society of Worcester. P, 1816. Pan 12(1816):511.

Rutland. Thompson Lodge. M, 1812. Mass GL (1857).

Female Auxiliary Charitable Society. P, 1816. Pan 12(1816):511.

Salem. Marine Society. M, 1766. *Laws* (Salem, 1873).

Essex Lodge. M, 1779, 1791. Mass GL (1857).

East India Marine Society. M, 1799. Ms.

Female Charitable Society. H, 1801. Ms.

Society for Promoting the Education of Religious Young Men. P, 1803. *Constitution* (Salem, 1803).

Baptist Female Cent Society. P, 1805. BR, Aug. 7, 1816.

Tabernacle Female Charitable Society. P, 1806. BR, Aug. 7, 1816.

Bible Society. P, 1810. Ms.

Dorcas Society. H, 1811. Ms.

Washington Chapter, Royal Arch Masons. M, 1811. Mass RA (1819), 19.

Baptist Bible, Translation, and Foreign Mission Society. P, 1812. BR, Aug. 7, 1816.

Female Charitable Library. R, 1812. BR, Aug. 7, 1816.

Female Tract Society. P, 1812. BR, Aug. 7, 1816.

Foreign Mission Society. P, 1812. BR, Aug. 7, 1816.

Humane Society. H, 1812. BR, Aug. 7, 1816.
Baptist Female Reading Society. P, 1813. BR, Aug. 7, 1816.
Female Book and Tract Society. P, 1814. BR, Aug. 7, 1816.
Female Charitable School. H, 1814. BR, Aug. 7, 1816.
Associated Females in Brown Emerson's Society. P, 1815. Pan 11(1815):329.
Baptist Female Education Society. P, 1815. BR, Aug. 7, 1816.
Female Auxiliary Education Society. P, 1815. BR, Aug. 7, 1816.
Juvenile Benevolent Society. H, 1815. BR, Aug. 7, 1816.
Juvenile Bible Society. P, 1815. BR, Aug. 7, 1816.
Second Charity School. H, 1815. BR, Aug. 7, 1816.
Tabithean Society. P, 1815. BR, Aug. 7, 1816.
Auxiliary Missionary Society. P, 1816. BR, Aug. 7, 1816.
Children's Auxiliary Missionary Society. P, 1816. BR, Aug. 7, 1816.
Children's Reading and Bible Society. P, 1816. BR, Aug. 7, 1816.
Female Society for Promoting the Education of Heathen Children. P, 1816.
    BR, Aug. 7, 1816.
Sabbath School. P, 1816. BR, Aug. 7, 1816.
Young Misses Society for the Improvement of Youthful Minds. R, 1816. BR,
    Aug. 7, 1816.
Auxiliary Society to Disseminate the Gospel Among the Destitute Within
    Our Own State. P, 1817. Pan 13(1817):379.
Charitable Mechanic Association. M, 1817. Ms.
Essex Auxiliary Education Society. P, 1817. AES (1817), 38.
Female Cent Society. P, 1817. ABM 1(1817):149.
Salisbury. Association. P, 1816. ABCFM (1817), 44.
Sandisfield. Rising Sun Lodge. M, 1808. Mass GL (1857).
Scituate. Auxiliary Society for the Suppression of Intemperance. R, 1817. Ms.
Sheffield. Sheffield Lodge. M, 1803. Mass GL (1857).
    Female Charitable Society. P, 1812. ABCFM (1812), 23.
    Female Foreign Mission Society. P, 1815. ABCFM (1815), 30.
Shrewsbury. Branch, Religious Charitable Society of Worcester. P, 1816. Pan
    12(1816):511.
    Female Auxiliary Society, Religious Charitable Society of Worcester. P,
    1816. Pan 12 (1816):511.
Somerset. Association for the Reformation of Morals. R, 1815. *Constitution* (n.p., 1815).
South Brimfield. Humanity Lodge. M, 1811. Mass GL (1857).
South Hadley. Jerusalem Lodge. M, 1797. Mass GL (1857).
    Female Foreign Mission Society. P, 1815. ABCFM (1815), 30.
    Female Charitable Society in Aid of Foreign Missions. P, 1817. ABCFM
    (1817), 39.
South Reading (Wakefield). Cent Society. P, 1814. Pan 10(1814):331.
    Auxiliary Society for the Suppression of Intemperance. R, 1817. MSSI
    (1818), 8.
Southampton. Society to Discountenance Vice and Encourage Virtue. R, 1814. MSSI
    (1816), 21.

Southboro. Branch, Religious Charitable Society of Worcester. P, 1816. Pan
12(1816):511.

Southbridge. Branch, Religious Charitable Society of Worcester. P, 1816. Pan
12(1816):511.

Southwick. Sylvan Lodge. M, 1807. Mass GL (1857).

Springfield. Foreign Mission Society. P, 1812. ABCFM (1812), 39.

    Hampden Bible Society. P, 1813. BSCM (1816), 21.

    Hampden Lodge. M, 1817. Mass GL (1857).

    Morning Star Chapter, Royal Arch Masons. M, 1817. Mass RA (1819), 19.

Stockbridge. Berkshire Lodge. M, 1777. Mass GL (1857).

    Missionary Society of Berkshire and Columbia. P, 1798. *Constitution and
Address* (Stockbridge, 1798).

    Female Cent Society. P, 1813. MSBC (1813), 36.

Stoneham. Female Charitable Society. P, 1816. Pan 12(1816):328.

Stoughton. Rising Star Lodge. M, 1799. Mass GL (1857).

Sturbridge. Charitable Female Society. P, 1815. MSPCK (1816), 34.

    Branch, Religious Charitable Society of Worcester. P, 1816. Pan
12(1816):510.

Sunderland. Pacific Lodge. M, 1801. Mass GL (1857).

Sutton. Branch, Religious Charitable Society of Worcester. P, 1816. Pan 12(1816):511.

    Female Cent Society. P, 1816. Pan 12(1816):511.

Taunton. King David Lodge. M, 1798. Mass GL (1857).

    Bible Society in the County of Bristol. P, 1814. BSCM (1816), 21.

    Norfolk Missionary Society. P, 1816. Mass. Reg. (1817), 149.

Templeton. Female Cent Society. P, 1816. EMS (1816), 9.

Topsfield. Association. P, 1816. ABCFM (1817), 44.

Townsend. Female Cent Society. P, 1815. Pan 11(1815):329.

    Society of Young Men. P, 1815. ABCFM (1815), 26.

Truro. King Hiram Lodge. M, 1795. Mass GL (1857).

Tyringham. Female Foreign Mission Society. P, 1813. ABCFM (1813), 23.

Upton. Branch, Religious Charitable Society of Worcester. P, 1816. Pan 12(1816):511.

    Female Cent Society. P, 1816. Pan 12(1816):511.

Uxbridge. Female Cent Society. P, 1815. ABCFM (1815), 30.

    Religious Society of Females. P, 1815. ABCFM (1815), 26.

    Female Prayer Society. P, 1817. BR, June 10, 1817.

Waltham. Female Cent Society. P, 1816. EMS (1816), 9.

Ware. Foreign Mission Society. P, 1812. ABCFM (1813), 39.

    Female Cent Society. P, 1813. ABCFM (1813), 23.

    Female Mite Society. P, 1817. MBMS (1818), 10.

    Female Society. P, 1817. ABM 1(1817):149.

Wareham. Benevolent Society. P, 1812. Thomas Andros, *Zion Enlarged* (Boston, 1812).

    Society of Females. P, 1815. ABCFM (1815), 25.

    Female Cent Society. P, 1817. ABCFM (1817), 59.

Watertown. Meridian Lodge. M, 1797. Mass GL (1857).

    Female Cent Society. P, 1816. EMS (1816), 9.

Wellfleet. Adams Lodge. M, 1797. Mass GL (1857).
    Cent Society. P, 1811. MSPCK (1811), 33.
Wenham. Association. P, 1816. ABCFM (1817), 43.
    Female Mite Society. P, 1817. MBMS (1818), 10.
West Boylston. Female Cent Society. P, 1815. ABCFM (1815), 26.
    Branch, Religious Charitable Society of Worcester. P, 1816. Pan
        12(1816):511.
    Female Auxiliary Charitable Society, Religious Charitable Society of Wor-
        cester. P, 1816. Pan 12(1816):511.
West Cambridge (Arlington). Charitable and Reading Society. H, 1816. *Massachusetts*
    Register and United States Calendar . . . 1816 (Boston, 1815), 220.
West Springfield. Mite Society. P, 1817. ABM 1(1817):198.
West Stockbridge. Wisdom Lodge. M, 1803. Mass GL (1857).
    Female Cent Society. P, 1815. MSBC(1815), 10.
Westborough. Female Cent Society. P, 1815. ABCFM (1815), 30
    Branch, Religious Charitable Society of Worcester. P, 1816. Pan 12(1816):
        510.
    Female Auxiliary Charitable Society, Religious Charitable Society of Wor-
        cester. P, 1816. Pan 12(1816):511.
    Female Society. P, 1817. ABM 1(1817), 239.
Western (Warren). Female Charitable Society. P, 1816. ABCFM (1817), 37.
Westfield. Female Foreign Mission Society. P, 1815. ABCFM (1815), 30.
Westford. Female Cent Society. P, 1815. ABCFM (1815), 30.
    Female Charitable Society. P, 1815. ABCFM (1815), 26.
    Female Charitable Cent Society. P, 1817. AES (1817), 39.
Westminster. Branch, Religious Charitable Society of Worcester. P, 1816. Pan 12(1816):
        511.
    Female Cent Society. P, 1816. Pan 12(1816):511.
Weston. Cent Society. P, 1814. Pan 10(1814):523.
Weymouth. Union Society. P, 1813. ABCFM (1813), 23.
    Female Cent Society. P, 1815. Pan 12(1816), 79.
    Society for the Reformation of Morals in Weymouth and Braintree. R,
        1817. MSSI (1818), 12.
Wilbraham. Rising Virtue Lodge. M, 1802. Mass GL (1857).
Williamstown. Friendship Lodge. M, 1785. Mass (1857).
    Female Charitable Society. P, 1813. MSBC (1813), 36.
    Auxiliary Education Society. P, 1815. BR, Jan. 28, 1817.
    Auxiliary Society for Promoting Good Morals. R, 1815. William Allen,
        Sermon (Pittsfield, 1815).
Wilmington. Cent Society. P, 1814. Pan 10(1814), 523.
Winchendon. Female Cent Society. P, 1814. ABCFM (1814), 51.
    Branch, Religious Charitable Society of Worcester. P, 1816. Pan 12(1816):
        511.
Windsor. Female Cent Society. P, 1816. ABCFM (1816), 28.
    Auxiliary Education Society. P, 1817. AES (1817), 37.

Woburn. Female Reading Society. P, 1815. BR, Jan. 28, 1817.

Worcester. Morning Star Lodge. M, 1793. Mass GL (1857).

>Social Club. M, 1805. [William Samuel Buel], *Address* (Worcester, 1806).

>Evangelical Missionary Society. P, 1807. *Address and Constitution* (Cambridge, Mass., 1807).

>Religious Charitable Society in the County of Worcester. P, 1812. Ms.

>Female Cent Society. P, 1814. ABCFM (1814), 51.

>Auxiliary Bible Society in Worcester County. P, 1815. BSCM (1816), 21.

>Branch, Religious Charitable Society of Worcester. P, 1816. Pan 12(1816):510.

>Female Baptist Charitable Society. P, 1817. ABM 1(1817):150.

>Female Reading and Charitable Society. P, 1817. Charles Augustus Goodrich, *Address* (Worcester, 1817).

Worthington. Female Charitable Society. P, 1815. BR, Jan. 28, 1817.

Wrentham. Associated Females. P, 1813. ABCFM (1813), 24.

>Cent Society. P, 1814. Pan 10(1814):332.

>Society of Young Ladies. P, 1814. ABCFM (1814), 49.

>Auxiliary Society for the Suppression of Intemperance. R, 1815. Daniel Clarke Sanders, *Sermon* (Dedham, 1815).

>Norfolk Auxiliary Education Society. P, 1816. Pan 13(1817):92.

>Female Reading Society. P, 1817. ABCFM (1817), 37.

Yarmouth. Association for the Suppression of Intemperance. R, 1817. MSSI (1818), 14.

New Hampshire

Acworth. Female Charitable Society. P, 1816. ABCFM (1817), 36.

>Moral Society. R, 1816. ABCFM (1817), 37.

Alstead. Cent Society (East Branch). P, 1814. NHCI (1814), 8.

>Cent Society (West Branch). P, 1815. NHCI (1815), 8.

Amherst. Benevolent Lodge. M, 1797. NHGL2, 558.

>Religious Tract Society. P, 1816. BR, Dec. 17, 1816.

>Bible and Tract Society. P, 1817. *New Hampshire Register . . . 1818* (Concord, N.H., 1817), 73.

>Female Foreign Mission Society. P, 1817. ABCFM (1817), 59.

>Female Reading Society. P, 1817. ABCFM (1817), 37.

>Foreign Mission Society. P, 1817. ABCFM (1817), 48.

>Hillsboro Bible and Charitable Society. P, 1817. BR, June 17, 1817.

Antrim. Female Cent Society. P, 1815. ABCFM (1816), 23.

>Association. P, 1817. ABCFM (1817), 39.

Bath. Female Cent Society. P, 1814. ABCFM (1814), 51.

>Meridian Sun Lodge. M, 1815. NHGL2, 558.

Bedford. Female Cent Society. P, 1812. Ms.

>Female Association. P, 1817. ABCFM (1817), 47.

Boscawen. Moral Society. R, 1815. Charles Carleton Coffin, *The History of Boscawen and Webster* (Concord, N.H., 1878), 182–183.

>West Parish Cent Society. P, 1815. NHCI (1815), 8.

[unnamed association #1]. P, 1817. ABCFM (1817), 46.

[unnamed asociation #2]. P, 1817. ABCFM (1817), 46.

Canaan. Moral Society. R, 1814. NHCI (1814), 10.

Mount Moriah Lodge. M, 1815. NHGL2, 558.

Canterbury. Female Association. P, 1817. ABCFM (1817), 38.

Foreign Mission Society. P, 1817. ABCFM (1817), 37.

Male Association. P, 1817. ABCFM (1817), 38.

Charlestown. Faithful Lodge. M, 1788. MGL 1, 486.

Chester. Female Cent Society. P, 1817. ABCFM (1817), 59.

Claremont. Hiram Lodge. M, 1798. NHGL2, 558.

Female Heathen School Society. P, 1817. BR, Oct. 9, 1817.

Society for the Religious Education of an Orphan Under the Care of the American Missionaries in Asia. P, 1817. BR, Oct. 9, 1817.

[unnamed association]. P, 1817. ABCFM (1817), 59.

Concord. Blazing Star Lodge. M, 1799. NHGL2, 558.

New Hampshire Missionary Society. P, 1801. Ms.

Female Cent Society. P, 1805. New Hampshire Missionary Society Records, New Hampshire Historical Society, June 4, 1805.

Female Charitable Society. H, 1811. Ms.

New Hampshire Bible Society. P, 1812. NHBS (1812).

Society for Discountenancing Vice and Immorality. R, 1813. *The Concord Society for Discountenancing Vice and Immorality* (Concord, N.H., 1813).

New Hampshire Society for the Relief of Widows and Children of Deceased Presbyterian and Congregational Clergymen. H, 1816. BR, Sept. 24, 1816.

Female Association. P, 1817. ABCFM (1817), 56.

Foreign Mission Society. P, 1817. ABCFM (1817), 37.

Juvenile Charitable Society. H, 1817. Concord Female Charitable Society Records, New Hampshire Historical Society, 44.

Cornish. Cent Society. P, 1812. NHBS (1812), 18.

Female Foreign Mission Society. P, 1814. ABCFM (1814), 47.

Ladies' Society. P, 1815. ABCFM (1815), 30.

Association of Young Men. P, 1817. ABCFM (1817), 45.

Deerfield. Sullivan Lodge. M, 1807. NHGL2, 558.

Dover. Federal Lodge. M, 1792. NHGL2, 558.

Strafford Lodge. P, 1817. NHGL2, 559.

Dublin. Altemont Lodge. M, 1815. NHGL2, 558.

Society Auxiliary to the Baptist Board for Foreign Missions. P, 1817. ABM 1(1817):73.

[unnamed association]. P, 1817. ABCFM (1817), 47.

Dunbarton. Cent Society. P, 1806. NHMS (1806), 7.

Female Foreign Mission Society. P, 1817. ABCFM (1817), 59.

Society in Aid of Foreign Missions. P, 1817. ABCFM (1817), 38.

Exeter. Society of the Cincinnati of New Hampshire. M, 1783. Myers, 43.

Washington Lodge. M, 1801. NHGL2, 558.

Cent Society. P, 1808. NHMS (1810), 5.

Society for the Reformation of Morals. R, 1816. Jonathan French, *Sermon* (Exeter, 1816).

Fitzwilliam. Charity Lodge. M, 1806. NHGL2, 558.

Cent Society. P, 1813. NHBS (1813), 4.

Francestown. Cent Society. P, 1806. NHMS (1806), 7.

Ladies' Society. P, 1812. NHBS (1812), 19.

Female Association. P, 1817. ABCFM (1817), 46.

Gentlemen's Association. P, 1817. ABCFM (1817), 46.

Gilsum. Female Cent Society. P, 1816. NHBS (1816), 30.

Goffstown. Bible Lodge. M, 1816. NHGL2, 558.

[unnamed association]. P, 1817. ABCFM (1817), 38.

Greenland. Female Charitable Society. P, 1814. Pan 11(1815):432.

Hampstead. Female Charitable Society. P, 1815. ABCFM (1815), 26.

Hancock. Cent Society. P, 1814. NHCI (1814), 8.

Foreign Mission Society. P, 1817. ABCFM (1817), 37.

Hanover. Dartmouth Lodge. M, 1788. MGL 1, 486.

Franklin Lodge. M, 1796. NHGL2, 558.

Cent Society. P, 1806. NHMS (1806), 6.

St. Andrew's Chapter, Royal Arch Masons. M, 1807. NHRA (1819), 18.

Bible Society of Dartmouth College. P, by 1816. BR, July 3, 1816.

Haverhill. Union Lodge. M, 1799. NHGL2, 558.

Female Cent Society. P, 1815. NHCI (1815), 7.

South Parish Junior Cent Society. P, 1816. NHCI (1816), 6.

Hillsboro. Hillsboro County Bible and Charitable Society. P, 1817. NHMS (1817), 6.

Female Reading Society. P, 1817. ABCFM (1817), 37.

Foreign Mission Society. P, 1817. ABCFM (1817), 37.

Hollis. Philanthropic Society. P, 1801. Ms.

Cent Society. P, 1805. NHMS (1806), 4.

Moral Benevolent Society. R, 1815. NHMS (1815), 18.

Hopkinton. Trinity Chapter, Royal Arch Masons. M, 1807. NHRA (1819), 18.

Cent Institution. P, 1809. NHMS (1810), 5.

Association of Females. P, 1817. ABCFM (1817), 46.

Association of Males. P, 1817. ABCFM (1817), 46.

Jaffrey. Cent Society. P, 1813. NHBS (1813), 4.

[unnamed association]. P, 1817. ABCFM (1817), 59.

Female Missionary Society. P, 1817. ABCFM (1817), 36.

Keene. Rising Sun Lodge. M, 1784. MGL 1, 486.

Cent Society. P, 1815. NHCI (1815), 4.

Auxiliary Tract Society. P, 1815. ATS (1824), 208.

Cheshire Chapter, Royal Arch Masons. M, 1816. NHRA (1819), 18.

Monthly Prayer Meeting. P, 1816. NHBS (1816), 30.

Cheshire County Bible Society. P, 1817. *Sixth Report of the New-Hampshire Bible Society* (Concord, N.H., 1817), 9.

Kingston. Cent Society. P, 1815. MSPCK (1816), 34.

Lancaster. Female Cent Society. P, 1816. ABCFM (1816), 23.

Lebanon. Cent Society. P, 1809. NHMS (1810), 5.

Londonderry. Female Cent Society. P, 1812. NHBS (1812), 19.

Lyman. Cent Society. P, 1817. P, 1817. *Seventeenth Annual Report of the Board of Trustees of the New-Hampshire Missionary Society . . . 1818* (Concord, N.H., 1818), 21.

Marlborough. Cent Society. P, 1814. NHCI (1814), 8.

Meredith. Female Cent Society. P, 1815. MSPCK (1816), 34.

Merrimac. Bible Society. P, 1817. ABS (1817), 33.

      [unnamed association. P, 1817. ABCFM (1817), 59.

Milford. Society of Females. P, 1815. ABCFM (1816), 23.

Moultonborough. Morning Star Lodge. M, 1804. NHGL2, 558.

Mount Vernon. Association for Educating Heathen Children. P, 1817. ABCFM (1817), 48.

New Boston. Cent Society. P, 1813. NHBS (1813), 4.

      Female Mite Society. P, 1817. ABM 1(1817):149.

New Ipswich. Cent Society. P, 1809. NHMS (1810), 5.

      Bethel Lodge. M, 1815. NHGL2, 558.

      [unnamed association]. P, 1815. ABCFM (1815), 30.

      Second Prayer Society. P, 1815. ABCFM (1815), 26.

      Auxiliary Education Society. P, 1817. AES (1817), 39.

New London. King Solomon's Lodge. M, 1802. NHGL2, 558.

      Cent Society. P, 1817. *Report on the Concerns of the New-Hampshire Cent Institution . . . 1817* (Concord, N.H., 1817), 3.

Newport. Corinthian Lodge. M, 1816. NHGL2, 558.

North Hampton. Charitable Society. P, 1814. NHCI (1814), 8.

Northumberland. North Star Lodge. M, 1797. NHGL2, 558.

Nottingham. Columbian Lodge. M, 1790. NHGL2, 558.

      Female Cent Society. P, 1817. ABM 1(1817), 239.

Orford. Cent Society. P, 1809. NHMS (1810), 5.

Pelham. Cent Society. P, 1809. NHMS (1810), 5.

      Praying Society of Females. P, 1815. ABCFM (1816), 23, 24.

      Auxiliary Society for Promoting Missions. P, 1816. *Fifteenth Report of the Trustees of the New-Hampshire Missionary Society . . . 1816* (Concord, N.H., 1816), 19.

      Knitting Society. P, 1816. BR, Sept. 16, 1817.

Pembroke. Cent Society. P, 1809. NHMS (1810), 5.

Peterborough. Cent Society. P, 1815. NHCI (1815), 8.

Plainfield. Cheshire Lodge. M, 1815. NHGL2, 558.

Plymouth. Olive Branch Lodge. M, 1803. NHGL2, 558.

      Cent Society. P, 1809. NHMS (1810), 5.

Portsmouth. St. John's Lodge. M, 1734. MGL 1, 482.

      Marine Society. M, 1765. Ronald H. Quilici, "The Portsmouth Marine Society: Social Diversity in a Colonial Maritime Community," *Historical New Hampshire* 30 (1975):101–112.

      St. Patrick's Lodge. M, 1780. MGL 1, 485.

Grand Lodge of New Hampshire. M, 1790. NHGL2.

Associated Mechanics and Manufacturers of the State of New Hampshire. M, 1802. *Constitution* (Portsmouth, 1802).

Female Charity School. H, 1803. Joseph Buckminster, *A Discourse Delivered Before the Members of the Portsmouth Female Charity School* (Portsmouth, 1803).

Piscataqua Missionary Society. P, 1804. Ms.

Female Asylum. H, 1804. Timothy Alden, *A Discourse, Delivered Before the Members of the Portsmouth Female Asylum* (Portsmouth, 1804).

Marine Society (reestablished). M, 1808. *Laws* (Portsmouth, 1808).

Piscataqua Branch of the Foreign Mission Society. P, 1812. ABCFM (1812), 20.

Foreign Mission Society. P, 1813. ABCFM (1813), 23.

Female Society for the Promotion of Christian Knowledge. P, 1815. MSPCK (1816), 34.

Washington Chapter, Royal Arch Masons. M, 1815. NHRA (1819), 18.

Rockingham Charitable Society. P, 1817. *Constitution* (Portsmouth, 1817).

Society for the Suppression of Vice. R, 1817. *Extracts from a Report* (Portsmouth, 1817).

Raymond. Cent Society. P, 1806. NHMS (1806), 6.

Rindge. Female Cent Society. P, 1812. ABCFM (1812), 20.

Ladies' Foreign Mission Society. P, 1813. ABCFM (1813), 39.

Female Catechetical Society. P, 1815. ABCFM (1816), 22.

Rochester. Humane Lodge. M, 1811. NHGL2, 558.

Roxbury. Female Benevolent Society. P, 1816. Christopher Paige, *The Nature and Necessity of Good Works* (Keene, 1816).

Salisbury. Association of Females in Aid of Foreign Missions. P, 1817. ABCFM (1817), 38.

Association of Males in Aid of Foreign Missions. P, 1817. ABCFM (1817), 38.

Sanbornton. Centre Lodge. M, 1809. NHGL2, 558.

Female Cent Society. P, 1812. Abraham Bodwell, *Sermon* (Concord, N.H., 1813).

Society of Young Females. P, 1815. NHMS (1815), 18.

Somersworth. Female Cent Society. P, 1809. NHMS (1810), 5.

Stoddard. Female Cent Society. P, 1815. ABCFM (1815), 30.

Sullivan. Female Mite Society. P, 1813. MBMM 3(1813):381.

Female Cent Society. P, 1817. ABM 1(1817), 73.

Tamworth. Children's Society. P, 1813. NHBS (1813), 4.

Female Cent Society. P, 1816. Ms.

Templeton. Female Cent Society. P, 1816. MBMM 4(1816):417.

Walpole. Female Cent Society. P, 1814. NHCI (1814), 8.

Warner. Female Cent Society. P, 1816. NHBS (1816), 30.

Association for Educating Heathen Children and Youth. P, 1817. ABCFM (1817), 48.

Auxiliary Tract Society. P, 1817. BR, July 22, 1817.

Warren. Cent Society. P, 1815. NHCI (1815), 8.
Washington. Mount Vernon Lodge. M, 1802. NHGL2, 558.
Westmoreland. Jerusalem Lodge. M, 1792. NHGL 2, 558.
        Female Mite Society. P, 1817. ABM 1(1817):73.

Rhode Island

Bristol. St. Alban's Lodge. M, 1800. RIGL, 53.
        Evangelical Society of Bristol and Newport Counties. P, 1814. ESBN (1816).
        Female Mite Society. P, 1816. ESBN (1816), 3.
Coventry. Hamilton Lodge. M, 1816. RIGL, 296.
Cranston. Pawtuxet Female Mite Society. P, 1817. ABM 1(1817):149.
Cumberland. Morning Star Lodge. M, 1810. RIGL, 168–169.
East Greenwich. King Solomon's Lodge. M, 1806. RIGL, 109.
Glocester. Friendship Lodge. M, 1800. RIGL, 53.
Newport. St. John's Lodge. M, 1749. MGL 1, 482.
        Marine Society. M, 1752. Ms.
        African Union Society. M, 1787. Ms.
        Association of Mechanics and Manufacturers. M, 1791. Ms.
        Female Benevolent Society. H, 1805. William Patten, *The Advantages of Association* (Newport, 1805).
        Newport Chapter, Royal Arch Masons. M, 1806. RIRA, 44.
        Female Cent Society. P, 1807. MMM, July 1807, 71.
        African Benevolent Society. H, 1808. Ms.
        African Humane Society. M, 1811. Ms.
        Washington Encampment, Knights Templar. M, 1814. GC, 93.
        St. Paul's Lodge. M, 1816. RIGL, 293.
Pawtucket. Harmony Lodge. M, 1805. RIGL, 98.
        Union Lodge. M, 1808. RIGL, 123.
Providence. St. John's Lodge. M, 1757. MGL 1, 483.
        Society of the Cincinnati of Rhode Island. M, 1783. Myers, 39.
        African Union Society. M, 1789. Newport African Union Society Records, Newport Historical Society, Sept. 22, 1789.
        Association of Mechanics and Manufacturers. M, 1789. Ms.
        Society for Abolishing the Slave-Trade. R, 1789. *Constitution of a Society for Abolishing the Slave-Trade* (Providence, 1789).
        Grand Lodge of Rhode Island. M, 1791. RIGL.
        Providence Chapter, Royal Arch Masons. M, 1793. RIRA, 44.
        Marine Society. M, 1798. *Charter, Laws, &c.* (Providence, 1799).
        Rhode Island Grand Chapter, Royal Arch Masons. M, 1798. Voorhis, 7.
        Mount Vernon Lodge. M, 1799. RIGL, 45.
        Female Charitable Society. H, 1801. Ms.
        Massachusetts and Rhode Island Grand Commandery, Knights Templar. M, 1805. Voorhis, 10.
        St. John's Encampment, Knights Templar. M, 1805. GC, 93.
        Rhode Island Missionary Society. P, 1806. MMM, July 1807, 71–72.

Female Mite Society. P, 1806. *Constitution* (Providence, 1814), 3.

Association for Promoting Christian Knowledge. P, 1807. *Constitution* (Providence, 1807).

Bible Society of the State of Rhode Island. P, 1813. Ms.

Auxiliary Bible Society. P, 1815. *First Annual Report* (Providence, 1816).

Female Tract Society. P, 1815. *First Annual Report* (Providence, 1816).

Dorcas Society. H, 1816. BR, May 8, 1816.

Smithfield. Mount Moriah Lodge. M, 1804. RIGL, 91.

Tiverton. Female Mite Society. P, 1816. ESBN (1816), 3.

Warren. Mechanics Society. M, 1795. Providence Association of Mechanics and Manufacturers Records, Rhode Island Historical Society, vol. 2, June 17, 1795.

Philanthropic Society. M, 1795. *By-laws* (Warren, 1795).

Washington Lodge. M, 1796. RIGL, 30.

Female Mite Society. P, 1816. ESBN (1816), 1.

Temple Chapter, Royal Arch Masons. M, 1817. RIRA, 45.

Westerly. Washington Lodge. M, 1798. RIGL, 40.

Vermont

Addison. Female Cent Society. P, 1816. ABCFM (1816), 23.

Female Charitable Society. P, 1817. ABCFM (1817), 37.

Arlington. Newton Lodge. M, 1797. VtGL, 419.

Barnard. Windsor County Bible Society. P, 1814. VtBS (1814), 6.

Barnet. Female Cent Society. P, 1817. ABCFM (1817), 39.

Barre. Female Cent Society. P, 1816. VtBS (1816), 15.

[unnamed society]. P, 1817. ABCFM (1817), 48.

Barton. Female Cent Society. P, 1815. VtMS (1818), 8.

Bennington. Temple Lodge. M, 1793. VtGL, 419.

Bennington County Bible Society. P, 1816. VtBS (1816), 14.

Female Charitable Society. P, 1816. VtMS (1818), 8.

Benson. Female Cent Society. P, 1816. ABCFM (1816), 24.

Brandon. Washington Lodge. M, 1802. VtGL, 419.

[unnamed society]. P, 1817. ABCFM (1817), 48.

Brattleboro. Columbian Lodge. M, 1812. VtGL, 419.

Female Friendly Association. P, 1816. *Annals of Brattleboro, 1681–1895*, comp. Mary R. Cabot (Brattleboro, 1921), 1:355–356.

Bridport. Morning Sun Lodge. M, 1800. VtGL, 419.

Female Cent Society. P, 1815. ABCFM (1815), 30.

Female Charitable Society. P, 1817. ABCFM (1817), 37.

Brookfield. Female Cent Society. P, 1817. VtMS (1818), 20.

[unnamed society]. P, 1817. ABCFM (1817), 48.

Burke. Female Society. P, 1817. VtMS (1818), 15.

Burlington. Washington Lodge. M, 1795. VtGL, 419.

Cambridge. Lamouille Lodge. M, 1806. VtGL, 419.

Charlotte. Friendship Lodge. M, 1801. VtGL, 419.

Chelsea. George Washington Lodge. M, 1804. VtGL, 419.

Chester. Olive Branch Lodge, M, 1797. VtGL, 419.

Concord. Female Cent Society. P, 1816. ABCFM (1816), 23.

Cornwall. Young Ladies' Society. P, 1810. VtMS (1810), 4.

Danby. Farmers Lodge. M, 1811. VtGL, 419.

Danville. Harmony Lodge. M, 1797. VtGL, 419.

   Female Charitable Society. P, 1807. VtMS (1808), 5.

   Female Society. P, 1808. MBMM 2(1810):352.

   Caledonia County Bible Society. P, 1814. VtBS (1814), 6.

Derby. Lively Stone Lodge. M, 1803. VtGL, 419.

   Orleans County Bible Society. P, 1815. VtBS (1815), 14.

Dorset. Female Cent Society. P, 1815. ABCFM (1815), 30.

   Moral Society. R, 1815. Pettengill, *Sermon.*

Enosburgh. Missisquoi Lodge. M, 1814. VtGL, 419.

Essex. Female Cent Society. P, 1815. ABCFM (1815), 30.

   Female Charitable Society. P, 1817. ABCFM (1817), 37.

Fairfield. Female Society. P, 1817. VtBS (1817), 27.

Glover. Female Cent Society. P, 1817. VtMS (1818), 16.

Grafton. Female Cent Society. P, 1817. ABCFM (1817), 39.

Greensboro. Meridian Sun Lodge. M, 1800. VtGL, 419.

Halifax. Female Cent Society. P, 1815. ABCFM (1815), 30.

   Auxiliary Missionary Society. P, 1817. Ms.

Hardwick. Female Alms Society. P, 1816. VtBS (1816), 15.

   Female Society. P, 1817. VtMS (1818), 20.

Hartford. United Brethren Lodge. M, 1812. VtGL, 419.

   Associated Females. P, 1817. VtMS (1818), 16.

Hyde Park. Mount Vernon Lodge. M, 1813. VtGL, 419.

Irasburg. Female Society. P, 1817. VtMS (1818), 20.

Jericho Center. Ladies' Cent Society. P, 1805. Ms.

Kingston (Granville). Female Cent Society. P, 1816. VtMS (1818), 8.

Londonderry. Female Cent Society. P, 1817. ABCFM (1817), 39.

Ludlow. Green Mountain Lodge. M, 1813. VtGL, 419.

   Female Cent Society. P, 1816. ABCFM (1816), 23.

Manchester. North Star Lodge. M, 1785. VtGL, 419.

   Adoniram Lodge. M, 1817. VtGL, 419.

Marlborough. Female Cent Society. P, 1815. ABCFM (1815), 30.

Marshfield. Female Cent Society. P, 1817. VtMS (1818), 19.

Middlebury. Union Lodge. M, 1794. VtGL, 419.

   Female Society. P, 1810. VtMS (1810), 3.

   Young Ladies' Society. P, 1810. VtMS (1810), 3.

   Middlebury College Charitable Society. P, 1813. Ms.

   Addison County Bible Society. P, 1814. VtBS (1814), 6.

   Young Ladies' Bible Society. P, 1817. ABCFM (1817), 47.

Middletown. Rainbow Lodge. M, 1807. VtGL, 419.

Montpelier. Grand Lodge of Vermont. M, 1794. VtGL.

   Aurora Lodge. M, 1796. VtGL, 419.

Vermont Missionary Society. P, 1807. VtMS (1808)

Vermont Religious Tract Society. P, 1808. ATS (1824), 208.

Vermont Bible Society. P, 1812. Ms.

Female Cent Society. P, 1814. ABCFM (1814), 48.

Vermont Missionary Society, Auxiliary to the Board of Foreign Missions. P, 1815. MBMM 4(1816):293.

Washington County Bible Society. P, 1815. VtBS (1815), 12.

Female Foreign Mission Society. P, 1817. ABCFM (1817), 36.

Vermont Colonization Society. R, 1817. David M. Ludlum, *Social Ferment in Vermont, 1791–1850,* 2d ed. (Montpelier, 1948), 54.

Vermont Foreign Mission Society. P, 1817. ABM 1(1817):199.

Newbury. Charity Lodge. M, 1811. VtGL, 419.

Newfane. Blazing Star Lodge. M, 1811. VtGL, 419.

Female Cent Society. P, 1815. VtMS (1818), 8.

Norwich. Female Society. P, 1816. ABCFM (1817), 37.

Orwell. Independence Lodge. M, 1815. VtGL, 419.

Female Cent Society. P, 1816. ABCFM (1817), 37.

[unnamed society]. P, 1817. ABCFM (1817), 48.

Pawlet. Hiram Lodge. M, 1796. VtGL, 419.

Evangelical Society. P, 1804. Pan. 2(1806):237.

Charitable Christian Society. P, 1808. *Detroit Society for Genealogical Research Magazine* 37(1973):137–140.

Peacham. Moral Society. R, 1815. Pettengill, *Sermon,* 2.

Poultney. Morning Star Lodge. M, 1807. VtGL, 419.

Evangelical Society. P, 1817. Nathaniel Hall, *Discourse* (Middlebury, 1816).

Pownal. Tabernacle Lodge. M, 1809. VtGL, 419.

Putney. Golden Rule Lodge. M, 1797. VtGL, 419.

Female Cent Society. M, 1816. VtMS (1818), 8.

Randolph. Federal Lodge. M, 1798. VtGL, 419.

Female Cent Society. P, 1816. VtMS (1818), 8.

[unnamed society]. P, 1817. ABCFM (1817), 48.

Reading. Eastern Star Lodge. M, 1815. VtGL, 419.

Richmond. Female Cent Society. P, 1816. ABCFM (1816), 23.

Female Society. P, 1817. VtMS (1818), 15.

Rockingham. King Solomon's Lodge. M, 1816. VtGL, 419.

Royalton. Rising Sun Lodge. M, 1807. VtGL, 419.

Female Bible Society. P, 1817. VtBS (1817), 8.

Rupert. Morning Flower Lodge. M, 1815. VtGL, 1815.

Female Cent Society. P, 1816. ABCFM (1816), 24.

Rutland. Center Lodge. M, 1794. VtGL, 419.

Royal Arch Chapter of the State of Vermont. M, 1804. Voorhis, 7.

Female Charitable Society. P, 1812. Heman Ball, *Discourse* (Rutland, 1812).

Rutland County Bible Society. P, 1814. VtBS (1814), 6.

[unnamed society]. P, 1817. ABCFM (1817), 48.

St. Albans. Franklin Lodge. M, 1797. VtGL, 419.

Champlain Chapter, Royal Arch Masons. M, 1806. VtRA, 82.

Franklin County Bible Society. P, 1814. VtBS (1814), 6.

Female Cent Society. P, 1816. ABCFM (1816), 23.

St. Johnsbury. Juvenile Society. P, 1816. ABCFM (1817), 37.

Shaftsbury. Auxiliary to the Baptist Board of Foreign Missions. P, 1816. *Origins and Constitution* (Bennington, 1816).

Shelburne. Female Religious Society. P, 1816. Ms.

Shoreham. Female Cent Society. P, 1814. ABCFM (1814), 48.

Springfield. Vermont Lodge. M, 1781. VtGL, 419.

St. John's Lodge. M, 1811. VtGL, 419.

Thetford. Female Cent Society. P, 1810. VtMS (1810), 3.

Female Charitable Society. P, 1814. Pan 12(1816):238.

Orange County Bible Society. P, 1814. VtBS (1814), 6.

St. John's Lodge. M, 1815. VtGL, 419.

Vergennes. Dorchester Lodge. M, 1791. VtGL, 419.

Waitsfield. King Hiram Lodge. M, 1817. VtGL, 419.

Wardsboro. Mount Moriah Lodge. M, 1799. VtGL, 419.

Female Cent Society. P, 1816. VtMS (1818),8.

Weathersfield. Female Cent Society. P, 1817. ABCFM (1817), 44.

Female Charitable Society. P, 1817. ABCFM (1817), 46.

West Haven. Cement Lodge. M, 1800. VtGL, 419.

Westford. Female Cent Society. P, 1816. ABCFM (1816), 23.

Westminster. Society of the Friends of Morals and Missions in the West Parish. P, 1815. ABCFM (1815), 30.

Female Charitable Society, East Parish. P, 1817. VtMS (1818), 15.

Williamstown. [unnamed society]. P, 1817. ABCFM (1817), 48.

Wilmington. Female Cent Society. P, 1815. ABCFM (1815), 30.

Social Lodge. M, 1815. VtGL, 419.

Windham. Windham County Bible Society. P, 1813. VtBS (1814), 6.

Female Charitable Society. P, 1817. ABCFM (1817), 37.

Windsor. Female Charitable Society, East Parish. P, 1814. ABCFM (1814), 48.

Ladies' Association. P, 1814. ABCFM (1814), 5.

Woodstock. Warren Lodge. M, 1804. VtGL, 419.

Female Cent Society. P, 1816. ABCFM (1816), 22.

[unnamed society]. P, 1817. ABCFM (1817), 38.

A Note on Primary Sources

BECAUSE the notes to this study are relatively full, I have considered it neither necessary nor desirable to conclude it with a comprehensive bibliography. In the course of my research, I have tried to read everything relevant to the history of charity in New England in the late colonial and early national periods. If I have failed in this objective, it is because the quantity of this material is enormous. Published election, funeral, and ordination as well as charity sermons; newspaper articles and advertisements; magazine essays and reviews; institutional reports, constitutions, and by-laws; and edited personal and institutional papers all contribute to an understanding of charity, as do manuscript correspondence, diaries, and organizational records.

I have drawn heavily on all these sources, paying special attention to printed addresses of various kinds and to institutional records, including edited works in print and manuscript collections. Of the thousands of sermons, orations, and other works printed before 1830, I have read almost all those published through 1810, a considerable proportion of those issued between 1811 and 1815, and a sampling of those printed thereafter. Of the institutional records, both manuscript and printed, I have read all but ten of those that I am aware of, a total of more than 150 collections.[1] The ten collections I have not examined are American Board of Commissioners for Foreign Missions, Prudential Committee Records, Congregational House, Boston, Mass.; Boston Asylum for Indigent Boys, Records, Healy Library, University of Massachusetts—Boston; Portsmouth Marine Society, Records, Portsmouth Athenaeum, Portsmouth, N.H.; Providence Society for Abolishing the Slave Trade, Record Book, Rhode Island Historical Society, Providence; Scots' Charitable Society, Records, and New England Company, Records, New England Historic Genealogical Society, Boston, Mass., as well as the records at the New Haven Colony Historical Society, New Haven, Ct., of four organizations: Charitable Society of New Haven, Dorcas Society for the Relief of Poor Female Professors, Female Auxiliary Bible Society of New Haven, and the Foreign Mission Society of the Eastern District of New Haven County.

Thanks to the *American Bibliography* of Charles Evans for material through 1800 and of Ralph R. Shaw and Richard H. Shoemaker for post-1800 material, information on most of the printed primary sources for this study is readily available. The citations indicate the works that have been of particular use. Because no guide to manuscript sources provides similar direction to unpublished material useful for the study of charity in New England, I have compiled the following list.

Institutional Records

Bath, Me. Humane Society. New York Public Library, New York

Bedford, Mass. Gentleman's Association . . . Auxiliary to the American Board of Commissioners for Foreign Missions. Houghton Library, Harvard University, Cambridge

Bedford, N.H. Female Cent Society. New Hampshire Historical Society, Concord

Bennington, Vt. Friendly Society. Wilbur Collection, University of Vermont, Burlington

Boston, Mass. American Board of Commissioners for Foreign Missions. Houghton Library, Harvard University, Cambridge

——. American Education Society. Congregational Library, Boston

——. Assistant Fire Society. Massachusetts Historical Society, Boston

——. Charitable Irish Society. Massachusetts Historical Society, Boston

——. Company for Promoting Good Order. Massachusetts Historical Society, Boston

——. Corban Society. New York Public Library, New York

——. Dispensary. Countway Library, Harvard Medical School, Boston

——. Episcopal Charitable Society. Massachusetts Historical Society, Boston

——. Female Asylum. Boston Children's Service Association, Boston

——. Female Asylum. Massachusetts State Library, Boston

——. Female Bible Society. Schlesinger Library, Radcliffe College, Cambridge

——. Fire Society. Massachusetts Historical Society, Boston

——. Fragment Society. Schlesinger Library, Radcliffe College, Cambridge

——. Massachusetts Bible Society. Massachusetts Bible Society, Boston

——. Massachusetts Charitable Fire Society. Massachusetts Historical Society, Boston [Microfilm edn., Boston, 1974]

——. Massachusetts Charitable Mechanic Association. Massachusetts Historical Society, Boston

——. Massachusetts [Charitable] Society. Massachusetts Historical Society, Boston

——. Massachusetts Congregational Charitable Society. Andover-Harvard Library, Harvard Divinity School, Cambridge

——. Massachusetts Congregational Charitable Society. Massachusetts Historical Society, Boston

——. Massachusetts Convention of Congregational Ministers. Congregational Library, Boston

——. Massachusetts Fire Insurance Company. Baker Library, Harvard Graduate School of Business Administration, Boston

——. Massachusetts Society for the Suppression of Intemperance. Massachusetts Historical Society, Boston

————. Provident Institution for Savings. Massachusetts Historical Society, Boston

————. St. Andrew's Lodge. Widener Library, Harvard University, Cambridge [Microfilm]

————. Society for the Promotion of Christianity in India. Andover-Harvard Library, Harvard Divinity School, Cambridge

————. Society for Propagating the Gospel among the Indians and Others in North America. Massachusetts Historical Society, Boston

————. Washington Benevolent Society of Massachusetts. Massachusetts Historical Society, Boston

Bradford, Mass. Female Charitable Society. Essex Institute, Salem

Brimfield, Mass. Female Benevolent Society. Old Sturbridge Village, Sturbridge

Cambridge, Mass. Female Humane Society. Schlesinger Library, Radcliffe College, Cambridge

————. First Church. Houghton Library, Harvard University, Cambridge

————. Society for Promoting Theological Education at Harvard University. Harvard University Archives, Cambridge

Concord, Mass. Charitable Society. Concord Free Public Library, Concord

————. Female Charitable Society. Concord Free Public Library, Concord

Concord, N.H. Female Charitable Society. New Hampshire Historical Society, Concord

————. New Hampshire Missionary Society. New Hampshire Historical Society, Concord

Coventry, Ct. Female Fragment Society. Old Sturbridge Village, Sturbridge [Photocopy]

————. Female Friendly Society. Old Sturbridge Village, Sturbridge [Photocopy]

Deerfield, Mass. Female Benevolent Society. Pocumtuck Valley Memorial Association Library, Deerfield

————. Franklin County Temperance Society. Pocumtuck Valley Memorial Association Library, Deerfield

————. Temperance Society. Pocumtuck Valley Memorial Association Library, Deerfield

Goshen, Ct. Moral Society. Connecticut State Library, Hartford

Hadlyme, Ct. Temperance Society. Connecticut State Library, Hartford

Halifax, Vt. Auxiliary Missionary Society. Vermont Historical Society, Montpelier

Hartford, Ct. Charitable Society. Connecticut Historical Society, Hartford

————. Connecticut Bible Society. Christian Conference of Connecticut, Hartford

————. Connecticut Bible Society. Connecticut Historical Society, Hartford

————. Missionary Society of Connecticut. Beinecke Library, Yale University, New Haven

————. Missionary Society of Connecticut. Christian Conference of Connecticut, Hartford [Microfilm edn., Glen Rock, N.J., 1976]

Haverhill, Mass. Fire Society. Essex Institute, Salem

Hingham, Mass. Temperance Committee. Hingham Public Library, Hingham

Hollis, N.H. Philanthropic Society. New Hampshire Historical Society, Concord

Jericho Centre, Vt. Ladies Cent Society. Congregational Library, Boston

Kennebunk, Me. Temperance Society. New-York Historical Society, New York

Lebanon, Ct. Female Cent Society. Connecticut State Library, Hartford

Litchfield, Ct. County Home and Foreign Missionary Society. Christian Conference of
    Connecticut, Hartford
Lynn, Mass. Female Benevolent Society. Lynn Historical Society, Lynn
———. Female Fragment Society. Lynn Historical Society, Lynn
Middlebury, Vt. Middlebury College Charitable Society. Sheldon Art Museum, Middle-
    bury
———. Orphan School Fund. Sheldon Art Museum, Middlebury
Middlesex and Worcester Counties, Mass. Evangelical Missionary Society. Andover-
    Harvard Library, Harvard Divinity School, Cambridge
Montpelier, Vt. Vermont Bible Society. Wilbur Collection, University of Vermont, Bur-
    lington
———. Vermont Colonization Society. Vermont Historical Society, Montpelier
New Braintree, Mass. Thief Detecting Society. Old Sturbridge Village, Sturbridge
New Haven, Ct. Auxiliary Female Bible Society. Sterling Memorial Library, Yale Univer-
    sity, New Haven
———. Connecticut Education Society. Sterling Memorial Library, Yale University, New
    Haven
———. Moral Society. Connecticut Historical Society, Hartford
New York, N.Y. American Home Missionary Society [Microfilm edn., Glen Rock, N.J.]
Newbury, Mass. First Fire Society. Essex Institute, Salem
Newburyport, Mass. Adelphi Society. Essex Institute, Salem
———. Female Charitable Society. Newburyport Public Library, Newburyport
———. Fourth Engine Company. Essex Institute, Salem
———. Leonidas Fire Society. Essex Institute, Salem
———. Merrimack Humane Society. Essex Institute, Salem
———. Relief Fire Society. Essex Institute, Salem
Newport, R.I. African Benevolent Society. Newport Historical Society, Newport
———. African Humane Society. Newport Historical Society, Newport
———. African Union Society. Newport Historical Society, Newport
———. Association of Mechanics and Manufacturers. Newport Historical Society,
    Newport
———. First Congregational Church. Rhode Island Historical Society, Providence
———. Newport Marine Society. Newport Historical Society, Newport
———. Second Baptist Church. Rhode Island Historical Society, Providence
———. Second Congregational Society. Rhode Island Historical Society, Providence
Northampton, Mass. Hampshire Bible Society. Forbes Library, Northampton
———. Hampshire Education Society. Forbes Library, Northampton
———. Jerusalem Lodge. Forbes Library, Northampton
———. Society for the Detection of Thieves and Robbers. Forbes Library, North-
    ampton
———. Society for the Reformation of Morals. Forbes Library, Northampton
Old Saybrook, Ct. Auxiliary Foreign Mission Society. Christian Conference of Connecti-
    cut, Hartford.
Phillips, Me. Temperance Society. Maine Historical Society, Portland

Portland, Me. Benevolent Society. Maine Historical Society, Portland

————. Bible Society for the District of Maine. Bible Society of Maine, Scarborough

————. Contribution for Sufferers at Newburyport, Massachusetts, 1811. Maine Historical Society, Portland

————. Maine Branch, American Society for Educating Pious Youth for the Gospel Ministry. Congregational Library, Boston

————. Maine Missionary Society. Maine Historical Society, Portland

————. Marine Bible Society. Bible Society of Maine, Scarborough

Portsmouth, N.H. Peace Society. New Hampshire Historical Society, Concord

————. Piscataqua Missionary Society. New Hampshire Historical Society, Concord

Providence, R.I. Association of Mechanics and Manufacturers. Rhode Island Historical Society, Providence

————. Female Charitable Society. Rhode Island Historical Society, Providence

————. Insurance Company. Rhode Island Historical Society, Providence

————. Mutual Fire Society. Rhode Island Historical Society, Providence

————. Rhode Island Bible Society. Rhode Island Historical Society, Providence

Rupert, Vt. Tract Society. Vermont Historical Society, Montpelier

Salem, Mass. Active Fire Club. Essex Institute, Salem

————. Bible Society. Essex Institute, Salem

————. Bible Translation and Foreign Mission Society. Essex Institute, Salem

————. Charitable Mechanic Association. Essex Institute, Salem

————. Dorcas Society. Essex Institute, Salem

————. East Church. Essex Institute, Salem

————. East India Marine Society. Peabody Museum, Salem

————. Engine Company Number Two. Essex Institute, Salem

————. Enterprise Fire Club. Essex Institute, Salem

————. Female Charitable Society. Essex Institute, Salem

————. Fire Club. Essex Institute, Salem

————. Friend Engine Company. Essex Institute, Salem

————. Hamilton Fire Club. Essex Institute, Salem

————. Marine Bible Society. Essex Institute, Salem

————. Social Fire Club. Essex Institute, Salem

————. Society for the Moral and Religious Instruction of the Poor. Essex Institute, Salem

————. Union and Naumkeag Fire Company. Essex Institute, Salem

————. York Fire Club. Essex Institute, Salem

Salisbury, Ct. Society for the Purpose of Securing Our Horses From Thieves. Connecticut State Library, Hartford

Salisbury, Mass. Benevolent Cent Society. Essex Institute, Salem

Scituate, Mass. Auxiliary Society for the Suppression of Intemperance. American Antiquarian Society, Worcester

Shelburne, Vt. Female Religious Society. Vermont Historical Society, Montpelier

South Berwick, Me. Fire Society. Maine Historical Society, Portland

South Farms, Ct. Moral Society. Christian Conference of Connecticut, Hartford

Tamworth, N.H. Female Cent Society. New Hampshire Historical Society, Concord

Vernon, Ct. Charitable Society. Connecticut State Library, Hartford
————. Temperance Society. Connecticut State Library, Hartford
Washington, D.C. American Colonization Society. Library of Congress, Washington
Windham, Ct. Charitable Society. Christian Conference of Connecticut, Hartford
Wiscasset, Me. Female Charitable Society. Wiscasset Public Library [Records kept at county courthouse]
————. Lincoln Lodge. Maine Historical Society, Portland
Woodstock, Ct. Society for Detecting Thefts. Connecticut State Library, Hartford
Worcester, Mass. Religious Charitable Society. Congregational Library, Boston
————. Washington Benevolent Society of Worcester County. American Antiquarian Society, Worcester
————. Worcester County Bible Society. American Antiquarian Society, Worcester

Personal Papers

Abbot, Ephraim. Missionary Journal. Rhode Island Historical Society, Providence
————. Papers. American Antiquarian Society, Worcester
Appleton, Jesse. Papers. Bowdoin College Library, Brunswick
Baldwin Family. Papers. Sterling Memorial Library, Yale University, New Haven
Boudinot, Elias. Correspondence. American Bible Society, New York
Clerc, Laurent. Papers. Sterling Memorial Library, Yale University, New Haven
Cogswell, Mason Fitch. Papers. Beinecke Library. Yale University, New Haven
Colman, Benjamin. Papers. Massachusetts Historical Society, Boston
Day Family. Papers. Sterling Memorial Library, Yale University, New Haven
Evarts Family. Papers. Sterling Memorial Library, Yale University, New Haven
Gallaudet, Thomas Hopkins and Edward Miner. Papers. Library of Congress, Washington
Hawley, Gideon. Journals and Letters. Congregational Library, Boston
Keith, Israel, to Joseph Palmer. Letter on annuitant society, April 11, 1780. Boston Public Library, Boston
Lathrop, John, to Rev. Ward. Account of Massachusetts Congregational Charitable Society, Aug. 30, 1792. Holmes Papers, Massachusetts Historical Society, Boston
Mitchell, Ammi R., et al., to Samuel Freeman. Letter concerning moral reform, Oct. 13, 1814. Maine Historical Society, Portland
Morse, Jedidiah. Papers. New-York Historical Society, New York
————. Papers. New York Public Library, New York
Morse, Jedidiah, to George Lewis, Jan. 15, 1793. Transcript of letter concerning Immigrant Aid Society. Massachusetts Historical Society, Boston [Original in National Library of Wales]
Morse Family. Papers. Sterling Memorial Library, Yale University, New Haven
Park Family. Papers. Sterling Memorial Library, Yale University, New Haven
Price, Ezekiel. Papers. Massachusetts Historical Society, Boston
Sewall, Jonathan. Missionary Journal. Maine Historical Society, Portland
Stafford, Ward. Account of the Formation of the Marine Bible Societies in New England. American Bible Society, New York

Tuckerman, Joseph. Papers. Andover-Harvard Library, Harvard Divinity School, Cambridge

———. Papers. Massachusetts Historical Society, Boston

Wheelock, Eleazar. Papers. Baker Library, Dartmouth College, Hanover [Microfilm edn., Hanover, N.H., 1971]

Worcester, Noah. Papers. Massachusetts Historical Society, Boston

Worcester, Samuel. Papers. American Board of Commissioners for Foreign Missions Papers. Houghton Library, Harvard University, Cambridge

Notes

Introduction

1. Except where otherwise noted, the source for all statements about Stafford's tour is his manuscript report, Account of the Formation of the Marine Bible Societies in New England, American Bible Society, New York City.

2. On Stafford's career, see Franklin Bowditch Dexter, *Biographical Sketches of the Graduates of Yale College* (New Haven, 1912), 6:496–499; Carroll Smith Rosenberg, *Religion and the Rise of the American City: The New York City Mission Movement, 1812–1870* (Ithaca, 1971), 57–58.

3. Marine Bible Society of Salem and Beverly, Constitution and Annual Report, Essex Institute, Salem, Mass., 1.

4. Portland Marine Bible Society, Records, Bible Society of Maine, Scarborough, Maine, Sept. 11, 1820. For an account of the annual meeting the following year, see Sarah Connell Ayer, *The Diary of Sarah Connell Ayer* (Portland, 1910), 227.

5. Clifford Geertz, *The Interpretation of Cultures* (New York, 1973), 14.

6. Geertz, *Interpretation of Cultures,* 14–16.

7. In my concern for the nuances of language, I have been influenced by the work of Raymond Williams. See *Culture and Society, 1780–1950* (New York, 1958) and *Keywords: A Vocabulary of Culture and Society* (New York, 1976).

8. Peter Clark, *The Banner of Love Displayed* (Boston, 1744), 18.

9. Williams, *Keywords,* 45–46; Christine Leigh Heyrman, "A Model of Christian Charity: The Rich and the Poor in New England, 1630–1730" (Ph.D. diss., Yale Univ., 1977).

10. Samuel Clarke, *The Works of Samuel Clarke, D.D.* (London, 1738), 1:291.

11. Samuel Johnson, *The Christian Indeed: Explained, in Two Sermons, of Humility and Charity* (New Haven, 1768), 16–17.

12. Cotton Mather, "The True Way of Thriving," in *Durable Riches* (Boston, 1695), 5, 8–9.

13. For examples of this approach, see Charles I. Foster, *An Errand of Mercy: The Evangelical United Front, 1790–1837* (Chapel Hill, 1960), and Oliver Wendell Elsbree, *The Rise of the Missionary Spirit in America, 1790–1815* (Williamsport, Pa., 1928). Carroll Smith Rosenberg also emphasizes connections between organized evangelism and orthodoxy in *Religion and the Rise of the American City.* But Suzanne Lebsock notes that organized

charity preceded revivals in Petersburg, Virginia: see *The Free Women of Petersburg: Status and Culture in a Southern Town, 1784–1860* (New York, 1984), 217.

14. *Letters from John Pintard to his Daughter Eliza Noel Pintard Davidson. Collections of the New-York Historical Society,* LXX (New York, 1937–1940), 1:308.

15. Massachusetts Bible Society, Records, Massachusetts Bible Society, Boston, 1:9–11; Bible Society of the State of Rhode Island, Records, Rhode Island Historical Society, Providence, vol. I, Aug. 10, 1813.

16. Studies that stress the organizational response to economic and moral need ordinarily draw their evidence from institutional promotional literature. They do so at their peril, since such publications were clearly intended to persuade potential donors, not to provide impartial accounts of socioeconomic conditions, and sometimes magnified the problems they faced. See, for example, Charles Roy Keller, *The Second Great Awakening in Connecticut* (New Haven, 1942). This approach is less common than it once was, but for a recent example, see W. J. Rorabaugh, *The Alcoholic Republic* (New York, 1979). For a study emphasizing the place of anomie in the founding of voluntary societies, see Mary P. Ryan, *Cradle of the Middle Class: The Family in Oneida County, New York, 1790–1865* (New York, 1981).

17. In addition to the approaches discussed below, some historians of the post-1830 period have also proposed that the status anxieties of merchants, declining economically vis à vis rising industrialists, also produced philanthropy and reform. See, for example, David Donald, "Toward a Reconsideration of Abolitionists," in *Lincoln Reconsidered: Essays on the Civil War* (New York, 1956), 19–36, and Stanley Elkins, *Slavery* (Chicago, 1959). Opposition to reform, however, has also been attributed to status anxieties: see Leonard L. Richards, *"Gentlemen of Property and Standing": Anti-Abolition Mobs in Jacksonian America* (New York, 1970). For a related effort to link humanitarian sensibilities to capitalism, see Thomas L. Haskell, "Capitalism and the Origins of Humanitarian Sensibilities," *American Historical Review* 90:339–361, 547–566 (1985).

18. Foster, *Errand of Mercy,* and Clifford S. Griffin, *Their Brothers' Keepers: Moral Stewardship in the United States, 1800–1865* (New Brunswick, N.J., 1960), both take this line. Others who have followed this approach include John R. Bodo, *The Protestant Clergy and Public Issues, 1812–1848* (Princeton, 1954), Charles C. Cole, Jr., *The Social Ideas of the Northern Evangelists, 1820–1860* (New York, 1954), and Raymond A. Mohl, *Poverty in New York, 1783–1825* (New York, 1971). For a devastating attack on this approach, see Lois W. Banner, "Religious Benevolence as Social Control: A Critique of an Interpretation," *Journal of American History* 60:23–41 (1973). Barbara J. Berg also points out flaws in this approach in *The Remembered Gate: Origins of American Feminism: The Woman & the City, 1800–1860* (New York, 1978), 146–149. Since Banner's article, social control arguments have appeared less frequently than they once did, but see John K. Alexander, *Render Them Submissive: Responses to Poverty in Philadelphia, 1760–1800* (Amherst, 1980), Paul Boyer, *Urban Masses and Moral Order in America, 1820–1920* (Cambridge, Mass., 1978), and Ryan, *Cradle of the Middle Class,* 105–111. The desire for social control undeniably underlay other institutional movements in postrevolutionary America, notably the establishment of prisons, insane asylums, and almshouses: see David J. Rothman, *The Discovery of the Asylum: Social Order and Disorder in the New Republic* (Boston, 1971).

19. In recent years, Gary B. Nash has argued this case most forcefully. See *The Urban Crucible: Social Change, Political Consciousness, and the Origins of the American Revolution* (Cambridge, Mass., 1979), 189–194, and especially "The Failure of Female Factory Labor in Colonial Boston," *Labor History* 20:165–188 (1979). Nash draws heavily on the controversial work of Alan Heimert, who portrayed the charitable activities of religious liberals as cynical and self-interested: see Heimert, *Religion and the American Mind: From the Great Awakening to the Revolution* (Cambridge, Mass., 1966), 246–253. For a related argument stressing the interrelationship of business corporations and charitable corporations, see Peter Dobkin Hall, "The Model of Boston Charity: A Theory of Charitable Benevolence and Class Development," *Science and Society* 38:464–477 (1974–1975).

The Lawyer's Question

1. Luke 10:25–37.
2. Timothy Dwight, *Travels in New England and New York*, ed. Barbara M. Solomon (Cambridge, Mass., 1969), 3:68.
3. Gideon Hawley to unidentified recipient, n.d. but probably Oct. 1753, Journals and Letters of Gideon Hawley, Letterbook, Congregational Library, Boston, Mass.
4. Hawley, Journals and Letters, Jan. 1, 1756.
5. Hawley, Journals and Letters, Dec. 27, 1756.
6. Hawley, Journals and Letters, Feb. 11, 1757.
7. Hawley, Journals and Letters, Feb. 12, 1757.
8. Hawley, Journals and Letters, Feb. 16, 1757.
9. Hawley, Journals and Letters, Feb. 17, 1757.

Chapter One

1. Jonathan Mayhew, *Seven Sermons* (London, 1750), 116.
2. Solomon Williams, *The Duty of Christians* (Norwich, Conn., 1773), 8, 10.
3. Arthur Browne, *Universal Love Recommended* (Boston, 1755), 15.
4. Andrew Eliot, *Twenty Sermons* (Boston, 1774), 145.
5. For a recent account of English deism, see Margaret C. Jacob, *The Newtonians and the English Revolution, 1689–1720* (Ithaca, 1976), 201–250.
6. Jacob, *Newtonians*, 143–200; G. R. Cragg, *From Puritanism to the Age of Reason: A Study of the Changes in Religious Thought within the Church of England, 1660 to 1700* (Cambridge, 1950).
7. Jared Eliot, *The Two Witnesses; or, Religion Supported by Reason and Divine Revelation* (New London, Conn., 1736).
8. Andrew Eliot, *A Discourse on Natural Religion* (Boston, 1771), 24, 29.
9. John Calvin, *Institutes of the Christian Religion*, trans. Henry Beveridge (Grand Rapids, Mich., 1979), 2:10.
10. Calvin, *Institutes*, 1:359.
11. Calvin, *Institutes*, 2:11.
12. Eliot, *Twenty Sermons*, 140.

13. Charles Brockwell, *Brotherly Love Recommended* (Boston, 1750), 10.

14. Joseph Sewall, *The Second Commandment Like to the First* (Boston, 1742), 12.

15. Jonathan Ashley, *The Great Duty of Charity, Considered and Applied* (Boston, 1742), 10.

16. I Cor. 13:4–5.

17. David MacGregore, *Christian Unity and Peace Recommended* (Boston, 1765), 12.

18. Thomas Clap, *An Essay on the Nature and Foundation of Moral Virtue and Obligation* (New Haven, 1765), 7.

19. Thomas Pollen, *Universal Love* (Boston, 1758), 10.

20. Benjamin Wadsworth, *The Imitation of Christ, a Christian Duty* (Boston, 1722), 3–4, 21.

21. Brockwell, *Brotherly Love Recommended,* 12.

22. Browne, *Universal Love Recommended,* 10.

23. Mayhew, *Seven Sermons,* 116.

24. Amos Adams, *Ministerial Affection Recommended* (Boston, 1769), 8.

25. Thomas Foxcroft, *A Discourse Concerning Kindness* (Boston, 1720), 24.

26. Jeremiah Condy, *Mercy Exemplified, in the Conduct of a Samaritan* (Salem, 1769), 9.

27. Mayhew, *Seven Sermons,* 115.

28. Pollen, *Universal Love,* 8.

29. Charles Chauncy, *Charity to the Distressed Members of Christ Accepted as Done to Himself* (Boston, 1757), 18.

30. Joseph Sewall, *A Tender Heart Pleasing to God, and Profitable to Men* (Boston, 1756), 4.

31. Benjamin Colman, *The Unspeakable Gift of God* (Boston, 1739), 4–5.

32. Browne, *Universal Love Recommended,* 13.

33. Thomas A. Horne, *The Social Thought of Bernard Mandeville: Virtue and Commerce in Early Eighteenth-Century England* (New York, 1978).

34. John Beach, *The Duty of Loving Our Enemies* (Boston, 1739), 7.

35. Andrew Eliot, *An Evil and Adulterous Generation* (Boston, 1753), 13.

36. Ebenezer Devotion, *Fortitude, Love and a Sound Judgment, Very Needful Qualifications for the Christian Minister* (New Haven, 1762), 11.

37. Nathaniel Appleton, *The Usefulness and Necessity of Gifts* (Boston, 1746), 22.

38. John 3:18. For examples of the use of this text, see Simeon Howard, *A Sermon on Brotherly Love* (Boston, 1779), 5, and Charles Chauncy, *The Idle-Poor Secluded from the Bread of Charity by the Christian Law* (Boston, 1752), 5.

39. Ezechiel Carré, *The Charitable Samaritan* (Boston, 1689), 2. On the same subject, see Jedidiah Jewett, *The Necessity of Good Works, as the Fruit and Evidence of Faith* (Boston, 1742).

40. Cotton Mather, *Compassion Called For* (Boston, 1711), 9.

41. Wadsworth, *Imitation of Christ,* 21.

42. Peter Clark, *The Banner of Divine Love Displayed* (Boston, 1744), 7.

43. Eliphalet Adams, *A Discourse Putting Christians in Mind to be Ready to Every Good Work* (Boston, 1706), 5.

44. Kenneth A. Lockridge, "Land, Population and the Evolution of New England Society, 1630–1790," *Past and Present* 39:62–80 (1968).

45. As Robert Middlekauff has pointed out, some members of New England's first generation felt such strong ties to their English roots that life in New England seemed like exile. See Middlekauff, *The Mathers: Three Generations of Puritan Intellectuals, 1596–1728* (New York, 1971), 31–33. For examples of correspondence, see Everett Emerson, ed., *Letters from New England: The Massachusetts Bay Colony, 1629–1638* (Amherst, 1976).

46. Quoted in Stephen Foster, *Their Solitary Way: The Puritan Social Ethic in the First Century of Settlement in New England* (New Haven, 1971), 136.

47. See Richard D. Pierce, ed., "The Records of the First Church in Boston, 1630–1868," *Publications of the Colonial Society of Massachusetts*, XXXIX, Collections (Boston, 1961); Cambridge, Mass., First Church and Shepard Congregational Society [*sic*], Account Book, 1638–1716, Houghton Library, Harvard University; Richard D. Pierce, ed., *The Records of the First Church in Salem, Massachusetts, 1629–1736* (Salem, 1974). Note that this interpretation coincides with Kenneth Lockridge's data on charitable bequests. Although Lockridge did not provide an explanation, his analysis of a sample of seventeenth- and eighteenth-century New England wills showed a growing reluctance to make charitable bequests, especially outside the testator's home community, after 1650. See his *Literacy in Colonial New England: An Enquiry into the Social Context of Literacy in the Early Modern West* (New York, 1974), 33–36.

48. Quoted in Marcus Lee Hanson, *The Atlantic Migration, 1607–1860: A History of the Continuing Settlement of the United States* (Cambridge, Mass., 1940), 32.

49. For studies that show the growing overcrowding of New England, see Lockridge, "Land, Population and the Evolution of New England Society"; Charles S. Grant, *Democracy in the Connecticut Frontier Town of Kent* (New York, 1961); and Sumner Chilton Powell, *Puritan Village: The Formation of a New England Town* (Middletown, 1963).

50. Daniel F. Vickers, "Maritime Labor in Colonial Massachusetts: A Case Study of Cod Fishing and the Whaling Industry of Nantucket, 1630–1775" (Ph.D. diss., Princeton Univ., 1981), 78.

51. Pierce, "First Church in Salem," 87; Pierce, "First Church in Boston," 92, 100, 120; Cambridge, Mass., First Church, Account Book, 20–22; *Records of the First Church at Dorchester in New England, 1636–1734* (Boston, 1891), 46, 51, 52, 53, 56, 60–61, 75, 78, 83, 84, 87, 90, 91. It should be noted that New England's churches were beginning to limit their charitable reach at about the same time that generational pressures were calling into question the nature of membership and were leading to increased use of the Half-Way Covenant. In this context, the constriction of charity becomes an element of the "tribalism" that Edmund S. Morgan describes in *The Puritan Family: Religion and Domestic Relations in Seventeenth-Century New England* (New York, 1966), 161–186. For a commentary on Morgan's use of the idea of tribalism, see Gerald F. Moran and Maris A. Vinovskis, "The Puritan Family and Religion: A Critical Reappraisal," *William and Mary Quarterly*, 3d ser., 39:31–38 (1982).

52. Calvin, *Institutes*, 2:187.

53. Morgan, *Puritan Family,* 21–25. See also Walter J. Ong, *Ramus, Method, and the Decay of Dialogue* (Cambridge, Mass., 1958).

54. William Perkins, *The Work of William Perkins,* ed. Ian Breward (Appleford, 1970), 382; Foster, *Solitary Way,* 34–36; Morgan, *Puritan Family,* 29–86, 109–160.

55. J. Sears McGee, *The Godly Man in Stuart England: Anglicans, Puritans, and the Two Tables, 1620–1670* (New Haven, 1976), 171–189.

56. William Ames, *The Marrow of Theology,* ed. John Eusden (Boston, 1968), 303–304.

57. Cotton Mather, *Bonifacius: An Essay Upon the Good. . . .* (Boston, 1710).

58. Although it is always difficult to reconstruct the attitudes of those colonial New Englanders who were neither clergymen nor secular leaders, their assumptions about charity do come through from time to time. The files of the Boston Committee of Correspondence during the blockade of the port in 1774 contain letters from many of the towns that answered the capital's request for help. In many cases, contributing towns took advantage of the occasion to comment on charity. These brief discourses, which are much in keeping with the more elaborate and formal statements of contemporary leaders, provide insight into popular beliefs about charity on the eve of the Revolution. See "Correspondence in 1774 and 1775, between a Committee of the Town of Boston and Contributors of Donations for the Relief of Sufferers by the Boston Port Bill," Massachusetts Historical Society, *Collections,* 4th ser. (Boston, 1858), 4:1–278.

59. Thomas S. Kuhn, *The Copernican Revolution: Planetary Astronomy in the Development of Western Thought* (Cambridge, Mass., 1957).

60. Joseph Ellis, *The New England Mind in Transition: Samuel Johnson of Connecticut, 1696–1772* (New Haven, 1973), 46–47; Charles W. Akers, *Called Unto Liberty: A Life of Jonathan Mayhew, 1720–1766* (Cambridge, Mass., 1964), 29.

61. Akers, *Called Unto Liberty,* 29; Jacob, *Newtonians,* 143–200.

62. William Whiston, *The Astronomical Principles of Religion, Natural and Reveal'd* (London, 1717), 130–131.

63. Francis Hutcheson, "An Inquiry Concerning the Original of our Ideas of Virtue or Moral Good," in L. A. Selby-Bigge, ed., *British Moralists* (Oxford, 1897), 127–128.

64. Hutcheson, "An Inquiry," 130.

65. Samuel Cooper, *A Sermon Preached in Boston, New-England, Before the Society for Encouraging Industry and Employing the Poor* (Boston, 1753), 12–13.

66. Sewall, *Second Commandment,* 6, 8.

67. Pollen, *Universal Love,* 12.

68. Clark, *Banner of Divine Love,* 39.

69. Samuel Andrews, *A Discourse, Delivered in St. Paul's Church at Wallingford* (New Haven, 1770), 9.

70. Cooper, *Sermon Preached in Boston,* 6–7.

71. Benjamin Wadsworth, *Vicious Courses, Procuring Poverty* (Boston, 1744, 1st ed. 1719), 5–7.

72. Wadsworth, *Vicious Courses,* 6.

73. Chauncy, *Idle-Poor,* 8.

74. Eliphalet Adams, *Eminently Good and Useful Men* (New London, Conn., 1720), 40.

75. Eliot, *Twenty Sermons,* 131–132.

76. Clap, *Moral Virtue,* 59.

77. William Balch, *The Duty of a Christian Church to Manage their Affairs with Charity* (Boston, 1735), 13.

78. Robert Breck, *The Surest Way to Advance a People's Happiness and Prosperity* (Boston, 1721), 9.

79. Edmund March, *The Necessity of Brotherly Love* (Boston, 1762), 7.

80. Balch, *Duty of a Christian Church,* 2, 4–7.

81. See George Silsbee Hale, "The Charities of Boston and Contributions to the Distressed of Other Parts," in Justin Winsor, ed., *The Memorial History of Boston* (Boston, 1880–1883), 4:660; Boston Quarterly Charity Lecture, Record, 1719–1873, in Boston Second Church, Records, vol. 21, Massachusetts Historical Society, Boston. Harold F. Worthley, "An Historical Essay: The Massachusetts Convention of Congregational Ministers," *Proceedings of the Unitarian Historical Society* 12:51, 56 (1958).

82. Balch, *Duty of a Christian Church,* 8; Browne, *Universal Love Recommended;* Pollen, *Universal Love.*

83. Scots' Charitable Society, *Constitution and By-Laws* (Cambridge, Mass., 1878), 30; Charitable Irish Society, *Constitution and By-Laws* (Boston, 1876), 21; Boston Episcopal Charitable Society, Records, Massachusetts Historical Society, Boston, 1758 Charter, art. 5.

84. "Extracts from the Journal of Charles J. Stratford," ed. Mrs. Jared Sparks, *Proceedings of the Massachusetts Historical Society* 15:389 (1877); [Margarette Matilda Odell], *Memoir and Poems of Phillis Wheatley, A Native African and Slave,* 2nd ed., (Boston, 1835), 12.

85. Benjamin Wadsworth, *Essay for the Charitable Spreading of the Gospel into Dark Ignorant Places* (Boston, 1718); Ellis, *New England Mind in Transition,* 3; John Sergeant, *A Letter from the Revd. Mr. Sergeant of Stockbridge* (Boston, 1743), 3.

86. William Kellaway, *The New England Company, 1649–1776: Missionary Society to the American Indians* (London, 1961).

87. R. Pierce Beaver, ed., *Pioneers in Missions: The Early Missionary Ordination Sermons, Charges, and Instructions* (Grand Rapids, Mich., 1966), 33–38.

88. Samuel Hopkins, "Historical Memoirs Relating to the Housatonic Indians," *The Magazine of History with Notes and Queries,* extra no. 17:120 (1911).

89. S. E. Dwight, *The Life of President Edwards* (New York, 1830), 270; Carl Bridenbaugh, *Mitre and Sceptre: Transatlantic Faiths, Ideas, Personalities, and Politics, 1689–1775* (New York, 1962), 209–210; Michael G. Kammen, *A Rope of Sand: The Colonial Agents, British Politics, and the American Revolution* (Ithaca, 1968), 78–79.

90. Hopkins, "Historical Memoirs," 120–123.

91. Eleazar Wheelock, *A Continuation of the Narrative of the State &c. of the Indian Charity School, at Lebanon, in Connecticut* (Boston, 1765), 7. This figure covers the period Nov. 27, 1763-Nov. 27, 1764.

92. Cotton Mather, "True Way of Thriving," 8.

93. *Records of the Church in Brattle Square, Boston, 1699–1872* (Boston, 1902); Pierce, ed., "Records of the First Church at Boston"; Hamilton Andrews Hill, *A History of the Old South Church* (Boston, 1890).

94. "The Diary of the Rev. Thomas Prince, 1737," *Publications of the Colonial Society of Massachusetts. Transactions, 1916–1917* (Boston, 1918), 19:347; Annual Convocation of the Ministers in the Province of New Hampshire, "A Record of the Transactions of the Annual Convocation. . . ." *New Hampshire Historical Society. Miscellaneous Historical Collections,* 9:20.

95. Jonathan Rockwell and John Newcomb to Wheelock, Oct. 9, 1763, *Papers of Eleazar Wheelock* (Hanover, N.H., 1971, microfilm ed.). Eben Loomis to Wheelock, Aug. 10, 1765, *Papers of Eleazar Wheelock.* Eleazar Wheelock, *A Continuation of the Narrative* (Hartford, 1771), 25.

96. Dudley W. Bahlmann, *The Moral Revolution of 1688* (New Haven, 1957), 31; the quotation is from Josiah Woodward, *An Account of the Rise and Progress of the Religious Societies* (London, 1701), 63, quoted in Bahlmann, *Moral Revolution,* 37–38.

97. Middlekauff, *The Mathers,* 270–273. Company for Promoting Good Order, Memorandum Book, 1761, Smith-Carter Family Papers, Massachusetts Historical Society, Boston; *Plymouth Church Records, 1620–1859* (New York, 1920–1923), 1:202, 205–206; Edwards A. Park, "Memoir," in Samuel Hopkins, *The Works of Samuel Hopkins, D.D.* (Boston, 1852), 1:138. Isabel M. Calder, ed., *Letters & Papers of Ezra Stiles, President of Yale College, 1778–1795* (New Haven, 1933), 39. Park indicates that Hopkins and Stiles actually founded an association in Newport in 1773 for the education and subsequent maintenance of African missionaries. Although the colonization project itself is well known, information on the organization is otherwise quite meager.

98. For examples, see the collections taken up for fire sufferers in Charleston, S.C., in 1741: Hill, *Old South Church,* 1:521; Pierce, ed., "Records of the First Church at Boston," 188.

99. William Whitwall, *A Discourse, Occasioned by the Loss of a Number of Vessels, with their Mariners, belonging to the Town of Marblehead* (Salem, 1770).

100. Carl Bridenbaugh, *Cities in Revolt: Urban Life in America, 1743–1776* (New York, 1964), 21, 230.

101. See Bridenbaugh, *Cities in Revolt,* 131–132.

102. Ebenezer Turell, *The Life and Character of the Reverend Benjamin Colman, D.D.* (Boston, 1749), 70–77.

103. *The Report of the Committee to the Society for Encouraging Industry, and Employing the Poor* (Boston, 1752); *Advertisement . . . For the Encouragement of the Raising and well-curing of Flax. . . .* (Boston, 1752); Eric G. Nellis, "Misreading the Signs: Industrial Imitation, Poverty, and the Social Order in Colonial Boston," *New England Quarterly* 59:486–507 (1986); Gary B. Nash, "The Failure of Female Factory Labor in Colonial Boston," *Labor History* 20:165–188 (1979).

104. Gary B. Nash, *The Urban Crucible: Social Change, Political Consciousness, and the Origins of the American Revolution* (Cambridge, Mass., 1979), 190–193.

105. *Boston Evening-Post,* Mar. 24, 1760.

106. Bridenbaugh, *Cities in Revolt,* 101–102.

107. *Boston Evening-Post,* Mar. 24, 1760.

108. Boston Records Commissioners, *Reports* (Boston, 1880–1902), 29:100.

109. William Pencak, "The Social Structure of Revolutionary Boston: Evidence from the Great Fire of 1760," *Journal of Interdisciplinary History* 10:267–278 (1979).

110. Richard D. Brown, *Revolutionary Politics in Massachusetts: The Boston Committee of Correspondence and the Towns, 1772–1774* (Cambridge, Mass., 1970).

111. John Russell Bartlett, ed., *Records of the Colony of Rhode Island and Providence Plantations in New England* (Providence, 1862), 7:250.

112. Massachusetts Historical Society, *Collections,* 4th ser., 4:16n.

113. John Gerry, Marblehead, to Boston Committee of Correspondence, July 30, 1774, Massachusetts Historical Society, *Collections,* 4th ser. 4:29.

114. Massachusetts Historical Society, *Collections,* 4th ser., 4:1–278. There is no way to know what proportion of the contributions was actually recorded in the books of the town's committees responsible for overseeing relief measures, nor is it always possible to reconcile the amounts that donors claimed to be sending with the amounts for which they received acknowledgment. Some cover and acknowledgment letters, moreover, do not specify the size of contributions or their composition. Freight rates also pose a problem: some contributors paid for freightage at their end, others depended on the committees in Boston and Charlestown or their agents in such towns as Salem, Marblehead, Gloucester, Providence, and New York to pay carting fees out of the proceeds of the sale of certain contributions. At a minimum, however, New Englanders contributed the following: 2,772 sheep; 4,186 1/4 bu. assorted grains and peas; 5 barrels flour; 233 5/8 cords wood; 224 quintals fish; 1 3/4 casks olive oil; 86 cattle; 25 swine; 14 oxen; 42 cheeses; 593 lbs. beef; 1/2 lb. pink flowers; 34 pr. shoes; 3 bags cocoa; 1/2 barrel pork; and £1,775 currency. Other colonies donated at least: 21,516 1/2 bu. assorted grains; 475 casks rice; 896 barrels flour; 63 barrels pork; 1 barrel beef; 81 barrels bread; 18 firkins butter; 16 tons iron (to keep Boston's smiths busy making hoes and axes); 200 barrels "ship stuff"; and £1,375 currency. The monetary equivalents used to translate commodities into cash are drawn either from the records themselves (for example, Marblehead's contribution of fish), or from the probate listings in Alice Hanson Jones, *American Colonial Wealth: Documents and Methods* (New York, 1977). The values for livestock are averages for Suffolk and Essex counties in 1774. I have used rough approximations for other commodities: sheep, £0.8.0; grain, bu., £0.3.0; flour, bu. £0.12.0; wood, cord, £0.15.0; fish, quintal, £0.14.0; cattle £4.0.0; swine £1.0.0; ox £5.0.0; cheese, lb., £0.0.3; beef, lb., £0.0.2; handkerchief, £0.1.0; shoes, pr., £0.2.0; pork, barrel, £2.0.0; beef, barrel, £2.0.0; butter, firken, £4.13.8; iron, ton, £16.0.0. No values survived for cocoa, "ship stuff," rice, olive oil, or bread.

115. Nathaniel Appleton to Committee of Correspondence of Brooklyn, Ct., Aug. 22, 1774, Massachusetts Historical Society, *Collections,* 4th ser., 4:52.

116. Society for Encouraging Industry and Employing the Poor, *Whereas it is found by Experience. . . .* (Boston, 1754), 2.

117. Butterfield et al., eds., *Diary and Autobiography of John Adams* (Cambridge, Mass., 1961), 2:150; Mather Byles, *Affections on Things Above* (Boston, 1740), 13.

118. Mather Byles, *The Man of God Throughly Furnished to Every Good Work* (New London, Conn., 1758), 9.

119. Samuel Johnson, *The Christian Indeed* (New Haven, 1768), 17.

120. Clap, *Moral Virtue*, 4.

121. George Lesslie, *The Nature and Tendency of the Sin of Selfishness Considered* (Newbury, 1779), 9.

122. Sewall, *Second Commandment*, 10.

123. Calvin, *Institutes*, 2:186–187; Ames, *Marrow of Theology*, 302; *Select Practical Writings of Richard Baxter*, ed. Leonard Bacon (New Haven, 1831), 1:448–455.

124. Sewall, *Second Commandment*, 6.

125. Browne, *Universal Love Recommended*, 21.

126. For different interpretations of the "household of faith," see Mather, *Durable Riches*, 16; Nathaniel Clap, *The Duty of All Christians Urged* (New London, Conn., 1720), 24; Beach, *Duty of Loving Our Enemies*, 12.

127. Mark 12:41–44.

128. For example, see East Haddam Committee of Correspondence to Boston Committee of Correspondence, Aug. 4, 1774, Massachusetts Historical Society, *Collections*, 4 ser., 4:57.

129. Francis Hutcheson, *An Essay on the Nature and Conduct of the Passions and Affections* (London, 1728), 7–8, 29.

130. Hutcheson, *Passions*, 28.

131. Solomon Stoddard, *Three Sermons Lately Preach'd at Boston* (Boston, 1717), 35.

132. Samuel Willard, *A Compleat Body of Divinity in Two Hundred and Fifty Expository Lectures* (Boston, 1726), 584.

133. Joseph Morgan, *Love to Our Neighbors Recommended, and the Duties Thereof Importunately Urged* (New London, Conn., 1727), 8.

134. Andrew Eliot, *An Inordinate Love of the World, Inconsistent with the Love of God* (Boston, 1744), 7.

135. Isaac Backus, "An Appeal to the Public for Religious Liberty," in William G. McLoughlin, ed., *Isaac Backus on Church, State, and Calvinism: Pamphlets, 1754–1789* (Cambridge, Mass., 1968), 309–310.

136. Cooper, *Sermon Preached in Boston*, 2–3.

137. Eliot, *Two Witnesses*, 34.

138. Mayhew, *Seven Sermons*, 132, 134.

139. Richard Warch, *School of the Prophets: Yale College, 1701–1740* (New Haven, 1973), 193, 234–238.

140. Johann Wollebius, "Compendium Theologiae Christianae," in John W. Beardslee III, ed., *Reformed Dogmatics* (New York, 1965), 224.

141. Samuel Hopkins, "An Inquiry into the Nature of True Holiness," *Works of Samuel Hopkins*, 3:28.

142. Jonathan Edwards, "Christian Charity: Or, The Duty of Charity to the Poor, Explained and Enforced," *The Works of President Edwards* (Leeds [Eng.], 1806–1811), 5:443.

143. Jonathan Edwards, *Charity and Its Fruits* (Philadelphia, 1874), 4. In placing Edwards in an American context I follow a different course from the one followed by Norman Fiering, whose interest in philosophical issues led him to divorce the Northampton pastor from his New England contemporaries. See Fiering, *Jonathan*

Edwards's Moral Thought and Its British Context (Chapel Hill, 1981). For an important study placing Edwards squarely among his New England contemporaries, see Patricia J. Tracy, *Jonathan Edwards, Pastor: Religion and Society in Eighteenth-Century Northampton* (New York, 1980).

144. Edwards, *Charity and Its Fruits,* 73–95.

145. Edwards, *Charity and Its Fruits,* 5.

146. Jonathan Edwards, *A Treatise Concerning Religious Affections* (Boston, 1746).

147. Jonathan Edwards, *An Account of the Life of the Late Reverend Mr. David Brainerd* (Boston, 1749).

148. Jonathan Edwards, *A Careful and Strict Inquiry into the . . . Freedom of Will* (Boston, 1754).

149. Jonathan Edwards, *The Nature of True Virtue,* ed. William K. Frankena (Ann Arbor, 1960), 3.

150. Edwards, *True Virtue,* 45.

151. Edwards, *True Virtue,* 40.

152. Hopkins, "True Holiness," 26.

153. Hopkins, "True Holiness," 24.

154. Jedidiah Mills, *An Inquiry Concerning the State of the Unregenerate Under the Gospel* (New Haven, 1767), i. See also Israel Holly, *Old Divinity Preferable to Modern Novelty* (New Haven, 1780), v.

155. On the influence of Edwards's edition of *The Life of David Brainerd* in the nineteenth century, see Joseph A. Conforti, "Jonathan Edwards's Most Popular Work: 'The Life of David Brainerd' and Nineteenth-Century Evangelical Culture," *Church History* 54:188–201 (1985).

156. Joseph A. Conforti, *Samuel Hopkins and the New Divinity Movement* (Grand Rapids, Mich., 1981), 41.

157. Franklin Bowditch Dexter, ed., *The Literary Diary of Ezra Stiles, D.D., Ll.D.* (New York, 1901), 1:363. For an annotated list of New Divinity men, see Conforti, *Samuel Hopkins,* 227–232.

158. William Hart, *Brief Remarks on a Number of False Propositions, and Dangerous Errors* (New London, Conn., 1769), 7.

159. For example, see Ebenezer Gay, *Natural Religion, as Distinguish'd from Revealed* (Boston, 1759), 22.

160. Samuel Moody, *An Attempt to Point out the Fatal and Pernicious Consequences of the Rev. Mr. Joseph Bellamy's Doctrines, Respecting Moral Evil* (Boston, 1759); Mills, *State of the Unregenerate;* Holly, *Old Divinity.*

161. Moses Mather, *The Visible Church, in Covenant with God* (New Haven, 1770).

162. William Hart, *Remarks on President Edwards's Dissertations Concerning the Nature of True Virtue* (New London, Conn., 1771), and Hart, *A Sermon of a New Kind, Never Preached nor Ever Will Be* (New Haven, 1769).

163. Hart, *Remarks,* 19.

164. Hart, *Remarks,* 5.

165. Hart, *Remarks,* 8, 9.

166. Hart, *Remarks,* 34.
167. Hart, *Remarks,* 46.
168. Hart, *Remarks,* 51.
169. Hart, *Remarks,* 47.
170. Mather, *Visible Church;* Mills, *Inquiry;* Holly, *Old Divinity.*
171. Gay, *Natural Religion,* 6, 19, 21.

The Blind Doctor Moyes

1. On Moyes and his career, see John Anthony Harrison, "Blind Henry Moyes, 'An Excellent Lecturer in Philosophy,'" *Annals of Science* 13:109–125(1957), and Robert E. Schofield, *The Lunar Society of Birmingham: A Social History of Provincial Science and Industry in Eighteenth-Century England* (Oxford, 1963), 246–247.

2. Francisco de Miranda, *The New Democracy in America: The Travels of Francisco de Miranda in the United States, 1783–1784,* trans. Judson P. Wood, ed. John S. Ezell (Norman, Okla., 1963), 145–151.

3. Freeman soon became the first New England clergyman publicly to proclaim unitarian principles. In 1787 he led the Stone (formerly King's) Chapel out of the Episcopal fold, and gradually he developed a new relationship with local Arminian ministers. Dexter was already professor of chemistry and materia medica at Harvard, where he taught from 1783 to 1816. Tyler moved in 1791 to Vermont, where he soon became a jurist and then a law professor. His greatest modern recognition, however, is due to his place as one of America's earliest novelists and playwrights. See Conrad Wright, *The Beginnings of Unitarianism in America* (Boston, 1955), 210–212, 286; M. A. DeWolfe Howe, *The Humane Society of the Commonwealth of Massachusetts: An Historical Review* (Boston, 1918), 40–41; G. Thomas Tanselle, *Royall Tyler* (Cambridge, Mass., 1967).

4. Howe, *Humane Society,* 5–7.

Chapter Two

1. Philo Pacificus, "Peace Societies Compared with Other Benevolent Institutions," *Friend of Peace* 1:219 (1816).

2. In his survey of charitable organizations, Philo Pacificus compared the work of peace societies with the activities of humane, temperance, moral reform, medical, Bible, missionary, and widows' and orphans' societies. "Peace Societies," 219–225.

3. John Eliot, *A Sermon Delivered in the Chapel, Boston, Before the Society of Ancient and Honorable Free and Accepted Masons, on Monday, June 24, 1782* (Boston, 1782), 10.

4. The nine marine societies were in Boston (1742), Newport (1752), Salem (1766), Newburyport (1772), Portland (1796), Marblehead (1798), Providence (1798), Salem East India (1798), and Portsmouth (1808). Fragmentary evidence suggests that Portsmouth's maritime community may also have established an earlier marine society sometime before 1765; see Ronald H. Quilici, "The Portsmouth Marine Society: Social Diversity in a Colonial Maritime Community," *Historical New Hampshire* 30:101–112 (1975).

5. The nine mechanic associations were in Providence (1789), Newport

(1791), Boston (1795), Warren (1795), Portsmouth (1803), Newburyport (1806), New Haven (1807), Portland (1815), and Salem (1817).

6. *The Constitutions of the Grand Lodge of Massachusetts* (Boston, 1857), 165–167; *Proceedings of the Grand Lodge of Connecticut* (Hartford, 1797), 1–4; *Grand Royal Arch Chapter of Massachusetts* (Boston, 1819); Evarts B. Greene and Virginia D. Harrington, *American Population Before the Federal Census of 1790* (New York, 1932), 58–60.

7. *Return of the Whole Number of Persons Within the Several Districts of the United States* (Washington City, [D.C.] 1802), 29.

8. On the history of Freemasonry in Connecticut, see *The Freemason's Library and General Ahiman Rezon* (Baltimore, 1817), appen. p. 69; E. G. Storer, *Records of Freemasonry in the State of Connecticut* (New Haven, 1859); *Grand Royal Arch Chapter of Massachusetts,* 19; and Dorothy Ann Lipson, *Freemasonry in Federalist Connecticut, 1789–1835* (Princeton, 1977). Between 1818 and 1826, Freemasonry again grew rapidly in Connecticut; by 1826 there were 74 lodges. See Lipson, *Freemasonry in Federalist Connecticut,* 114–115.

9. *Grand Lodge of the Most Ancient and Honorable Society of Free and Accepted Masons of the State of Vermont* (Montpelier, 1819), 17–20; *Summary of the Proceedings of the Grand Lodge of New-Hampshire* (Amherst, N.H., 1817), 8–9; *Regulations of the Grand Royal Arch Chapter of . . . New-Hampshire* (Concord, N.H., 1819), 18; *Freemason's Library,* appen. pp. 67–70; *Grand Royal Arch Chapter of Massachusetts,* 19.

10. Scots' Charitable Society, *Constitution and By-Laws* (Cambridge, Mass., 1878), 30; Charitable Irish Society, *Constitution and By-Laws* (Boston, 1876), 21; Boston Episcopal Charitable Society, Records, Massachusetts Historical Society, Boston, 1758 Charter, art. 5.

11. *Proceedings in Masonry: St. John's Grand Lodge, 1733–1792, Massachusetts Grand Lodge, 1769–1792* (Boston, 1895), 267–268.

12. *Reprint of the Early Proceedings of the MW Grand Lodge of Free and Accepted Masons of the State of Rhode Island From the Date of Organization, June 27th 1791 to June 19th, 1820 Inclusive* (Providence, 1888), 9, 15, 23, 26, 30. For the grand lodge's later involvement in public relief, see ibid., 269–270.

13. Records of the Humane Society in Bath, Maine, 1793–1812, New York Public Library, 3; *Whereas in a State of Civil Society . . . .* (Boston, 1794).

14. *Massachusetts Charitable Fire Society Papers, 1792–1973* (Boston, 1974, microfilm ed.).

15. Boston Dispensary, Managers' Record Book, 1796–1827, Countway Library, Harvard Medical School, Boston.

16. M. A. DeWolfe Howe, *The Humane Society of the Commonwealth of Massachusetts: An Historical Review, 1785–1916* (Boston, 1918); Merrimack Humane Society, Correspondence, Essex Institute, Salem, Mass.; *Information for Immigrants to the New-England States* (Boston, 1795).

17. Hartford Charitable Society, Papers, 1792–1871, Connecticut Historical Society, Hartford.

18. *Boston Fuel Society* (Boston, 1813).

19. Boston Female Asylum, Records, Massachusetts State Library, Boston;

Salem Female Charitable Society, Secretary's Records, Essex Institute, Salem; Newburyport Female Charitable Society, Records, Newburyport Public Library, Newburyport; *Piscataqua Evangelical Magazine* 1:34 (1805); Providence Female Charitable Society, Records, Rhode Island Historical Society, Providence; Wiscasset Female Charitable Society, Secretary's Book, Wiscasset Public Library (kept in the Lincoln County Courthouse), Wiscasset, Me.; Female Humane Society of Cambridge, Records, 1814–1848, Schlesinger Library, Radcliffe College, Cambridge, Mass.; Concord [Mass.] Female Charitable Society, Records, Concord Free Public Library, Concord, Mass.; Concord [N.H.] Female Charitable Society, Records, New Hampshire Historical Society, Concord.

20. Margaret Gerteis, "The Massachusetts General Hospital, 1810–1865: An Essay on the Political Construction of Social Responsibility During New England's Early Industrialization" (Ph.D. diss., Tufts Univ., 1985); Charles E. Rosenberg, *The Care of Strangers: The Rise of the American Hospital System* (New York, 1987); Charles Roy Keller, *The Second Great Awakening in Connecticut* (New Haven, 1942), 168–171.

21. *Proceedings of the First Ten Years of the American Tract Society* (Boston, 1824), 208.

22. Auxiliary Foreign Missionary Society of Middlesex, Records, 1812–1881, Christian Conference of Connecticut, Hartford.

23. *Report of the American Board of Commissioners for Foreign Missions* (Boston, 1817).

24. *Third Report of the American Bible Society* (New York, 1819), 30. Note that many local and county associations were affiliated with the national society indirectly as auxiliaries of state organizations.

25. *Constitution of a Society for Abolishing the Slave-Trade* (Providence, 1789); *The Constitution of the Connecticut Society for the Promotion of Freedom, and the Relief of Persons Unlawfully Holden in Bondage* (New Haven, 1792); Nathanael Emmons, *A Discourse, Delivered September 3d, MDCCXCIII, to the Society for the Reformation of Morals, in Franklin* (Worcester, 1793).

26. Massachusetts Society for the Suppression of Intemperance, Letter-book, 1813–1829, Massachusetts Historical Society, Boston.

27. *Address of the Connecticut Society for the Promotion of Good Morals* (New Haven, 1814).

28. Jesse Appleton, *A Discourse, Delivered at Bath, before the Society for Discountenancing and Suppressing Public Vices* (Boston, 1813); *The Concord Society for Discountenancing Vice and Immorality* (Concord, N.H., 1813).

29. *A Circular Letter from the Massachusetts Peace Society* (Cambridge, Mass., 1816); P. J. Staudenraus, *The African Colonization Movement, 1816–1865* (New York, 1961).

30. *Salem Gazette,* Aug. 2, 1816. Note that the *Gazette's* list was actually a partial one that betrayed an evangelical bias in its incompleteness, since it omitted the town's masonic lodge and an auxiliary to the largely Arminian (or liberal) Evangelical Missionary Society. See *Constitutions of the Grand Lodge of Massachusetts,* 20, and "Subscription to Evangelical Missionary Society by Members of the Salem North Church," Saltonstall Papers, Massachusetts Historical Society, Boston.

31. Concord [N.H.] Female Charitable Society, Records, 37.

32. Appleton, *Discourse Delivered at Bath,* 7.

33. Daniel Appleton White, *An Address to the Members of the Merrimack Humane Society* (Newburyport, 1805), 20.

34. Massachusetts [Charitable] Society, Records, Massachusetts Historical Society, Boston, 126.

35. Bettye Hobbs Pruitt, ed., *The Massachusetts Tax Valuation List of 1771* (Boston, 1978), 32.

36. Massachusetts [Charitable] Society, Records, 126.

37. Massachusetts [Charitable] Society, Records, 81.

38. [James Anderson], *The Constitutions of the Free-Masons* (London, 1723), 50.

39. *Rules and Articles of the Massachusetts Charitable Society* (Boston, 1811).

40. *Rules and Articles of the Massachusetts Charitable Society,* 19–27; Massachusetts [Charitable] Society, Records; Pruitt, ed., *Massachusetts Tax Valuation List of 1771;* James Henretta, "Economic Development and Social Structure in Colonial Boston," *William and Mary Quarterly,* 3d ser., 22:82 (1965).

41. *Rules and Articles of the Massachusetts Charitable Society,* 19–27; "The Statistics of the United States Direct Tax of 1798, as Assessed on Boston," *Report of the Record Commissioners of the City of Boston* (Boston, 1890), 22:1–442; *History of Saint John's Lodge of Boston* (Boston, 1917), 16; Benjamin Huntoon, *An Address Delivered at New Haven* (New Haven, 1850), 5.

42. Lipson, *Freemasonry in Federalist Connecticut,* 132–149.

43. Providence Association of Mechanics and Manufacturers, Journal, Rhode Island Historical Society, Providence, Feb. 13, 1792, Apr. 2, 23, 1792, July 9, 1798.

44. William H. Bayley and Oliver O. Jones, comps., *History of the Marine Society of Newburyport, Massachusetts* (Newburyport, 1906), 30; Massachusetts [Charitable] Society, Records, 60.

45. Newport Marine Society, Minute Book, 1799–1859, Newport Historical Society, Newport, Jan. 6, 1813.

46. *Boston Gazette,* Sept. 28, 1801.

47. For a description of Stillman, see William B. Sprague, ed., *Annals of the American Pulpit* (New York, 1857–1869), 6:71–79. *Boston Gazette,* Sept. 28, 1801; Samuel Stillman, *A Discourse, Delivered before the Members of the Boston Female Asylum* (Boston, 1801), 12n.

48. *The Institution of the Boston Female Asylum* (Boston, 1801).

49. Thaddeus Mason Harris, *A Discourse Preached before the Members of the Boston Female Asylum* (Boston, 1813), 15.

50. *An Account of the Rise, Progress, and Present State of the Boston Female Asylum* (Boston, 1803), 12–19.

51. Boston Female Asylum, Records, Massachusetts State Library, Boston, Oct. 27, Nov. 25, Dec. 28, 1800, Feb. 8, 1802.

52. Boston Female Asylum, Records, vol. 1, Mar. 1802.

53. *Institution of the Boston Female Asylum; The Boston Directory* (Boston, 1798); *The Boston Directory* (Boston, 1800); "Direct Tax of 1798."

54. Boston Female Asylum, Records, vol. 1, Sept. 1802.

55. Joseph Eckley, *A Discourse, Delivered before the Members of the Boston Female Asylum* (Boston, 1802), 15, 16.

56. *Boston Gazette,* Sept. 28, 1801; Stillman, *Boston Female Asylum,* 16–18.

57. Sumner was the father of Charles Sumner, the abolitionist senator from Massachusetts, born in 1811.

58. Boston Female Asylum, Records, vol. 1, May, June, Sept., Oct., 1802; vol. 2, Oct. 1806.

59. Stillman, *Boston Female Asylum,* 12.

60. Thomas Clark to Hannah Stillman, Boston, Mar. 9, 1801, in Boston Female Asylum, Records, vol. 1, Mar. 31, 1801.

61. Boston Female Asylum, Records, Boston Children's Service Association, Box 101, Register of the Orphan Children; *The Boston Directory* (Boston, 1803), 66.

62. Boston Female Asylum, Register of the Orphan Children.

63. Boston Female Asylum, Records, vol. 1, Apr. 28, May 26, 1801; Register of the Orphan Children.

64. *Account of the Rise, Progress, and Present State,* 18.

65. Boston Female Asylum, Records, vol. 1, loose pages inserted after May 26, 1801.

66. Harris, *Boston Female Asylum,* 18–19.

67. Daniel Dana, *An Address to the Members of the Merrimack Humane Society* (Exeter, 1813), 3.

68. Benjamin Pollard, *An Address, to the Massachusetts Charitable Fire Society* (Boston, 1811), 16.

69. Timothy P. Gillet, *Charity Profitable; Or, God a Surety for the Poor* (New Haven, 1813), 13.

70. Samuel Spring, *An Address to the Members of the Merrimack Humane Society* (Newburyport, 1807), 17.

71. James Richardson, *An Address, Delivered before the Members of the Massachusetts Charitable Fire Society* (Boston, 1810), 7.

72. Difficult, but not impossible. Note the opposition to female asylums and Freemasons discussed on pp. 113–114 and 164–168.

73. William Walter, *A Charge: Delivered at Charlestown* in Josiah Bartlett, *A Discourse on the Origin, Progress and Design of Free Masonry* (Boston, 1793), 24.

74. For a conservative tabulation of these organizations, see Richard D. Brown, "The Emergence of Urban Society in Rural Massachusetts, 1760–1820," *Journal of American History* 61:40–41 (1974). The trustees of the most prominent of these organizations formed a kind of interlocking directorate of considerable influence. See Ronald Story, *The Forging of an Aristocracy: Harvard and the Boston Upper Class, 1800–1870* (Middletown, 1980), and Peter Dobkin Hall, *The Organization of American Culture, 1700–1900: Private Institutions, Elites, and the Origins of American Nationality* (New York, 1982).

75. Walter Buckingham Smith and Arthur Harrison Cole, *Fluctuations in American Business, 1790–1860* (Cambridge, Mass., 1935), 12.

76. Smith and Cole, *Fluctuations in American Business,* 4–33.

77. David Brion Davis, *The Problem of Slavery in the Age of Revolution, 1770–1823* (Ithaca, 1975), 240–241.

78. [Peter Thacher], *Brief Account of the Society for Propagating the Gospel among the Indians and Others in North America* (Boston, 1798), 2. Note that the Society in Scotland for Propagating Christian Knowledge eventually resumed activities in New England, notwithstanding the organization of the SPGNA. See *The Massachusetts Register and United States Calendar . . . 1811* (Boston, 1810), 44.

79. Recent scholarship has depicted the American Revolution itself as the adolescent striving and coming of age of the American colonies. The early history of the SPGNA would seem to support this provocative thesis. See Jay Fliegelman, *Prodigals and Pilgrims: The American Revolution Against Patriarchal Authority, 1750–1800* (Cambridge, 1982), and Melvin Yazawa, *From Colonies to Commonwealth: Familial Ideology and the Beginnings of the American Republic* (Baltimore, 1985).

80. On the participation of business leaders and their families in charity, see: Story, *Forging of an Aristocracy,* 24–56; Robert F. Dalzell, Jr., *Enterprising Elites: The Boston Associates and the World They Made* (Cambridge, Mass., 1987), 113–163; Gerald T. White, *A History of the Massachusetts Hospital Life Insurance Company* (Cambridge, Mass., 1955).

81. Samuel Hopkins to Moses Brown, Mar. 7, 1787, Moses Brown Papers, Rhode Island Historical Society, Providence, quoted in Joseph A. Conforti, *Samuel Hopkins and the New Divinity Movement* (Grand Rapids, Mich., 1981), 140.

82. Mary P. Ryan, *Cradle of the Middle Class: The Family in Oneida County, New York, 1790–1865* (New York, 1981), 105–144.

83. *Early Records of the Grand Lodge of the State of Vermont,* 80.

Chapter Three

1. See, for example, Charles Roy Keller, *The Second Great Awakening in Connecticut* (New Haven, 1942), and Perry Miller, *The Life of the Mind in America: From the Revolution to the Civil War* (New York, 1965), 3–95.

2. Philip Schaff, *America: A Sketch of Its Political, Social, and Religious Character,* ed. Perry Miller (Cambridge, Mass., 1961), 96–97.

3. Schaff, *America,* 74–77.

4. Richard L. Bushman, *From Puritan to Yankee: Character and the Social Order in Connecticut, 1690–1765* (Cambridge, Mass., 1967), 235–266.

5. William G. McLoughlin, *New England Dissent, 1630–1833: The Baptists and the Separation of Church and State* (Cambridge, Mass., 1971), 1:281, 1:504–505, 2:700–701.

6. McLoughlin, *New England Dissent,* 1:505–511.

7. McLoughlin, *New England Dissent,* 2:698–699, 1115–1121.

8. Clara O. Loveland, *The Critical Years: The Reconstruction of the Anglican Church in the United States of America* (Greenwich, Conn., 1956), 236–272; quotation, p. 51.

9. Conrad Wright et al., *A Stream of Light: A Sesquicentennial History of American Unitarianism* (Boston, 1975), 11.

10. Joseph W. Phillips, *Jedidiah Morse and New England Congregationalism* (New Brunswick, N.J., 1983), 123–124, 144–146.

11. Conrad Wright, *The Beginnings of Unitarianism in America* (Boston, 1955), 252–280.

12. Wright, *Stream of Light,* 30–32.

13. Wright, *Stream of Light,* 28–29.

14. See Stephen A. Marini, *Radical Sects of Revolutionary New England* (Cambridge, Mass., 1982).

15. *The Religious History of New England* (Cambridge, Mass., 1917), 55.

16. Chauncy to Wheelock, Feb. 15, 1762, *Papers of Eleazar Wheelock* (Hanover, N.H., 1971, microfilm ed.). Admittedly, this relationship was marked by constant tensions: see Wheelock to Chauncy, Mar. 13, 1769, *Papers of Eleazar Wheelock,* for an example of the anger that sometimes boiled over when they corresponded.

17. Jonathan Edwards, "The Life and Diary of the Rev. David Brainerd: with Notes and Reflections," in *The Works of President Edwards* (Leeds [Eng.], 1806–1811), 3:475–476.

18. *Records of the General Association of the Colony of Connecticut* (Hartford, 1888), 76, 79, 80, 85, 86, 120, 141, 148, 154, 160.

19. *A Brief Account of the Present State of the Society for Propagating the Gospel among the Indians and Others in North-America* (Boston, 1790), 1.

20. The Alford bequest was substantial: £1,152 in specie bonds, £418 in Commonwealth notes, and $8,420 in continental securities. See Society for the Propagation of the Gospel among the Indians and Others in North America (SPGNA), Records, Massachusetts Historical Society, Boston, vol. 1:11, 19, 24, 13, 14, 15.

21. SPGNA, Records, 1:11–12.

22. SPGNA, Records, 1:12, 24.

23. SPGNA, Records, 1:13, 14, 19, 24, 26, 29, 67–69; SPGNA, Select Committee, Records, 6–8, 10–11, 22.

24. Elihu Thayer, *A Sermon, Preached at Hopkinton, at the Formation of the New-Hampshire Missionary Society* (Concord, N.H., 1801), 17.

25. *A Statement of the Affairs of the New-Hampshire Missionary Society* (Concord, N.H., 1803), 7.

26. Jere R. Daniell, *Experiment in Republicanism: New Hampshire Politics and the American Revolution, 1741–1794* (Cambridge, Mass., 1970), 49.

27. "A Humble Petition" to Wheelock from Theadford [sic], Mar. 16, 1768, *Papers of Eleazar Wheelock.*

28. Marini, *Radical Sects,* 40–59.

29. Once established with both Baptist and Congregationalist members, the Boston Cent Society continued to support the work of both denominations; see *Panoplist* 13:179 (1817). On early minimizing of denominational lines, see *Instructions of the Trustees of the Hampshire Missionary Society* (Northampton, 1802), 5.

30. *The Memoir and Journals of Rev. Paul Coffin, D.D.,* ed. Cyrus Woodman (Portland, Me., 1855), 80, 81, 138.

31. *The Constitution and Address of the Congregational Missionary Society* (Stockbridge, 1798), 8–11.

32. Missionary Society of Connecticut, *A Summary of Christian Doctrine and Practice* (Hartford, 1804); New Hampshire Missionary Society, *A Summary of Christian Doctrines and Duties* (Concord, N.H., 1807).

33. Hampshire Missionary Society, *Instructions of the Trustees,* 6; Hampshire Missionary Society, *Report of the Trustees* (Northampton, 1803), 3, 18; John Lathrop, *A Discourse before the Society for "Propagating the Gospel"* (Boston, 1804), 21; Levi Frisbie, *A*

Discourse, before the Society for Propagating the Gospel (Charlestown, 1804), 21; Thomas Barnard, *A Discourse before the Society for Propagating the Gospel* (Charlestown, 1806).

34. Frederick Lewis Weis, *A Brief Historical Sketch of the Evangelical Missionary Society in Massachusetts, 1807–1951* (Lancaster, Mass., 1951).

35. *The Constitution and Address of the Bible Society of Salem and Vicinity* (Charlestown, 1810), 12.

36. *The Constitution and Address of the Merrimack Bible Society* (Newburyport, 1810), 3.

37. *Bible Society of Salem and Vicinity,* 12.

38. Peter Thacher, *A Brief Account of the Society for Propagating the Gospel* (Boston, 1798), 4. On Doddridge, see Geoffrey F. Nuttall, ed., *Philip Doddridge, 1702–51* (London, 1951).

39. *The Constitution of the Providence Association for Promoting Christian Knowledge* (Providence, 1807), 17.

40. *Constitution of the Massachusetts Society for Promoting Christian Knowledge* (Charlestown, 1803), 3, 7–8.

41. *The Massachusetts Register and United States Calendar for . . . 1811* (Boston, 1810), 45.

42. David F. Allmendinger, Jr., *Paupers and Scholars: The Transformation of Student Life in Nineteenth-Century New England* (New York, 1975), 58.

43. *The Constitution of a Society for Promoting the Education of Religious Young Men for the Ministry* (Salem, 1803), 7.

44. On the history of the society, see Natalie Ann Naylor, "Raising a Learned Ministry: The American Education Society, 1815–1860" (Ed.D. diss., Columbia Univ., 1971).

45. See, for example, Maine Branch of the American Society for Educating Pious Youth for the Gospel Ministry, Directors' Records, Congregational Library, Boston, June 8, 1820.

46. Society for Promoting Theological Education, Records, Harvard University Archives, Cambridge, Mass.

47. Keller, *Second Great Awakening,* 37.

48. Quoted in Keller, *Second Great Awakening,* 38.

49. Keller, *Second Great Awakening,* 41–42.

50. *A Missionary Address from the Trustees of the Missionary Society of Connecticut* (Hartford, 1813), 15–16.

51. Joseph Dana, *A Sermon Delivered before the Merrimack Humane Society* (Newburyport, 1804), 22.

52. Charles Brockwell, *Brotherly Love Recommended* (Boston, 1750), 13.

53. Tina Levitan, *The Firsts of American Jewish History* (Brooklyn, N.Y., 1957), 50.

54. John Sylvester John Gardiner, *An Address, Delivered before the Members of the Massachusetts Charitable Fire Society* (Boston, 1803), 12.

55. Dana, *Merrimack Humane Society,* 22.

56. Robert Louis Hampel, "Influence and Respectability: Temperance and Prohibition in Massachusetts, 1813–1852" (Ph.D. diss., Cornell Univ., 1980), 33.

57. Massachusetts Bible Society, Records, Massachusetts Bible Society, Boston, 1:9–11.

58. Bible Society of the State of Rhode Island, Records, Rhode Island Historical Society, Providence, vol. 1, Aug. 10, Sept. 3, 1813.

59. Hampel, "Influence and Respectability," 33.

60. M. A. DeWolfe Howe, *The Humane Society of the Commonwealth of Massachusetts: An Historical Review, 1785–1916* (Boston, 1918), 290.

61. Lucius Bolles, *A Discourse, Delivered before the Members of the Salem Female Charitable Society* (Salem, 1810), 3–4.

62. William Bentley, *The Diary of William Bentley, D.D.* (Salem, 1905–1914), 3:541.

63. Salem Female Charitable Society, Secretary's Records, Essex Institute, Salem, Mass., Dec. 2, 1801, 26–27.

64. Salem Female Charitable Society, Secretary's Records, Feb. 1, 1802, 29; Mar. 11, 1802, 31.

65. Boston Female Asylum, Records, Massachusetts State Library, Boston, Aug. 1810.

66. Board to Miss Bacon, Boston Female Asylum, Records, Aug. 1810.

Chapter Four

1. Menzies Rayner, *A Charity Sermon* (Hartford, 1811), 9.

2. *Address of the Board of Trustees of the Massachusetts General Hospital to the Public* (Boston, 1814), 3–5.

3. Benjamin W. Labaree, *Patriots and Partisans: The Merchants of Newburyport, 1764–1815* (Cambridge, Mass., 1962), 132.

4. See, for example, Town of Cornwallis, N.S., to Eleazar Wheelock, Cornwallis, Dec. 1, 1760, and Jonathan Rockwell and John Newcomb to Eleazar Wheelock, Cornwallis, N.S., Oct. 9, 1763, *Papers of Eleazar Wheelock* (Hanover, N.H., 1971, microfilm ed.).

5. Lynne Withey, *Urban Growth in Colonial Rhode Island: Newport and Providence in the Eighteenth Century* (Albany, 1984).

6. On the growing problem of widowhood in the late 18th century in one New England town, see Barbara E. Lacey, "Women in the Era of the American Revolution: The Case of Norwich, Connecticut," *New England Quarterly* 53:529–535 (1980). On the growing number of public wards, see Sheila Anne Culbert, "Sturdy Beggars and the Worthy Poor: Poverty in Massachusetts, 1750–1820" (Ph.D. diss., Indiana Univ., 1985), 12–43. Boston's almshouse had 270 residents during the summer of 1790. Ibid., 29.

7. For an example of such a collection, of which there were many, see Weston's after the great Newburyport fire of 1811 in Town of Weston, *Births, Deaths and Marriages, 1707–1850* (Boston, 1901), 546.

8. Wiscasset Female Charitable Society, Secretary's Book, Wiscasset Public Library, Wiscasset, Me. (stored at Lincoln County Courthouse), 1–7.

9. *J. Russell's Gazette, Commercial and Political,* Dec. 2, 9, 1799, July 31, 1800.

10. Ronald F. Banks, *Maine Becomes a State: The Movement to Separate Maine from Massachusetts, 1785–1820* (Middletown, 1970), 7, 8.

11. Banks, *Maine Becomes a State,* 57.

12. *Records of the General Association of the Colony of Connecticut* (Hartford, 1888), 166–167, 172–173, 177.

13. David Freeman Hawke, *Benjamin Rush: Revolutionary Gadfly* (Indianapolis, 1971), 320–322; John K. Alexander, *Render Them Submissive: Responses to Poverty in Philadelphia, 1760–1800* (Amherst, 1980), 132–133.

14. Raymond A. Mohl, *Poverty in New York, 1783–1825* (New York, 1971), 143–144.

15. *Letters of Benjamin Rush,* ed. L. H. Butterfield (Princeton, 1951), 1:447–448, 478.

16. *Institution of the Boston Dispensary* ([Boston, 1797]), 1.

17. Boston Dispensary, Managers' Record Book, 1796–1827, Countway Library, Harvard Medical School, Boston, Mass., 74–76, 84.

18. Massachusetts Congregational Charitable Society, Records, Massachusetts Historical Society, Boston, 10, 15, 23, 25–28.

19. For donations, see Massachusetts Congregational Charitable Society, Journal, Andover-Harvard Library, Harvard Divinity School, Cambridge, Mass. The abandonment of the annuity scheme came shortly after the Society considered a new private subscription to increase funds. See Records, 42, 44, 47, 56, 74.

20. E. G. Storer, *The Records of Freemasonry in the State of Connecticut* (New Haven, 1859), 49, 56; *Early Proceedings of the MW Grand Lodge of . . . Rhode Island* (Providence, 1888), 1:5–6; *Proceedings of the Grand Lodge of New Hampshire* (Concord, 1860), 1:1; *Records of the Grand Lodge of . . . Vermont* (Burlington, 1879), 55–59. *Proceedings in Masonry: St. John's Grand Lodge, 1733–1792; Massachusetts Grand Lodge, 1769–1792* (Boston, 1895), 222–223, 341–381.

21. Mack E. Thompson, "The Ward-Hopkins Controversy and the American Revolution in Rhode Island: An Interpretation," *William and Mary Quarterly,* 3rd ser., 16:363–375 (1959); Sydney V. James, *Colonial Rhode Island: A History* (New York, 1975), 294–313. *Early Proceedings of the MW Grand Lodge of . . . Rhode Island,* 5, 6, 59. Storer, *Freemasonry in . . . Connecticut,* 68. *Records of the Grand Lodge of . . . Vermont,* 103.

22. *Records of the Grand Lodge of . . . Vermont,* 72. *Proceedings in Masonry,* 357–361. *New Hampshire Grand Lodge,* 10. Storer, *Freemasonry in . . . Connecticut,* 74. *Records of the Grand Lodge of . . . Vermont,* 72.

23. *Records of the Grand Lodge of . . . Vermont,* 87–90. *Proceedings of the Most Worshipful Grand Lodge of Ancient Free and Accepted Masons of the Commonwealth of Massachusetts* (Cambridge, Mass., 1905), 282–284, 290–291.

24. The 1791 Constitution of the Grand Lodge of Rhode Island referred to the "districts" of Newport and Providence. See *Early Proceedings of the MW Grand Lodge of . . . Rhode Island,* 5. See also *Grand Lodge of . . . Massachusetts,* 2:191–192; *Grand Lodge of New Hampshire,* 77–78; *Records of the Grand Lodge of . . . Vermont,* 103.

25. *The Diary of William Bentley, D.D.* (Salem, 1905–1914), 2:396, 411.

26. *Report of the Trustees of the Bible Society of Salem and Vicinity* (Salem, 1812), 8.

27. *Piscataqua Evangelical Magazine* 1:34 (1805).

28. William Kellaway, *The New England Company, 1649–1776: Missionary*

Society to the American Indians (London, 1961), passim; see also the so-called "Eliot Tracts," collected in one place in Massachusetts Historical Society, *Collections,* 3rd ser. 4:1–288 (1834).

29. *Institution of the Boston Dispensary,* 2.

30. Providence Female Charitable Society, Records, Rhode Island Historical Society, Providence, 6–7.

31. New Haven Moral Society, Minute Book, Connecticut Historical Society, Hartford. Charles Roy Keller believed that the local auxiliaries of the Connecticut Moral Society were simply in advance of public opinion and failed for lack of public support. The later persistence of many other reform groups, however—peace, temperance, abolition—is a reminder that the survival of reform organizations (as opposed to their success) never depended on broad support. See Keller, *The Second Great Awakening in Connecticut* (New Haven, 1942), 153–154.

32. *Whereas It is Found by Experience. . . .* (Boston, 1754).

33. Eleazar Wheelock, *A Plain and Faithful Narrative of the Original Design, Rise, Progress, and Present State of the Indian Charity-School at Lebanon, in Connecticut* (Boston, 1763); *A Continuation of the Narrative* (Boston, 1765); *A Continuation of the Narrative* (Hartford, 1771); *A Continuation of the Narrative* (Portsmouth, 1772); *A Continuation of the Narrative* (Hartford, 1773); *A Continuation of the Narrative* (Portsmouth, 1773); *A Continuation of the Narrative* (Hartford, 1775).

34. Richard H. Shoemaker, comp., *A Checklist of American Imprints for 1820* (New York, 1964), passim.

35. Patricia Cline Cohen, *A Calculating People: The Spread of Numeracy in Early America* (Chicago, 1982), 150.

36. Cohen, *Calculating People,* 150–174; James H. Cassedy, *American Medicine and Statistical Thinking, 1800–1860* (Cambridge, Mass., 1984), 25–51.

37. Keller, *Second Great Awakening,* 165–168.

38. *Circular Addressed to the Members of the Massachusetts Society for Suppressing Intemperance* (Boston, 1814), 4–5, 14–15.

39. *Friend of Peace* 1:131 (1816).

40. On the development of "scientific philanthropy," see Robert H. Bremner, *American Philanthropy* (Chicago, 1960), 89–104; Michael B. Katz, *In the Shadow of the Poorhouse: A Social History of Welfare in America* (New York, 1986), 58–84; James Leiby, *A History of Social Welfare and Social Work in the United States* (New York, 1978), 90–110; Walter I. Trattner, *From Poor Law to Welfare State* (New York, 1974), 75–95.

Curtius

1. *National Aegis,* Sept. 14, 1803.

2. *National Aegis,* Sept. 14, 1803.

3. *National Aegis,* Sept. 14, 1803.

4. *National Aegis,* Oct. 19, 1803.

Chapter Five

1. John Bartlett, *A Discourse, Delivered before the Roxbury Charitable Society* ([Boston, 1796]), 6–7.

2. [Samuel] Seabury, *A Sermon Delivered before the Boston Episcopal Charitable Society in Trinity Church* (Boston, 1788), 17–18.

3. Samuel Stillman, *A Discourse, Delivered before the Members of the Boston Female Asylum* (Boston, 1801), 3.

4. Edward D. Griffin, *A Sermon, Preached August 11, 1811* (Boston, 1811), 28, 18.

5. Arthur Browne, *The Advantages of Unity* (Portsmouth, 1758).

6. Daniel Appleton White, *An Address, to the Members of the Merrimack Humane Society* (Newburyport, 1805), 20.

7. William Patten, *The Advantages of Association to Promote Useful Purposes* (Newport, 1805), 10–12.

8. Eccles. 4:9.

9. Thomas Barnard, *A Discourse, Delivered before the Humane Society* (Boston, 1794), 12.

10. Andrew Yates, *A Sermon Delivered in the North Presbyterian Church in Hartford* (Hartford, 1812), 8.

11. Patten, *Advantages of Association,* 11.

12. Luther Baker, *An Address, Delivered to the Philanthropic Society* (Warren, R.I., 1806), 10.

13. Patten, *Advantages of Association,* 11.

14. Patten, *Advantages of Association,* 12.

15. Daniel Dana, *An Address to the Members of the Merrimack Humane Society* (Newburyport, 1813), 4.

16. Charles Paine, *An Address, Delivered Before the Members of the Massachusetts Charitable Fire Society* (Boston, 1808), 6.

17. John Lathrop, *A Discourse before the Massachusetts Charitable Fire Society* (Boston, 1796), 15–16.

18. Stillman, *Discourse,* 8.

19. Samuel Cary, *An Address to the Members of the Merrimack Humane Society* (Newburyport, 1806), 6–7.

20. *A Dissertation, on the Subject of Procuring the Education of Pious Youth for the Christian Ministry* (Boston, 1814), 3.

21. Joseph Eckley, *A Discourse, Delivered before the Members of the Boston Female Asylum* (Boston, 1802), 10.

22. Jedidiah Morse, *A Sermon Preached before the Humane Society* (Boston, 1801), 9.

23. Isaac Hurd, *A Discourse Delivered in the Church in Brattle Street* (Boston, 1799), 8.

24. Baker, *Philanthropic Society,* 7.

25. Joseph Sewall, *The Second Commandment Like to the First* (Boston, 1742), 7.

26. Andrew Eliot, *A Sermon Preached at the Ordination of the Reverend Mr. Joseph Roberts* (Boston, [1754]), 15.

27. See, for example, Philanthropos, *A Valediction, for New Year's Day. 1763* (Boston, 1763); see also a 1756 reprint of a London pamphlet, [Philanthropos], *A Serious Address to the Clergy* (Boston, 1756), 13.

28. John Eliot, *The Charge,* in Christopher Gore, *An Oration: Delivered at the Chapel, in Boston* (Boston, [1783]), 19.

29. Zabdiel Adams, *Brotherly Love and Compassion, Described and Recommended* (Worcester, 1778), 8.

30. George Rawson Burrill, *An Oration, Delivered before the Providence Association of Mechanics and Manufacturers* (Providence, 1796), 10.

31. Hurd, *Humane Society,* 7–8.

32. Zechariah Eddy, *Philandrianism: An Oration* (Providence, 1800), 19.

33. On colonial millennialism, see James West Davidson, *The Logic of Millennial Thought: Eighteenth-Century New England* (New Haven, 1977); Nathan O. Hatch, *The Sacred Cause of Liberty: Republican Thought and the Millennium in Revolutionary New England* (New Haven, 1977).

34. *The Constitution and Address of the Congregational Missionary Society* (Stockbridge, 1798), 14.

35. *Constitution and Address,* 17, 19, 20–22.

36. Samuel Niles, *A Sermon, Delivered before the Massachusetts Missionary Society* (Cambridge, Mass., 1801).

37. Samuel Spring, *A Sermon, Delivered before the Massachusetts Missionary Society* (Newburyport, 1802), 6.

38. *An Address of the Congregational Missionary Society* (Stockbridge, [1805]), 6.

39. Paul Litchfield, *A Sermon, Preached before the Massachusetts Missionary Society* (Salem, 1805), 17. The text is from Haggai 1:8.

40. Joseph Barker, *A Sermon, Preached before the Massachusetts Missionary Society* (Salem, 1806), 11.

41. Joseph Eckley, *A Discourse Before the Society for Propagating the Gospel* (Boston, 1806), 21.

42. Missionary Society of Connecticut, *A Narrative on the Subject of Missions* (Hartford, 1806), 13.

43. Elijah Parish, *A Sermon, Preached before the Massachusetts Missionary Society* (Newburyport, 1807), 4.

44. Timothy Mather Cooley, *The Universal Spread of the Gospel* (Northampton, 1808), 4.

45. Parish, *Massachusetts Missionary Society,* 7.

46. Cooley, *Universal Spread,* 10.

47. Parish, *Massachusetts Missionary Society,* 7, 11.

48. Abiel Holmes, *A Discourse, Delivered before the Society for Propagating the Gospel Among the Indians and Others* (Boston, 1808), 16–17.

49. John Emerson, *The Duty of Christians to Seek the Salvation of Zion, Explained and Urged* (Northampton, 1809), 14, 13.

50. Eliphalet Gillet, *A Sermon Delivered Before the Maine Missionary Society* (Hallowell, Me., 1810), 22.

51. *Fourth Report of the Trustees of the Bible Society of Salem and Vicinity* (Salem, 1815), 8.

52. Samuel Spring, *An Address to the Members of the Merrimack Humane Society* (Newburyport, 1807), 17, 18.

53. Thaddeus Mason Harris, *A Sermon, Preached before Union Lodge* (Boston, 1807), 12.

54. Cooley, *Universal Spread*, 5.

55. *The Diary of William Bentley* (Salem, 1905–1914), 3:298.

56. *The Monthly Anthology and Boston Review*, 8:135 (1810).

57. Thomas Baldwin, *A Discourse, Delivered before the Members of the Boston Female Asylum* (Boston, 1806), 22.

58. Manasseh Cutler, *A Discourse, Delivered in Salem, Before the Bible Society* (Salem, 1813), 5.

59. Robert Nisbet, *History of the Idea of Progress* (New York, 1980), 10–46, 179–212.

60. Drew R. McCoy, *The Elusive Republic: Political Economy in Jeffersonian America* (Chapel Hill, 1980), 19.

61. John Bartlett, *A Discourse, on the Subject of Animation* (Boston, [1792]), 6.

62. Arnold Welles, *An Address, to the Members of the Massachusetts Charitable Fire Society* (Boston, 1797), 8, 10, 9.

63. Benjamin Whitwell, *An Address to the Members of the Massachusetts Charitable Fire Society* (Boston, 1814), 9, 8, 5.

64. Lyman Beecher, *The Autobiography of Lyman Beecher*, ed. Barbara M. Cross (Cambridge, Mass., 1961), 1:179–184.

65. Thomas Barnard, *A Sermon Preached before the Salem Female Charitable Society* (Salem, 1803), 11.

66. Jedidiah Morse, *A Sermon, Preached in Brattle-Street Church* (Boston, 1807), 10.

67. See, for example, Moses Stuart, *A Sermon, Delivered by Request of the Female Charitable Society in Salem* (Andover, 1815), 6.

68. Lyman Beecher, *The Practicability of Suppressing Vice, by Means of Societies Instituted for that Purpose* (New London, 1804).

69. Scituate, Massachusetts, Auxiliary Society for the Suppression of Intemperance, Records, 1817–1836, American Antiquarian Society, Worcester, Mass., May 24, 1820.

70. *Circular Address to the Members of the Massachusetts Society for Suppressing Intemperance* (Boston, 1814), 3.

71. Parker Cleaveland, *An Address, Delivered at Brunswick, April 27, 1814* (Boston, 1814), 5.

72. Beecher, *Autobiography*, 1:180–181.

73. Lyman Beecher, *A Reformation of Morals Practicable and Indispensable* (New-Haven, 1813).

74. Massachusetts Society for the Suppression of Intemperance, Letterbook, Massachusetts Historical Society, Boston.

75. Beecher, *Autobiography*, 1:182.

76. See, for example, Clifford S. Griffin, *Their Brothers' Keepers: Moral Stewardship in the United States, 1800–1865* (New Brunswick, N.J., 1960); W. J. Rorabaugh, *The Alcoholic Republic: An American Tradition* (New York, 1979); Ian Robert Tyrell, "Drink and the Process of Social Reform: From Temperance to Prohibition in Ante-Bellum America, 1813–1860" (Ph.D. diss., Duke Univ., 1974).

77. New Haven Moral Society, Minute Book, Jan. 25-Feb. 4, 1814, Connecticut Historical Society, Hartford; Northampton Society for the Reformation of Morals, Papers, Forbes Library, Northampton, Mass., 1st Annual Report, March 1, 1815, and Report of the Tythingmen . . . March 1815.

78. Moral Society of Goshen, Conn., Minutes or Transactions of the Society for the Promotion of Good Morals in the Town of Goshen, Conn., 1813–1816, April 6, 1814. See also Connecticut Society for the Promotion of Good Morals, *Address . . . to the Respective Branches* ([New Haven?], 1814), 14.

79. Concord Society for Discountenancing Vice and Immorality, "There are times when outward vice. . . ." ([Concord, N.H., 1813]), 2.

80. Heman Humphrey listed good laws as the third tool for the promotion of good morals, following education and institutions for moral and religious purposes. See Humphrey, *The Efficacy and Importance of Combined and Persevering Action* (New-Haven, 1815), 13–21. See also Newburyport Society for the Suppression of Vice and Immorality, *Articles of Association* (Newburyport, 1813), 4–5.

81. Moral Society of Goshen, Minutes, April 6, 1814.

82. Massachusetts Society for the Suppression of Intemperance, Letter-book, Constitution, art. 8. Note that in Rowley and Byfield, "persuasion and caution" were considered the "first and chief means" of encouraging public morality, but if they proved ineffectual the members of the local reform society pledged to consider it their "duty to aid and strengthen the arm of the law." *Constitution of the Moral Society of Rowley and Byfield* (Newburyport, 1814), 4.

83. *Constitution of the Brunswick, Topsham and Harpswell Society for the Suppression of Intemperance, and Other Immoralities* (Portland, 1814), 4.

84. Peace Society of Maine, "At a meeting of a number of Gentlemen. . . ." ([Portland, 1817]).

85. [Noah Worcester], *A Solemn Review of the Custom of War* (Cambridge, Mass., 1815), 23.

86. Portsmouth Peace Society, Second Annual Report, Nov. 1, 1820, Papers of Noah Worcester, New Hampshire Historical Society, Concord.

87. Massachusetts Peace Society, *Second Annual Report of the Committee of Inquiry* (Cambridge, Mass., 1819), 11.

88. Peace Society of Maine, "At a meeting of a number of Gentlemen. . . ."

Chapter Six

1. Boston Episcopal Charitable Society, Records, Massachusetts Historical Society, Boston, vol. 1.

2. Boston Episcopal Charitable Society, Records, 1:123–125.

3. Boston Episcopal Charitable Society, Records, 1:128.

4. [Samuel] Seabury, *A Sermon Delivered before the Boston Episcopal Charitable Society* (Boston, 1788), 20.

5. On self-interest and economic competition, see Joyce Appleby, *Capitalism and a New Social Order: The Republican Vision of the 1790s* (New York, 1983). Appleby correctly indicates that the Jeffersonians appreciated the advantages of competition

before the Federalists, but by the early nineteenth century a new generation capable of effective political organization and competition was coming to power within the Federalist establishment; see David Hackett Fischer, *The Revolution of American Conservatism: The Federalist Party in the Era of Jeffersonian Democracy* (New York, 1965).

6. John Clarke, *A Discourse, Delivered before the Humane Society of the Commonwealth of Massachusetts* (Boston, 1793), 24–26.

7. *Connecticut Courant,* Jan. 28, 1793.

8. Humane Society in Bath, Maine, Records, 1793–1812, Rare Books and Manuscript Division, New York Public Library, Astor, Lenox and Tilden Foundations, New York, 3.

9. Roxbury Charitable Society, *Whereas in a State of Civil Society. . . .* (Boston, 1794).

10. Clarke, *Humane Society,* 26; Thomas Barnard, *A Discourse, Delivered before the Humane Society* (Boston, 1794), 7, 9.

11. Massachusetts [Charitable] Society, Rules and Records, Massachusetts Historical Society, Boston, 1:130, 158–159.

12. Massachusetts [Charitable] Society, Rules and Records, 1:130, 158–159; *Proceedings in Masonry: St. John's Grand Lodge, 1733–1792, Massachusetts Grand Lodge, 1769–1792* (Boston, 1895), 267–268; Grand Lodge of Rhode Island, *Reprint of the Early Proceedings of the MW Grand Lodge. . . .* (Providence, 1888), 9, 15, 23, 26, 30.

13. Massachusetts Congregational Charitable Society, Records, Massachusetts Historical Society, Boston, 74, 86; Massachusetts [Charitable] Society, Rules and Records, 1:229–231, 247–248, 2:313.

14. M. A. DeWolfe Howe, *The Humane Society of the Commonwealth of Massachusetts: An Historical Review, 1785–1916* (Boston, 1918), 48–124.

15. Howe, *Humane Society,* 12.

16. Howard S. Miller, *The Legal Foundations of American Philanthropy, 1776–1844* (Madison, 1961), 14. Miller adds that as early as 1684, a Connecticut statute provided "that all estates that had been, or ever would be, granted for the support of religion, education, poor relief, 'or for any other public and charitable use,' should be confirmed for the uses intended by the donor." Miller, *Legal Foundations,* 17–18.

17. William Blackstone, *Commentaries on the Laws of England in Four Books* (Oxford, 1770), 1:467–485. Quotations, pp. 467, 479–480.

18. Zephaniah Swift, *A System of the Laws of the State of Connecticut* (Windham, Conn., 1795), 224–228; Nathan Dane, *A General Abridgement and Digest of American Law* (Boston, 1823–1829), 5:143–165; Francis Hilliard, *The Elements of Law: Being a Comprehensive Summary of American Civil Jurisprudence* (Boston, 1835), 32–39; James Kent, *Commentaries on American Law* (New York, 1826–1830).

19. Blackstone, *Commentaries,* 1:467. It is worth recalling that incorporation did not yet confer its most important modern benefit, limited liability. In New England, the first steps toward a doctrine of limited liability did not become evident until 1817, when Connecticut began to move in this direction. See Oscar Handlin and Mary F. Handlin, "Origins of the American Business Corporation," *Journal of Economic History* 5:8–17 (1945), and William C. Kessler, "Incorporation in New England: A Statistical Study, 1800–1875," *Journal of Economic History* 8:52 (1948).

20. Blackstone, *Commentaries*, 1:470–471.

21. Society for Propagating the Gospel among the Indians and Others in North America, Journal, Massachusetts Historical Society, Boston, 1:18–19.

22. Rupert Tract Society, Constitution and Records dating from Dec. 28, 1819, to Jan. 1834, Vermont Historical Society, Montpelier, Dec. 21, 1827, Dec. 5, 1828; *The Constitution of the Piscataqua Missionary Society* (Portsmouth, 1804), 2; *The Constitution of the Missionary Society of Connecticut* (Hartford, 1800), 3.

23. Swift, *Laws of . . . Connecticut*, 226.

24. Kent, *Commentaries*, 2:239. In their fidelity to corporate purposes, New England trustees seem to have been more strict than some of their contemporaries. For a useful comparison between activities in Boston and a southern city, see William H. Pease and Jane H. Pease, *The Web of Progress: Private Values and Public Styles in Boston and Charleston, 1828–1843* (New York, 1985), 138–152.

25. Kent, *Commentaries*, 2:240–245. There was, of course, one serious challenge to the rights of trustees to the exercise of their power—Board of Trustees of Dartmouth College *v.* Woodward (1819), the so-called Dartmouth College case. In this case, the State of New Hampshire tried to reorganize the board and rewrite the college's charter, but it met resistance from the trustees, who contended that the state had no right to revise a grant already in effect. In deciding in favor of the trustees, Chief Justice John Marshall recognized the college's status as an "eleemosynary" corporation and the right of both the board and the donors who supported Dartmouth to maintain it within the terms of the original grant and without the interference of the state. See Jurgen Herbst, *From Crisis to Crisis: American College Government, 1639–1819* (Cambridge, Mass., 1982), 232–234.

26. Josiah Hussey, *An Oration, Pronounced before the Fraternity of Masons* (Boston, [1793]), 6; [Anon.], *An Address Delivered at Manchester* (Bennington, 1786), 9; Grand Lodge of New Hampshire, *Proceedings of the Grand Lodge of New Hampshire from July 8, 5789, to June 8, 5841, Inclusive* (Concord, N.H., 1860), 49.

27. Arthur Browne, *Universal Love Recommended in a Sermon Before the . . . Free Masons, in Trinity-Church, Boston, 1st of October, 1755* (Boston, 1755), 20.

28. E. G. Storer, ed., *The Records of Freemasonry in the State of Connecticut* (New Haven, 1859), 68; *Records of the Grand Lodge of Free and Accepted Masons of the State of Vermont from 1794 to 1846 Inclusive* (Burlington, 1879), 75.

29. Storer, ed., *Freemasonry in . . . Connecticut*, 72.

30. For the appeals for acceptance of the Black Masons, see [John] Marrant, *A Sermon Preached on the 24th Day of June, 1789* (Boston, 1789), and Prince Hall, *A Charge Delivered to the Brethren of the African Lodge* (Boston, [1792]), 12.

31. Abraham Lynson Clarke, *The Secrets of Masonry Illustrated and Explained* (Providence, [1799]), 6.

32. Josiah Dunham, *An Oration, Delivered at Hanover before the Franklin Lodge* (Hanover, N.H., 1796),19–20.

33. Thomas W. Hooper, *An Oration, Delivered before the Right Worshipful Master, Wardens and Brethren of St. Peter's Lodge* (Newburyport, 5796 [1796]), 13.

34. E. Styles, *An Oration . . . upon the Festival of St. John the Evangelist* (Westminster, Mass., 1782), 6.

35. Thaddeus M. Harris, *A Masonic Eulogy, Preached at Worcester* (Worcester, 1794), 10.

36. Newport Mechanics to Providence Association of Mechanics and Manufacturers, Oct. 20, 1791, Providence Association of Mechanics and Manufacturers, Journal, Rhode Island Historical Society, Providence, vol. 1.

37. Providence Association of Mechanics and Manufacturers, Journal, 2:Jan. 27, 1800.

38. William H. Bayley and Oliver O. Jones, comps., *History of the Marine Society of Newburyport, Massachusetts* (Newburyport, 1906), 39, 91, 105.

39. Providence Association of Mechanics and Manufacturers, Journal, 1:66, 97.

40. Joseph Tinker Buckingham, comp., *Annals of the Massachusetts Charitable Mechanic Association* (Boston, 1853), 6, 83, 95.

41. Buckingham, *Annals,* 12, 16; "Recollections, 1840," John Howland Papers, Rhode Island Historical Society, Providence.

42. Massachusetts Society for Promoting Agriculture, *Laws and Regulations* (Boston, 1793).

43. Gary John Kornblith, "From Artisans to Businessmen: Master Mechanics in New England, 1789–1850" (Ph.D. diss., Princeton Univ., 1983), 15.

44. Providence Association of Mechanics and Manufacturers, Select Committee, Minutes of Proceedings, 1:5; Journal, vol. 1, Feb. 13, 1792, vol. 2, July 9, 1798.

45. *Salem Gazette,* Aug. 3, 1813.

46. *Salem Gazette,* Aug. 6, 1813.

47. For a list of those baptized, see Salem Female Charitable Society, Secretary's Records, Essex Institute, Salem, 1:168.

48. Salem Female Charitable Society, Secretary's Records, 1:152.

49. Salem Female Charitable Society, Secretary's Records, 1:152.

50. Salem Female Charitable Society, Secretary's Records, 1:152–153.

51. Salem Female Charitable Society, Secretary's Records, 1:153.

52. Salem Female Charitable Society, Secretary's Records, 1:155–158.

53. Charles Stearns, *A Sermon, Delivered at Concord, Before the Bible Society in the County of Middlesex, Massachusetts, 26 April, 1815* (Cambridge, Mass., [1815]), 25.

54. Joseph Eckley, *A Discourse, Delivered before the Members of the Boston Female Asylum* (Boston, 1802), 9. See also Henry Cumings, *A Discourse, Addressed to the Roxbury Charitable Society* (Boston, 1802).

55. Zechariah Eddy, *Philandrianism: An Oration* (Providence, 1800), 8.

56. John Sylvester John Gardiner, *A Sermon Delivered before the Humane Society* (Boston, 1803), 9.

57. Alden Bradford, *An Address Delivered before the Wiscasset Female Asylum* (Hallowell, Me., 1811), 10.

58. Daniel Dana, *A Discourse Delivered May 22, 1804* (Newburyport, 1804), 7–8.

59. Chandler Robbins, *A Discourse Delivered before the Humane Society* (Boston, 1796), 10.

60. Samuel Cary, *An Address to the Members of the Merrimack Humane Society* (Newburyport, 1806), 27.

61. Alexander Townsend, *An Address, to the Charitable Fire Society* (Boston, 1809), 12.

62. Edward Bass, *A Sermon, Delivered in St. Paul's Church* (Newburyport, 1803), 6–7.

63. Jedidiah Morse, *A Sermon, Preached in Brattle-Street Church* (Boston, 1807), 6.

64. Samuel Stillman, *A Discourse, Delivered Before the Members of the Boston Female Asylum* (Boston, 1801), 12n., 14–15.

65. John Lathrop, *A Discourse, Delivered before the Members of the Boston Female Asylum* (Boston, 1804), 22n., 21.

66. John Gorham Coffin, *An Address Delivered Before the Contributors of the Boston Dispensary* (Boston, 1813), 14.

67. Joseph Buckminster, *A Sermon, Delivered Before the Members of the Female Charitable Society* (Newburyport, 1809), 5, 4.

68. John Prince, *Charity Recommended from the Social State* (Salem, 1806), 11–12.

69. Buckminster, *Female Charitable Society*, 10.

70. Andrew Yates, *A Sermon, Delivered in the North Presbyterian Church, in Hartford* (Hartford, 1812), 8.

71. Lucius Bolles, *A Discourse, Delivered before the Salem Female Charitable Society* (Salem, 1810), 7.

72. Boston Society for the Religious and Moral Improvement of Seamen, *An Address to Masters of Vessels* (Boston, 1812), 7.

73. For criticism of the allegedly selfish motives of these doctors, see John Eliot to Jeremy Belknap, Boston, Jan. 24, 1786, Massachusetts Historical Society, *Collections*, 6th ser. 4:307.

74. *A Missionary Address from the Trustees of the Missionary Society of Connecticut* (Hartford, 1813), 4.

75. Eckley, *Boston Female Asylum*, 8.

76. James Wilson, "A Sermon Preached Extempore before the Providence Female Charitable Society," Providence Female Charitable Society, Records, Rhode Island Historical Society, Providence, 17.

77. Benjamin Gleason, *An Address Pronounced at the Visitation* (Boston, 1807), 8–10. For a discussion of the doctrine of woman's sphere in postrevolutionary New England, see Nancy F. Cott, *The Bonds of Womanhood: "Woman's Sphere" in New England, 1780–1835* (New Haven, 1977).

78. For a refutation of such objections, see Moses Stuart, *A Sermon, Delivered by Request of the Female Charitable Society in Salem* (Andover, 1815), 19.

79. Dana, *A Discourse, Delivered May 22, 1804*, 15.

80. Morse, *Brattle-Street Church*, 5.

81. Dana, *A Discourse, Delivered May 22, 1804*, 16.

82. Bradford, *Wiscasset Female Asylum*, 9.

83. Laurel Thatcher Ulrich, *Good Wives: Image and Reality in the Lives of Women in Northern New England, 1650–1750* (New York, 1982), 57.

84. *The Institution of the Boston Female Asylum* (Boston, 1801), 3.

85. William Bentley, *A Discourse, Delivered in the East Meeting-House* (Salem, 1807), 5.

86. Bentley, *Discourse,* 19.

Chapter Seven

1. *Christian Spectator* 4:113–120 (1822).

2. Carl Bridenbaugh, *Cities in the Wilderness: The First Century of Urban Life in America, 1625–1742* (New York, 1938), 359–360; F. C. Oviatt, "History of Fire Insurance in the United States" in Lester W. Zartman, ed., *Yale Readings in Insurance: Property Insurance* (New Haven, 1934), 70–98; Lester W. Zartman, "History of Life Insurance in the United States," in Zartman, ed., *Yale Readings in Insurance: Life Insurance* (New Haven, 1934), 75–94.

3. *An Act to Incorporate the Newport Insurance Company* (Newport, 1799); P. Henry Woodward, *Insurance in Connecticut* (Boston, 1897), 6.

4. (Boston, 1772).

5. Massachusetts Congregational Charitable Society, Records, Massachusetts Historical Society, Boston, 11–12, 25–28.

6. Massachusetts Mutual Fire Insurance Company, Records, Baker Library, Harvard Business School, Boston, vol. 2, Mar. 10, 1800. The quotation is from a notice placed by the company in eight Massachusetts newspapers.

7. Gerald T. White, *A History of the Massachusetts Hospital Life Insurance Company* (Cambridge, Mass., 1955), 7–22.

8. On the Washington Benevolent societies of New England, see David Hackett Fischer, *The Revolution of American Conservatism: The Federalist Party in the Era of Jeffersonian Democracy* (New York, 1965), 110–128; William Alexander Robinson, "The Washington Benevolent Society in New England: A Phase of Politics during the War of 1812," *Proceedings of the Massachusetts Historical Society* 49:274–286 (1915–1916); Harlan H. Ballard, "A Forgotten Fraternity," *Collections of the Berkshire Historical and Scientific Society* III, 4:279–298 (1913).

9. The New England affiliates of the Tammany Society were located in Providence, Newport, Bristol, and Warren, Rhode Island, and in Attleborough, Rehoboth, Seekonk, and Dedham, Massachusetts. On the Tammany Society, see Marcus W. Jernegan, "The Tammany Societies of Rhode Island," *Papers from the Historical Seminar of Brown University* (Providence, 1897), esp. 14–16, 33–36.

10. See, for example, Washington Benevolent Society, Minutes of the Standing Committee, Massachusetts Historical Society, Boston, 23, 29, 40.

11. Washington Benevolent Society for the County of Worcester, Records, 1812–1836, American Antiquarian Society, Worcester, Mass., vol. 1.

12. Quoted in Robinson, "Washington Benevolent Society," 278.

13. Robinson, "Washington Benevolent Society," 279.

14. Robinson, "Washington Benevolent Society," 280.

15. On the early history of savings banks, see Lance Edwin Davis and Peter Lester Payne, "From Benevolence to Business: The Story of Two Savings Banks," *Business History Review* 30:386–406 (1958).

16. On James Savage and the Provident Institution for Savings, see Walter Muir Whitehill, *The Provident Institution for Savings in the Town of Boston, 1816–1966* (Boston, 1966), 3–21, 71–87; and Theodore Chase and Celeste Walker, eds., "The Journal of James Savage and the Beginning of Frederic Tudor's Career in the Ice Trade," *Proceedings of the Massachusetts Historical Society* 97:115 (1985).

17. Davis and Payne, "From Benevolence to Business."

18. "Dissertation upon Masonry, Delivered to a Lodge in America, June 24th, 1734," in *The Freemasons' Monthly Magazine* 8, 10:293 (1849).

19. On the practice of secrecy by other mutual societies, see, for example, Boston Fire Society, Records, Massachusetts Historical Society, Boston, art. 7 and Mar. 3, 1742, to Sept. 3, 1747. On colonial antimasonry, see *Boston Evening-Post*, Jan. 7, 1751; [Joseph Green], *Entertainment for a Winter's Evening* (Boston, 1750); Joseph Green, "A True and exact account of the celebration of the Festival of St. John the Baptist. . . ." *American Apollo* 1:281 (1792).

20. On Morse and the Bavarian Illuminati, see Vernon Stauffer, *New England and the Bavarian Illuminati* (New York, 1918); Richard Hofstadter, *The Paranoid Style in American Politics* (New York, 1964), 10–18; Joseph W. Phillips, *Jedidiah Morse and New England Congregationalism* (New Brunswick, N.J., 1983), 73–102.

21. This is, in fact, Stauffer's and Hofstadter's interpretation.

22. Dorothy Ann Lipson, *Freemasonry in Federalist Connecticut, 1789–1835* (Princeton, 1977), 97–111, esp. 102.

23. Jedidiah Morse, *A Sermon, Delivered at the New North Church in Boston* (Boston, 1798), 21–23.

24. Nath'l Spooner, comp., *Gleanings From the Records of the Boston Marine Society, Through its First Century, 1742 to 1842* (Boston, 1879), 31–32, 36, 38, 45, 69; William H. Bayley and Oliver O. Jones, comps., *History of the Marine Society of Newburyport, Massachusetts* (Newburyport, 1906), 39, 52, 60, 62, 76–77, 81; Salem East India Marine Society, Records, Peabody Museum, Salem, Mar. 2, Sept. 7, 1814.

25. Providence Association of Mechanics and Manufacturers, Journal, Rhode Island Historical Society, Providence, vol. I, Jan. 9, 1792.

26. Spooner, *Gleanings*, 32, 39–40; Salem East India Marine Society, Records, May 6, 13, 1801; Bayley and Jones, *Marine Society of Newburyport*, 39.

27. [William Bentley], *Extracts From Professor Robison's "Proofs of a Conspiracy"* (Boston, 1799); [John Cosens Ogden], *A View of the New-England Illuminati* (Philadelphia, 1799); Bentley, *An Address, Delivered in the Essex Lodge* (Salem, 1799), 6–9; Grand Lodge of Massachusetts, *Proceedings of the Most Worshipful Grand Lodge. . . .* (Cambridge, Mass., 1905), 2:131, 134.

28. William [Henry] Woodward, *An Oration, Pronounced at Hanover, New Hampshire, January 9, 1800* (Hanover, 1800), 15.

29. *Proceedings of the . . . Grand Lodge*, 2: 161–164, 156, 157–158, 159, 160.

30. *Monthly Anthology* 1:320 (1804). See also *Monthly Anthology* 4:395–396 (1807).

31. See Samuel Johnson, *A Dictionary of the English Language* (London, 1755), vol. 1. Note that Raymond Williams believes that in England as early as the sixteenth century "charity" had already assumed "the predominant sense of help to the needy." I think he unduly accelerates a process that had proceeded far less swiftly toward fruition than he allows. See Williams, *Keywords: A Vocabulary of Culture and Society* (New York, 1976), 45.

32. Noah Webster, *An American Dictionary of the English Language* (New York, 1828), vol. 1.

33. Jasper Adams, *Elements of Moral Philosophy* (Cambridge, Mass., 1837), viii–ix, xxii, 242–248. On the development of moral philosophy after 1800, see D. H. Meyer, *The Instructed Conscience: The Shaping of the American National Ethic* (Philadelphia, 1972), and Daniel Walker Howe, *The Unitarian Conscience: Harvard Moral Philosophy, 1805–1861* (Cambridge, Mass., 1970).

34. For the constitution of 1778, see Oscar Handlin and Mary Handlin, eds., *The Popular Sources of Political Authority: Documents on the Massachusetts Constitution of 1780* (Cambridge, Mass., 1966), 190–201. *A Constitution or Frame of Government, Agreed upon by the Delegates of the People of the State of Massachusetts-Bay. . . .* (Boston, 1780), 37. On the place of organized charity in state constitutions, see Irwin G. Wyllie, "The Search for an American Law of Charity, 1776–1844," *Mississippi Valley Historical Review* 46:205–206 (1959).

35. *A Constitution, Containing a Bill of Rights, and Form of Government, Agreed upon by the Delegates of the People of the State of New Hampshire. . . .* (Portsmouth, 1783), 39.

36. *The Constitution of the State of Vermont . . . July 2d, 1777. . . .* (Hartford, 1778), 22–23; *The Constitution of Vermont . . . June 1786* (Windsor, 1786), 28; *The Constitution of Vermont . . . October 1792* (Rutland, 1792), 10; *The Constitution of Vermont . . . July Fourth, One Thousand, Seven Hundred and Ninety-Three* (Windsor, 1793), 27–28.

37. *Monthly Anthology* 4:505–506 (1807).

38. *Monthly Anthology* 2:94 (1805); 3:552 (1806); 2:602 (1805). See also 1:608 (1804); 2:319–320 (1805).

39. *Monthly Anthology* 2:320 (1805).

40. Thaddeus Mason Harris, *A Discourse, Delivered before the Humane Society* (Boston, 1806), 11.

41. Joseph Eckley, *A Discourse Before the Society for Propagating the Gospel Among the Indians and Others in North America* (Boston, 1806), 3.

42. Connecticut Bible Society, *Address, Constitution, and Subscription Proposal* (n.p., [1808]), 10.

43. *An Address of the Bible Society of Maine* (Portland, 1809), 8.

44. Jedidiah Morse, *A Sermon Preached before the Humane Society* (Boston, 1801), 27, 14.

45. Eliphalet Porter, *A Discourse Delivered before the Humane Society* (Boston, 1802), 12.

46. John Lathrop, *A Discourse, Delivered before the Members of the Boston Female Asylum* (Boston, 1804), 17.

47. Jedidiah Morse, *A Sermon, Preached in Brattle-Street Church* (Boston, 1807), 11, 12.

48. *The Winthrop Papers* (Boston, 1929–   ), 2:283.

49. See above, ch. 3.

50. *A Brief Account of the Present State of the Society for Propagating the Gospel Among the Indians and Others in North America* (Boston, 1790), 1.

51. Nathan Perkins, *A Narrative of a Tour through the State of Vermont* (Woodstock, Vt., 1930), 20.

52. Missionary Society of Connecticut, *A Second Address. . . .* (Hartford, 1801), 9.

53. *Instructions of the Trustees of the Hampshire Missionary Society* (Northampton, 1802), 12.

54. *A Brief Account* (1790), 1.

55. Timothy Mather Cooley, *The Universal Spread of the Gospel* (Northampton, 1808), 24.

56. Missionary Society of Connecticut, *A Second Address,* 8.

57. Missionary Society of Connecticut, *A Narrative on the Subject of Missions* (Hartford, 1802), 12–13.

58. Jacob Cram, *Journal of a Missionary Tour in 1808* (Rochester, 1909), 10, 9.

59. Peter Thacher, *Brief Account of the Society for Propagating the Gospel Among the Indians and Others in North America* (Boston, 1798), 4.

60. *Instructions of the Trustees . . . Hampshire Missionary Society,* 12.

61. Society for Propagating the Gospel among the Indians and Others in North America (SPGNA), Records, Massachusetts Historical Society, Boston, 107.

62. Ephraim Abbott, Journal of a Mission to Rhode Island, 1812, Rhode Island Historical Society, Providence, Nov. 20, 1812.

63. *The Constitution and Address of the Bible Society of Salem and Vicinity* (Charlestown, 1810), 16.

64. Massachusetts Bible Society, *A Circular Address* (Boston, 1809), 6, 9.

65. *Report of the Trustees of the Hampshire Missionary Society* (Northampton, 1804), 11.

66. SPGNA, Select Committee, Records, 58–59.

67. Lincoln and Kennebec Religious Tract Society, *The Importance of Sobriety* (Wiscasset, Me., [1805?]).

68. SPGNA, Select Committee, Records, 85.

69. *Minutes of the First Fifteen Annual Meetings of the General Convention of Ministers in the State of Vermont, From 1795 to 1810 Inclusive* (Montpelier, 1877), 34–35, 39.

70. SPGNA, Select Committee, Records, 85.

Anniversary Week

1. Lyman Beecher, *The Autobiography of Lyman Beecher,* ed. Barbara M. Cross (Cambridge, Mass., 1961), 1:315–316; *Letters from John Pintard to his Daughter Eliza Noel Pintard Davidson. Collections of the New-York Historical Society* (New York, 1940), 70:290.

2. Charles I. Foster, *An Errand of Mercy: The Evangelical United Front, 1790–1837* (Chapel Hill, 1960), 148–155.

3. *The Diary of William Bentley* (Salem, 1905–1914), 4:225–228.

4. Foster, *Errand of Mercy,* 153–155.

5. William E. Channing, *The Works of William Ellery Channing, D.D.* (Boston, 1882), 139.

6. Alexis de Tocqueville, *Democracy in America,* trans. Henry Reeve, rev. Francis Bowen and Phillips Bradley (New York, 1960), 2:109. See also, George Wilson Pierson, *Tocqueville in America,* abr. Dudley Lunt (Garden City, N.Y., 1959), 233–295, and Tocqueville, *Journey to America,* trans. George Lawrence, ed. J. P. Mayer (New Haven, 1960), 212, 252–253.

7. Michael Aaron Rockland, trans., *Sarmiento's "Travels in the United States in 1847"* (Princeton, 1970), 208.

Chapter Eight

1. United States, *Census for 1820* (Washington, D.C., 1821).

2. Josiah Quincy, *An Address to the Citizens of Boston* (Boston, 1830), 43–45, 65–68.

3. [Samuel A. Eliot], "Public and Private Charities in Boston," *North American Review* 61:136 (1845).

4. James T. Patterson, *America's Struggle Against Poverty, 1900–1980* (Cambridge, Mass., 1981), 56–77.

5. Quincy, *An Address,* 45–45, 65–68.

6. See Appen. 3 and *Massachusetts Register, and United States Calendar . . . 1830* (Boston, 1829), 108, 140–156, 247–249; *The Boston Directory* (Boston, 1830), 32–35; Quincy, *An Address,* 43–45, 65–68; *A Checklist of American Imprints for 1830,* comp. Gayle Cooper (Metuchen, N.J., 1972); *Annual Communication of the Most Worshipful Grand Lodge . . . of Massachusetts . . . A.L. 5834* (Boston, 1835), 19–20; Spencer Lavan, *Unitarians and India: A Study in Encounter and Response* (Boston, 1977), 63; Daniel T. McColgan, *Joseph Tuckerman: Pioneer in American Social Work* (Washington, D.C., 1940); Society for the Promotion of Christianity in India, Records, Andover-Harvard Library, Harvard Divinity School, Cambridge, Mass.

7. Richard D. Brown, "The Emergence of Urban Society in Rural Massachusetts, 1760–1820," *Journal of American History* 61:40–41 (1974). Included in this figure are new charitable, mechanic, and Masonic associations. Such calculations inevitably understate the population they attempt to count because some institutions, especially small, rural ones that functioned independently of parent organizations, have left few or no traces of their existence.

8. Noah Worcester to David Tomlinson, Brighton, July 9, 1819, Noah Worcester Papers, Massachusetts Historical Society.

9. Margaret Gerteis, "The Massachusetts General Hospital, 1810–1865: An Essay on the Political Construction of Social Responsibility During New England's Early Industrialization" (Ph.D. diss., Tufts Univ., 1985), 65–142.

10. Clifford S. Griffin, *Their Brothers' Keepers: Moral Stewardship in the United States, 1800–1865* (New Brunswick, N.J., 1960), 75–80.

11. *The Fourth Report of the American Home Missionary Society . . . May 12, 1830* (New York, 1830), 12–39.

12. *Fourteenth Annual Report of the American Education Society* (New York, 1830), 32.

13. *American Almanac and Repository of Useful Knowledge for the Year 1831* (Boston, 1830), 165.

14. Lois Wendlund Banner, "The Protestant Crusade: Religious Missions, Benevolence, and Reform in the United States, 1790–1840" (Ph.D. diss., Columbia Univ., 1970); Fred J. Hood, *Reformed America: The Middle and Southern States, 1783–1837* (University, Ala., 1980), 113–168.

15. Oscar Handlin, *Boston's Immigrants: A Study in Acculturation* (rev. ed., New York, 1969), 162; Donald B. Cole, *Immigrant City: Lawrence, Massachusetts, 1845–1921* (Chapel Hill, 1963), 153.

16. Ray Allen Billington, *The Protestant Crusade, 1800–1860: A Study in the Origins of American Nativism* (Chicago, 1962), 120, 168, 186.

17. On the role of organization in the development of the woman's rights movement, see Keith E. Melder, *Beginnings of Sisterhood: The American Woman's Rights Movement, 1800–1850* (New York, 1977); Barbara J. Berg, *The Remembered Gate: Origins of American Feminism: The Woman and the City, 1800–1860* (New York, 1978); Lori D. Ginzberg, "Women and the Work of Benevolence: Morality and Politics in the Northern United States, 1820–1885" (Ph.D. diss., Yale Univ., 1985); Nancy F. Cott, *The Bonds of Womanhood: "Woman's Sphere" in New England, 1780–1835* (New Haven, 1977); and Suzanne Lebsock, *The Free Women of Petersburg: Status and Culture in a Southern Town, 1784–1860* (New York, 1984), 195–249. There is no sign that individual members, themselves, gravitated from moderate to increasingly radical organizations; for a revealing study of membership patterns, see Anne M. Boylan, "Women's Benevolent Organizations in New York and Boston, 1797–1840," *Journal of American History* 71:497–523 (1984).

18. On the union of the Old Calvinists and the Consistent Calvinists, see Leonard Woods, *History of the Andover Theological Seminary* (Boston, 1885), 449–638; Joseph W. Phillips, *Jedidiah Morse and New England Congregationalism* (New Brunswick, N.J., 1983), 129–194; and Daniel Day Williams, *The Andover Liberals: A Study in American Theology* (New York, 1941), 1–30.

19. Woods, *Andover Theological Seminary,* 509–515.

20. Phillips, *Jedidiah Morse,* 137.

21. Woods, *Andover Theological Seminary,* 533–584.

22. R. Pierce Beaver, ed., *Pioneers in Misions: The Early Missionary Ordination Sermons, Charges, and Instructions* (Grand Rapids, Mich., 1966), 251.

23. *Report of the American Board of Commissioners for Foreign Missions . . . Twenty-First Annual Meeting . . . Boston, Oct. 6, 7, 8, and 9, 1830* (Boston, 1830), 121–124; *General Catalogue of the Andover Theological Seminary, Andover, Massachusetts, 1808–1908* (Boston, [1909]), 31–115; *Minutes of the General Association of Massachusetts . . . June 1830* (Boston, 1830), 9; *Annual Report of the Directors of the Massachusetts Society for Promoting Christian Knowledge* (Boston, 1831).

24. *Christian Register,* Apr. 15, 1826.

25. Newburyport Female Charitable Society, Records, 1824–1832, New-

buryport Public Library, Newburyport, Mass., Apr. 3-May 8, 1832, and Rev. Thomas B. Fox to the Society, May 5, 1832.

26. Woods, *Andover Theological Seminary,* 564.

27. Phillips, *Jedidiah Morse,* 139–140.

28. Sidney Earl Mead, *Nathaniel William Taylor, 1786–1858: A Connecticut Liberal* (Chicago, 1942), 229–232.

29. Edmund S. Morgan, *Roger Williams: The Church and the State* (New York, 1967), 39–40. On the psychology of radical commitment, see Michael Waltzer, *The Revolution of the Saints: A Study in the Origins of Radical Politics* (Cambridge, Mass., 1965); Silvan S. Tomkins, "The Psychology of Commitment: The Constructive Role of Violence and Suffering for the Individual and for His Society," in Martin B. Duberman, ed., *The Antislavery Vanguard: New Essays on the Abolitionists* (Princeton, 1965), 270–298; Kenneth Kenniston, *Young Radicals: Notes on Committed Youth* (New York, 1968).

30. On the history of antebellum reform, see John L. Thomas, "Romantic Reform in America, 1815–1865," *American Quarterly* 17:656–681 (1965); Paul Boyer, *Urban Masses and Moral Order in America, 1820–1920* (Cambridge, Mass., 1978), 3–64; Ronald G. Walters, *American Reformers, 1815–1860* (New York, 1978), 77–144.

31. See John Allen Kraut, *The Origins of Prohibition* (New York, 1925), 83–152; W. J. Rorabaugh, *The Alcoholic Republic: An American Tradition* (Oxford, 1979), 185–222; Ian Robert Tyrell, "Drink and the Process of Social Reform: From Temperance to Prohibition in Ante-Bellum America, 1813–1860" (Ph.D. diss., Duke Univ., 1974); Robert Louis Hampel, "Influence and Respectability: Temperance and Prohibition in Massachusetts, 1813–1852" (Ph.D. diss., Cornell Univ., 1980).

32. Merle E. Curti, "Non-Resistance in New England," *New England Quarterly* 2:34–57(1929); Merle Eugene Curti, *The American Peace Crusade, 1815–1860* (Durham, 1929); Peter Brock, *Pacifism in the United States: From the Colonial Era to the First World War* (Princeton, 1968), 449–615; Jayme A. Sokolow, "Henry Clarke Wright: Antebellum Crusader," *Essex Institute Historical Collections* 111:122–137(1975); Charles DeBenedetti, *The Peace Reform in American History* (Bloomington, 1980), 32–58; David Clifton Lawson, "Swords into Plowshares, Spears into Pruninghooks: The Intellectual Foundations of the First American Peace Movement, 1815–1865" (Ph.D. diss., Univ. of New Mexico, 1975); Clyde W. MacDonald, Jr., "The Massachusetts Peace Society, 1815–1828: A Study in Evangelical Reform" (Ph.D. diss., Univ. of Maine, 1973).

33. P. J. Staudenraus, *The African Colonization Movement, 1816–1865* (New York, 1961); John L. Thomas, *The Liberator: William Lloyd Garrison, a Biography* (Boston, 1963); Aileen S. Kraditor, *Means and Ends in Abolitionism: Garrison and His Critics on Strategy and Tactics, 1834–1850* (New York, 1967); Lewis Perry, *Radical Abolitionism: Anarchy and the Government of God in Antislavery Thought* (Ithaca, 1973); William H. Pease and Jane H. Pease, "Antislavery Ambivalence: Immediatism, Expediency, Race," *American Quarterly* 17:682–695(1965); John Demos, "The Antislavery Movement and the Problem of Violent 'Means,'" *New England Quarterly* 37:501–526(1964).

34. Efforts to win over existing temperance societies to the cause of teetotalism sometimes met successful resistance. For an example of such a conflict, see

Temperance Society of Kennebunk [Maine], Minutes, 1829–1838, New-York Historical Society, New York, 29–30 (Dec. 15, 1836).

35. Melder, *Beginnings of Sisterhood,* 95–112; Eleanor Flexner, *Century of Struggle: The Woman's Rights Movement in the United States* (rev. ed., Cambridge, Mass., 1975), 62–70.

36. Quoted in James Brewer Stewart, *Holy Warriors: The Abolitionists and American Slavery* (New York, 1976), 48.

37. Charles M. Snyder, ed., *The Lady and the President: The Letters of Dorothea Dix and Millard Fillmore* (Lexington, Ky., 1975), 63.

38. Rupert, Vermont, Tract Society, Constitution and Records, Vermont Historical Society, Montpelier, Constitution.

39. See Albert K. Weinberg, *Manifest Destiny: A Study of Nationalist Expansion in American History* (Baltimore, 1935); Frederick Merk, *Manifest Destiny and Mission in American History: A Reinterpretation* (New York, 1963); and Ernest Lee Tuveson, *Redeemer Nation: The Idea of America's Millennial Role* (Chicago, 1968), 91–136.

40. Robert F. Dalzell, Jr., *Enterprising Elite: The Boston Associates and the World They Made* (Cambridge, Mass., 1987).

41. George Rogers Taylor, *The Transportation Revolution, 1815–1860* (New York, 1951), 338.

42. John Winthrop, "A Modell of Christian Charity," *Winthrop Papers* (Boston, 1929–   ), 2:283.

43. Luther Baker, *An Address, Delivered to the Philanthropic Society* (Warren, R.I., 1806), 5.

44. Jedidiah Morse, *A Sermon, Preached in Brattle-Street Church* (Boston, 1807), 17.

45. Clifton Jackson Phillips, *Protestant America and the Pagan World: The First Half Century of the American Board of Commissioners for Foreign Missions, 1810–1860* (Cambridge, Mass., 1969); John A. Andrew, III, *Rebuilding the Christian Commonwealth: New England and Foreign Missions, 1800–1830* (Lexington, Ky., 1976).

46. Merle Curti, *American Philanthropy Abroad: A History* (New Brunswick, N.J., 1963), 3–40.

Appendix One

1. John R. Bodo, *The Protestant Clergy and Public Issues, 1812–1848* (Princeton, 1954); Charles C. Cole, Jr., *The Social Ideas of the Northern Evangelists, 1820–1860* (New York, 1954). The best historiographical treatment of the social-control thesis is Lois W. Banner, "Religious Benevolence as Social Control: A Critique of an Interpretation," *Journal of American History* 60:23–41 (1973).

2. *Mississippi Valley Historical Review* 44:423–444 (1957).

3. Clifford S. Griffin, *Their Brothers' Keepers: Moral Stewardship in the United States, 1800–1865* (New Brunswick, N.J., 1960), 23.

4. I am indebted to Robert A. Gross for emphasizing to me the importance of this distinction.

5. Walter I. Trattner effectively sets the context for the acceptance in many

circles of this view in his introduction to Trattner, ed., *Social Welfare or Social Control? Some Historiographical Reflections on "Regulating the Poor"* (Knoxville, 1983), 3–6.

6. Charles I. Foster, *An Errand of Mercy: The Evangelical United Front, 1790–1837* (Chapel Hill, 1960); Raymond A. Mohl, *Poverty in New York, 1783–1825* (New York, 1971); David J. Rothman, *The Discovery of the Asylum: Social Order and Disorder in the New Republic* (Boston, 1971); John K. Alexander, *Render Them Submissive: Responses to Poverty in Philadelphia, 1760–1800* (Amherst, 1980); Gary B. Nash, *The Urban Crucible: Social Change, Political Action, and the Origins of the American Revolution* (Cambridge, Mass., 1979); Paul Boyer, *Urban Masses and Moral Order in America, 1820–1920* (Cambridge, Mass., 1978).

7. *Labor History* 20:165–188 (1974).

8. On the historiographical consequences of the work of Cloward and Piven, see Trattner, ed., *Social Welfare or Social Control?*

9. (Rutherford, N.J., 1985), 20.

10. M. J. Heale, "Humanitarianism in the Early Republic: The Moral Reformers of New York, 1776–1825," *Journal of American Studies* 2:161–175 (1968); Carol S. Lasser, "A 'Pleasingly Oppressive' Burden: The Transformation of Domestic Service and Female Charity in Salem, 1800–1840," *Essex Institute Historical Collections* 116:160 (1980); Charles E. Rosenberg, *The Care of Strangers: The Rise of America's Hospital System* (New York, 1987), 15–46.

11. For one of the last examples of this approach, see Carl Bridenbaugh, *Cities in Revolt: Urban Life in America, 1743–1776* (New York, 1955).

12. (New York, 1965), 56–58.

13. (Williamsport, Pa., 1928).

14. Alan Heimert, *Religion and the American Mind: From the Great Awakening to the Revolution* (Cambridge, Mass., 1966), 11, 239–293.

15. Nash, *Urban Crucible,* 192.

16. Nancy A. Hewitt, *Women's Activism and Social Change: Rochester, New York, 1822–1872* (Ithaca, 1984), 260–261, 265–267, 271.

17. See, for example, Michael Kraus, *The Atlantic Civilization: Eighteenth-Century Origins* (Ithaca, 1949), 123–158.

18. Daniel T. McColgan, *Joseph Tuckerman: Pioneer in American Social Work* (Washington, D.C., 1940); Daniel Walker Howe, *The Unitarian Conscience: Harvard Moral Philosophy, 1805–1861* (Cambridge, Mass., 1970); Sydney V. James, *A People Among Peoples: Quaker Benevolence in Eighteenth-Century America* (Cambridge, Mass., 1963); Mack Thompson, *Moses Brown, Reluctant Reformer* (Chapel Hill, 1962).

19. (New York, 1941, 1969), 151–177.

20. Kathleen Neils Conzen, *Immigrant Milwaukee, 1836–1860: Accommodation and Community in a Frontier City* (Cambridge, Mass., 1976), 154–191; Humbert S. Nelli, *The Italians of Chicago, 1880–1930* (New York, 1970), 156–200; Moses Rischin, *The Promised City: New York's Jews, 1870–1914* (Cambridge, Mass., 1962), 95–111; Donald B. Cole, *Immigrant City: Lawrence, Massachusetts, 1845–1921* (Chapel Hill, 1963), 138–153.

21. Keith E. Melder, *Beginnings of Sisterhood: The American Woman's Rights Movement, 1800–1850* (New York, 1977); Barbara J. Berg, *The Remembered Gate: Origins of American Feminism: The Woman and the City, 1800–1860* (New York, 1978).

22. Nancy F. Cott, *The Bonds of Womanhood: "Woman's Sphere" in New England, 1780–1830* (New Haven, 1977); Suzanne Lebsock, *The Free Women of Petersburg: Status and Culture in a Southern Town, 1784–1860* (New York, 1984), 195–236; Anne M. Boylan, "Women in Groups: An Analysis of Women's Benevolent Organizations in New York and Boston, 1797–1840," *Journal of American History* 71:497–520 (1984).

Appendix Two

1. Dorothy Ann Lipson, *Freemasonry in Federalist Connecticut, 1789–1835* (Princeton, 1977), 141; Gary John Kornblith, "From Artisans to Businessmen: Master Mechanics in New England, 1789–1850" (Ph.D. diss., Princeton Univ., 1983), 18, 185.

2. Steven C. Bullock, "The Revolutionary Transformation of American Freemasonry, 1752–1792," *William and Mary Quarterly,* 3rd ser., 47:346–369 (1990).

3. Peter R. Virgadamo, "Charity for a City in Crisis: Boston, 1740–1775," *Historical Journal of Massachusetts* 10:26–27 (1982).

4. Robert F. Dalzell, Jr., *Enterprising Elites: The Boston Associates and the World They Made* (Cambridge, Mass., 1987), 128.

5. The existence of a network of Baptist institutions suggests the limits of another proposition, the attempt to tie organized charity to Federalist politics. Although conclusions on the subject must be tentative in the absence of direct efforts to link political party membership with participation in charitable associations, it is clear that most Baptists were Democrats and likely that most supporters of Baptist missionary organizations also belonged to that party. On Baptist participation in the Democratic Party, see Paul Goodman, *The Democratic-Republicans of Massachusetts: Politics in a Young Republic* (Cambridge, Mass., 1964), 94; Ronald P. Formisano, *The Transformation of Political Culture: Massachusetts Parties, 1790s-1840s* (New York, 1983), 15, 154, 166–167, 168; and William G. McLoughlin, *New England Dissent, 1630–1833* (Cambridge, Mass., 1971), 2:751, 784–786.

6. Robert Louis Hampel, "Influence and Respectability: Temperance and Prohibition in Massachusetts, 1813–1852" (Ph.D. diss., Cornell Univ., 1980), 36–39.

7. Susan Lynne Porter, "The Benevolent Asylum—Image and Reality: The Care and Training of Female Orphans in Boston, 1800–1840" (Ph.D. diss., Boston Univ., 1984), 99–100.

8. Anne M. Boylan, "Women in Groups: An Analysis of Women's Benevolent Organizations in New York and Boston, 1797–1840," *Journal of American History* 71:512–513 (1984).

9. Unitarians were especially numerous among wealthy Bostonians. During the Federalist and Jacksonian periods approximately two-thirds of wealthy Bostonians were Unitarians. See Robert Stanley Rich, "Politics and Pedigrees: The Wealthy Men of Boston, 1798–1852" (Ph.D. diss., U.C.L.A., 1975), 277, 279.

10. George Leon Walker, *History of the First Church in Hartford, 1633–1883* (Hartford, 1884); Edwin Pond Parker, *History of the Second Church of Christ in Hartford* (Hartford, 1892); *Centennial Memorial of the First Baptist Church of Hartford, Connecticut* (Hartford, 1890); *Contributions to the History of Christ Church, Hartford* (Hartford, 1895, 1908).

11. The members of St. John's Grand Lodge and its subordinate lodges

were also apparently affluent merchants and professionals. See Bullock, "Revolutionary Transformation," 347–369, and Tables 2, 3a, and 3b.

12. M. A. DeWolfe Howe, *The Humane Society of the Commonwealth of Massachusetts: An Historical Review* (Boston, 1918), 6.

13. See, for example, Robert K. Lamb, "The Entrepreneur and the Community," in William Miller, ed., *Men in Business: Essays in the History of Entrepreneurship* (Cambridge, Mass., 1952), 91–119, 318–321; Ronald Story, *The Forging of an Aristocracy: Harvard & the Boston Upper Class, 1800–1870* (Middletown, 1980), 3–23; Conrad Wright, *The Beginnings of Unitarianism in America* (Boston, 1955), 252–280; and Wright, "Ministers, Churches, and the Boston Elite, 1791–1815," in Conrad Edick Wright, ed., *Massachusetts and the New Nation* (forthcoming).

Index